In The Clea

A Spiritu

Part Two

(India and Beyond)

Prajna (Sanskrit: or panna: Pali) is wisdom, understanding, discernment, insight, or cognitive acuity. It is one of three divisions of the Noble Eightfold Path. Such wisdom is understood to exist in the universal flux of being and can be intuitively experienced through meditation.

From Wikipedia, the free encyclopedia

The highest devotion is attained by slow degrees by the method of constant endeavor for self-realization with the help of scriptural evidence, theistic conduct, and perseverance in practice.

Sri Brahma Samhita 5.59

Table of Contents

Preface

If you are reading this book, you have probably read Volume One in one of its incarnations. I hope you read the "revised and expanded" version, as it is infinitely better than the original. When I expanded the original, I made a concerted effort to escape the tried, true, and hackneyed chronological approach and write something more thoughtful and stimulating. This time, I hope to get far away from the straight chronological approach and write something more closely approaching a series of essays linked by a common narrative.

Volume One also featured a series of photographs meant to evoke a time and place. I wrote of events that took place in a totally different era. For younger readers, born long after those events, it can be a confusing and disconcerting time. I hoped the photographs provided a visual context and made the material more relatable. This time, I largely eschewed the photos. As the chronological train chugs rapidly forward, the context becomes easier to comprehend and appreciate, and the need for visual context less pressing.

The first volume emphasized the difficult path towards India and South Asia culminating in my initial India/Nepal trip. It took place primarily in the United States and Europe. Much of this volume deals with an ongoing relationship with India, and takes place in South Asia (India, Pakistan, Bangladesh, Sri Lanka). This significant shift in emphasis and experience marks the transition from an aspirational stage to a more mature and realized one.

Another notable development is my transition from a "single" person existing within a communal social milieu, to a family man with wife and children. This transition is among the most significant events in any person's life. A person as colorful as Norman Mailer can lead a tumultuous life that expands to include numerous marriages and children. This has not been the case with me. My family life has been calmer and more prosaic, and has centered around my wife Nilu.

In the first Volume "Buck" and I often journeyed together, and he played a crucial role in developments. In this Volume, while Buck makes his appearance, entering and leaving the narrative, Nilu plays the crucial role. Nilu and I, and later our two children, travel together throughout much of this journey.

I am immensely grateful to Nilu for her patience, persistence, and dedication. I would never have been able to make it without her. Her unrelenting support has been invaluable, and I dedicate this volume to her.

Chapter I

Getting Chronology Out of the Way – 1976-1978

"There is an irony which usually defeats the memoir and makes it an inferior art. The man who can tell a good story in company about his friends, is usually not able to find a prose which can capture the nuances of his voice. Invariably, the language is leached out – the account tends to have a droning episodic quality as if some movie queen were recounting the separate toils of her lovers to a tape recorder."[1]

--Norman Mailer

As Norman Mailer so cogently points-out, there is a genuine problem with autobiography. The elephant in the room is that no matter how significant the person, hardly anyone is really interested in a linear recitation of events placed in a chronological row, one event following the other in a boring train.

This problem becomes particularly acute when the person relating the memoir is not famous, and is not a rock star. How many memoirs of famous politicians and statesmen have we seen in which the protagonist moves ponderously from one momentous meeting to another, with one Prime Minister, General, or dictator to the next.

Likewise, rock star memoirs are often utterly predictable, consisting of a series of sexual encounters, one after the other, while the protagonist consumes ever greater quantities of ever-more unusual drugs (think of Keith Richards and his bestselling recent memoir) or inordinate amounts of alcohol (in the case of British rockers – Keith Moon comes readily to mind).

If these accounts of the lives of famous and glamorous people can grow stale and tiresome, imagine how pallied and uninteresting are the accounts of "seeker," academics, and just plain Joes? They cannot even rely on the innately colorful aspects of their lives to drag the reader along.

One way to overcome this inherent shortcoming is to focus on the life of the mind, and try to capture great thoughts. This approach dictates that the work stress less sex and color and more thoughtfulness. In the case of people like James Baldwin, and Norman Mailer, who are well known literati, this approach can be quite

---

[1] Norman Mailer, "Punching Papa: A Review of *That Summer in Paris*, The New York Review of Books, February 1963, excerpted from *Collected Essays of the 1960's,* page 148

attractive, as these people are noted for the depth of their thought. Persons interested in a life of the mind, find their essays eminently stimulating and encouraging of personal development.

I would not be so presumptuous as to imagine that millions of readers are anxiously awaiting my essays, wanting to gain exposure to my great thoughts. However, I find such an approach has more benefits than drawbacks. It would be even more presumptuous to fool myself into believing that the events of my life are more attractive than my intellectual development.

In my case, this series of memoirs is more than intellectual. The subtitle is "spiritual memoir." The intellectual development is thus subservient to self-realization. This involves pressing philosophical questions. "What is the purpose of life?" "Why are we put on this planet, in this particular time, in this particular milieu." "What are we meant to accomplish?" These questions are, in our Western civilization, considered both philosophical and religious/spiritual. These "ultimate questions" form the basis of metaphysics.

The *Gaudiya Vaishnava Sampradaya* (of which I will be writing a lot more about in the pages to come), is known for the breadth and depth of its philosophy. It answers the question of why we are here by stating that "The purpose of life is self-realization." I heartily concur with this conclusion. This means that for me the ideal biography documents the individual soul's efforts to attain self-realization. Such a work qualifies as a "spiritual memoir," not to be confused with a more mundane work based on lengthy descriptions of significant achievements, and conventionally determined success.

However, it is not possible to string together a series of spiritual revelations with no support, as the events must be elucidated within their proper contexts. This underlies the pattern of this work. The principal focus is on spiritual realizations, and the life of the mind as it relates to these realizations. However, these emphases are contextualized within chapters placing events within a solid chronological context. Some readers may find these intervening chapters quite interesting. But from my point of view, the goal is to get these boring details out of the way, so I can get into subjects of more import. This is the first of such chapters.

The first volume, left off with my 1976 graduation from the University of Arizona, Department of Oriental Studies, with a Master's Degree in South Asian Studies, with an emphasis on the Social Sciences, Modern India. At this point, I had made an initial trip to India.

Here is the chronology of events that transpired between this event and the next significant phase (a return to India). Like a fish swimming in the sea, I swim within these events, and they serve as the environment in which I pursue self-realization. As such, while the events themselves are not the focus, it is necessary to be cognizant of them. I wrestle with these events, experience them, and attempt

5

to use them to make spiritual progress. We saw this taking place in Volume One. Hopefully, this volume documents progress, as events unfold and realization proceeds.

Here are the events I will wrestle with in this chapter. They are perhaps not terribly significant in and of themselves, but remain necessary to comprehend what comes after:

Upon graduation from my master's program, I immediately entered the doctoral program, with the goal of completing a PhD in South Asian studies. This process culminated in my final graduation from the PhD program in 1981. This entire academic experience was conducted under the watchful eye of my mentor, Dr. James M. Mahar (called "Mike"). He was more than simply an academic mentor. I spent lots of time with him and his family. I socialized at his house with a wide variety of people, usually at his informal Saturday night soirees, and we discussed anything and everything under the sun. I got to know his wife and children, participating in their daily lives. The interaction between Mike and I was not confined to academic mentorship.

Mike was an anthropologist, and his principal research focus was on rural India. He had been conducting long-term research in the village of Rankhandi since he was a Cornell doctoral student in the late 1950's. Rankhandi is located in the North Indian state of Uttar Pradesh. Mike's decades-long interaction with this village allowed him to follow the lives of individual Indians, families, castes, and the village community, and document and analyze the course of change over time.

In addition, Mike had access to mountains of quantitative data collected by the Indian census. Mike tried to use his own observations and the quantitative data to determine the impact of this long-term change (both positive and negative) on the residents of Rankhandi. In Mike's teaching, he used Rankhandi as an example that could be extended to the people of India as a whole. He argued that the Rankhandi data could be used to make generalizations about India, and that the lives of the Rankhandi's people could be used to draw wider conclusions about the state of India and its society.

I was a penniless graduate student. I had no money for travel, entertainment, or conspicuous consumption. My parents had paid for my tuition and some of my expenses while I was an undergraduate, but that ceased when I entered graduate school. I supported myself as a teaching and research assistant, and by performing odd jobs, usually of a clerical nature. The lion's share of my time was devoted to serious study of all things Indian. After entering graduate school, all my courses dealt with Asia in general and South Asia in particular.

My particular circumstances enabled me to rapidly acquire academic credits. Largely free of distractions, I took a full course load every semester. My parents lived in Germany. With no money for travel back and forth, I remained in Tucson during the long hot summers. I took advantage of these intervals to speed up my time to graduation. I not only took a full course load every semester, I registered for back to back summer school courses, enabling me to compress an entire semester of courses into intense summer study, effectively cutting my time in school by 50 percent.

I arrived at the University of Arizona as a senior and graduated right on time (1975). I immediately registered for a Master's Degree and finished it in record time (1976). I also zipped through the course work for the PhD. I maintained a 4.0 average throughout. This strategy enabled me to compress my doctoral studies (including a year of fieldwork) into a five year intensive program. I graduated in 1981, as the youngest PhD in the history of the department.

I lived frugally. My principal entertainment was hanging out with friends, while devising ways to have fun while spending as little money as possible. My friends and I did things like hiking, walking around the campus and Tucson, and going to the drive-in (smuggling in our own food in the trunk of the car, as we could not afford to patronize the snack bar). Although I did not drink alcohol and did not go to bars or clubs, I did scrape together money for occasional concerts.

When George Harrison and Ravi Shankar and an Indian ensemble came to the Tucson Community center, I bought a ticket. George Harrison had been engaged in intensive interaction with Ravi Shankar that included traditional study of the sitar and extended trips to India. As a result, George was determined to work with Ravi Shankar to present a cross-section of Indian music to Western audiences. The two collaborators presented these efforts in a series of albums. I had been listening to their albums "Ravi Shankar's Music Festival from India," and "Shankar Family and Friends," over and over again. Both albums feature a large ensemble of Indian musicians and singers playing a wide variety of Indian classical, folk, and devotional music. I particularly liked the song "I am Missing You," a simple declaration of love for God in the form of Krishna, sung by Ravi Shankar's sister Lakshmi Shankar.

George was determined to escape his seemingly eternal legacy as an "ex-Beatle" and explore new territory. George and Ravi Shankar put together a traveling ensemble of Indian musicians and set out to tour America. I was very excited to hear they would be performing in Tucson and was determined to see the concert. With considerable excitement I made my way downtown to Tucson's clunky concrete "convention center," but found the experience trying. It was quickly apparent that George Harrison had taken a gamble by presenting Indian music to a Western rock audience, and that it had not paid off.

My fellow concert goers had come to hear George sing Beatles songs, and had zero interest in listening to Indian music. At the Tucson performance, the audience quickly became bored and started getting up from their seats, walking around the auditorium, drinking and eating, while ignoring the music. At the quieter musical moments, the din of conversation almost drowned out the music.

This displayed serious disrespect for the music and the musicians, and made it difficult for me to appreciate what I was listening to.

On another occasion my friends and I went to a drag strip South of Tucson to hear a triple bill. Dan Hicks and his Hot Licks, Commander Cody and his Lost Planet Airmen, and Hot Tuna, were playing on the same bill. It was the middle of the afternoon and the sun beat down on the asphalt. The audience brought coolers loaded with cold beer and quickly became quite lubricated. The bands played on, as the audience grew more raucous. I have always been a big fan of Dan, who was noted for his off-beat, acerbic sense of humor ("How can I Miss You When You Won't Go Away?"). He shared this trait with Frank Zappa. While Zappa could drift into the adolescent toilet humor genre, Dan's was always on point. I saw Dan play three times at Tucson's Rialto Theatre. The last time I saw him he was dying of cancer, and everyone in the audience knew it. He kept up his deadpan sense of humor throughout.

After completing my BA, our little commune abandoned its rented house on Speedway boulevard. The carpenter landlord had told us he was just holding on to the place until he could sell it for a huge profit and he did. Soon after we left, it was bulldozed and a brand new office building came up on the spot. It still stands today. Everything transpired just as our landlord predicted. Afterwards, I moved from one student apartment to the next, in neighborhoods around the University, always sharing with different configurations of fellow travelers. Life in Tucson remained cheap, laid back, and largely carefree.

During this period I had encounters with Tibetan Buddhists, followers of noted Indian guru Paramhansa Yogananda, Christians, and ISKCON devotees ("Hare Krishnas"). I met an assistant to the Dalai Lama, who had been sent by the government in exile to study in Tucson. He invited me to his apartment for further discussions, but for some reason I felt shy, and did not follow up. I somehow discovered a small group of Yogananda followers (members of the Self Realization Fellowship – SRF). I attended their meetings at a church hall just off campus every week for several months. We meditated together. I enjoyed the experience, finding it quite therapeutic. I don't know why it progressed only so far and no further. I don't remember why I stopped going. I will deal with the ISKCON encounters later.

Mike and I worked closely together throughout this period. As his research assistant, I helped catalog the mountain of data he had collected in Rankhandi. Computers were still massive and difficult to use, and I entered data onto paper sheets for entry into the computer to construct a data base for quantitative analysis. Mike had census data on births, education, residency patterns, occupation, income, deaths, and family size, for everyone in the village, divided by caste, and family. It had all been collected by Indian census workers. The families in Rankhandi were the traditional extended families then common in rural India. They were multigenerational, including grandparents, their children, and grandchildren, and extended to cousins, aunts and uncles, all living together in clusters of buildings within the village.

In addition to my research assistant gig, I was a teaching assistant, teaching classes in Hinduism, and Asian Humanities to undergraduates. Mike was a co-founder of the University's Department of Oriental Studies. He and his compatriots convinced the University and the legislature which provided the funding, that an Oriental Studies Department would open new doors to Arizonans with limited access to Asia. Although the Department's founding was miraculous, reaching the students was often an uphill battle. Most had little or no concrete exposure to the Asian continent, and many were not highly motivated.

While I was a teaching assistant, we held an initial briefing for the new students who had registered for "Oriental Humanities." Hundreds of them assembled in the "Modern Languages Auditorium" for their initial orientation. A large group of football players signed up, thinking it would be easy. The professor I worked for was an Anglo American totally committed to Zen Buddhism. He had been a Zen monk in Japan and brought the Zen approach to everything he did. He laid out his expectations. The next week, the hall was almost empty. The vast majority of students had dropped the course. There were no football players in sight.

My concentrated study pattern enabled me to complete the course work for my PhD by 1978, in record time. It was time to finalize preparations for the necessary field work. Mike and I decided I would go to Rankhandi, reside there for one year and gather the onsite data needed to complete the necessary research for my doctoral dissertation. I would then return to Tucson to integrate this data with textual data to draft the dissertation and defend it. Money was still a problem. I worked with Mike to try to obtain a Fulbright scholarship to fund the fieldwork. We put together a proposal that would document the impact of changes in agricultural technology over time in Rankhandi. I presented it to the Fulbright committee, but failed to win the grant.

Mike and I decided I would have to self-fund the fieldwork. I approached my parents and they graciously agreed to pay for my ticket to India and provide a small amount of money to cover my expenses. Other than the air ticket, my expenses were marginal. I purchased a small portable typewriter to type up my notes while in India, a battery powered cassette tape machine, that I would use to conduct interviews, and a camera to take photographs. This was the only equipment I would need.

Over the course of his many trips to Rankhandi, Mike had always stayed with the family of Dhoom Singh. I would be doing the same, living as they lived, and eating whatever they ate. Mike said I could work out an arrangement to pay Dhoom Singh after my arrival. India was very cheap compared to the United States, and it cost next to nothing to travel around, provided I lived as Indians lived, and avoided five star enclaves reserved for foreign tourists. The air travel was the only major expense.

Mike decided my research methodology would be based around "participant observation," and that my research would isolate variables that provided insight into the high degree of alcohol abuse already documented by Mike's earlier research among the Rajput subcaste. Dhoom Singh and his family were Rajput farmers. The Rajputs are probably the largest subcaste of the Kshatriya Varna (caste). Kshatriyas are Hinduism's martial caste, whose traditional duty has been to defend Hinduism during wars and serve as rulers. The Maharajahs (kings and princes) of India were predominantly from this caste.

Participatory observation calls for the researcher to integrate him/herself into the lives of his/her subjects. It requires the researcher to spend sufficient time living with the subjects to overcome any consciousness among them that he/she is an outsider. Over time, the subjects lose their inhibitions and behave around the researcher as they would around any other family member. The researcher can then discreetly record his/her observations. The result is hopefully honest data recording the actual lives of the subjects. The goal is to break through the personas that anyone erects when they are presented with strangers. Participatory observation removes the formality of formal interviews and allows the researcher to catch his/her subjects in casual moments. The object is to gain access to the genuine thoughts of the subjects. In addition, the researcher gains a firsthand experience of the lives of the subjects by sharing their lives, and can write about this shared experience as a participant rather than an observer.

Mike told Dhoom Singh's family he would one day send a student to live with them in Rankhandi. He had tried over the years to interest a student into moving to Rankhandi to conduct research, but none had ever taken up his offer. Rankhandi is located only five kilometers from the town of Deoband, which is a Muslim town of approximately 100,000 population, and home to the Deobandi sect of Islam.

This conservative Sunni sect was founded in Deoband, and is centered around the Darul ul Islam seminary, which trains Deobandi Mullahs from all over the world. The Deobandis have become famous (or infamous) as the sect of the Taliban. Deobandis established a series of madrassas (religious schools) in Pakistan to educate the male children of Afghan refugees, who had fled to Pakistan to escape the Soviet invasion of Afghanistan. The Taliban (which is the plural of the Urdu word "*Talib*" or student), was founded by graduates of these madrassas. The Taliban leadership continues to patronize these schools and many of its foot soldiers continue to attend.

There was no regular communication between Mike and Rankhandi. Although it was a large village (population approximately 15,000) at the point of transforming into a town, it had only intermittent electricity and a handful of telephones, which often did not function. Correspondence with the Rajputs of Rankhandi was infrequent. Although most Rajput males were literate, they were not in the habit of putting their thoughts down on paper. Mike therefore usually did not correspond with the people of Rankhandi and did not call them on the phone.

Mike did not tell the Dhoom Singh family that I had set out from Tucson, and would be arriving in their village.

Chapter II

Absorbed Into Rankhandi – 1978-1979[2]

I

The first time I flew to India everything made an enormous impression. I remembered everything in graphic detail. I remembered the airport (JFK in New York) and everything that transpired on the plane. It was not the same the second time. This second Indian journey involved two flights. For the first leg, I got on the plane at our little airport in Tucson and flew to Germany. The Indian government was dragging its heels on my visa. It was not an ordinary tourist visa. It was a researcher visa and required more clearances. I had already been exposed to the intricacies of Indian bureaucracy on my first trip. I remembered, for example, how long it took to change money at the bank, and get through the passport line at the airport, or to buy a rail ticket. I was therefore not surprised when the visa approval remained in limbo.

Because I did not yet have an Indian visa, I first flew to Germany. My parents lived in the tiny German village of Ockstadt, located in the German state of Hesse. I flew into the Frankfurt airport, where my parents picked me up and drove me back to the village. I moved into a room on the ground floor (American first floor) of their two storied apartment. I used this interval to study up on Hindi. Mike emphasized that once I arrived in Rankhandi, it would be sink or swim, with Hindi as the only language. I was travelling to Rankhandi alone. Unlike all previous researchers in that village, I did not have an interpreter.

Since all conversation with anyone would only be in Hindi, all interviews and interaction necessary for the research would be stillborn if my Hindi skills were not up to the mark. I brought my Hindi textbook and notes and sat at my parent's dining room table reviewing and practicing for hours each day. Later, my father gave me an assignment. Someone had presented him with a history of Ockstadt published locally in German. Since he could not read German, he asked me to translate it into English for him. Part of my day was therefore all Hindi and part all German.

My parents spent their evenings watching German television. When I watched television with my father, I translated the dialog on the screen into English for him. After they went to bed early, around 10 PM or so, I stayed up until the wee hours reading and watching the cool stuff that came on after midnight on German television. Germans (and I assume Europeans in general) do not believe in

---

[2] This long chapter is a book within a book and stands alone as its own narrative. This type of narrative is part of a specific subgenre I call "The Indian Village Narrative," in which a westerner describes his/her absorption into an Indian village milieu. My favorite in this genre is, *An Indian Attachment*, by Sarah Lloyd

censoring films or breaking them up with advertising. They view films as works of art, and believe that television networks do not have the right to mess with them. They always show the entire film with no commercial breaks of any kind. Germans also believe that the obscene parts of movies are the violence, and that depictions of sex are in and of themselves not obscene. They view sex as an integral part of life and readily comprehend that it is impossible to realistically depict human life without realistically depicting human sexuality.

Germans viewed American films as inherently violent, lacking in character development, and overly dependent on big budgets, violence, and special effects. German movies are generally low budget by American standards and therefore place a much stronger emphasis on acting and the interactions of highly-developed characters. Many Americans viewed German films to be obscenely obsessed with sex and nudity. It was beyond comprehension of most Americans, for example, that Germans have a film genre called "sex comedies," which deal with all the funny aspects of sexuality, and include lots of nudity. German television showed uncut films dealing with adult subjects late at night, when all children were in bed. These were primarily Avant Garde and underground films from all over the world, dubbed into German.

Eventually, the Indian government came through and I went to the Indian Consulate in downtown Frankfurt, had the visa stamped into my passport, and was on my way. The flight was uneventful, landing this time in Delhi rather than Bombay.

This was a far different trip than my first sojourn in India. Then, I was an undergraduate going on a study tour with a small group of fellow students, under the tutelage of a retired professor. Although I stayed on in India alone for six weeks or so after the group departed, in the back of my mind I knew it was a relatively short excursion, and that I would be returning to everything familiar soon enough.

This was an entirely different ball game. I would reside in India for a full year, cut off from everything I knew, and living entirely on my own. I felt a bit frightened during the flight, and that underlying anxiety only increased during my stay in Delhi.

There was not much commercial air travel in India in those days. Indian airports were small affairs, left over from the British Raj. Most Indian commercial airports were former British military "aerodromes." During the Raj, there were almost no domestic flights. This had not changed much since independence. Travel by air was still unheard of for the average Indian. Only the wealthiest elites could afford to fly. There were no commercial airlines in India. There were only two government-owned airlines. Air India was the international carrier and Indian

Airlines the domestic carrier. They were socialist affairs with none of the glitz and glamour of American commercial airlines.

Although Delhi was the capital of a major country, its airport was a small building, consisting of a few rooms. It had changed little since the British departed. I landed at Delhi Airport and quickly caught a cab to Connaught Circle, New Delhi's shopping district and the commercial centerpiece of the British planned city. I was quite familiar with CP (as the people of Delhi call it) from my first Indian sojourn.

I found a cozy guest house just behind the "Madras Coffee House." I had discovered the establishment during my first trip, and have returned many times since. The coffeehouse dated from the 1930's and nothing had been changed (or maintained) since it was first built. With each succeeding decade it just got shabbier. It was very dark and served simple South Indian "*Thallis*" (metal plates divided into sections that contained rice, and South Indian delicacies such as Idlis and Dosas), and strong Indian coffee. Last time I was in India I heard talk that the Madras Coffee house was set to be closed down, another victim of "progress." Apparently the younger generation of Indians has no use for such old fashioned venues.

I stayed in the Connaught Place guest house for several days before contracting to stay with a Brahmin family (quite westernized) called the Naths. Mike had told me to rely on the Fulbright House in New Delhi, which looked after visiting American scholars, and the people there must have referred me to the Naths. The family lived in the posh Rabindra Nagar area of Delhi.

Rabindra Nagar was part of the "imperial quarter" built by the British as part of "New Delhi," and meant originally for British senior civil servants and high officials that ran the imperial government. After independence, it became the favored residence of high-level civil servants in the central government and Indian politicians. Although it dates from the 1930's, it is still considered one of Delhi's "posh" areas. It is noted for its fantastic Anglo Indian architecture, beautiful parks and gardens, and is centered around the Khan Market (established in 1951, it is a favorite shopping spot and watering hole for Indian elites, foreign diplomats and other expats). I would become intimately acquainted with this neighborhood over the succeeding decades.

Everything is planned in this part of New Delhi, as it was built from scratch by the British. The streets are broad and tree-lined. The trees had grown out since the British first planted them and they create a shaded canopy protecting pedestrians from the sun. Almost everyone was a pedestrian in those days, as there were very few cars in India. During the British period, cars were a total rarity, and there may have been only a few thousand personal autos in the whole country then. It was not much different when I arrived this time (1978).

The neighborhood consisted of a series of walled in "bungalows," long one-storied houses with attached covered porches that personify Anglo-Indian architecture. Each bungalow was on its own green lot, featuring spacious green lawns and flower beds, assiduously maintained by platoons of gardeners.

During my research year, I stayed at the Nath residence whenever I came to Delhi. They were a cultured, gracious, anglophile family. On Sundays, we sat in wicker chairs in the back garden, drank tea, ate sandwiches, and listened to Western classical music on the radio. Like many of the westernized Indians I encounter, they were amazed that I could speak Hindi, could not comprehend how an American could live in a village, and were concerned for my health and well-being.

Before I could depart for Rankhandi, I was required to meet with my Academic Advisor. It was a stipulation of my visa. He was a Sikh Anthropology Professor from the University of Delhi. I had one short meeting with him and never saw him again. We drank tea, as was the custom, and shared nothing of substance. He made no serious enquiries regarding my research and did not proffer any assistance. It was quite clear he was merely checking a box and expected me to do the same.

During this Delhi interval, I freaked out and got cold feet. This is an essential element of living and traveling alone in a foreign country, far away from everyone and everything familiar. I wondered what the hell I was doing in a guesthouse in New Delhi. I became filled with dread about my upcoming trip to Rankhandi, and determined I would bag the whole thing, as I could not go through with it. I decided to go back to the airport, and catch the first flight back to Tucson.

There were no cellphones or internet then. Phone service in India was practically non-existent. The few telephones were big black affairs. On the few occasions when I had an opportunity to use a telephone, I often heard only noise. International calls were almost unheard of. During my yearlong stay in India, I never called anyone back in the US. I communicated by writing messages on small postcards, and folded-up aerogrammes. These were pieces of blue paper that folded up into a defacto envelope. The sides contained glue and the user was supposed to lick them to seal the envelope, but the glue never worked, so every post office had a "glue pot" with a big brush. The patrons smeared huge amounts of glue all over the aerogrammes, which arrived at their destinations brown and sticky. I therefore had no immediate contact with Mike or anyone else in the USA and relied solely on my own resources.

Since I was on my own, I reached deep down within myself and confronted my irrational fears. This was a wonderful moment for me, as I discovered my capability for true self-reliance and maturity. I discovered resources I did not know I possessed. I discovered the strength to calm myself and carry on. The key

15

was to give it all up and just let go. I gave up my attachment to my former life in Tucson, Arizona, in the United States of America. I determined that Rankhandi, in the Saharanpur District of Uttar Pradesh state in India was now my only home. I dismissed my former existence and created the illusion that I had been born and raised in India/Rankhandi and had never been exposed to anything different. I existed solely in the Indian present. The American past and future were pushed aside. This inner strength was necessitated by my anomalous situation. My circumstances were different from those of the other Western researchers in Rankhandi. Since I was in uncharted territory, I had to devise my own coping mechanisms.

The first American researchers that came to Rankhandi (including Mike), came as a group from Cornell and other American universities. American anthropologists had not done much research in India prior to this, as India was a British colony. The British did not want American academics poking around the Crown Jewel of the British Empire. Americans had few ties to India, in any case. In the great rush to colonize and dominate Asia that took place in the 19th and early 20th centuries, the Americans had opened up Japan and staked their claim there and in China. American Asianists focused on China and Japan, where US businessmen, academics, and missionaries were active. There had been scant interaction between American academia and India and no Indian studies programs at American universities.

Throughout the two century long British colonial era, the British had shown little interest in the Indian population and almost no interest in their welfare. Under the British, Indians remained rural, illiterate, malnourished and in poor health. While the British provided a modicum of security, the lives of average Indians tended to be nasty and short.

Once the British had departed, Nehru and his Congress Party were determined to right this wrong and bring India into the 20th Century. As part of this effort, the Nehru government established "development blocks" all over the country. In each block the government built schools, and clinics, and staffed villages with civil servants. Rankhandi was one of these villages. Jawaharlal Nehru, removed earlier British restrictions on American academics and opened up India to American researchers. He wanted to show off the independent government's development efforts.

As a larger village, Rankhandi acquired an "intercollege" (similar to an American Junior College), a clinic staffed with a government doctor and a "compounder" (pharmacist), and a bank. Nehru wanted the Americans to come see this new emerging India. He wanted to demonstrate to the world that unlike the British colonialists, who had largely neglected Indians, the independent government cared about its citizens and wanted to help them make rapid progress.

I suspect that the Indian government wanted to ensure that the American researchers had the best possible experience in rural India and presented India in the best possible light. The government was probably concerned that the American researchers would not be able to adjust to the inherent hardship of Indian village life. It wanted them to be comfortable, and able to bear the rigors that are an integral part of living in an Indian village. The government set aside quarters at the inter-college for the visiting anthropologists. I assume they brought their own cook and their own food, and that unlike the villagers, slept in beds with matrasses, and enjoyed some cooling provided by ceiling fans (although electricity was practically nonexistent). The previous researchers also did not speak enough Hindi to conduct their research in that language and relied on Indian interpreters and assistants.

Mike was a bit more adventurous than his counterparts. Once he completed his initial stint in Rankhandi, he kept coming back. He returned to Rankhandi many times over subsequent decades, eventually bringing his wife and children with him. During his first stint, Mike befriended the family of Dhoom Singh. They lived in the compound of their extended family (*Khandan*) in Khaala patti (the Khaala neighborhood).

While I, like Mike, would stay with Dhoom Singh and his family, I came to Rankhandi alone. I also did not bring lots of equipment and nothing to provide creature comfort. I came to Rankhandi with only a backpack containing some clothes, and my portable typewriter, battery-operated cassette tape machine, camera, and some notebooks.

Having overcome my initial panic attack, I set out for Rankhandi with my meager luggage. I first went to the Old Delhi Railway station, the same station I had used to travel around India during my first trip. It was legendary for its bustle, crowding, and chaos.

India was (and remains) an economy of scarcity. It seems there are never enough resources to meet demand. During the Nehru years, it was not a consumer economy. The British Raj had maintained India as a subsistence rural economy. It had subsumed India's economic interests to those of the British Empire. While Nehru wanted to break out of this economic cycle as quickly as possible, he relied on socialism to do it. Nehruvian socialism was egalitarian and spartan, emphasizing the need to meet the basic needs of the many over selfish personal consumerism. During this era, even many of those with money lived lives considered spartan and frugal by American standards. For most of rural India, it was still a subsistence economy, and the average Indian was a rural peasant who lived in his ancestral village, and grew crops on a small plot of land to feed himself and his family, and perhaps sell something for a little cash. Except for a few small enclaves reserved for foreigners and the very wealthy, India was universally simple. There were few luxuries.

17

Like almost everyone in India, I lined up to gain access to scarce commodities. This experience is epitomized at the train station. The economy of scarcity breeds an excess of aggressiveness. The mentality is that without aggression, one will be denied access to scarce resources, such as a train ticket. Aggression is the best way to survive and thrive in such an environment. The aggression is not personal. It was not aimed at any particular person among the faceless masses of people one encounters everywhere, every day. They were simply impediments and competitors that must be overcome at all costs in the all-pervasive fight for survival. Aggression was widely accepted as a simple survival mechanism, a Darwinian survival of the fittest.

The trains were always filled to overflowing, with little or no guarantee of a seat. The only way to ensure access to a seat was to buy a first class ticket, and that was not always a guarantee. First class ticketholders paid four or five times as much for their train ticket as the average traveler. This was a completely unaffordable luxury for the average Indian, who went through life with very little cash. First Class travel was supposed to ensure an assigned seat in a relatively private compartment. The trains were filled with "ticketless travelers," however, who snuck on the train and grabbed space wherever they could find it. It was not unknown for them to wander into the first class section and make themselves at home.

In this scarcity economy, Indians were always lining up to receive access to goods and services. Whenever people lined up, there were problems, as aggressive people shoved their way to the head of the line. At the ticket window, no one waited for the ticket, each person put money in his (it was always a him, as women did not participate) hand and shoved it through the tiny ticket window and yelled to get the ticket seller's attention. The ticket seller was confronted with a sea of hands reaching into his space. To try and compel people to line up the railroad station had put up iron railings on either side of the ticket booths. These did not prevent people from cutting in line by climbing over the railings and forcing their way in.

I was ill-equipped for this exercise. I had come from America, a prosperous country with more than enough for all. With an economy of plenty, Americans had the luxury of privacy and personal space. Each American had his "personal bubble," which was inviolate. Americans were so conscious of this personal bubble, that they constantly said "excuse me" whenever they came too close to another person. Americans were taught that this was basic politeness. None of this existed in India. There was no privacy, no personal space, no personal bubbles, and no concept of Western "politeness." No one ever said "excuse me."

When I stood in the ticket line, I was immediately shoved aside. People constantly cut in front of me. Since I lacked the basic resolve and aggression, it took me much longer to get to the front of the line. When I finally got to the window, I was again shoved aside. This meant that it took me much longer to get my train ticket. Incapable of displaying the necessary aggression, my only option was to cultivate unlimited patience. The economy of scarcity cultivates a mentality of fear. There is an underlying fear that if you do not push and shove and cut your way into the head of the line, you will get to the ticket booth and all the tickets will be sold. Although I never learned to forget my conditioning and join the pushing and the shoving, I was always able to get a ticket, eventually. I also learned to patiently endure lots of pushing, shoving, and yelling. It was like water off of a duck's back.

Once I bought a ticket, I carried my luggage over the long pedestrian bridge that ran over the nine or 10 tracks in front of the station. Another aspect of my Indian experience is that many individuals feel under no compulsion to follow rules. There were large signs on each platform saying in English and Hindi, "Do not cross the tracks. Use the pedestrian bridge." Many Indians are illiterate and cannot read the signs, but they all know what the signs say. Despite the signs with their extensive warnings of potentially fatal consequences, individuals lowered their luggage onto the tracks crossed them, and raised their luggage onto the next platform. They appeared casual and unconcerned that a train could run over them at any time. They did not want to take the trouble of climbing the long steps packed with people.

I also had to adjust to living in a society with widespread illiteracy. Approximately half of the population could not read, and the proportion was much higher among women, who were still deprived of access to education. It seemed ludicrous to me that there were signs in English. Here in North India, where Hindi was the most common language and the lingua franca, at best, perhaps five percent of the population could have read and comprehended English. The most significant thing about this tiny minority was that it was totally literate. English was prestigious and a status symbol because it signified an educated status. Although Hindi was the universal language, half of the population could not read it. Hindi speakers have the highest illiteracy rate in India. Time and again, I was approached by illiterates and asked to read signs, and letters, and train schedules for them. It did not seem the least bit odd to them that a western foreigner could read Hindi.

Like many other Westerners, I had been socialized into following the rules. I was naïve enough to always read the signs and follow the rules written on them. I therefore did not jump off the platform and cross the tracks, like so many others. I carried my luggage up the many steps, fighting my way through the crowds on the pedestrian bridge.

Poorer Indians could not afford hotels or guest houses. They simply camped out in the station until their train arrived. The trains were often late, often by many hours, and sometimes they were days late.

These campers slept and ate on every platform and on every available space on the pedestrian bridge. They laid out a blanket or towel or other piece of cloth and simply camped out, often surrounded by all manner of luggage. Poorer Indians had no money for suitcases or formal luggage. They carried their belongings in salvaged bags, made of cloth or nylon. Fertilizer bags were very popular. Farmers bought chemical fertilizer in big nylon bags and after removing the fertilizer, used them for many different purposes. This was a common pattern all over India. Indians recycled everything before there was a concept called recycling.

I travelled all over India on the train during this period and quickly devised my own strategy. Since there was no concept of personal space, it was contingent upon me to fight for a little space of my own within the greater space I shared with many other people. Comfort was rarely an option, and I quickly learned the stoic approach of the average Indian. In India, one quickly learns to be satisfied with whatever comes your way. There is no point in getting agitated or entertaining high expectations. To do so would be a recipe for disaster and a ticket to quick mental breakdown. Once I fought my way onto the train, I settled in and made the best of my situation.

When in the train station, I quickly learned to discount time. Train schedules were set up on the platform and trains scheduled to arrive and depart at various times at various platforms, but it really had no meaning, for the trains arrived randomly (almost always late but never early and sometimes at their assigned platforms, and other times at a random platform). A scratchy voice projected from ancient cobweb covered speakers hung from the rafters above the din on the platform, made announcements of various kinds in Hindi and English, but I was rarely able to make sense of these garbled and fuzzy announcements.

I learned to do what Indians did, which was to always keep track of what was happening by asking random strangers. Indians find this to be perfectly normal, and are not the least bit annoyed if strangers ask them questions. I have seen Indians answer multiple enquiries one after the other, without the least hint of annoyance. This is also the result of widespread illiteracy. Illiterates must constantly ask other people for information, as they cannot read signs, schedules, and guidebooks. I was in the same boat as everyone else. If I did not keep track of incoming trains, my train could show up at a random platform and depart without me.

When the train arrived at the platform, it set off a mad melee, as people rushed to get on board, grab a seat and get their families and luggage in place before the train departed. It was the assigned task of one male member of each family group to elbow his way into the train and grab the seats. He then signaled family members outside on the platform who rushed to the window and handed him the luggage. Anyone who hesitated was lost, and could spend the entire train journey standing next to the foul smelling bathroom, or perhaps not make it on to the train

20

at all. I have experienced this myself, standing for nine or ten hours engulfed by foul odors as passengers go in and out of the bathroom, doomed to suffer because of my lack of aggressiveness.

I quickly learned to join the mad rush. I also quickly learned that I would not be able to grab a seat, as the families would have already staked them all out. Instead, I learned to quickly climb up into the overhead luggage racks with other single men travelling alone. Family groups travelling with wives and children had to have seats on the benches. Parents knew they had to maintain a constant watch over children to ensure they were not harassed or separated. From our perch in the luggage racks, we single men looked out onto the benches where family groups were arrayed below us. The husband, wife, grandparents, and little children lined up along the benches. Often, young wives held babies in their arms. Sometimes, they held the babies out over the floor to urinate, as the babies wore no diapers.

Once I had procured my luggage rack space, I knew I could not leave it until the train arrived at the destination. This meant I could not get down, step between all the passengers camped out in the aisles and make my way to the "latrine," at the end of the car to urinate. If I did so, my spot would be taken by someone else in my absence.

The latrine consisted of an Indian squat toilet, two porcelain footpads on either side of a hole in the floor. Everyone squatted on the two footpads, perched over the hole to urinate and defecate (Indian men often urinate sitting down). Urine and feces were supposed to fall through the hole onto the tracks below, but that was literally a hit or miss proposition. As a result, there were always piles of feces and puddles of urine around the squat toilet. There was a small sink in the latrine but it often did not work. There was usually no soap. Signs urged passengers not to use the toilet while the train was parked in the station, but many people ignored them. As a result, the space between the tracks at the station was often carpeted with human feces and well-watered with urine.

The Indian custom is not to use toilet paper, but rather water. The right hand is the clean hand and never used for this purpose. The left hand is the dirty hand. Needless to say, it is not considered good to be left handed. With everyone using water, the latrine is always flooded. The water sloshes around as the train moves. When using a squat toilet in a moving train rattling down the tracks at speed, the passenger must balance over the hole to prevent falling off into the sloshing water.

I was traveling to Deoband, which meant I had to ride a local rather than an express. Express trains stop only at big cities, while locals stop everywhere. Deoband is on the Delhi/Hardwar railway line. Hardwar, the train's ultimate destination, is a Hindu pilgrimage city and the gateway to the Himalayas. It is where the holy Ganges emerges from the mountains. Deoband is 178 kilometers from Delhi, at roughly the midway point between Delhi and Hardwar.

The trip from Delhi to Deoband is supposed to take 3 hours and 32 minutes. On the local train, it takes between 9 and 10 hours because of frequent and lengthy stops. The train clacks along for hours on end and then inexplicably stops and does not move for long periods of time. There is never any explanation for these long delays. Because of this, I was often ensconced in my luggage rack perch the entire time, with no chance to urinate. I quickly learned to go great lengths of time without urinating. I recently spoke with my urologist who informed me that this practice damages the bladder.

The westerner's first reaction to all the chaos is to get angry and deride Indians as "rude." This is not actually the case. This is an example of cultural miscomprehension. While Indians have no personal space and must aggressively compete with each other, Indian society has its own well-developed system of manners. It is just not the same as that of the West. It is impossible to practice the western system of etiquette in this situation. Manners must adapt to the circumstances.

For example, once everyone is settled into their seats there is little to do for amusement. This is especially true once it gets dark and it is no longer possible to watch the countryside roll by. In this part of India, the countryside is not very interesting in any case. It consists of flat farm fields, broken by intermittent groves of trees and villages that all tend to look alike after a while.

Indians fill these intervals with friendly conversation. Since I speak Hindi, I find myself conversing at great length with people I have never met before. The people I converse with are generally warm and friendly and by the end of the journey, you feel you have made fast friends.

Throughout the journey, hawkers of various kinds make their way up the aisles offering all manner of foodstuffs. They shout out in loud voices, using melodic chants to advertise their wares. Between the hawkers, blind singers pass down the aisles. They usually sing religious songs and hold out their hands for alms. Sales of the proffered snacks and drinks are not brisk, however. When riding a local, most passengers are peasants, and peasants have little access to cash. They prefer to bring their own food from home. This usually consists of cold vegetable curries and chapatis, which are then wrapped in newspaper and kept in a recycled shopping bag. The passengers sharing the benches inevitably break out their food and share it with the others in the compartment.

Another common accusation levelled by many westerners is that Indians are "dirty." They say this because the common environment that Indians venture into when they leave their homes is dirty. While there exist some cultural factors that contribute to this sad state of affairs, the impact of poverty cannot be overemphasized. The Indian public environment is often dirty, not because of a willful choice, but because of the pervasive impact of poverty.

Because of poverty, infrastructure of all kinds is often lacking in much of India. It takes a highly developed infrastructure to keep public spaces neat and clean. Those who so casually accuse Indians of being "dirty" need only look into Indian private homes. Their cleanliness puts the homes of many westerners to shame. Indians are assiduous about all aspects of personal cleanliness and generally keep personal spaces immaculately clean. The common observation is that Indian housewives meticulously sweep every inch of their homes every morning, and often sweep all the dirt out into the street in front of their homes. It is commonly acknowledged in India that public spaces are someone else's responsibility. With everyone ascribing this responsibility to someone else, there is often no one willing to take up the challenge. Indians must contend with this fact of life. It is not going to go away anytime soon. As a result, they develop a thick skin and learn to live with this grim reality. They do not find it pleasant. It is not something they enjoy. It is something they bear.

I have taken the train journey from Delhi to Deoband many times over the years, and it seems that no matter what time the train leaves the Delhi station, it does not arrive in Deoband until late at night. The Deoband station is small, consisting of the ticket booth, the second and first class waiting rooms and a small room with beds and mattresses that can be rented out by first class passengers who find themselves stranded in Deoband overnight and must catch an early train out of town. This is where I disembarked to journey to Rankhandi for the first time.

When the train stops, the mayhem begins all over again. There is no concept that those entering the train must wait until all detraining passengers depart the car before trying to enter. Instead, those entering push against those departing in a perpetual shoving match. There seems to be an underlying fear that the train will depart. This causes everyone to conclude they must enter or depart as quickly as they possibly can or face being stranded on the platform.

Everyone in the train is very conscious of their luggage. There is a perpetual fear of thieves and pickpockets. Many buy chains that they wrap around their wrists and lock to their luggage. This enables them to sleep without fear that someone will take their luggage. It is common to hear gruesome tales of the thieves who cut off the fingers of sleeping passengers to get their rings. I suspect such stories are apocryphal, as I have never met anyone who witnessed such a robbery, and everyone seems to have all their digits.

The trains are routinely guarded by uniformed soldiers from the paramilitaries, however, who walk up and down the aisles carrying World War II era Enfield rifles and lots of ammunition in canvas bandoliers. These are meant to prevent train robbers from boarding the train and robbing the passengers at gunpoint. I always stayed with my luggage on the luggage rack, using my backpack as a pillow. As soon as the train entered the station, I climbed down from the luggage rack grabbed my luggage and fought my way off the car and onto the platform.

The only bathroom in the Deoband station is in the first class waiting room. Although I was not traveling first class, everyone assumed I was. This was because I was a white foreigner. This enabled me to go into the first class waiting room to relieve myself after the long journey. The stationmaster is very particular about who gets to use the restroom and watches the First Class Waiting Room with an eagle's eye. The secret is to enter with confidence. Although Deoband was a city of 100,000 people, I confirmed that the only public restroom in the city is in the first class waiting room.

II

Upon leaving the platform, I walked through the sleepy train station and out to the tonga stand. Tongas are small horse-drawn carts and were then the sole way for arriving train passengers to get from Deoband to Rankhandi. Each tonga was drawn by a single horse, and the drivers stood in a group conversing, waiting for passengers. I entered a tonga with my luggage. Men dressed in the rural uniform of a short *kurta* (traditional shirt) and western style trousers with sandals were seated in the benches on either side. In the space between the rows of seated men, women dressed in saris and holding babies and small children, sat on the floor. This was the custom. The women kept their saris over their faces, preventing any man from getting a glimpse of their face, as dictated by the *purdah* system prevalent in this part of India.

Once the tonga was full, it set out for the five kilometer journey to Rankhandi. It was a trip I have taken many times since. The tonga reached a brisk pace. No one talked and the only sound was the clip clop of the horses hooves on the road, and the birds scouring the fields for bugs. We travelled past the sugar mill, the mainstay of the local economy. *Buggis* (handmade flat carts drawn by water buffalo) were lined up at the unloading area. *Buggis* consist of a flat piece of wood fabricated from boards by a village carpenter. The axle underneath is recycled from a junked car, as are the rubber tires. The buggi is pulled by a water buffalo kept in harness. The water buffalo are lazy and lethargic. The driver of the buggi has a stick in his hand that he uses to prod the testicles of the water buffalo. This ensures an increase of speed for 50 meters or so, until the water buffalo returns to his natural pace.

In later years, some villagers dispensed with the lackadaisical water buffalo and converted their *buggis* into motorized vehicles. They mounted an irrigation pump on the buggi and connected it to a primitive drive shaft. Totally illegal and unregulated, these vehicles are called "*jugard*" (which means improvisation in Hindi, and is an example of village humor).

The *buggis* parked in front of the sugar mill were topped high with piles of cut sugar cane to be sold to the mill for processing. This was the primary source of cash for peasants from the surrounding villages. In previous times, they had been subsistence farmers, growing vegetables for their families (vegetarianism was and is the norm). After the mill was built during the British colonial period, local

24

farmers became greedy for more and more money and converted their land to growing cane. Instead of growing their own food, they were forced to purchase it from stores. The word store is somewhat of a misnomer. There were no actual stores in Rankhandi, only little cubbyholes, small rooms opening on to the street. Shopkeepers sat inside surrounded by their wares, which in those days consisted of bags of lentils (dal), rice, and some vegetables.

After leaving the environs of the sugar mill, the city of Deoband fell away and the tonga trotted slowly down the dirt road with fields of sugar cane on both sides. The fields were interspersed with small groves of trees, and trees lined the road. When the tonga approached Rankhandi it passed the small campus of the intercollege, the health clinic, and the bank. These were built in the usual Indian fashion, walls of bricks covered with stucco painted a pale ochre. These public buildings demarcated Rankhandi, but were outside the village proper.

III

The village of Rankhandi lay on the other side of a river crossed by a bridge. When my tonga approached the village, the water around the bridge was filled with water buffalo. Every afternoon, their owners took them to the river to cool off. Otherwise, they overheat. Some owners stood beside their precious water buffalo and washed them down. There were very few tractors in Rankhandi, owned only by the most prosperous. Almost all farmers plowed their holdings using water buffalo, and used *buggis* for transportation. In a previous era, high caste village men had used horses for transportation, but most had disappeared.

The *tonga* crossed the bridge and stopped in a public area where people congregated to chat and gossip and wait for tongas to take them into Deoband. I got off and asked one of the many men hanging around where I could find the *chopal* of Dhoom Singh. The streets of Rankhandi had no names and there were no street signs. They were not really streets, but rather glorified alleys.

There was no running water and no sewage system in Rankhandi. For centuries the villagers had relied on wells, which still stood abandoned and unused all over the village. In the 19th Century, villagers installed hand pumps, which became the common source of water. All the water from the pumps in front of each home ran into ditches that ran along the streets. The ditches filled with animal waste and dead plants, converting the water into a dark smelly muck. In Rankhandi one learned to avoid these rivulets and not step in them. To do so would result in a foot covered in brown effluent.

Although many homes were rigged for electricity, it was only available for a few hours in the dead of night. This meant the village was totally dark at night. It was impossible to go anywhere without a flashlight. In this period, there were no foreign products available in India. The government had erected tariff barriers to all imports to guarantee markets for Indian producers. With industry in a nascent stage and no competition, the resulting products were often substandard. This included flashlight batteries, which generally lasted only a few hours. I quickly learned to buy these by the case and to keep fresh batteries at hand, as otherwise, I could be stranded in the middle of the dark village surrounded by fetid water. To fall into those noxious streams would be a most unpleasant experience and was to be avoided at all costs.

The combination of the open sewage streams in the street and the presence of so much livestock gave a powerful odor to the village. It was an odor that would likely have been very familiar to 19th Century farmers in the United States. When I first arrived, it was overwhelming, but I quickly got used to it.

No one not resident in Rankhandi could find his/her way through the maze without help from a villager. A young man took me down one street and stopped. On my left was a two storied structure. This was the central building of my extended family compound. Some 92 persons lived in our compound and most lived within the confines of this building and its attached courtyards. Dhoom Singh was eccentric and chose not to live with his extended family. He established his own smaller courtyard across the street. On my right, an inclined bricked path led to the residence of Dhoom Singh and his entourage. "Dhoom Singh is on the right," the young man said, and pointed the way. I walked up the path and into a small courtyard surrounded by buildings. On my right was a barn. In front of me a small building which appeared to be a single room residence. On the other sides were blank adobe walls. Everything seemed ancient and in some disrepair.

The courtyard was filled with straw and manure, as it was home to four or five water buffalo. They had large rings through their noses attached to chains, which ran to large stakes pounded deep into the ground. They were enormous animals, and almost totally passive. They stood with no expression on their faces and placidly chewed their cud.

Just past them were arrayed several string cots (called *charpoy*).

They consisted of a rectangular wooden frames with twine strung between to form a bed. Charpoys were the ubiquitous furniture of Rankhandi. For most villagers, they were the only furniture. Some families kept chairs and tables, but these were merely status symbols, kept around for show, and were not actually used. The residents sat on their charpoys during the day, ate their meals there, socialized there, and slept on them at night. There were no mattresses and the only bedding was a quilt stuffed with cotton (called a *rezai*). One of these *charpoy* would be my bed for the entire time I stayed in Rankhandi, and this courtyard my home.

Rajput men were seated on the charpoys chatting and smoking hookah. The water pipes, like almost everything in Rankhandi, were made in the village and represented timeless technology. The base containing the water, was made of clay, and the stem of bamboo wrapped in twine with a mouthpiece. The smoker took a few puffs and passed the stem on to the person next to him. I later learned that the hookah was popular primarily with older men of a different generation. The younger generation preferred *bidi* (filterless Indian cigarettes made of a rolled tobacco leaf). *Bidi* are usually made by hand. Those with money to burn smoked cigarettes made in factories.

These Rajputs were typically peasant in their appearance. Their bodies were lanky, with no fat whatsoever. They all had a standard short haircut, which would be familiar to anyone in the American Army and bushy mustaches, which would be familiar to anyone in the British Army. Their skin was taut and burned dark brown by the sun. The older men wore a *dhoti*.

The younger men did not wear dhotis. They considered them old fashioned and out of date. They wore either baggy white cotton "pajama"[3] pants or trousers. There were almost no ready-made clothes available in India then. Everyone bought bolts of cloth and took them to the village tailor for sewing.

Dhoom Singh was there socializing with his cronies. He was obviously an old man, with solid white hair and a bushy white mustache, but was not wrinkled or frail. He was dressed in a white kurta and dhoti like the other old men, but sported his own trademark, a "Gandhi" cap, worn by followers of Mahatma Gandhi during the freedom movement.

Dhoom Singh had been the patriarch of his clan for a long time, but was beginning to retire from active life and hardly spent any time in the fields any more. Instead, he spent his days socializing with his circle of old cronies. While they chatted for hours, their principal recreation was to read aloud the Hindu epic the *Ramayana*. The group of old men took turns reading the book, and when they reached the end, they simply turned the book over, started right back to the beginning and read it again.

In the days of Dhoom Singh's youth, all was different for the Rajputs of Rankhandi. Then they were true nobility, and did not engage in manual labor. They were landlords who collected rents from their tenants and spent their days in leisure. Dhoom Singh had proudly ridden his horse through the village and caroused with his circle of Rajput young men. They rode into town on weekends to frequent the brothels and drink lots of liquor. After he was married, Dhoom Singh kept a *dalit* (untouchable) woman in a low shed behind his sleeping quarters, and fathered several children with her. The Rajputs could, in those days, walk through the *dalit* quarter and take home any pretty girl they found. Those days were gone now.

---

[3] The English word "pajama" is a Hindi loan word. The British adapted common Indian pajama as a comfortable sleeping garment in a very hot and often muggy climate.

The economy had changed. Rapid population growth had shrunk the size of Rajput landholdings. The low caste tenants had moved on to other jobs, with many emigrating to cities to work in factories or offices. While other castes took advantage of the new schools to gain education and leave the village to seek their fortunes elsewhere, the Rajputs remained tied to the land.

As practicing Hindus, Rankhandi's Rajputs practiced village exogamy. Hindus view incest with great repugnance. For them, it would be incestuous to have sexual relations with a cousin. In a village setting, it would be all but impossible to find a bride that is not a relative. South Asian Muslims do not define incest in the same way, with many seeing female cousins as desirable brides. This is one of the many cultural bones of contention between India's Hindus and Muslims. Hindus are forbidden to marry women from their own village. This means that all the girls born in Rankhandi will eventually marry and leave.

Rankhandi's Rajputs were tied to their landholdings, and the village exogamy system was part of this cultural pattern. They stayed where they were born and continued to divide up their land between the sons, with the plots shrinking with each new generation. Forced to economize, they hired low-caste farm laborers to help with the backbreaking work of farming without mechanized equipment, but they now had to work the fields themselves. The days of leisure and nobility had faded away. Dhoom Singh was a relic of that era. His children and grandchildren had no experience of such times.

Dhoom Singh was a legally registered opium addict. Each month he took his addict card to a government shop and procured his supply of opium. It was a yellow grassy substance he kept in a bag in the men's quarters, cooked up every morning in water and drank.

He was what we would now call a fully functional addict. His addiction did not impair his ability to lead a normal life. His speech was not slurred. He did not nod off. He was lively and entertaining with a twinkle in his eye and a keen sense of humor. He liked to joke and laugh. Since I was a family member, I called him by his family name "Baba," which would be similar to grandpa.

I introduced myself to Baba, who was sitting with one of his sons. I would call him "Pita" or "father." Everyone seemed quite relaxed. No one seemed surprised to see me, even though they had no idea that I was coming. "Where have you been" said Baba, "We have been expecting you for a long time."

Village life was timeless. Village houses were filled with calendars. They were given to households for free as advertising by local businesses. Most featured pictures of Hindu gods and goddesses, and the Hindu hero Rama and his consort Sita.

Although villagers grew up surrounded by calendars, they paid no attention to them and rarely knew the date. It was never clear to me whether everyone even knew how to read a calendar. Those who were illiterate probably could not. Likewise, all Rajput men were expected to wear a wristwatch, but it had little practical function. Villagers continued to follow the course of the day by keeping track of the path of the sun across the sky, and had no appointments. Wristwatches were a status symbol. Women did not wear wristwatches, but many had wristwatches tattooed on their arms. It was the female status symbol, although for them, their watch always had the same time. No one sitting there in the courtyard on the charpoys had any real idea how long it had been since Mike had been in Rankhandi and had told them to expect one of his students.

Baba told me to have a seat and proudly showed me the room at the head of the compound. This is where "Mike Sahib" had stayed while living in Rankhandi. It was the only room in the compound with a table and chairs. Mike must have purchased these to create a de-facto office where he could work. The family had framed several pictures of Mike and his family and hung them above the desk, which had remained unused since Mike's departure. It had the appearance of a shrine. In later years, my picture was hung there as well, and remains in that spot to this day. Baba told me this had been set aside as my workspace. He said Mike had insisted on sitting there and typing away and that they expected me to do the same thing.

I took my things inside and placed them at the work desk. I worked here every evening transcribing my notes and writing in my journal, but only slept there under special circumstances. Like everyone else, I slept outdoors in the courtyard. However, the year that I lived in Rankhandi was marked by a drought and extremely hot weather. With no cooling of any kind, our only way to cope with the heat was to go inside the room out of the sun during the heat of the day and cover ourselves with thin cotton dhotis pressed into service as makeshift blankets. We rolled ourselves up like cocoons and lay motionless for hours waiting for the arrival of the night and cooler temperatures. Every once and a while, someone would douse the sleepers with water.

My courtyard sleeping spot was beside the water buffalo. My head abutted their stakes where they stood placidly sleeping at night. Some nights I dreamed I was standing beside a giant waterfall and awoke to the sound of the water buffalo loudly urinating on the cobblestones.

When I arrived in Rankhandi, I wore a simple outfit of pants and short sleeved shirt and had a brimmed hat with a feather in it. Pita got up from his *charpoy* and told me formally that as good Hindus, we were not to wear anything polluting and that I must throw away the feather. He then told me my hair was too long and that he would take me to the barber in the morning for a proper haircut. He dutifully

29

took me to the barber for the requisite military style haircut sported by all the Rajputs. I would maintain this style throughout my Rankhandi year.

Pita was a devotee of the powerful hallucinogenic drug Datura. In my doctoral dissertation, I described this drug as follows:

Datura (Datura Fastuosa). This is an extremely powerful intoxicant (hallucinogen) which is occasionally taken in villages. It has traditionally been taken by sadhus (religious ascetics), who use it as an aid to their religious quests. Datura is the name given to seeds of a flowery plant that commonly grows like a weed throughout northern India. The drug is so powerful that it can cause vomiting, gastric irritation, headaches, temperature and a bright red rash, among other effects. An overdose of the drug can be fatal.[4]

Pita had a long history of mental illness compounded by his fondness for Datura and Hashish. While Baba was an opium addict, Pita and his circle of friends used these intoxicants on a daily basis. In the past, he had become incoherent and had wandered around muttering to himself. His family chained him to the furniture to keep him in place.

Pita eventually broke free of his bonds and wandered away from the village and rode for free on trains all over India. He was so obviously insane that no train conductor ever bothered him. No one in Rankhandi heard anything from him for years, until one day he showed up back in the village. He was again coherent and resumed his former life. The entire time I knew him and interacted with him, he spoke in a slow deliberative way with an impassive face. He was gentle and liked a good joke, laughing softly.

After I left Rankhandi, he wandered off again, and no one has seen or heard from him since. The Rajput members of my family were incredibly stoic about everything, including the disappearance of Pita. It was taken in stride, like all the events of life.

This was my first night in Rankhandi.

IV

The next day was my first full day in Rankhandi and the beginning of my acculturation, my absorption into my village. It was akin to not knowing how to swim and being taken into the middle of a large lake and dropped into the water. I had to quickly learn all the essentials, or I would not survive in my new environment. Every aspect of my life from this day on would be different from my previous life. I would have to learn new ways to perform all essential tasks.

---

[4] Jon Peter Dorschner, *Alcohol Consumption in a Village in North India*, UMI Research Press, Ann Arbor Michigan, page 194

When I awoke, I was introduced to the toilet habit. The men gathered together and each of us carried a small metal jug with a spout (called a *lotha*) and a dry washcloth. We walked into the fields, where we squatted to defecate. After defecation, we used the water to clean ourselves (using only the left hand), and the wash cloth to dry. I not only learned this process, I learned that in India, people train themselves to ensure defecation takes place at roughly the same time every morning. This absence of toilet facilities ensures that everyone keeps "regular," but this cultural norm persists even after indoor toilets are introduced. Toilets, which in India are almost always squat toilets, were almost non-existent in Rankhandi.

This is still the case throughout India, with a large percentage of the population defecating outside every day. As a result, it is not uncommon to encounter human feces when walking unknowingly into a "toilet area," and it is common to see men urinating in public areas. The villager men of Rankhandi would squat to urinate when they were out in public to preserve a modicum of privacy. When women had to urinate in crowded public areas, several of them created a private space by extending their saris over the squatting woman.

The current Indian government has put in place a crash program to end the practice of outdoor defecation. It has built hundreds of thousands of toilets in villages, but it is hard for many villagers to adjust to this new reality. Some have converted their new toilets into storage sheds and continue their old ways.

I asked Baba how I should pay for my stay in Rankhandi. He told me to pay for the building of a "modern" toilet for the chopal. Village craftsmen duly arrived and built a brick outhouse attached to Mike's room. Inside was an Indian squat toilet with a septic tank below. After the construction of this new building I no longer went to the fields in the morning. I also used this building to bathe every day. Baba had determined that it would be unseemly for me to bathe under the hand pump and defecate in the fields. He was also aware that Westerners preferred to take off all their clothes when bathing and could therefore not bathe in the open air like the villagers. The women heated water for me so I would not have to take a cold bath. They put it into a bucket and I dipped my wash cloth into the bucket and washed myself from head to foot. At the end of my bath, I dumped all the warm water over my head to wash away all the soapy residue. This was a genuine luxury and one of the few ways in which my life differed from that of my family members.

The other men in the chopal bathed at the hand pump. The old men never seemed to take off their dhotis and bathed with them on. The younger men stripped down to their underwear. While I did not bathe under the hand pump in Rankhandi, I have done so numerous times when wandering through rural India.

Villagers could not afford expensive packaged soaps and used a cheap harsh soap similar to "Lava" soap in the United States. It was scratchy and was like washing with a piece of rock. It had no perfumes and smelled like harsh disinfectant.

31

I was the only resident of the chopal who used the new bathroom on a regular basis. Most still preferred the morning ritual. When I returned to Rankhandi in 2014 it was being used as a storage shed. Baba had clearly intended to take advantage of my residence to acquire a rare status symbol.

There were two ways to defecate in Rankhandi. One could go into the fields every morning, or squat inside an space enclosed by bricks on three sides and otherwise open to the air on the family compound and defecate into powdery dirt. Every day the *bhangis* (a dalit/untouchable caste), took the feces away and disposed of it.

The Rankhandi men always preferred the first method to the second. They had an inherent repulsion for shared toilets and preferred to defecate in the open air. It was considered the most pleasant and civilized method. The few public toilets I used in India were often broken, with feces in piles, and often covered with flies. I still have vivid dreams of Rankhandi and India, with me encountering such piles of human feces or stepping through fields covered with it.

After the defecation ritual, I was taken to the women's quarters for breakfast and introduced to the women of the family. Unlike previous researchers, I religiously followed the participatory observation methodology, adopting the life of a village Rajput. This meant I ate the precise diet as the rest of my family. I did not have any special foods stashed away anywhere. I did, however, acquire peanuts on several occasions, which I then ate up on the roof.

Since there was no privacy in Rankhandi, villagers marked out areas where they could do things without being observed. One of these was on the roofs of buildings. The roofs were used to dry harvested grain and store animal feed. Rajput women, subject to purdah, could venture outside the zenana (women's quarters) surreptitiously and observe what was going on by sticking to the rooftops. When I wandered the narrow alleys of Rankhandi, I often spied women and teenaged girls eyeing me from above. When Baba learned I was eating peanuts, he admonished me, saying that I was a *brahmacharya* (celibate) and could therefore not eat peanuts. According to Baba, peanuts fell into the category of *Rajasic* (passion inducing) foods, and eating them increased the sex drive and made *brahmacharya* more difficult.

I quickly discovered that the standard Rankhandi diet was monochromatic, that is, it never changed. Each meal was the same as the last. We went for weeks eating the same thing. Our diet consisted of *dal* (spicy lentil soup), and *roti* (Indian flat bread). In Hindi this meal is often described simply as *dalroti*. Most of the time, we ate only these two items, but once in a while, someone acquired vegetables to vary our diet. The most common vegetable dish was potatoes and peas. When I travelled outside Rankhandi with village men, they took advantage of the trip to purchase fruit to supplement their monochromatic diet. The favorites were bananas, apples, and mangos. The Indian custom is to always present a gift when visiting anyone. Before stopping at the homes of people outside Rankhandi we always bought fruit for our hosts, usually bananas, apples, or mangos. When given fruit on these rare occasions, we ate it with great gusto.

American multinational corporations had not yet introduced processed junk foods into the Indian diet, and for Indians, snacks consisted of nuts, and fruit. The people of Rankhandi loved to eat Indian sweets (which are incredibly sweet since they consist of massive amounts of sugar boiled down with milk and formed into shapes – with some topped with tissues of edible silver). These sweets tended to be expensive, however, and reserved only for special occasions, such as religious festivals and weddings. The Coca Cola corporation had introduced Coke to India some time before and had heavily marketed it, but it was considered too expensive by villagers, and most were quite unfamiliar with it in any case. The only place it was consumed was during weddings, where it was served as an expensive status symbol. The villagers did not really like it, preferring to drink milk, tea, and fruit juice instead.

During the course of my day I routinely wandered the village engaging in friendly conversation with all and sundry. I regularly chatted with a fellow who sold snacks from a small cart by the bridge. One morning he took great delight in showing me a Coke can. I read the label and saw that it was from Singapore. It must have made its way to India on an international flight. No canned drinks were sold in India at that time, and all the Coke was sold in returnable bottles. Only the most cosmopolitan Indians had seen canned Coke. The man assumed that I, like everyone in Rankhandi, had never seen a Coke can. He expected me to be as amazed as the other villagers.

Other examples of our rural isolation abound. The entire time I was in Rankhandi I only saw cars once or twice. I believe these private cars belonged to wealthy politicians who were making calls on our village headman. When these cars appeared, they caused a great uproar in the village. Children ran from their homes to get a glimpse of the cars and when they drove down the narrow streets, many children followed behind, laughing and shouting in their excitement.

On another occasion we listened to an address by the Prime Minister on the radio. As is the practice in India, after speaking in Hindi, he then spoke in English. The villagers immediately turned to me and asked why the Prime Minister was speaking in a foreign language on the radio. I explained to them that most Indians did not speak Hindi and therefore did not understand the Hindi speech and needed to hear it in English. They did not believe me. They insisted everyone in India spoke Hindi and that it was impossible that there were Indians who could not understand Hindi.

Since the Rajputs had given up subsistence farming in favor of cash farming, they had converted all their land holdings to sugar cane. They purchased flour to make chapattis and lentils to make dal at small village shops, and when finances permitted, purchased vegetables to supplement these essentials. The vegetables and dal were cooked in ancient metal pots. The women (who did all the cooking),

33

kept their spices in equally ancient wooden boxes divided into squares. They resembled the pillboxes that sick people use in the west to keep track of their medications. Because of the drought, monsoon rains had been sparse and crops were bad. This meant that the price of food skyrocketed and was at times too expensive to purchase. On these occasions, we went to culverts and harvested the green weeds that grew there. The women made them into a dish to replace our usual *roti* and *dal*.

As is the Indian custom, we drank only water with our meals. Throughout the day, the men who congregated in Baba's chopal made tea. Indian tea is boiled. The tea maker places tea, sugar, water and milk in a pot and boils them all together. Indians generally put lots of sugar in their tea, and when it is boiled it becomes sticky sweet and syrupy. This was particularly true in Rankhandi. Since we were in a sugar producing area, sugar was cheap and ubiquitous, and villagers used prodigious amounts of it.

Baba, who had lived in Rankhandi during the British colonial period, told me the British got Indians addicted to tea. This was a clever British ploy. They got the Chinese addicted to opium and the Indians addicted to tea, creating mutually supportive captive markets. British merchants then imported Indian opium to China and Chinese tea to India, charged everyone high prices and made more money than they ever imagined.

Over the course of the British raj, the British created an Indian tea industry, setting up tea estates that produced some of the best tea in the world. Ironically, all of the high grade tea is sold for export to the UK and other wealthy tea drinking countries. Only wealthy Indians can afford it. Only the unwanted remains of a quality too poor to sell abroad are sold in the Indian domestic market and consumed by the average Indian. The Indian way of making tea and the poor quality of the tea produces a heavily caffeinated drink. Many Indians are "addicted" to tea, as it is an interwoven part of their life that they cannot live without.

According to Baba, the villagers of Rankhandi drank only water and buffalo milk before the British raj. Then one day, a cart appeared in the village advertising a new drink called tea. The purveyor of the new drink offered free samples to everyone, until all acquired the tea drinking habit. He then stopped providing free samples and demanded cash. The people of Rankhandi have been drinking tea ever since.

Baba was elated when the water buffalo started producing milk. It was unpasteurized and unhomogenized and very thick. We boiled the milk for a long time (of course with lots of sugar), and drank it several times a day. All cooking was done on a *chulla* (a small enclosure of adobe bricks). The cooking fuel is *gobar* (cakes made of dried manure), which gives off a pungent odor when burned.

34

The buffalo milk was boiled for long periods. As a result, the milk absorbed the odor of the *gobar*. The thick mixture emitted a pungent earthy odor and took some getting used to.

My family also ate homemade yogurt, which they kept in an earthen pot. In the absence of refrigerators, this was supposed to keep the yogurt from spoiling. We received our electricity for only one hour every night, when everyone was asleep. The farmers woke up then to use electrically powered fodder cutting machines to prepare the food for their livestock. No one used electricity for any other purpose. I tried to eat this yogurt, but it was not always fresh and several times it made me retch. To this day, I still have trouble eating plain yogurt.

Under the then dominant purdah system, the residence pattern was divided, with women living in the women's quarters (*zenana*), and the men living in the men's quarters (*mardana*). Our men's quarters was the little courtyard that I and the male members of my family shared with the water buffalo and the single room dwelling/office. We reached the women's quarters by walking along a narrow pathway between ancient and decaying walls, with water buffalo tethered on both sides.

The Rajputs strictly followed *purdah* (the seclusion of women). Although they were Hindus, and this is a Muslim practice, they insisted they were forced to adopt this custom to protect the honor of their women. The story goes that during the Muslim period, Rajput women were renowned throughout India for their great beauty and were therefore often kidnapped by Muslim rulers for their harems. This, according to the story, compelled the Rajputs to place their women in *purdah*. They therefore spend their lives secluded within the *zenana,* and left only in the company of male relatives and only for special occasions like religious rituals, and the annual fair (*mela*) in Deoband. The lower caste women had more freedom, as they were expected to work in the fields. Rajput women always covered their heads and faces with their saris when outside the *zenana*. Lower caste women wore pants and blouses (*shalwar kameez*) and did not cover their heads.

While the story, like most Rajput stories, lauds the inherent superiority of the Rajputs, it is likely not the real explanation for this phenomenon. In reality, the Rajputs interacted closely with their Muslim conquerors, with many serving in the Muslim armies, and due to this close cultural interaction, the Rajputs adopted some common Muslim practices, such as *purdah*. It does contain a grain of truth, however. As the Mughul Empire went into decline Rankhandi's North Indian region no longer enjoyed the security provided by the government. A variety of groups took advantage of this situation to loot villages. I do not doubt that these robbers kidnapped attractive women and that Rajput men felt duty bound to prevent this at all costs.

The Rajputs distort this narrative in their own favor, however. One of the principal groups engaged in this looting was the Marathas, a Hindu group of horsemen which ranged far and wide engaging in plunder. Today, this ethnic group dominates the Indian state of Maharashtra. In the Rajput narrative, these robbers are always Muslim.

In response to this situation, every Rajput family in Rankhandi kept weapons in their home. All Rajputs, including women and children, were expected to know how to use them. Watchmen manned watchtowers around the village and rang the alert on bells if they spotted the approach of robber bands. Every male Rajput then grabbed his weapons and went to his assigned area to defend the village.

This reliance on weapons continues into the present day. Rajput males commonly carried long staffs (*lathi*), similar to the staffs used by the peasantry in medieval England. They used these staffs for herding livestock, but they were deadly weapons. The Rajputs increased their efficiency by pouring molten lead into both ends, or wrapping them in heavy wire. A blow on the head from a lathi would likely be fatal. In addition, the Rajputs kept firearms hidden in secluded places, and brought them out in times of threat or disorder.

Although we were living in the 20th Century, the security situation in Saharanpur District, in which Rankhandi was located, was still poor. Articles in the Indian press had christened our district "the bandit capital of India" (bandits are called *dacoits* in local parlance). There were no police in Rankhandi. The police station was located in Deoband. The police were commonly assumed to be cowardly, corrupt, and sadistic. They had only one forensic method. When called to solve a crime, they rounded up suspects and tortured them until someone confessed. They often refused to take on a case unless bribed.

As a result, the Rajputs relied on themselves to provide security. The Rajputs had no faith in modern cash and banks. They placed their faith in gold, and kept their gold in buried stashes. It was their security in bad times, and was used to pay for lavish village weddings, or medical and other emergencies. The dacoits were well-aware of these stashes and used a standard methodology to convince the villagers to part with their gold. They threatened to torture the family's small children unless they revealed the locations of their hidden stashes. To avoid getting into such a situation, the village maintained an informal watch system to provide some warning of the approach of armed robbers. This gave the Rajputs time to access their firearms and mount a defense.

The government knew full well that it could not rely on local police to maintain order. When a dacoit band got out of hand, the government deployed federal paramilitaries to resolve the situation.

India has several such groups, each with their appointed tasks. For example the Central Reserve Police Force (CRPF) was fully equipped to take on and "nullify" robber bands. They boasted armored vehicles, automatic weapons, and mortars, and did not hesitate to use them. When called in to clean up a robber band, they first went to the home village of the robbers and "convinced" their families to reveal their hideouts. This coercion often consisted of torture. They then drove to the hideout with a large force and killed everyone in the band. They did not take prisoners, and no robbers were ever put on trial.

Sushma was Pita's wife. Her sole job was to cook for us. She cooked all day long, sitting on the floor in front of a small mud fireplace (*chula*) feeding a fire that burned dried cow dung cakes. She cooked *roti* on a griddle suspended over the flames in a small adobe room. It was always filled with smoke. Almost everyone ignored her, and I made a point of eating my morning *roti* and *dal* with her and conversing about her and her life. She was very appreciative and very affectionate. Stoicism is the principal component of the Rajput ethos and a huge facet of the Rajput personality. As such, they make no overt displays of affection and never speak to each other in affectionate terms. People living in this culture learn to communicate affection in other ways. As I became acculturated to Rajput life, I learned how to perceive the subtle signals Rajputs used to communicate affection.

The women lived in close quarters within the confines of the zenana. On three sides of the zenana were bare adobe walls. The fourth side consisted of a series of rooms. Some women slept in these rooms on occasion, but they were actually used for storage. The family's possessions, mostly clothing and bedding, were kept there in aluminum trunks stacked up to the ceiling. Some 25 women and girls lived in the zenana and they slept outdoors, with their cots side by side. When husbands wanted to have sex with their wives, they made an appointment. The wife stayed awake and when everyone was asleep, the husband slipped into the zenana. I assume that if anyone was still awake or was awakened by such a nocturnal visit, they pretended to be asleep.

Indian culture is often stereotyped as being puritanical, as many aspects of sexuality are not openly acknowledged or talked about. This generalization can be over-stressed, however, especially when talking about rural people. They grow up with farm animals and are well-aware of the facts of life from an early age. The Rajputs of Rankhandi also live in close quarters with no privacy and are, as a matter of course, exposed to sexual behavior. In my long conversations with family members and other villagers, I discovered that there were no taboo topics, and that everyone in the village discussed many aspects of sexual behavior with no shame or embarrassment.

It was in the zenana that I met Mataji for the first time. She was Baba's wife and the family matriarch.

She controlled the finances and did not allow Baba access to much money. She also was in charge of his meals. They had an acrimonious relationship. She freely yelled at him and insulted him in front of everyone, and he was meek and mild in her presence. The Rajput custom was to never use the spouse's name. Baba called his wife "*gharwali*" (housewife). While Mataji ruled with an iron hand, I managed to get on her good side, probably because I took the time to converse with her and the other women and showed interest in them as persons. In this patriarchal, sexually divided society, the men lived in their own realm and had minimal interaction with their female family members. Rajput men did not have the concept of female companionship. The viewed women primarily as the providers of cooked food, children, and sex.

As such, they placed a low premium on girls and did not take any role in child care. Girls were quickly assigned child care duties. Girls as young as six years old were given infants to care for. Pita had a child who was mentally handicapped. Although he was several years old, he was so small that he could easily be mistaken for an infant. He was skinny and unresponsive, and his face covered with mucus. Flies were everywhere in Rankhandi, and they settled in great numbers on his eyes and the mucus covering his face. One of Pita's daughters, a young girl of perhaps seven or eight, carried this baby everywhere. Her job was to make sure he did not wander off or was stepped on. The families of Rankhandi did not use diapers. The babies and toddlers were kept naked and urinated and defecated wherever they happened to be.

After some time, mataji told me I was not a guest but a member of their family. My kinship status was readily acknowledged by all within the *zenana*. The women who lived there freely interacted with me without embarrassment. We spent pleasant hours talking about all manner of subjects and joking and laughing together. Women were kept in the *zenana* and not allowed to show their faces to anyone outside their family, but when I entered the *zenana* women were often bathing naked under the water pumps in front of me. They showed no embarrassment and conversed freely with me while bathing. After all, I was a member of the family and the rules of *purdah* did not apply to me.

The other person in my immediate family group was Krishan. He was not actually Pita's son, but Pita's nephew. Earlier, Pita had gone to Baba and said he needed a son and Baba had told his other son Amarnath to hand Krishan over to him. This happened when Krishan was small. No one ever mentioned the fact that Pita was not Krishan's natural father, and I only discovered this much later when it came up in conversation.

Krishan was a typical village farmer. He got up in the middle of the night every night of the week to cut grain stalks as feed for the water buffalo. During the day, he took a short sickle to the road side and cut plants growing there and carried them back to the chopal to feed the livestock. He made sure all the animals were fed and the cows milked before going out into the fields, where he worked from dawn until dusk.

Although he was not a religious devotee, Krishan had seen the impact of intoxication and addiction on his grandfather and uncle and abjured all intoxicants. Unlike most in Rankhandi, he had graduated from high school, and therefore was able to converse in standard Hindi. Most villagers spoke only the village dialect. Under village exogamy, the wives of Rankhandi all came from other villages. This means that none of the mothers were natives of Rankhandi. Our wives came from the state of Punjab and often spoke more Punjabi than Hindi. The village dialect was therefore a mixture of grammatically incorrect Hindi and poor Punjabi, that could be unintelligible to standard Hindi speakers.

Baba told Krishan to become my assistant, and the two of us went everywhere in the village together. When in the course of conversation, I had difficulty understanding someone's village dialect, Krishan translated into standard Hindi. He also helped me improve my vocabulary. Every evening we sat together and he taught me eight or ten new words. Krishan, unlike many villagers, could also read and write Hindi, which made him very useful. While there were 92 people in my extended family, I interacted primarily with this nuclear family group, and these persons were the most significant.

Pita, as promised, took me to a village barber. As is the custom in India, the barber worked outdoors. He had an old wooden chair set up by the tonga stand. He provided me with a standard Indian men's haircut that I maintained throughout my stay in India. I wore western clothes for the first few days in Rankhandi, but quickly adopted Indian dress. I preferred the more traditional *kurta/pajama* outfit (always white), while many younger Rajputs preferred to wear trousers rather than *pajama*. Later, I also started wearing a *lungi* (a piece of cloth wrapped around the body and tied at the waist). Baba and the older men wore only white *dhotis* and *kurta*.

After my haircut I was taken to the intercollege. I thought I was only going to get a tour, but discovered the entire student body sitting in the school parade ground awaiting my arrival. In India, students have an outdoor morning assembly in which they are often addressed by the principal, perform exercises, sing patriotic songs, or conduct prayers or religious ceremonies. I was taken in front of the student body and told to address them. This caught me completely unawares and I had to make up something on the spot. Over the years this would happen to me on different occasions, and I would do extemporaneous speaking in German, Hindi, Urdu, and Bengali to different audiences. While what I said was never that profound, the audiences were always polite.

I was also introduced to the village doctor and to Khaala Singh, one of the senior teachers. He was one of the educated Rajputs and part of a group trying to bring social change to the village. Unlike most villagers, he had been to big cities and had an inkling of life outside Rankhandi. In one conversation with villagers, he tried to explain the concept of a napkin to people who had never heard of it. They did not believe him and thought he had made the whole thing up. Khaala Singh tried to convince village families to plant vegetable gardens to supplement their monochromatic diet of *roti* and *dal* and improve their health. He maintained his own garden as an example to the other villagers and sat in his courtyard enjoying vegetables in full view of everyone in the village.

I later learned that his weakness was teenaged girls. He used his status as a village teacher and high caste Rajput to coerce female students into having sex with him. He once offered to procure for me any village girl that I wanted. I explained to him that I was a "*bhagat*" (religious devotee) and *brahmacharya* who did not engage in such things, and he never brought up the subject again.

Our village was a "Congress village," meaning that everyone was expected to vote a straight Congress Party ticket in elections. This makes perfect sense. Congress governments had invested a lot of time and money in Rankhandi, and its leaders were grateful.

The village headman was devoted to the Congress Party and worked with Khaala Singh to bring change to the village. The headman was very popular and well-respected (and wealthy). He had a large home in the center of the village. His big concerns were what we would now call "female empowerment" and family planning.

He called a big meeting of everyone in the village and told the men they needed to limit the size of their families. He told them that the best way to do so was male sterilization, as the operation was short and relatively painless. He said that they should not put their wives through a complex and painful sterilization process. Indian men are often reluctant to undergo sterilization out of fear that they will lose their virility. Our head man bragged that he had already had the operation and was as good as he ever was.

He built a covered verandah around his home (the only one in the village) and instead of *charpoy*, he put tables and chairs there. Every morning, he had his daughters sit in chairs on the verandah and read the newspaper. He wanted to demonstrate to the villagers that girls should go to school and be taught to read, and should be fully involved in village affairs. He had a big impact on Rankhandi. When I went to the school, I saw that it was not just boys. There were many girl students, as well.

I was also introduced to the village doctor. He was a Brahmin, not a Rajput, and was not from Rankhandi. He was a government employee, and came from a town high up in the Himalayas (called a "hill station" in Indian parlance). Over the course of my travels through the Himalayas, I travelled to his home town and enjoyed it immensely. Like me, he was an educated outsider. The doctor and the teacher and I spent hours together discussing many things outside the purview of the average villager. They followed national politics and knew something of the world, while the average villager talked of more mundane things. These two men were the only persons I knew of in Rankhandi who could converse in English, although with some difficulty.

Krishan and most villagers were enamored of Hindi movies. Since there was no electricity, it was dark at night and there was almost nothing to do to pass the time after sundown. We lay on our *charpoys* making small talk and looking up at a sea of stars in the sky. I could see the entire night sky clearly, as there were no electric lights for many miles and therefore no light pollution, and picked out numerous falling stars every night.

The younger men had battery powered transistor radios and spent endless hours listening to Hindi film music. They particularly enjoyed listening to "dialogs." These are scenes lifted out of Hindi movies and played over the radio. Since Hindi movies are usually melodramas, the dialogs are quite melodramatic. The village boys recited them by heart and took turns, going from one scene to the next.

VII

Working in agriculture without mechanization is a lot of hard work. Krishan and Pita were away in the fields all day, while Baba enjoyed his retirement in the *mardana* with his old buddies, drinking tea, taking his opium, and reading the *Ramayana* over and over again.

As part of my acculturation process I did some work in the fields as well. I grabbed a scythe and cut grain, and helped with the harvesting. The family also taught me how to drive the *buggi*, sitting directly behind the water buffalo, hitting him with a stick, and jabbing his testes to make him run faster. I was also supposed to learn how to drive a tractor, but somehow this got overlooked.

I was familiar with the life of the livestock that I shared my space with. They were always fed at the same time and taken out into the fields at the crack of dawn, and after a hard day's work, were taken to the river for their swim and to cool down. I specifically asked my family about the names of the animals. They said that they did not give names to animals.

A pack of semi-feral dogs hung around the chopal. No one fed them or showed them any affection. They waited around when we ate and grabbed whatever they could. Sometimes someone threw them a piece of *roti*, which they eagerly devoured. The men did not hesitate to throw rocks at them or kick them. Since the people of Rankhandi had no concept of family pets, I was not quite sure why the dogs were there. Perhaps they served as yet another security device in this bandit-infested region.

While family members engaged in their routines, I had my own. I spent my days wandering the village and getting to know people from all castes and walks of life and income levels. I observed what was happening all over the village and administered questionnaires. You can read all about my research in *Alcohol Consumption in a Village in North India*. In the evening I had my language lesson with Krishan. Of course my Hindi fluency was already expanding rapidly just

41

through extensive daily interaction. Constant use of a second language is how it is developed. It is just like any other skill, in that it improves with practice. You can tell you have reached a certain level of fluency when you are no longer conscious of which language you are speaking. Two other things happen. You begin to dream in your new language, and you learn to appreciate humor. It was while I lived in Rankhandi that I started having extensive dreams in Hindi. These have continued up to the present.

After my language lesson, I retreated into the room in the *chopal* and wrote up all of my data. I had a little portable typewriter and typed up my notes. I also took lots of pictures that were later turned into slides for use in presenting my research, and made some audio tapes of conversations, and interviews.

Mike and I had devised a cover story before my departure. I originally told everyone I was studying the history of the Rajputs. Rajput villagers were always ready and willing to talk about Rajput history. They were very conscious of their heritage and their role in Indian history. They regaled me with long tales of life in medieval and colonial times.

I learned that we belonged to the Pundir *gotra*, (lineage), and were directly descended from Arjun. He was one of the five Pandavas in the *Mahabharata* and was Lord Krishna's close friend and confidant. The *Bhagavad Gita* is a conversation between Arjuna and Krishna in which they discuss all manner of spiritual topics. They are able to do so because they are such close friends. Arjun is thus a human being who was a close friend of God. At one point Arjun's close friend reveals his true identity as the Lord of all creation, but Arjuna cannot stand to look at this form and begs Krishna to resume his human form.

This connection to the Hindu epics was very real to everyone in my extended family. It was reconfirmed every year when the genealogist came to the village. He kept ancient books that must have gone back centuries, in which it was said were recorded all of the births and deaths of the Pundirs, from the time of Arjuna (5,000 years ago) to the present. I sat with him, as he pulled out a pen and wrote down the information in his huge book, and he showed me the lineage stretching back into the distant past.

I was actually studying the Rajput alcohol drinking pattern, including its many pathological aspects, and kept this aspect of my research hidden. Mike had told me that once I had spent sufficient time in Rankhandi, everyone would be so used to me that they would no longer be conscious of my presence. This was certainly true. After a certain point, no one held anything back from me. I joined the Rajput men in their drinking sprees, although I did not participate. As a *bhagat*, I was not expected to. We all sat on charpoys. The men uncorked bottles of homemade rum. They put the bottles to their lips and drank as much as they could. The drinking ended when they passed out unconscious.

One of the men I encountered was our next door neighbor. He took a special interest in me and tried to cultivate a relationship. One night he became particularly aggressive. I was put off by him and tried to make a polite exit, but he started to get angry and threaten me. Pita then intervened, pulling me away and taking me back to our chopal. He explained that the neighbor had a bad reputation and was a dangerous man.

One afternoon it became quite apparent just how dangerous he was. I was relaxing, when I heard a scattering of gunfire just down the street. Neighbors quickly ran into our *chopal* to inform us that this particular neighbor had decided to put the Brahmins in their place. He had just entered the home of a leading Brahmin family, killing the patriarch, his wife and other relatives, and then fleeing. We quickly ran to the scene of the crime. Villagers had taken the bodies and laid them out for all to see. They were arrayed in a line, with the gunshot wounds and the blood clearly evident. They were still wearing the clothes they wore when murdered and were covered with blood.

This was another aspect of my Indian acculturation. Indians do not possess the strong taboo against death and dying that is often found in Western countries. Over the course of my years in India, I saw dead bodies on numerous occasions. Like Indians, I took this to be part of my natural environment.

The man fled and started his own bandit gang and started looting and plundering local villages. The police were asked to intervene and showed up in Rankhandi, only to cart away his possessions. To keep the police at bay, my neighbor crept up to the police station and tossed a hand grenade inside. The police got the message and quietly closed the case and returned the purloined possessions to his family.

In the end, as was often the case, villagers took justice into their own hands and ended his bandit career. He had come to a local village and was invited to sit down for tea and snacks. While he was imbibing, a villager quietly approached him from behind and strangled him with a cord. His body was brought back to Rankhandi for cremation. As a fellow Rajput, I participated in the cremation ceremony, walking around the burning funeral pyre and tossing in pieces of wood to feed the flames, while the priest recited the funeral *mantras*. The bandit was not popular in Rankhandi and had revealed himself to be a cold-blooded killer, but in the end, was a son of the village.

VIII

I was not always in Rankhandi. Sometimes I took trips with family members, usually Baba. Everyone traveled on the train. Baba was very particular about money and determined to spend as little as possible. Before leaving, he wrapped money up in his undershirt (*banyan*). He told me this money was only for tea on the train, as it was impossible to travel anywhere without drinking tea. True to his word, he pulled out the coins at every stop and purchased tea from the hawkers manning the railway platforms. The tea cost only 40 paisa, less than one half of one rupee, a fraction of a cent in American money.

Once, when traveling with Krishan, we decided to engage in "ticketless travel" by riding on a freight train. We climbed onto a flat car with lots of other people also riding free. Our fellow passengers included a group of *sadhus*, (mendicants) wandering from town to town.

We did not only travel by train. Once Baba and I left the railway station, we often walked for miles along country roads, sometimes hitching rides with local farmers in their *buggis* or tongas.

I took a trip with Baba purely for fun. He decided we should go together and see the countryside. It was not clear to me whether Baba had any itinerary. It seemed we were wandering aimlessly. When Baba arrived in a village, he always asked for the residence of the wealthiest Rajput. We then went there and announced ourselves as fellow Rajputs. The wealthy Rajput always laid out a feast for us, consisting of a wide variety of delicious vegetarian dishes. It was no simple *dal/roti* for us. We were even given delicious *ghee* (clarified butter) to put on our food. *Ghee* is really delicious and makes everything taste wonderful. We rarely ate *ghee* at home.

We also traveled to the villages in which family daughters were married. Every Rajput girl born in Rankhandi knows she will be given away to another family and will not live in her ancestral village all her life. This village exogamy system ensures there are no incestual marriages, but also provides opportunity for widespread abuse of Rankhandi brides. Once they move from their village and their families, they belong to the family of their husbands, who can take advantage of them, as none of their relatives are around to protect them.

It is the duty of the bride's brother to protect her. The brother is expected to keep tabs on his sisters, and they are expected to keep him abreast of what is happening with them. That is why this brother/sister relationship is so important. It is demarcated by the Hindu festival of Rakhee. Hindu women tie a reddish saffron string around the wrist of a male friend, demarcating him as her "brother." While this is a great honor, it also entails great obligation. Just as the natural brother protects his sister, the new "rakhee brother" is supposed to protect his new sister. With the strong condemnation of incest in Hindu culture, this asexual relationship is considered "pure" and beyond reproach.

Since many Rankhandi brides were literate, they wrote letters home and could report ill treatment. Such a report would bring the brother from Rankhandi and could be the cause of serious conflict. As part of this system, we took periodic trips to villages Rankhandi women had married into. Everyone knew that the purpose of these visits was to check up on the Rankhandi daughters and make sure they were alright, but maintained the fiction that it was simply a friendly family visit.

Many observers say India is a country which exists in several centuries simultaneously. This became quite apparent to me on one such visit. We took the train, and walked, and hitched rides on farmers' carts to get to this village. We arrived at night. There was no electricity, so the village was dark, and I felt like I had slipped backward in time. The village was more remote and more traditional than Rankhandi. We went to the home where the Rankhandi daughter lived. It was a timeless mud brick building. We sat in the courtyard, and the only light came from traditional clay lamps. They were filled with ghee, with wicks laid in channels around the outside. The light was diffuse and wavering and reflected off the mud walls, which were adorned with folk art murals depicting Rajput warriors. The murals appeared as if they could have been painted in the Indian medieval period and not touched since. The men of the bride's family entertained us. We never saw a woman. Instead, *charpoys* were turned on their sides to form screens. Behind these makeshift screens sat women busily making fresh *chapattis* for us. As we ate, hands emerged from behind the *charpoys* to deliver freshly made roti.

The relationships between the groom's family and the bride's family were frosty and reserved and there was an underlying undercurrent of hostility despite the hospitality. They did not like being inspected and we were always looking for signs of abuse. Later, Baba and Pita met with the daughter privately to make sure she was safe and listen to her complaints. Sometimes the abuse became too much to bear, and these young brides committed suicide by jumping into village wells. Mike and other researchers had documented suicides by Rankhandi's Punjabi brides. Thankfully, none took place while I was resident there.

I also travelled with family members to the nearby towns of Deoband, Sharanpur, Muzaffarnagar and Meerut, where we walked through bazaars poking into stalls and ate generous portions of street snacks and fruit. During one such trip I found a huge Hindi/English copy of the *Ramayana*, and was determined to buy it. The shopkeeper, noticing my white face, refused to bargain and insisted on a high price. My companions then insisted he come down and I was able to purchase it. The book is still in my library.

There was only one television in Rankhandi and it was at the intercollege. The most popular television program in India was *Geet Mala* (necklace of songs) and the *Hindi Feature Film*, which ran every Sunday night. When this program was on, the living room of the TV owner was packed with viewers from all over the village and others congregated at the windows and watched the film from outside.

We went to cinemas and saw Hindi movies whenever we went to nearby towns. On one occasion we watched a film in Saharanpur called *Love in Canada*. Since the film was supposed to be about overseas Indians living in Canada, they sometimes spoke a few words in English. Whenever the characters spoke English, the entire crowd (all males) would start shouting "Hindi, Hindi, Hindi." They were most assuredly not aware of why English was being used and were quite angry.

The nearest town was Deoband, and we went there most frequently. It was a Muslim majority town and the site of a famous Islamic seminary. The town was incredibly filthy. Piles of rotting garbage were everywhere and sewage ran down the streets. We stopped to have tea at a local tea stall and sat outside. As soon as I put my cup down, it was covered with flies. It was such an incredible experience that I took a picture. The cup was no longer white. Every centimeter of its surface was covered by a living fly.

Once, while travelling on the train I got into a conversation with a young man from a Sikh family. His father was an engineer at a local factory and he was able to converse in perfect English. When he heard I was living in Rankhandi and existing on a diet of dal/roti, he took pity on me and said I could stop by his house and his mother would prepare me any dish I wanted. I thanked him for his gracious offer and duly showed up at his house several weeks later. It was a delight to meet his family. I told his mother that my favorite dish was an Indian vegetable called *Kereela* (bitter gourd). She made it for me, was a wonderful cook, and I never enjoyed a meal more.

During my Rankhandi stay I made several trips back to Delhi on the train. I took care of various administrative tasks and stayed with the Naths and enjoyed their hospitality. I took Krishan to Delhi with me on one such occasion.

He had never been to a big city and had never met westernized English-speaking Indians. I took him to the Ashoka Hotel, one of the only five star hotels in India and showed him an escalator. He was amazed and rode up and down on it over and over again. I indulged him and let him ride it as long as he wanted. I then took him to Khan Market, not far from the Nath residence, where I gave him ice cream and chocolate for the first time in his life. We then went to the cinema and saw the movie *Oh God*, starring George Burns. I explained to him that unlike Hindi movies, it did not contain any singing or dancing and thought he would find it very boring, especially since he spoke no English whatsoever. He was delighted by the whole experience. When he got back to Rankhandi, he regaled everyone with stories of the exotic foods he had eaten and the wonderful English movie. Miraculously, he had memorized several lines from the film, although he did not know what they meant, and, just like the Hindi "dialogs," he recited them to his friends.

On one such trip, my return journey from Delhi to Rankhandi was delayed and did not arrive until late in the night. When I arrived at the railway platform, I found a group of Rankhandi Rajputs waiting for me, armed with lathis and knives. They explained that there would be no way I could get back to Rankhandi in the dead of night without being robbed and killed, and they had come to ensure I got back safely. We all rode back on a tractor.

The big occasions for everyone to get a break from the endless drudgery and work were weddings and the annual fair in Deoband. When a wedding was held in Rankhandi, the women were allowed out of the zenana to participate and dressed in their best saris and jewelry. Loudspeakers placed on poles all over the village blasted out Bollywood tunes at maximum volume. The speakers were cheap and the music so distorted as to be unintelligible.

No one danced. That would have been totally out of character for Rajputs. In addition to the Hindi music, hijra were hired to provide entertainment.[5] The hijra dressed in full female regalia, including saris, heavy make-up and lots of jewelry, danced provocatively. My family members told me not to associate with them or get into conversations with them, as they were quite violent and dangerous. They were very loud and spoke rudely to everyone. In addition to dancing, hijra are also supposed to provide sexual services to men for a price.

The Rajput men also drank large amounts of country liquor (a home-brewed rum made from their own sugar cane) and everyone ate prodigious amounts of food. I participated in the wedding preparation. A large pot several meters in diameter was filled with sticky sweet paste consisting of butter fat and sugar and nuts. We sat in a long line and rolled this paste into balls. These were the wedding sweets.

To eat the food, we sat in lines along the ground (langur lines) with plates made of green leaves in front of us. Men with buckets of food and long ladles walked along the lines dishing out the food and placing it on our leaf plates. They kept serving for as long as we wanted to eat. Groups of dalits waited in the dark, just outside where we ate. After the caste Hindus had eaten, the dalits were served the leftovers.

The Hindu wedding ceremony is quite lengthy and goes on for hours. Most villagers ignored this part of the wedding and loudly conversed while it transpired. I was one of the only people paying attention.

A big part of the wedding is the presentation of the dowry. The bride's family must provide the correct items and in the desired quantity or problems could result. To verify that everything is being done correctly, the items are laid out for

[5] The definition of Hijra is: a person whose gender identity is neither male nor female, typically a person who was born male and dresses as a woman. Hijra can be hermaphroditic or male. In extreme instances, hijra are subjected to castration as part of their induction into hijra society.

all to see. The desired items included cookware, furniture, and bicycles, but the most important items were the gold jewelry. During this presentation, villagers armed with shotguns stood guard to ensure nothing was stolen.

I was often an honored guest at village weddings, but it was not the case when we attended weddings outside of our village. On one such occasion, large groups of village women congregated on the rooftops to get a glimpse of me when I walked with my family members to the festivities. This angered the men of the village, who said I was enticing their women and bringing dishonor to the community. They told my family that if I showed up at the wedding they would kill me. In order to prevent my murder, my family lied to me about the time of the wedding. They told me to get some sleep and that they would wake me up in time to join the festivities. They deliberately let me sleep and went to the wedding without me. The next morning they informed me of what happened.

Once a year, the entire village attended the Deoband mela. It took place on a large flat field. A series of tent booths served food and sold all manner of cheap trinkets, including lots of very cheap toys. This was one occasion when village people felt indulgent and loosened the purse strings. The children received cheap toys that they played with for a few hours, until all were broken and cast aside.

For many Rajput women, this was one of the few occasions they were allowed out of the zenana, and they were in a festive mood. We walked in a big group down the country road to the fairgrounds. Even though the women were out and about, they still kept their faces covered with their saris. They met other women from all over the village and socialized and talked loudly.

The high point for the women was the chance to see a Hindi movie in the movie tent. The film was projected on a screen inside the tent and the women squatted on the ground on top of tarpaulins and were captivated by the world of Bollywood. The principal reason for Bollywood films is to provide escape for people such as these, whose lives can be drab and difficult. Their sole purpose is to provide escape in an Indian cultural context. The educated English speaking Indians often deride Hindi films as facile and simple-minded, but they are not made for this audience. They are made largely for illiterate or barely educated villagers and slum dwellers. For the women of my family they provided an essential escape that they looked forward to all year. I sat with them on the ground and we all watched the film "Don" together. It was a blockbuster Hindi film filled with action, dancing, excitement, and lots of sentimentality. In traditional Indian culture women are considered overly "sentimental" and the Hindi film industry caters to this segment by including sappy scenes in each film that center around revered widows and religious themes. Hindi films are generally very long and contain scenes tailored to the various groups watching. Men are considered "lusty" and the movies thus include violent and sexy scenes meant for them.

Afterwards, I and a group of young village men walked together through the rows of stalls eating lots of snack food and sweets, laughing and joking together.

Everyone was in high spirits. Rajputs maintain their stoic persona year round and 24 hours per day. This was one of the rare occasions when they relaxed and allowed themselves to be spontaneous and have fun.

IX

As a member of the family, I was a full participant in its religious life. I discovered that Rankhandi was a place with many and varied religious options. The Rajputs had a reputation for taking their obligation to defend Hinduism against all comers very seriously, but were not renowned for their spirituality. Most Rajput men in my family said they did not have sufficient self-discipline to be a truly observant religious practitioner.

As Rajputs, they were members of the second highest of the four varnas (castes), just below the Brahmins. However, they did not lead a brahminical lifestyle, in that they were very fond of intoxication, and sexual exploits both in and out of marriage. In addition, as Rajputs they had a special dispensation that allowed them to eat meat. The rationale was that they required warrior strength to fulfill their dharma as defenders of Hinduism. The Rajput men in my family rarely worshipped at the village temple, although it was just a short distance away, had very little interaction with the temple priest, and did not conduct personal *puja* (worship) in their home. They did not maintain home altars like other high-caste Hindus. They left this type of piety to other castes.

A small group of religious adherents met at the temple regularly to sing religious songs (*bhajan*) and discuss religious topics. None of them were Rajputs. My family expressed a lot of respect for these persons and anyone who led a religious life. I once went with Baba and Pita to the village of the Tyagis, a caste renowned for its religious devotion. The Rajputs, known for their pride bordering on arrogance, went out of their way to show respect to their Tyagi hosts. Baba said it was a great privilege to eat with them and spend time with them. We should all admire them, he said, because they are sincere in their purity.

The Rajputs lack of spiritual practice was not because of any questioning of their faith. They held everything Hindu in high regard, and participated fully in all the rituals of their folk religion, and observed all Hindu festivals with great enthusiasm. The Rajput men were particularly enamored with the Hindu epics, the *Mahabharata* and the *Ramayana*, and were always happy to hear stories from these works, or to hear someone reading them. For them, these works were not mythology or fiction, but fact. To them, the events in these epics were absolutely real, and served as a working model for the daily conduct of their lives.

Baba told me his copy of the *Ramayana* was getting worn out because of repeated readings and asked me to buy him a new one. I told him I was happy to comply. "It must be in Urdu," he said, "I cannot read anything else." Baba was of the elder, pre-independence generation. During the British Raj, Urdu was the lingua franca, and Baba was educated in this medium.

Urdu is written in the Persian script and is almost non-existent in modern India. After independence, India adopted Hindi as the national language. It is rooted in Sanskrit and written in the devanagri script, just like Sanskrit. Indians of the post-independence generations cannot read anything in Urdu, as it largely confined to Muslim neighborhoods. Likewise, Baba could not read anything in Hindi. I wondered where I would be able to find an Urdu copy of the *Ramayana*, since this is a Hindu epic and Urdu is the language of Indian Muslims. Baba told me that there were many Urdu bookstalls by the Jama Masjid (the Mughul's imperial Mosque) in Delhi and that I would find one there. To my surprise, he was right. I found one in a bookshop filled with books on Islam. Baba was very happy to get a new copy.

Because Rankhandi was a Rajput village, the Rajputs held the political and economic power. However, it was the Brahmins that monopolized the religious status. As a result, the Rajputs were suspicious of the Brahmins, and viewed them as rivals. While all high-caste people in Rankhandi engaged in agriculture and worked hard in the fields, the Brahmins benefitted from their priestly status and used it to make extra money. They charged the Rajputs to perform the many ceremonies that marked the course of life.

Rajput men were also skeptical about the many *Sadhus* (mendicants) who passed through the village. High-caste Hindus in Rankhandi were expected to entertain these sadhus by preparing rich food for them. The Rajput men told me they suspected that many of these sadhus were not genuine, but were just lazy fellows who did not want to work. While sadhus were supposed to be celibate, the Rajput men suspected that they actually lusted after village girls. Whenever sadhus were in the village, the men made sure the women remained in the zenana and they did not allow the sadhus to visit while they were away in the fields.

This skepticism did not prevent the Rajput men from fulfilling their duty. The Rajputs (and other castes in the village) accorded me special status, as I was revered as a "bhagat" (devotee). I was highly regarded for my daily reading of the *Bhagavad Gita* and my abstinence from intoxication and sex, and everyone agreed I exhibited spiritual qualities. This meant I was accorded the same status as the Sadhus. When they came to the village, they were placed in a village square surrounded by other buildings. Sitting on the ground, they were then fed many courses of vegetarian food prepared by the village women. Whenever this occurred, I was placed next to the sadhus and provided this food. This is called "*darshan*" (viewing). The belief is that the observer acquires special merit just by viewing the holy person and feeding him. The women in particular, hoped the sadhus would bless them with children, good husbands and other wishes.

I found most sadhus to be pleasant and gentle folk and not nearly as nefarious as depicted by the Rankhandi Rajputs. One of them explained to me that before becoming a sadhu, he had been a high-ranking civil servant. He wanted to follow the traditional Hindu pattern of life and give up everything in his old age and pursue *moksha* (liberation). He had walked away from his wife and children and comfortable life to wander India among the sadhus. He was an educated and articulate fellow and quite sincere.

I had a different experience with the sadhus I encountered in a temple in Saharanpur. I had gone there with a neighbor active in the Congress Party. His political meeting was to last all afternoon. He explained to me that it was quite boring and I should go spend the time in a nearby temple. He took me there and placed me among a group of sadhus covered in ashes, with long plaited locks, dressed only in dirty loincloths. I spent the afternoon with them, but it was not very edifying. They pulled out their chillums (clay pipes) and stuffed them with pure oily hashish and smoked continuously for the entire time I was with them. They were so stoned that they were incapable of conversation. So I sat there in silence in the heart of the temple in a cloud of hashish smoke until my neighbor came to pick me up.

The strength of the belief in *darshan* was exhibited to me one day when I was busily working at my desk typing up my notes. I looked up to notice a man I had never seen before standing just a few feet away and staring at me. I asked him what he was there for. He said he had travelled from another village to come to Rankhandi to get a glimpse of me. "Now that I have seen you," he said, "I can go home," and he quickly left.

The women were more conventionally religious in Hindu terms than their husbands. They were strict vegetarians and would not cook meat or even touch dishes and utensils that had come into contact with meat. Unlike the men, the women abstained from all intoxication and never touched alcohol or the wide variety of drugs circulating in the village. The women conducted many religious rituals in the zenana, and gathered together regularly to sing religious songs (bhajan). Men were not allowed to participate. The women made elaborate images of village gods and goddesses on the walls of the family's buildings out of cow dung and surrounded them with folk designs in white paint.

All Rajputs maintained ancestral shrines in the fields and every year went there to conduct ceremonies in honor of their departed ancestors. I participated in this ritual, which was quite elaborate. It was another certification of my role as an esteemed member of the family.

Another aspect of the village religion was the belief in ghosts and spirits that haunted the village cremation ground. These spirits were malign, as they were souls unable to transmigrate into their next birth and cursed to haunt the cremation ground. I was told never to walk there at night, lest they attack me. I asked whether anyone had seen them, and was told many villagers had spotted them at night. They drift suspended about a meter off of the ground and their feet are backwards.

As I grew closer to my Rajput family, I felt free to talk about anything and everything with them. I asked the men why they did not wear *jeneuu* (the sacred thread). All high-caste (twice-born) men are supposed to wear a white thread over their right shoulder as a mark of their twice-born status, but no Rajputs I knew wore one. They all stated that to wear the sacred thread was a huge obligation, in that it required a pure life and lots of religious observance. No Rajput man I encountered felt up to the challenge. I had discussed this with Mataji and one day she called me to the zenana and presented me with the sacred thread.

In retrospect I should not have accepted it from her. High caste Hindus are not supposed to wear jeneuu without the necessary rituals. At the time of the twice born ceremony, the family priest gives the man the Gayathri mantra, which he is supposed to repeat daily as long as he wears the jeneuu. I did not meet any of these qualifications. Despite this, I wore jeneuu for the last several months I resided in Rankhandi. It must always be kept clean and a man who wears it must put it over his right ear when urinating or defecating. The Rajputs of my family were quite proud that one of their members was an actual jeneuu-wearing Rajput.

X

By the end of my stay in Rankhandi, it had been nine months of unrelenting village life. I was starting to feel disoriented and cut-off from the wider world. I concluded that there was no further benefit to be gained from remaining. I had concluded my research and was not going to acquire more valuable data. I longed to get back in touch with my previous life and the wider world. It was just a fact of life and nothing negative. I was grateful for the experience and grateful to my family. They had opened up to me, welcomed me into their midst and treated me like any other family member. In their Rajput way, they had displayed a lot of affection towards me. I had learned a lot from my Rajput family. The Rankhandi experience was intense. I spent years absorbing it and appreciating the lessons I learned there.

Perhaps the biggest lesson concerned the benefits of Rajput stoicism. When I first arrived in Rankhandi I did not possess Rajput stoic characteristics. One day Pita told me that Rajputs do not complain. They do not care whether it is too hot or too cold or whether they have enough to eat. They simply stay quiet. The Rajput boys in our family never cried, no matter what happened to them. When they fell down or had an accident, they did not go running to their mothers. They simply adopted a poker face and went on. While I did not witness this event, I was told that a boy from our family was about nine years old when his finger was nearly severed in a farming accident. He was taken to the clinic to have it stitched back together, but never shed a tear or complained of being in pain, although he underwent a painful procedure with no anesthesia.

The Rajputs also do not spend a lot of time worrying about their feelings. As long as they are treated with respect, they are satisfied. They do not need a lot of self-justification. They are very proud and have lots of self- esteem. The worst thing a

Rajput can do is feel sorry for himself. The Rajputs are independent. While they have huge families to provide support, they are capable of doing things on their own, and rarely ask for help. I think that by the end of my stay I had absorbed many of these Rajput characteristics.

When I arrived back in Tucson after my year-long stay in India, I went to the university clinic for a checkup. I had eight cavities from consuming so much sugar and from eating roti made from flour that had been ground between rocks. The village flour often contains little bits of stone that damage the teeth. I also had intestinal parasites and failed the TB tine test. Because I had been exposed to TB I cannot take this test for the rest of my life, but always have to take an X-Ray. I had to reacclimatize to the Western way of life.[6]

---

[6] Radhanath Swami had a similar experience after he returned from a two-year stay in India. He describes it in the final chapter of his book, *The Journey Home*.

Chapter III

Rankhandi Reprise

In 2014 I returned to Rankhandi. It was not the first time I had been back to my village. I visited Rankhandi many times in the decades since my residence there, and will likely return many times in the years to come. This was just the latest visit. Unlike the others, however, it was fully documented. It was part of a three and one half month odyssey through India. I kept detailed notes of the entire trip. This is my account of the return to Rankhandi. I travelled to Rankhandi with my brother in law Ranu[7].

The Trip to Rankhandi

Ranu and I got up early for our trip to Rankhandi. We were staying at the New Delhi YMCA and planned to go by bus. We ate our YMCA breakfast and took a taxi to the bus station with our back packs.

The bus station presented the usual picture of persistent confusion, with hordes of travelers and busses everywhere blaring their horns. Touts (the bus conductors) stood in front of each bus platform advertising their routes. We found an Uttar Pradesh government bus heading for Hardwar that would take us part of the way. It was the usual dilapidated vehicle rapidly filling with country people heading for disparate villages and towns. We found a seat in the front, but there was no room for our bags, so we put them on our laps.

The driver was fond of Bollywood film music, and kept it playing loudly throughout the trip. This mixed with the sound of his constantly blowing horn, as we weaved in and out of traffic and around pedestrians, bullock carts, rickshaws, motorcycles, trucks, and cars, as well as cows that strayed onto the road. Vehicles parked on the road, blocking traffic, and pedestrians continually wandered in front of oncoming vehicles, oblivious to the madly rushing traffic, hoping to make it to the other side of the street.

The noise was so loud that conversation was impossible, so I read a book on my kindle. I enjoyed the book despite the noise. We were not disturbed by people curious as to who I was and where I was from, as is usually the case. This is an aspect of Indian life that has changed considerably since I first started coming to India five decades ago. When I first came to India, foreigners were an oddity, and I was stared at everywhere I went. This is no longer the case, and I can now travel

---

[7] This chapter is excerpted from my previous publication, *My Indian Journey (Mera Bharatiya Yatra), Volume Three*, Createspace Independent Publishing, San Bernadino, CA, 2015

almost anywhere in India without attracting much attention, although the complete anonymity persons enjoy in a big American city is not there.

When I travel through rural India, people often try out their rudimentary English language skills by asking questions. Perhaps there was no one on this bus who possessed rudimentary English language skills. It has been my experience that almost no one in rural North India can speak English, although it is supposedly taught in school. I am more likely to encounter this phenomenon when I travel in South India, where more people, out of an animus against Hindi, prefer to use English as their lingua franca and are eager to practice their skills with a native speaker.

The city soon fell away and we drove through the North Indian countryside. Due to high population density, we were never out of the sight of large numbers of people, and even in the middle of the countryside the roadside was littered with mounds of trash.

We stopped for breakfast at a roadside *dhaba* (roadside rudimentary restaurant). Although the *dhaba* provided toilets, many men stood not far from the bus and urinated in public. We grabbed a good breakfast of aloo parathas, rice, and chick peas (*chole*), with tea. We would be subjected to highly sweetened tea for the next few days in this sugar producing region. The tea, milk and sugar, all boiled together, make something more resembling dark sweet syrup than what any westerner would recognize as tea. The amount of sugar in this mixture is incomprehensible.

We re-boarded the bus and got off at our first destination, the Muzaffanagar bypass. We flagged down a motor rickshaw and got in. The other passengers were a Muslim father and his daughter that looked curiously at us throughout our ride, but did not speak. Like many Muslim men his age, he carried himself with much dignity and was very caring about his daughter. The motor rickshaw carried us into Muzaffanagar town. The neighborhood was almost totally Muslim, characterized by bearded men with henna in their hair, women covered in black, many wearing veils, and men wearing traditional Indian Muslim dress, rather than the Western clothes preferred by men in other areas.

The driver had to let us off, as his vehicle could not proceed any further into the crowded bazaar, so we transferred to a cycle rickshaw and made our way further into the bazaar to the spot where we could catch a bus into Deoband, the town nearest to Rankhandi.

We stopped and found a Hindu man selling tea in the bazaar from a bubbling pot. We were required by Indian custom to bring some sweets to present to our Rankhandi hosts. The tea seller had a small glass case containing homemade Indian sweets. He provided us with samples. Like the tea, they were almost pure sugar and so sweet as to induce an overdose. We bought one half kilo of two kinds for Krishan and his family. The tea man placed the sweets in colorful boxes and wrapped them with string.

We then caught a small bus to Deoband, about 25 kilometers away. As soon as we left the bazaar, the decibel level decreased to a more normal level, and we found ourselves driving through quiet countryside. The fields were lush, green, and ready for harvesting. The scene quiet and bucolic, with farmers and field hands working the fields, cutting and harvesting grain, and plowing up the freshly harvested fields with tractors.

Deoband was a typical North Indian provincial town with a Muslim flavor due to its Muslim population and the presence of the Darul Aloom seminary, the headquarters of India's Deobandi religious sect. We drove up a muddy road and transferred to another smaller bus for the drive to Rankhandi. The Muslims got off at Deoband, and our new bus filled with stolid Hindu peasants, mostly Rajputs, in this Rajput dominated area.

We passed the sugar mill, the lifeblood of the local economy, which provides cash to the sugar cane growers, and headed up the eight kilometer road to Rankhandi. I began to see the familiar sights of the small roadside temples and businesses. We passed the intercollege, primary school and clinic, and pulled up before the bridge leading into the village. Although I was fairly confident I could find Krishan's house, after getting off the bus I confirmed its location with the man sitting in the small store at the bus stop.

We turned right past the *chopals* (compounds) of the Rajput families. Men sat on *charpoys* passing the time in conversation, with their water buffalo tethered nearby. We rounded the corner and spotted Krishan's brother coming out of his bath wrapped in a towel. In his stolid Rajput fashion, he showed no emotion and no surprise to see us appearing in the village. He led us into the compound he shared with Krishan and called for him to come down.

It was a two story compound built around a courtyard. The top floor ringed by a verandah that overlooked the dark courtyard, where the women did the cooking. When I lived with the extended family (*khandan*) in 1979, there were 92 of us housed in this and several other buildings across the lane, and it was very crowded.

Family sizes had decreased significantly since then, with two children now the norm, decreasing the overall size of the family. In addition, family members had built new compounds outside of town and moved their families outside the old cramped quarters. As a result, there was now lots of empty space where previously large numbers of people lived practically on top of each other.

Krishan had only two children. His daughter Renu had married and moved to her husband's village, as was the custom. His son Devinder had also married the previous year and he and his wife lived in the compound. Previously, under the purdah system, the men and women had lived separately. Devinder and his wife no longer followed this system and shared their own room. I soon discovered that this was happening all over Rankhandi.

Devinder's wife, Guruja Devi, still followed some of the old Rajput purdah tradition, however. She stayed out of our sight. Krishan's wife had no such compunctions. She came down and greeted us, wearing *shalwar kameez*. She spoke briefly, enquiring about my wife and children, but did not eat or sit with us, as per Rajput tradition. She did not keep her face covered in our presence as previously required, as she was quite comfortable with us and viewed me as a family member. Krishan and Guruja Devi had attended my daughter's wedding in New Delhi some years before and had met many members of my extended family, including Ranu. Likewise, I had attended Renu's wedding in Rankhandi, taking part in some of the ceremonies in the role of Renu's Uncle.

Krishan took us upstairs to our room. It was large, with a large bed, and other furniture, and had a punkah (ceiling fan). I had told Ranu I was eaten alive by mosquitoes on a previous visit, so he asked Krishan to provide a mosquito net. After washing up and depositing our luggage, we went downstairs for tea and snacks. Here, Krishan had a small sitting room off of the courtyard with sofas and chairs and a large coffee table. There were no such rooms in Rajput homes when I lived in Rankhandi before. There were no tables and chairs and sofas.

The three of us chatted for a time, enjoying the tea and snacks, as per custom, and Krishan then took us for a walk around the village. I showed Ranu the space outside, where I had slept on a charpoy with the water buffalo, the small room where I had written and typed up my notes, and the latrine I had built for the family. This was the former *mardana* (men's quarters) where Dhoom Singh (called Baba or grandfather by us family members) had sat with his friends, drinking tea, taking opium, and reading the *Ramayana*. He was the family patriarch, but now he and his wife were both dead and gone. There were no longer any water buffalo in the courtyard. Now, several tractors were parked there.

The remaining water buffalo were now tethered in the space between the old *mardana* and the old *zenana* (women's quarters). We walked into the former zenana. With the big drop in population and the erosion of the purdah system, it was no longer needed. Only a few women lived there now, mostly widows. There I met Somwati, who had looked after me while I lived with the family. Every day, she had sat in a small shed over a smoky *chula* (hearth) fed by *gobar* (cow dung cakes) cooking endless *roti* for everyone in our family. I used to sit with Somwati and chat with her as she made one chapati after another.

Somwati greeted me warmly, giving me a hug and blessing me by touching my head, as any Hindu mother would do with her son. She told Ranu she was like a mother to me. Almost all her teeth were gone, and she only had a few large ones left in front, giving her a distinctly bucktoothed appearance. As is the case with village people, she had aged considerably and I did not recognize her at first.

We went to the spot where Dhoom Singh's wife "Mataji" had once held court, ruling over 30 or more women and girls living in this small compound. The area was largely abandoned. The door leading into her room now led into an empty lot. The compound was only half of its former size, having been split in two by a high brick wall.

We headed out, past the bus stand and out of the village. Krishan wanted to show me his other compound. On the way, we met Dharamvir, the family patriarch and the largest landowner in the area. He had built an enormous compound to house his extended family and eight tractors. Dharamvir was herding his water buffalo back into the compound and invited us inside for tea. For all his wealth, power, and standing in the Rajput community, Dharamvir was a simple, open, and friendly man.

We had a pleasant discussion over our tea. He asked about agriculture in Arizona, and I told him of the large farms and ranches, and the typical crops of Arizona. (I did not tell him that we have large ranches in Arizona that raise cows for beef). In Rajput fashion, he said good bye warmly and invited us to stay at his compound any time we liked. His invitation was more than a mere formality. It was serious. I could turn up at his compound tomorrow and move in and stay indefinitely, as I am and always will be a member of the family.

We then walked down the road to Krishan's other compound. It was located outside the village. No one lived there, and Krishan used it for storage. Devinder was there sitting on a charpoy with several friends. I was surprised to learn they were selling liquor (whiskey and beer) out of a front window to village men, who drove up on motorcycles. I suspected the business was totally illegal and unlicensed. Liquor and alcohol consumption was the subject of my Rankhandi research. In 1979, Rajput men drank country liquor distilled from sugar cane and served in unmarked bottles. This has since been replaced by factory distilled liquor in labeled bottles. I did not make detailed enquiries, lest I be perceived to be overly interested in what could be an illegal operation. They allowed me to take pictures of the bottles and discreetly asked if we would like to join them for a drink, but we declined.

We visited the homes of several more of Krishan's relatives. In one home, two old men smoked a hookah. Krishan explained that this once common practice was dying out and that only the older generation engaged in it now. Ranu said he wanted to try it, and the smokers gladly let Ranu into their circle. I took several pictures of Ranu puffing away. He said afterwards that the tobacco was very strong and difficult to smoke.

Upon my first arrival in Rankhandi, many years before, I had told everyone at the outset that I was a Bhagat (devotee of God) and therefore did not drink, take intoxicants, or smoke tobacco. I therefore never shared the hookah with Baba and his circle of friends.

At one home, I noticed that the younger girls were far different than in 1979. They were not the least bit shy in my presence, but rather eager to engage me in conversation about all manner of subjects. This would not have been the case previously, when girl children were expected to remain silent and out of sight.

Krishan then showed us the new bank building, and the new additions to the town clinic and the various educational institutions lining the road leading into Rankhandi. These included a new commercial primary school, a new degree college, and the old intercollege, that had been founded and supported by a former patriarch of our family. While these educational institutions all claimed to be "English medium," I only met one person from Rankhandi who could converse in English.

Krishan's wife is a great cook and I have always enjoyed my meals in Krishan's home. She and Guriya Devi prepared a wonderful meal for us. The rotis were fresh and tasty, the vegetables delicious, and everything prepared with ghee (clarified butter). All of the ingredients used in the meal were grown on Krishan's farm and the ghee made from the milk of his own water buffalo.

After this wonderful repast, Krishan, Ranu and I sat in chairs on the verandah upstairs and chatted as it grew dark. In previous years darkness had descended with a heavy weight on Rankhandi, which had no electricity except for a few hours in the early morning. This was still the case, but now, Krishan's home had a "convertor" which stored energy during the few hours it was available. Krishan used this stored power for his electric lights.

The village was peaceful. There was a sea of stars over our heads. We enjoyed quiet conversation and went to bed early.

What Has Changed in Rankhandi?

I lived in the village of Rankhandi, in the Saharanpur District of Uttar Pradesh State, in 1979/80. A lot has changed since then. I have visited the village repeatedly in the intervening decades, and have witnessed a rapid rate of social and economic change. This is what I noticed during my last visit in October, 2014.

1. Water buffalo, once the mainstay of Rankhandi agriculture, are hardly used any more. Previously, farmers used water buffalo for a wide variety of farm tasks and used carts pulled by water buffalo (*bughi*) as their principal means of transportation. Now this is hardly the case. Now, water buffalo are primarily kept to provide milk.

2.   The farmers of Rankhandi gather feed crops from their fields and cut them up to feed their livestock. Previously, the feed was cut using a blade mounted on a large wheel and turned by hand. The long grasses were fed into a chute leading into the turning blade. Now, the wheel has been hooked up to a diesel irrigation motor, which turns a belt attached to the old hand driven cutting machine.

3.   Oxcarts were the principal means of transportation. Today, farmers haul their loads in trailers pulled by tractors, and use motorcycles to drive their families long distances. When I first arrived in Rankhandi, I took a horse cart (*tonga*) from the railway station in the nearby town of Deoband. Today, the trip is made by bus. The *tongas* have disappeared. I have fond memories of my many previous tonga rides and miss the peaceful clop clop of the horses hooves and the slow pace. Formerly, there were no motor vehicles in the village. Now there are many motorcycles and a few cars.

4.   Formerly, not all girls were educated. After puberty, they were married off to other villages, where they were routinely confined within a women's compound and could not go out in public unless they covered their faces and were accompanied by male family members (*purdah*). The age of marriage for women has increased, giving girls time to pursue their education to the high school level and beyond. Today, teenage girls no longer wear saris or cover their faces, and roam freely in public, even when not accompanied by male relatives. I was surprised to see girls dressed in jeans and pants, and sitting confidently on the bus. Newly married women seemed to generally follow the old *purdah* customs, but the restrictions are relaxed as the women have their children and grow older. Adult men and women still do not mix in public. Female literacy is universal. I saw young girls on their own riding to Deoband on the bus. This would have been unheard of in previous years. Young unmarried girls spoke freely with me, with no hint of shyness or embarrassment, and without hostility from nearby men. In previous years they would have been kept out of sight and I would only have spoken to men and older women. Any sign of familiarity with young girls would have placed me in danger. I could have been attacked or even killed by the girl's male relatives.

5.   The *Zenana/Mardana* (men's and women's quarters) residential system seems to still function, but has been seriously undermined, with many young married couples living together even while remaining in an extended family residential situation. This also reflects the decrease in crowded housing (at least among the Rajputs), as they construct elaborate new compounds to replace the former crowded quarters.

6. Untouchability is also being challenged. Formerly, dalits had to sit on the ground in the presence of Rajputs and others from the "twice born" castes, and were extremely circumspect in their speech when talking with upper caste members. This is no longer the case. Dalits no longer sit on the ground, and their interaction with Rajputs is more normal and less stilted. Rajputs will still not eat with *dalits* or accept food from them. *Dalits* and Rajputs receive the same education in the same schools, and many *dalits* are taking advantage of these educational opportunities to enter new occupations. The Rajputs still own the vast majority of farm land, although some *dalits* have become land owners and have taken up agriculture.

7. The Muslim population of Rankhandi has drastically reduced, with most moving to other locations. The Muslim Rajputs have left entirely. This reflects a violent clash between the Rajputs and the Muslims. One of the Muslim Rajputs decided the Muslim community needed to build a Mosque in Rankhandi. When he announced the project, he, his family, and followers were threatened with death. This convinced many Muslims and all Muslim Rajputs they were not secure in Rankhandi, and that it was best to pick up stakes and move elsewhere.

8. The entire village is more prosperous, with a general increase in the quality of life. Many people are better dressed. There is a wide variety of consumer goods available, which was formerly not the case. This includes furniture, refrigerators, ceiling fans, water filters, gas cookers, and televisions. These items were all practically non-existent previously. Although there is only electricity available from 2200 to 0500, when most people are sleeping, this does not deter villagers from buying electrical appliances, including television sets. People appeared healthier and better fed, with a more nutritious and varied diet. A generational difference was readily apparent. The younger children and adolescents were taller, better nourished and appeared generally healthier than previous generations.

9. The region is still plagued by violent crime and a lack of security, as it was when I resided in Rankhandi. This is due to the nexus between organized crime, politicians, and the police. The son of one of my contacts was kidnapped by criminals, who demanded a ransom of 2.1 million rupees. When the criminals learned the family had contacted the police, they murdered the boy, who was only 12 years old. Although the police arrested the killers, they were released after paying the police a sizeable bribe. In another incident, party workers from a regional political party openly murdered someone in the Deoband bazaar in broad daylight. Onlookers photographed the perpetrators, their vehicle, and the license plate number on the vehicle, as they fled the scene. Although all this information was provided to the police, no arrests were ever made.

In another incident, students from the Darul Uloom seminary in Deoband murdered someone in Deoband and the police took no action.

10. Formerly, there were only a handful of small stores in Rankhandi. There are now complete grocery stores similar to those found in major cities. They sell a complete line of products, including cosmetics, processed foods, cologne and shaving cream and a wide variety of soaps and detergents. None of these products were formerly available in Rankhandi.

11. There was previously no motorized traffic coming or going to Rankhandi. In my year there, I saw only one or two cars come to the village, and they were immediately surrounded by excited children. This time in just several hours, I saw several hundred motorcycles pass by Rankhandi on the main road leading to Saharanpur. They were almost all driven by young men. This is a phenomenon I noticed all over India. Young men with motorcycles drive aimlessly on the roads for hours at high speeds seeking thrills and excitement, while endangering the public. This phenomenon has been named the "motorcycle menace." Most of the driving appears pointless, as young men, often without employment, have lots of time on their hands and nothing constructive to do. I have often heard from my Indian interlocutors how these young men (who never seem to wear helmets, and often travel with as many as four persons on one motorcycle) find the money for expensive motorcycles (which start at 50,000 rupees) and expensive gasoline. The common assumption is that these young men make cash by doing errands for organized crime and political parties (which often overlap). I am told that many of these young men are unemployed and spend their days hanging around local bazaars. This could represent the dangerous intersection between an economy that fails to provide employment for its young men, and is increasingly driven by high demand for expensive consumer items.

12. Rankhandi used to be incredibly filthy. It is now much cleaner. The old mud tracks have been replaced by concrete roads, which have vastly increased the standard of cleanliness.

13. A large water tank is being built on the edge of town. This could mean that everyone in the village could eventually have access to running water. When I previously lived in Rankhandi there was no running water. Once the new water system is up and running and becomes universal, hand pumps will disappear, along with the puddles of water surrounding them. The next step would be a functioning sewage system. Krishan's home featured a bathroom with both Western and Eastern toilets, and a sink with running water. The water was pumped to a water tank on the roof with an irrigation pump and flowed down and out the faucets.

14. Many more affluent villagers own inverters. These store power and provide lighting, even when there is no power. This means that there is now electric light in many homes at night, in homes that formerly used oil wick and kerosene lamps. The homes without inverters are readily apparent, as they are still dark.

Returning to Delhi

Today is Sunday. We had two items on our agenda. We were scheduled to tour Darul Uloom Seminary in Deoband. We then had to get back to the YMCA in Delhi early enough to rest up for the next leg of our journey, as we head to Madhya Pradesh State and the ancient temple site of Khajuraho.

Krishan asked to accompany us to Deoband, as he wanted to tour Darul Aloom. We said farewell to everyone in the khandan. The Rajputs are stoic and make no displays of emotion. We took pictures of everyone. Devinder's wife did not want her picture taken, but acquiesced, standing meekly behind her parents in law.

I said good bye to Somwati in the street. She wanted to touch my head, but no physical contact is allowed in public, so she merely said good bye and to come back soon. The Rajputs were all affectionate in their stoic way. No words of affection or tears are allowed.

As I left the compound where I had slept with the water buffalo every night, I was particularly struck by a girl. She was from my extended family and was using this quiet space to study. She was seated in the driver's seat of one of the tractors parked there, studying the schoolbooks on her lap. She epitomized everything that has changed. She was sitting on a tractor in a space once occupied by water buffalo. She was studying in a village where girls once rarely went to school. She was in the men's quarters, where women were once not allowed. She was strong, courageous, and not afraid to be photographed. She looked up from her studying and gave me a bright smile.

We drove in the bus past the sugar mill and the bus parked behind the railway station. Many on the bus from Rankhandi were getting out and catching the train. We walked through Deoband to the old section where Darul Uloom is located.

The neighborhood became 100% Muslim, with all men and women dressed in traditional Muslim garb. The signs on the shops changed from Hindi to Urdu. The streets became narrow lanes, with 19th Century brick buildings on both sides and overhangs that obscured the light. We walked through the narrow lanes to the gate of Darul Uloom. The area was frequented almost entirely by seminary students, with beards, long white kurta pajamas and skull caps. We waited at a tea stall filled with these young *talib*, until we spotted my friend and guide Kazmi Sahib.

63

He was a genial gentleman who spoke with us in flawless Urdu, giving both Ranu and I a chance to practice. He took us straight inside and up a steep staircase to the office of Hadhrat Maulana Mufti Abdul Qasim Nomani, the President (Mohtamin) of the Seminary. We entered after removing our shoes.

He sat cross-legged on a mat working at a low desk. President Nomani appeared to be a kindly grandfather, with his white hair and beard and modified Gandhi topi (cap) on his head. He appeared kindly rather than the frightful head of the Taliban Deobandis, especially with his ready laugh and smile. We sat and chatted on a number of subjects. Like Kazmi Sahib, President Nomani spoke perfect Urdu. At one point Kazmi Sahib and the President starting disagreeing on various points and raising their voices. Kazmi Sahib alleged that the Muslim community was plagued by growing numbers of fake madrassas, all claiming to be sponsored by Darul Uloom.

The President disagreed, saying it was not proper to criticize fellow Muslims, rebuking Kazmi Sahib, saying discretion was in order. President Nomani was busy and dismissed us after we had finished the sugary tea.

Kazmi Sahib took us around the establishment. We saw the classrooms, with the all-male students sitting in rows on the floor in front of low desks and repeating verses from the Qu'ran. The air was filled with the sounds of students engaging in the "parrot method" in which they memorize the Qu'ran by repeating select verses over and over again.

There was a stark contrast between the various blocks. Darul Uloom was founded in 1866 by Maulana Muhammad Qasim Nonotvi. It is the headquarters of the Deobandi sect of Sunni Islam, which is devoted to expunging South Asian influences and practices from the Islam practiced in South Asian countries and bringing it closer to the "pure" Islam practiced in Saudi Arabia. The campus was clean throughout, with the older buildings showing their age, but well maintained. There was a block of more modern buildings from the late 20th Century in various architectural styles, and a block of most recent buildings in an elaborate Islamic style, with lots of white marble and ornamentation.

The new buildings include a huge mosque less than 10 years old, and an enormous block of buildings that Kazmi Sahib said would house a new library and classrooms. He explained that the Seminary also owned various student hostels throughout the old section of Deoband.

After completing the tour, we went to Kazmi Sahib's house for tea and snacks. He displayed the best Islamic hospitality. In the course of our conversation, he revealed that he was a PhD graduate in Islamic Studies from Aligarh Muslim University (AMU, which is a rival of Deoband in many ways). AMU, which teaches in English rather than Urdu, was established to bring modernity to India's Muslim community and create a class of English speaking Muslims familiar with

Western culture that could compete with the Hindus for positions in the civil service and the professions. Deoband completely rejects this approach.

Kazmi Sahib was quite critical of the Seminary and the Deobandi sect. He lampooned them for trying to force Muslims to live in their own separate world and not participate in Indian society with their fellow Indians. In his view, Deobandis will lead the Islamic community into disaster, because they view themselves as junior Arabs rather than Indians and are too quick to reject their Indian nationality, modernism, and integration. Kazmi Sahib was involved in the formation of a Muslim political party, which fizzled out. He wants Muslims to be active in politics and now concedes that they should participate in secular parties.

After thanking Kazmi Sahib for his hospitality, we walked all the way across town to the train station to catch a train for Delhi. It was a long walk, but the weather was good, the shops were closed and the streets quiet. Outside the station, we stopped at a stall run by a "ticket agent." These private businesses consist of young men with a computer, who make train reservations and print out the tickets for a small fee. One can purchase train tickets in the station, but it involves standing in long lines.

We purchased tickets for a train leaving later in the afternoon. Krishan then bade us farewell and headed back to Rankhandi and we went to the railway platform to wait for our train. It was very crowded. We were travelling during the Hindu holiday of Bhai Dhoom in which brothers visit their married sisters. It seemed like every Hindu brother in the region was traveling by train that day to visit his sister.

Everyone had clustered under the awnings on the platform to avoid the sun, so there was no place to sit there. We went to the station master who opened the first class waiting room for us so that we could use the bathroom. These were the only toilet facilities in the entire train station. While we waited a young girl approached us. Unlike the other children, she was dressed in western clothes, including jeans, and addressed us in simple English with a broad smile. I asked about her, and she said her father was a well-educated engineer who wanted his daughters to be independent, educated and have their own careers.

When our train arrived, it was absolutely packed with human beings. Almost no one got off and masses of people rushed to the doors to force their way in. We assessed the situation and decided to wait for the next train. A hawker on the platform told us it would be coming within 45 minutes. We sat on the platform for a few more hours (as the train was late). A blind Muslim beggar walking along the platform held out his hand and repeated verses from the Qu'ran. The tap of his stick and the sound of his voice provided our sonic background.

When the next train arrived, it was also full. We pushed our way on board. There were people everywhere, including sitting on all of the luggage racks and in every space of the aisles. The only place we could find to stand was next to the lavatory, which reeked with a pungent odor. The train stopped at every station along the way and slowly headed towards the Old Delhi Railway Station, its final destination.

The stops were only small provincial towns and practically no one got off the train. After several hours, we finally came to a major town and some people got off. This allowed us to move into the aisle and away from the bathroom, but we were both still standing. I was very tired by this time and cultivating the ability to sleep standing up.

After several more hours, we hit another city and more people got off and we made our way to the benched compartment, where we procured a spot to sit down (for one of us). The benches were made for four persons, but 7 or 8 sat on every one, with small children sitting on the laps of their mothers and falling asleep. Ranu and I took turns sitting down in our one spot.

After several more hours, we approached the outskirts of Delhi and lots of people got off, and we both were finally able to sit. By this time we had been standing in the train in a crush of other people for over eight hours.

We were happy when the train finally pulled into Old Delhi Station. We quickly exited the train station with our back packs and made our way through the crowds to the taxi stand, found a taxi and drove straight to the YMCA.

Our Rankhandi adventure was over. We had to get some sleep for our next trip. The next day we would travel by train to Jhansi and then by car or bus to Khajuraho in the state of Madhya Pradesh.

Chapter IV

Entr'acte

I returned from my year in India in 1979. While I was staying in Rankhandi, I started thinking about my return to Tucson, and thought it would be good to make the trip back overland to Europe. In Volume I of this work,[8] I recounted how my friends Buck and Eric and I planned to drive from Germany to India in our Volkswagen van in 1971, and why the trip never took place. I thought it would be good to finally make the trip, except in reverse.

I looked into it, and determined it would be too difficult to travel through Iran and Iraq, then both involved in a bloody military conflict, so it would be best to go through Afghanistan to the Soviet Union, and then on to Europe. I therefore went to the Soviet Embassy in New Delhi during one of my Delhi visits, to enquire about getting a visa. The Embassy was deserted when I went there. Unlike the scene at the US Embassy, there were no long lines of Indian visa seekers waiting to take their chances outside. I was actually the only person in sight.

I walked up to a receptionist and told him I wanted to apply for a visa. He told me to take a seat and I sat down alone on a sofa in the cavernous and dark lobby. After a few minutes a man came out and escorted me into a room. The two of us sat down and he asked me about my trip. He told me it would not be easy for me to get a visa, but did not shut the door entirely. In retrospect, it is not too far-fetched to assume he was a KGB officer sent to check me out. I told him I would think it over and get back to him.

It was while I was in Rankhandi that I heard the news that the Soviet Army had invaded Afghanistan. The US immediately applied sanctions on the USSR, and Afghanistan was plunged into war that has continued unabated up to the present day. This avenue was closed.

In any case, events quickly intervened, and I ended up getting married instead. The wedding took place on December 28, 1979 in Jamshedpur, Bihar, India.

My new bride and I flew back to Tucson via Frankfurt, Germany, where we stopped to spend some time with my parents. Back in Tucson, we settled into our new life. I was a graduate student, finishing up my PhD in South Asian studies. I had nothing left to do except write my dissertation. Dr. Mahar, my doctoral advisor, told me not to work, but to devote myself fulltime to dissertation writing, with the object of finishing as quickly as possible. We therefore scraped by on my wife's income as a law library clerk at the University of Arizona Law Library.

---

[8] Jon Dorschner, *In the Clear Light of Day (Revised and Expanded)*, Createspace Independent Publishing Platform (2nd Edition), 2018

I was assigned a windowless room in the basement of the University of Arizona library to complete the drafting and research process. It contained a small desk and a bookshelf mounted on the wall. I spent countless hours there conducting research and working on my manuscript. Since the library was open 24 hours, I often worked there throughout the night. I liked to break up the all-night research with stops at Seven Eleven stores to buy a slurpee. I typed the entire dissertation on a manual typewriter, sitting at a small table in my apartment. The manuscript was around 400 pages long, and I must have typed it seven or eight times during the revision process.

I completed the dissertation, defended it before the committee and was awarded my PhD in 1981. At 29, I was the youngest PhD in the history of the Department of Oriental Studies. I was pleasantly surprised when my dissertation was selected for publication, as the first in a series titled "Studies in Cultural Anthropology."[9]

While working on my dissertation, I went to a large hall at the University to take the Foreign Service Examination. I was one of hundreds of students taking the exam. I passed the written exam, was selected for the oral exam, and spent a small inheritance I received from my grandmother to fly to Dallas, Texas, for the oral examination. Even with my Grandmother's inheritance money, I was compelled to stay in the YMCA, as I could not afford a hotel. The YMCA was located practically next door to the examination site.

I rode back to the airport with the Foreign Service Officers who had examined me. They told me they were not supposed to tell anything to the applicants, but decided to end any suspense, informing me I had passed the oral exam with flying colors, and would be joining the United States Foreign Service as a Foreign Service Officer. As it turned out, I would not begin my diplomatic career until 1983. It took two years to complete my security clearance because of the many places around the world I had resided in and visited.

I spent this interregnum teaching at community colleges, doing odd jobs around the university, and taking a post-doctoral Hindi course at the University of Pennsylvania in Philadelphia.

I was at home at my small apartment in Tucson when I received "the call," from the State Department informing me I had been selected. The examination was divided into different categories to reflect the various occupational "cones" within the Foreign Service. These included, Consular, Economic, Political, Administrative, and Cultural. I passed all the tests and was put on the registers for all five. My name had come up first for selection as a Political Officer. This was the most prestigious of the five cones and the one most sought after by aspiring diplomats. I quickly accepted the offer, and the State Department informed me I

[9] Jon Peter Dorschner, *Alcohol Consumption in a Village in North India*, UMI Research Press, Ann Arbor Michigan, 1981, 1983

was to report for duty in Washington that coming Monday. That gave me only three days.

We quickly donated our few sticks of furniture to charity and packed all our worldly possessions in a couple of suitcases and flew to Washington DC in a matter of days. This was the beginning of a 27 year Foreign Service Career, during which I served in the following places:

Berlin (then under allied occupation) – Consular Officer

Islamabad, Pakistan – Economic Officer

Washington, DC – Intelligence Analyst for South Asian Terrorism, and India, at the Bureau of Intelligence and Research

Dhaka, Bangladesh – Political Officer

Lagos, Nigeria – Political Officer

Islamabad, Pakistan – Consul

Washington, DC – Staff Aide to the Assistant Secretary for Intelligence, at the Bureau of Intelligence and Research

Washington, DC - Political Military Advisor, at the Bureau of South Asian Affairs

The United States Military Academy, West Point, New York, visiting faculty, the Department of Social Sciences

New Delhi, India – Political Officer

Tallil, Iraq – Public Affairs Officer at the Italian Provincial Reconstruction Team (PRT)

Berlin (newly named as the Capital of the Federal Republic of Germany) – Economic Officer

I will deal with this career only tangentially in this work. It is a totally separate subject, dealing with international relations and foreign policy, and requires its own book.

Instead, I will refer to how the Foreign Service allowed me to live in South Asia (Pakistan, Bangladesh, India) for protracted periods of time, and make periodic trips to the subcontinent from Washington, and how I used these opportunities to make extensive trips throughout the region.

After I left the Foreign Service in 2011, these trips continue, including a trip to Sri Lanka.

These trips provide context for spiritual exploration.

Chapter V

Mysticism and Hinduism

Outside observers can approach another life with an objective eye. They do not carry the same baggage, acquired over the course of their lifetime, as their subject. This life I am currently narrating is dominated by an Indian attachment. The first thing any outside observer would ask is: Why India?

The answer of course is Hinduism.

India, the place, is dominant only because it is the home of the Hindu faith. Without Hinduism, there is no India.

But then…Why Hinduism?

Every individual born on our planet enters with choices. Social scientists have debated for a long time how much of our individual lives are the result of inherited social circumstance and how much comes down to individual choice (nature or nurture). Most social scientists assert that the overwhelming majority of responsibility for the outcome of our lives is the result of social conditioning, leaving only a small area that the individual can influence through personal choice or effort. We are born into poor families or rich families, well-educated or poorly-educated families, in rich or poor countries. Every human being is born healthy or unhealthy, with his/her own set of genes. These, and many other factors, outside our control, restrict our choices. In the end, say the social scientists, what we actually decide amounts to very little.

Those born without opportunities face life with the deck stacked against them. It has been statistically verified in thousands of studies that very few, escape poverty and rise to accomplish great things. We like to point at the person who has raised him/herself up by his/her bootstraps, but these cases are the anomalies rather than the norm, and we are often regaled with the same cases over and over again.

It is not, say the social scientists, a matter of ability or will, or the lack or presence of basic morality, although it is difficult to maintain high moral standards when faced with the imperative to survive in a harsh and unforgiving environment. It is just too hard to overcome poverty and other inherited negative factors, and the restricted opportunities associated with them.

Likewise, it has been well-documented that those born into opportunity find doors magically opening before them. In many cases, the doors open for people with limited abilities and limited ambitions. Despite their own inherent shortcomings, these individuals still rise to "greatness." They become famous, wealthy, and powerful, because they were born into the right circumstances. When it comes to looking at the choices individuals make, regardless of whether these choices actually play a crucial role in determining the outcome of the individual life, our

71

outlook is dominated by a scientific "western" world view, without much room for mysticism.

In this scientific world view, the outside observer would look at my life and try to find objective explanatory variables that answer the questions, "why India," and "why Hinduism." I suppose that if I looked long enough and hard enough, I would find such variables myself.

The social scientist would look for something in the social or economic realm. Karl Marx argued that economics determines everything. His world view was exclusive. For him there was no other viable explanation for what transpires in life. He did not come to that conclusion out of the blue. His views were based on his reading of social science research regarding the impact of an economic system, capitalism, on the lives of those who live within that system. This reliance on socio/economic factors to the exclusion of mystical explanations compels analysis pointing to non-mystical, mundane explanatory variables. That was the starting point for Marx's analysis of the human situation. His world view was strictly materialistic. Religion was a reactionary force supporting a capitalist status quo. It was "the opiate of the people," and would be eradicated as the march of progress proceeded.

For Example

My parents came from solid lower-middle class stock out of the great American Midwest. This defined them. They worked hard, were honest and looked for ways to better themselves, to rise above their roots and solidly establish themselves in the middle class. By the time I came along, they had done so.

My father was born in Manitowoc, Wisconsin, along the shores of Lake Michigan. His extended family all lived nearby, and worked in factories or were dairy farmers. They hunted and fished and liked to drink beer together after work. As long as the economy went well, they were content to lead simple lives and were not consumed by overweening ambition. They were content to graduate from high school, get a job, go to work, get married and have children. Some dropped out of high school, as they did not need much education to pursue their working class jobs. Most presumed their children would follow in their footsteps. They had no desire to leave their little corner of Wisconsin and examine the outside world.

My father was a reader. He was a bookworm from an early age. He devoured books. Maybe his reading led him to determine he could not remain in Manitowoc, Wisconsin. He came to the conclusion that he had to get out, but had no idea where to go, or how to do it. At the same time, he was not big on formal education, and had no desire to go to college or pursue a profession, avenues often used by exceptional working class kids as their ticket into the middle class.

Like all of us, his life was determined by larger historical forces outside his personal control. In his case it was the Second World War. This war was dreadful, killing millions, and bringing untold misery to humankind. At the same time, for people like my father, it opened doors to bigger and better things. It gave my father a way out of Manitowoc and out of Wisconsin. Once he left for the war, he never turned back.

In his case, the US Army provided him his way out. After the war, he returned to his parents in Manitowoc and tried to make a go of it, but was consumed by his overwhelming desire to get out. He could not settle down into the provincial life of his home town and was plagued by persistent discontent. In the end, he was so desperate that he rejoined the Army he had just left. This odd choice ran against the grain. Millions of GIs were happy to demobilize. Many were getting married, and using the GI bill to go to college and join the middle ranks of the booming economy. They dreamed of getting established, starting a family, and buying a home in the newly burgeoning suburbs. My father was different.

Like so many returning veterans, he married his high school sweetheart, but for some inexplicable reason I will never determine, did not use the GI bill to go to college, although the University of Wisconsin is one of the best public universities in the US. Perhaps such a possibility was simply outside his frame of reference. He instead joined the rapidly shrinking Army and settled into its peacetime doldrums, returning the Germany he had left after being liberated from a Nazi POW camp. This time, he would be a member of the Army of Occupation. Everyone was tired of military life after years of war, but my father could not wait to get back in.

He was grateful for the Army. It was his ticket out, and he adopted the Army wholeheartedly. It was not just a job for him, it was his life. He tried to inculcate this military identity into his three sons, and two of them pursued Army careers. Social scientists would have said that it would have been most logical for me to do likewise. My father wanted me to go to West Point and become an officer.

Social scientists have isolated powerful explanatory variables well-documented by prior research. One of these is birth order. It is very important, possessing potent explanatory power. I was the middle of three sons, and the middle child often rebels and pursues a different tack from the others, for a variety of reasons I will not delineate here.

Maybe social scientists would look at genetics. When the school system started IQ testing, I was off the charts. This intelligence is not the product of individual will or effort or morality, it is an inherited trait. It is a genetic dispensation. While genetic traits can be mapped-out, there is a strong element of randomness because of the presence of recessive genes. Some genetic traits can skip one generation and appear in the next, or some siblings can share genetic traits, while others inherit traits not present in the other siblings.

Although intelligence is not the result of individual effort, it can be nurtured in the right environment and applied to open doors to advancement and growth. Because of my father's military career, I was able to attend fairly good Department of Defense (DOD) schools. Some teachers there recognized my abilities and did their best to point me in the right direction and provide me with tools. Without these nurturing individuals, my life would likely have turned out much differently.

These schools were not the academic powerhouses that American elites attended; no prep-school education for me. The teachers and counselors told my parents, "Your child is gifted. You need to send him to a really good school and give him solid economic opportunities." My parents did not know what to make of this advice. It was from a different world they were not familiar with.

In the end, they fell back on what they knew. My father relied on the Army to take care of him, and in his eyes, it had a done a great job. He was happy to entrust his sons to the Army's care. Although he had only a high school education, the Army allowed my father to chalk out a firm spot in the middle-class. Despite his lack of a college degree, he was an officer, and served side by side with men (no women in those days) from more privileged backgrounds, all with a college education. He would be conscious of this inherent difference between himself and his colleagues his entire professional career. In the end, my father counted himself lucky that his son had the opportunity to attend Department of Defense schools on military bases.

These DOD schools were probably better than most public schools of this era. When my father was overseas, however, we moved "off-base" to humble (but still middle class) neighborhoods, and attended very ordinary public schools. I was bitten by the education bug and found opportunities to expand my horizons and learn new things even in these restricted circumstances. Social scientists would say I was a product of the times. The economy was booming. Public education was in great shape. The US was characterized by upward social mobility and education was the ticket.

I was riding with my father and another man in the car back in Albuquerque, New Mexico, where I grew up. I was sitting in the back seat and listening intently to their conversation. I must have been all of 10 years old. He was some kind of professional. Maybe he worked at Sandia Labs, located on the military base, doing top secret military research. I have no idea what relationship he and my dad enjoyed. They seemed cordial enough.

The subject of education came up, and the man was talking about the Doctor of Philosophy degree. I was absorbing the conversation from the back seat. He was talking about the value of higher education, and about graduate level education and how it opened doors. My parents never talked about such things. We did not know anyone with graduate level education. This was the first time I had ever heard anyone mention the existence of something called a PhD. The only professionals we knew were our public school teachers, the doctors at the Army hospital, and, of course, military officers. I made a quiet decision, right then and there, in the back seat of that car, that I was going to go all the way and get all the education I could and earn my own PhD.

During this same period, we visited my grandparents in Manitowoc. During these family visits, my parents re-entered the society they had grown up in. They visited with their many relatives and people they went to high school with, who had remained in Wisconsin. One of my father's friends owned a factory and took us on a tour. I saw how hard the workers toiled. It appeared a gray, depressing and tiresome place. When talking over dinner, outside on the lawn, I told my father and my hosts, I would make sure not to be stuck working in a factory. My father applauded my decision.

In the ensuing years I worked in warehouses, and a bottling plant and on a truck, and found the work just as denigrating and boring as I had observed as a child. The big difference was that it was not a life-long sentence for me. It was only temporary. I always knew I would be returning to school and acquiring ever more education, culminating in a PhD and that in the end, I would never do blue collar work again. While the work was distasteful, I took my succession of blue collar jobs (28 in all) as a learning experience. They provided me with insight into humanity and enabled me to connect with honest to God people from all walks of life. It developed character. I heartily recommend hard work with your hands to everyone. Those from privileged backgrounds who never perform work that gets them dirty, that is so hard and so stultifying that their entire body aches afterwards, have missed out on something genuine.

The best passages in Ken Kesey's novel "Sometimes a Great Notion"[10] concerns the travails of the main character, who is introduced to logging work. This is the first time he has ever worked so hard in his life. Kesey's description of how it feels to come home at the end of the day utterly exhausted and literally aching all over, with the complete knowledge that you will have to repeat the experience in toto the next day, is one of the most memorable passages of fiction I have ever read.

These vignettes from my life perhaps point to explanatory variables. They may explain why my life took the course it did, but not totally.

I would argue that while social science can explain many things about human behavior and outcomes, it seldom provides that all-encompassing explanation that definitely answers all the questions. Social science cannot, for example, adequately explain, why India? And why Hinduism?

---

[10] Ken Kesey, *Sometimes a Great Notion,* Penguin Books, New York, New York, 1977

India did not start to enter into American popular culture until I was in Junior High School in the mid-1960's, with the Beatles, and the Maharishi, and LSD, and meditation. But I decided on India well before that. I was only in fourth grade, when I made that decision. India was not on the national radar screen during that period.

I rely on mysticism. It is the only explanation I need.

To understand the mystical explanation, one must examine Hinduism itself.

Predictions Based on Background

Hinduism was a totally obtuse subject when I was growing up. No one in my realm could have told me anything whatsoever about it. I do not recall anyone ever talking about it in any context. This is an indication of just how provincial and restricted my life was. Although because of our military background we considered ourselves more worldly than the average American, entire areas of the world simply did not exist for us. This is not to say that we were in any way exceptional. We were no different from the vast majority of Americans, although my circumstances were perhaps somewhat unique. In retrospect, we had little reason to believe we were worldly in any way. We lived in New Mexico, which was such a backwater, that many Americans considered it an exotic foreign place. While I loved my childhood, there was much about the world I was not exposed to and was not aware of.

Once I learned of the existence of Hinduism and a match was lit under me, this overarching provinciality compelled me, as a child, to research this religion on my own, trying to take maximum advantage of the limited resources available to me. There was no one I could talk to about this subject, and no one could provide me objective information.

My impression was that Americans lived (and continue to live) highly-divided lives. In our world view there were the average everyday Americans we were familiar with, and there were sophisticates, who lived on the west and east coasts, and perhaps in separate enclaves in between. The sophisticates knew about such esoteric subjects as Hinduism. This is because sophisticates lived in an environment which exposed them to the broader world.

Unlike the vast majority of Americans, the Army had provided my parents with the opportunity to live abroad. As I small child, I had lived with my family in Japan and Germany. This military worldliness is in many ways illusory, however, as most military families are sequestered on military bases. Sociologists have determined that US military bases are deliberately structured to feel like a small town in the Midwest. The idea is to make the average military person feel at home.

When I was on the faculty at West Point, I was in the Social Sciences Department. There was a think tank in the basement that conducted extensive studies of the people in the US Army. They, and many other social scientists, have documented exactly who joins the Army and why. Many Army recruits are from small towns in the South and Midwest. The Army determined that it would not be able to send its personnel to disparate countries around the world if they had to live in a totally foreign environment, so the Army reproduced a familiar environment. This enables military personnel to step into an Army base anywhere in the world and lose all sense of being in a foreign country. Like most military people, my parents remained within this comforting cocoon, and only ventured out into the host country on periodic trips.

Despite our self-perceived worldliness, we were still a long way from the world of the sophisticates. Such people and places were outside our frame of reference.

For example, Amazon this year (2018) released its own television production "The Fabulous Mrs. Maisel," which deals with such people, living at the precise time (the early 1960's) that I was growing up in New Mexico. The main character lives on fifth Avenue in Manhattan and comes from a highly-educated Jewish family. Her father is a mathematics professor at Columbia. Barnard is listed as the best women's college in America. Both the main character and her mother went to Barnard, and on to Europe to study culture and art after graduation. The Maisels did not own a television, but spent their after-dinner hours conversing or reading, with Dr. Maisel often working late in his book-lined study.

My family was nothing like the Maisels, not even close. There was nothing in common between my family and the Maisels. Throughout my childhood, I never met people like them and had no concept such people even existed. I would not discover them until I was out of the house and on my own.

Had I been born into a family like the Maisels. I would have attended a terrific private school in Manhattan, followed by prep school, and an Ivy League university, probably my father's alma mater. If I had lived in such a family, I would have brought up my interest in India (probably during an extended dinner time discussion). It would not have raised eyebrows. My father would likely have said, "I can introduce to you my fellow faculty member Dr. ------, from the Religion Department. He is an acknowledged authority on India and can point you in the right direction." Or I would have brought up the subject with one of the brilliant teachers at my school, who would have set up a study program for me. These mentors would have pointed me to the vast resources of the New York Public Library, or the library at Columbia, which would have provided me with a surfeit of information. I would have dived in. One thing would have led to another, and I would be off and running.

Social scientists point to this difference in opportunity as an indication of just how little of our lives are determined by our own choice. They would say that in the society of this period, it would have been natural for someone from the Maisel family background to study India, and they would have been right. A statistical examination of the backgrounds of American South Asia scholars conducted in the early 1960's would have quickly verified that all, or almost all, came from the same social class as the Maisels, and emerged from Ivy League universities or a handful of top-notch public universities.

The same research would also have confirmed that none or almost none of American South Asian scholars shared my background and came from my social class. My experience is thus anomalous, falling outside statistical predictors. Social science has great difficulty explaining anomalies, although it is widely recognized that social science is not soothsaying or magic and is therefore not right 100 percent of the time. My experience and the outcome of my life is not predicted by my social environment.

That is why the mystical explanation carries so much weight, and why Hinduism can provide answers not available elsewhere.

Chapter VI

Hinduism and Mysticism II

Americans and Hinduism

My parents were Protestants, and Protestants carried a lot of weight when it came to how Americans perceived India/Hinduism. Organized religion and churches of all kinds are now in decline in the US. That was not the case when I was a child. Churches were going strong and had an all-pervasive influence on the way Americans lived and thought. This was particularly true of Protestant churches. Mainstream Protestants were the successful Americans. In New Mexico, when I was growing up, Catholicism was the religion of Mexican-Americans, who occupied the lower rungs of the socio-economic ladder. The "anglos" ran the show, and the anglos were Protestants.

Protestants are known for evangelism. This is a loaded word with many definitions, that has become even more confused in the present-day political climate, when the term "evangelical Protestants" carries a political meaning rather than a theological one.

When I was a child, evangelism was associated with proselytization. Evangelism meant that it was the devout Christian's proscribed duty to "spread the faith." This evangelism was based on "religious exclusivity." This concept states that there can only be one narrowly-defined religious truth totally encapsulated within one and only one religion, and all other religious concepts are false.

For many Protestants, this one and only religion was Protestant Christianity writ large. When I was a child, most Protestants belonged to what we now call "mainstream denominations," such as Methodists, Presbyterians, and Baptists. There were no such thing as the "non-denominational" Protestants seen in the US today, and no such thing as suburban mega-churches. All but the most liberal of Protestants believed in religious exclusivity.

The more conservative Protestants, who, in that time frame, fell outside the mainstream, took religious exclusivity to the furthest extreme. They preached that non-Protestant Christians were damned to hell fire for eternity, and that non-Christian faiths were "of the devil" and "doing the work of Satan." I did not know anyone who espoused these beliefs. They were outside our religious perception. Our Protestantism was of the "feel good" variety, and espoused success and good behavior.

Traditionally, American Protestants supported missionaries who journeyed to far-off corners of the world to "spread the gospel," that is the one true faith. The purpose of Christianity is salvation. While theologians have written thousands of books exploring the concept of salvation and addressing the issue in sophisticated and subtle terms, most Protestants defined salvation literally. Those not "saved," were not going to heaven after death, but to hell to spend eternity in torment. It was therefore inherent on all Christians to convert all non-Christians to save them from hell.

The people living in India, and most specifically the Hindus, were the particular object of Protestant attention. Although it was not part of my own experience growing up, many American Protestants supported missionaries sent to India specifically to convert Hindus to Christianity and save their souls.

Hindus attracted this attention because some Protestant theologians depicted this religion as strange, foreign, and totally outside the ken of practicing Christians. To many devout and sincere American Protestants, Hinduism was a faith that contravened every tenet of Christianity. Some of these Protestants depicted Hinduism as a "superstitious faith," while others declared it to be "satanic." These Protestants propounded their negative view of the Hindu religion far and wide throughout the United States. Some American missionaries and clergymen (no women in those days) used this depiction of Hinduism to raise money to support missionary programs. The absence of objective information on India and Hinduism often left these Protestants a wide-open field.

There was almost no immigration from India to the United States when I was growing up. The racial exclusion acts, passed by the US Congress in 1924, prohibited Asian immigration into the US, and were not repealed until 1965, when I was 13 years old. As a result, almost no Americans had met anyone from India and certainly not a practicing Hindu during my childhood years. I did not personally meet someone from India until I was in college.

This is certainly not the case today. Indian immigrants are found almost everywhere in the US, and practice the Hindu religion in Hindu temples located in towns and cities all across America. This exposure to the real thing makes it more difficult to propound all-encompassing racial and cultural stereotypes. It is another research verified fact that the more personal experience one has with an "outside group," the more difficult it is to stereotype the group. This is particularly true of negative stereotypes, which are those most grounded in ignorance. In today's globalized world, it is far easier to access objective information. This has fundamentally changed American society in many ways, while making it more difficult for religious exclusivism to hold sway.

What were some of the things most Americans commonly believed about Hindus when I was growing up? These included:

- Hindus worship idols
- Hindus are "superstitious"
- Hindus worship cows
- Hindus believe in salvation through "works" rather than grace
- Hindu scriptures are immoral and profane

In the modern academic context, such views would be dismissed as ignorant and indefensible. While such views may still be taught in certain Christian educational institutions, anyone studying Hinduism in the secular classroom today would be exposed to a far more objective view of the religion.

That is because the "exclusivism" of the past has been largely replaced in secular (and most religious) educational institutions by a different approach, called "relativism." Whereas exclusivism teaches that there is only one valid religious faith and all others are false, relativism teaches that there are no valid and invalid faiths. Likewise, it is not possible to construct a hierarchy of religious faiths, to determine which is more valid, more valuable, more beneficial than another. Instead, students are taught to look at each religious faith on its own merits and within its own cultural context.

It is important to recognize the extreme cultural variation found in the world, and recognize that religion is the principal expression of human culture. It is thus perfectly logical to assume that we will see a wide variety of religious practice and thought. This makes it difficult to propound the inherently illogical concept that one religion can meet the needs of everyone on the planet.

When relativism is applied in a cultural context, it teaches students that there is no such thing as a dominant legitimate culture that epitomizes human civilization. Rather, the world's cultures each make their own contributions to a many-faceted universal human civilization that is slowly emerging.

To see how much cultural change has occurred in this regard in a short period of time, one has only to turn to Turner Classic Movies (TCM) on cable television and watch American films made in the 1930's and 1940's. This time frame is not that long ago. We are separated from this era by only 80 to 90 years, but in so many regards their frame of reference is totally foreign. These films are completely Eurocentric, reflecting the American world view of the time. The not so subtle message they convey is that human civilization is white civilization, and comes from Europe, and no non-white civilization is valid. Rather, it is the duty of the world's non-white populations to gratefully acknowledge white supremacy and white dominance.

It is difficult to grasp that during this time frame, much of what we now call the developing world was colonized by Europe and the United States, and that the average person in the US honestly believed that we were raising up these ignorant people by exposing them to the benefits of our culture.

The films often revolve around the lives of American elites. The common man in the United States in the 1930's (at the height of the great depression), was fascinated by wealthy elites. Unemployment was running at 25%, many Americans were desperately poor. The social divide was great, and most Americans had no contact with those leading lives of wealth and privilege. Suffering Americans retreated into fantasy when they went to the movies, by sharing the imaginary lives of the wealthy. These fortunate few were depicted in American films as Europhiles, who spoke English with an ersatz British accent found nowhere in the US today. To our ears, it sounds like a self-conscious pretension (American film studios kept vocal coaches on contract to teach the actors how to speak in this accent, so it was not an innate to the actors, but rather a consciously acquired trait).

The reason why these films seem so odd today is because this old model has been largely supplanted by multiculturalism, which teaches that each of the world's individual cultures has its own merits and demerits, and that it is impossible to judge or rank them. Multiculturalism also emphasizes that the optimum is for cultures to interact and learn from each other, which requires mutual tolerance and respect. In this view, the optimum culture is one not restricted to one region, one culture, or one religion, but rather a "composite culture" taking traits from many sources.

Religious Overlap

I would argue that this old paradigm about the radical incongruity of Hinduism and western culture and the supposed natural antipathy between Christianity and Hinduism is based on a series of false premises and suppositions.

I would argue that a shift in perspective allows an observer to discover something closer to reality, that Christianity and Hinduism actually overlap and share many common perspectives, concepts and outlooks. It is a matter of approach. If you enter into your examination of Hinduism with the assumption that it is a false religion, you will search out data justifying this presupposition. If you enter into your examination with an open mind, you can follow the data where it leads and come to a different conclusion.

We must first define our terms. Christianity is a dogmatic faith. I do not mean this in a pejorative sense. This assertion is judgement free. Christianity is dogmatic in that when the faith was in its early stages, its leadership met in multiple conferences, debated the basic tenets and devised a series of "confessions" that encapsulate Christianity to its adherents. Christians thus recite on a regular basis the "Apostles Creed" for example, which lays out in a series of clear statements that all Christians agree is what they believe.

Hinduism, by contrast, is a non-doctrinal, non-dogmatic faith, in that there is no such common creed all Hindus can recite that encapsulates their shared belief system. That being said, I would argue that while Hinduism (like Christianity), is divided into countless sects with widely-differing beliefs, it is possible to state with certainty some basic tenets that the majority of Hindus believe. Since the faith is non-dogmatic, these beliefs can only be stated in general terms.

82

When the basic assertions of belief of Hindus and Christians are described and compared, it is possible to discover areas in which there is an overlap between Hinduism and Christianity.

The basic divide in Hinduism is between "personalists," who believe in a personal God, and "impersonalists," who believe there is a transcendent reality beyond a personal God. This "impersonalism" is epitomized by Vedanta within Hinduism, and has been passed on to Buddhism, which, as an offshoot of Hinduism, uses Hindu concepts as its basis.

This impersonalist approach has been espoused by mystics and theologians of all faiths all over the world. It is common in the United States, for example, where an increasing number of Americans are uncomfortable with personalist "religion," and prefer impersonalist "spirituality."

Most human beings do not find much solace in impersonalist religious concepts. Their attraction has been primarily for highly-intellectual persons, who aspire to a sophisticated faith. For the vast majority of the human race, religion is defined in personal terms and is centered on belief in a Supreme Being. They want to practice a faith that engages them emotionally rather than intellectually. Indians are no exception. The vast majority of Indians, whether they are Buddhists, Hindus, Sikhs, Muslims, or Christians, practice a faith based on worship of a Supreme Being.

I would argue that the average Hindu living in India believes the following:

- A divine being oversees the universe
- He/She loves humankind
- The human being's essential identity is as an eternal soul
- This soul lives on after the body dies
- The purpose of life is to reunite with God after this earthly life
- This process requires a strong ethical sense
- Without ethical behavior, it is impossible to get close to God
- These ethics are defined by devotion to family, marriage, non-violence, and a concern for other human beings, other living beings (animals), and the environment

I would argue that most Christians would not find these concepts to be foreign or strange. Most Christians would profess the same beliefs.

Hinduism is the integration of two religious strains within the Indian subcontinent. There is a high Hinduism (Brahmanism) centered around the Vedas, the original scriptures passed on orally for many years before finally being written down. These Vedic scriptures were in the Sanskrit language and the written Vedas of today are in Sanskrit, as are Hindu rituals. This high Hinduism is administered and interpreted by the Brahmin caste, which is supposed to be schooled in the

Sanskrit language, know how to perform Hindu rituals, and provide religious education.

The second strain, Indian folk religion, predates the Vedic/Sanskritic tradition and has been practiced in India since time immemorial. It is in the village vernacular, is not always scripturally-based, and doesn't rely on Brahmin priests.

The amazing thing about India is that its civilization is absorptive. Indian civilization prefers to find common ground rather than seek conflict. As a result, it is high syncretic, taking in ideas from many sources like a sponge, and integrating them into a colorful and disparate whole.

In this sense, Indian civilization embraces paradox, rather than simple solutions. This strong tendency for adoption and integration can require Indians to take in conflicting ideas and place them within the same context. Indians often therefore find no difficulty appreciating contradictory ideas and concepts. This is because for millennia India has integrated Brahmanism and folk religion into the daily life of average Indians, often with no consciousness of their differing bases and origins. Indians are often unconcerned about where an idea comes from. If something appeals to them, they take it on and absorb it into their syncretic world view.

Because of this overwhelming absorptive emphasis, Hinduism has evolved over millennia into a religion incorporating the entire spectrum of human religious thought. For example, for Indian Hindus, India is a land characterized by sacred places (geomancy). There are sacred places everywhere, sacred rivers, mountains, trees, plants, and animals. This reflects the Indian ability to retain ancient concepts and integrate them with modern ones.

This belief in sacred places reflects a perseverance of pantheism (the belief that nature is sacred, powerful and is to be revered – and feared/appeased). Religious scholars tell us that mankind's original religion was most likely pantheistic. Over the course of time, these natural forces became personified into divine personalities ("gods"). The Vedas are populated by a set of Vedic divinities, that evolved into the popular gods of modern Hinduism.

The Vedas speak of interaction with the Vedic deities and describe how to worship them. Some of these descriptions of ancient Vedic worship mirror descriptions of ancient Jewish worship found in the Old Testament of the Bible. Other Vedas allude to a powerful force that incorporates everything in existence and is a transcendent reality rather than a divine being. This is Brahman, the ultimate object of Vedanta philosophy. This belief is described as "monism." Everything is one, and the object of existence is not to be reunited with a personal God, but to merge into an impersonal all-encompassing reality. In both instances, the mundane earthly life we are currently leading is characterized by suffering, and religious enlightenment will free us from that suffering.

In the lives of most Hindu Indians Brahminical Hinduism and folk Hinduism have become inextricably merged, and they are most probably unaware and unconcerned about these two strains of their faith. For most Hindus, the most powerful motivating factor is devotion, the formation of a devotional relationship with the divine, a personal relationship with God.

Hindu literature/scripture is the most expansive on earth. The Hindu epics, the *Ramayana* and the *Mahabharata* are the world's longest poems. These epics are supplemented by the *Puranas*, which are an exhaustive series of stories involving interaction between human beings and the divine and many forms and manifestations.

A quintessential component of popular Hinduism is the belief that God "descends" from the spiritual realm to our earthly realm in the form of an "*avatar*" (incarnation) to interact personally with mankind, save us from evil (often of our own making), and ensure the triumph of good and the primacy of morality over immorality.

The descent/incarnation is depicted as an act of love aimed at helping human beings overcome illusion "*maya.*" Our attachment to *maya* prevents us from experiencing the reality of the divine. This attachment is motivated by hubris, a desire to be free and independent and in control and to deny the supremacy of God. This hubris gives us the false impression that we control everything around us. We become attached to our perceived position and do not want to acknowledge that it could be inherently false. This massive distraction makes us unable to chart a path to escape (transcend) our illusory earthly existence, characterized by suffering, and get back to our natural state, living with God and experiencing a personal relationship with Him/Her.

The Hindu epics describe the activities of avatars while they are on earth and places these activities squarely within a wider religious context. The Hindu epics often emphasize a playful Lord with a sense of humor. The Lord's activities are often described as "*lila*" or play. The average Hindu shares in the life of the avatars by participating in the epics. This can be in the form of reading the epics as books, listening to them being read or recited, or watching the epics acted out in the form of plays, movies and television programs.

Metaphysics

In my view, one of Hinduism's strongest attributes is its highly-developed metaphysical system. Metaphysics is the branch of philosophy that tries to answer the ultimate questions. Hindu metaphysics is sophisticated, and although ancient, is often consistent with modern science.

Hindu metaphysics postulates a view of time familiar to modern scientists. It describes various ages (*yugas*) that encompass extremely long periods of time, and mirror the geologic ages found in current scientific thought. Hindu thinkers early on wrestled with the concept of infinity (and devised the concept of zero in mathematics). They determined that infinity is defined not only by something extending endlessly into the future, but by the lack of any beginning. Something infinite, has no beginning and no end.

This means that the universe does not start from a specific point (such as the big bang) but has always existed. It does not progress to some final goal, for that would imply that the universe would reach a point of stasis, in which no further progress is possible. Instead, the universe has always existed and will always exist, and is characterized by cyclical trends. It progresses through a series of very long *yugas* to a maximum point, and then deteriorates into a state of limbo, from which creation again takes place. This cycle repeats endlessly.

Physics tells us that all matter shares the same trait. Matter is constantly decaying. Everything material deteriorates into its basic compounds. Every living thing dies and the body of every living things decays into its basic components. Hindu philosophers saw this as a basic effect of time, the destroyer of all things. "The Supreme Personality of Godhead said: Time I am, the great destroyer of the worlds, and I have come here to destroy all people."[11]

Hindu metaphysics likewise postulates a universe of extreme distances consistent with modern astronomy. It describes a universe not unfamiliar to 21st Century humans. It consists of infinite space populated by a huge variety of phenomena, including innumerable planets at great distances from the Earth. Unlike Christian metaphysics, in Hindu metaphysics, the Earth is not the center of a circumscribed universe, but one of a vast number of inhabited planets. These planets are inhabited by a seemingly infinite variety of life forms. Human beings are not the epitome of existence, but occupy a middle rung, with beings on these other planets in both lower and higher stages of development. In this world view, human beings are not the sole inhabitants of the universe. They are also not the epitome of God's creation. Instead they are conscious components of an integrated whole. God did not create the material world to be at the disposal of human beings. The animals and plants that inhabit this world are not placed there for mankind's benefit. Instead, the human race is just one of the many species found on this planet and is not meant to distance himself from creation but to integrate with it in a mutually beneficial relationship.

Hindu metaphysics incorporates evolutionary thought. Beings evolve from lower to higher life-forms and vice versa (devolution). Humans are described as capable of evolutionary progress into a higher state characterized by a higher level of consciousness, and vastly increased abilities (*siddhi* – supernatural powers). Human beings are therefore not static creatures. They are not meant to lord it over

---

[11] AC Bhaktivedanta Prabhupada, *The Bhagavad Gita as it is,* Text 32, page 577, Bhaktivedanta Book Trust, Los Angeles, 1998

material creation until some apocalyptic "end-time" when God will destroy the Earth. Mankind is a constantly changing entity and is capable of physical, intellectual and spiritual evolution. When Charles Darwin propounded his theory of evolution, it shocked the Christian world. It was decried as antithetical to all Christian beliefs. Evolution has never been controversial in the Hindu world, where it has been repeatedly described and discussed in holy books for many years.

These, and many other concepts now current in science, did not enter into Western thought and gain wide acceptance until the last several centuries.

Hindu metaphysical concepts such as the law of Karma and reincarnation, serve as the basis of the Hindu world view, and differentiate Hinduism from the Semitic religions. All living things, man, animal, and plant share the same divine ingredient (the soul). Some are merely more evolved than others. The degree of evolution is determined by the degree of consciousness (self-realization). Obviously, plants and most animals exhibit a low degree of consciousness, While human beings currently exhibit the highest level of consciousness, there is a wide variation of levels of consciousness within the human species. Since they share a soul, nature and animals live side by side with human beings, and are not inanimate "stuff" to be used to benefit humanity. Everything shares an essential spiritual nature. Everything is infused with spirit. This is because God is transcendent and immanent at the same time, a great paradox at the heart of Hinduism.

Existence does not move in only one direction and is cyclical rather than unidirectional. Souls, like God, have no beginning and no end, and share the same spiritual essence as God. Like God, souls have free will and are under no compulsion to associate with God, or even acknowledge His/Her existence. Some souls take full advantage of this free will and aspire to be free from God and gain mastery over material nature. They refuse to acknowledge that while they are powerful, their power is insignificant when compared to God's omnipotence. Such individual souls see this hierarchical relationship as too limiting and constricting. They refuse to accept their subordination to God. God enables these individual souls to descend from the spiritual to the material so they can try to live independently from God, and try to become masters of their own fate and lord it over material nature. This is because human beings have free will. Without free will there can be no love. If one is coerced into loving someone or something, that love is not genuine. To have free will, the individual must possess the ability to reject God and choose to live without Him.

God allows human beings the opportunity to live without Him/Her. God allows human beings to pursue the illusory belief that they can reject Him/Her and live independently. This is the basis of *maya* (ignorance). The result is suffering, which results from a willful distance from God, a rejection of the inherent spiritual nature of existence, and the embrace of the material as the be all and end all of existence. Sin is any activity that increases this distance from God. Since humans enjoy free will, they can remain enmeshed in *maya* in this material realm for as long as they like. They can even descend downward into other life forms and other planets where there is even more suffering than we find here on earth. Human beings are free to spend as much time as they like moving up and down the evolutionary ladder until they reach a point where they are capable of longing for a relationship with God and taking a conscious decision to rekindle this forgotten relationship.

While Christianity would traditionally find Hindu metaphysics quite strange, modern science does not. However, when the Hindu concept of salvation is extracted from its metaphysics and cultural context, the narrative would be quite familiar to practicing Christians.

Monotheism

Many Christians condemn Hinduism as a false religion because they believe it lacks the concept of monotheism. The Christian concept of monotheism (the belief in only one Supreme Being) is, of course, rooted in Judaism. Most Christians believe that the Jews were the people chosen by God to deliver the concept of monotheism to mankind.

Most modern Christians are proud to assert that their faith is monotheistic, that their monotheistic beliefs originated with the Jews, as described in the Old Testament, and that this monotheism establishes Christianity as the apotheosis of religion. Most modern Christians believe that the Jews' concept of monotheism was the same as that of modern Christians. Namely, that the Christian God is the only God that exists and that has ever existed and that all other gods postulated throughout the course of time are "false."

However, this modern Christian belief is far different from that of the biblical Jews. The old Testament describes the Jews as a people living in a world characterized by polytheism (the belief in many gods). The old testament Jews did not believe that these many gods did not exist, but that their God was supreme and superior to all the various gods in existence and worshipped by other peoples. Throughout the Old Testament, the Jews wrestle with an attraction to polytheism and veer back and forth between their own monotheistic faith and the polytheistic faith of their neighbors.

Modern theologians describe the religious beliefs of the ancient Jews not as monotheism, but as "monolatry." This is the belief that there is one Supreme Being – God, but that lesser spiritual beings "gods or godlings" exist and are worshipped by less spiritually evolved people.

Many modern Christians practice a modified form of monolatry, positing the existence of intermediate beings between the Supreme Being – God, and mankind. For modern Christians, these would be angels, who, like God, are immortal, and possess their own supernatural powers, and, like God, intervene in the earthly affairs of mankind. For modern Catholics, the Virgin Mary, and the Saints play a similar role. Catholics share their griefs, sorrows, and problems with the Virgin Mary and the Saints, who intervene with God on the worshipper's behalf. These Christian concepts would be quite familiar to modern Hindus.

Technically, modern Hindus are not polytheists, in that they do not believe that there are many gods and that they are all equal. The vast majority of modern Hindus share religious beliefs with modern Christians. They believe in a Supreme Being – God, and in lesser spiritual beings - gods. In this view, the other gods play a role similar to angels in the Christian world view. The other gods intervene in the world to accomplish specific tasks given to them by the Supreme God. This is similar to Christians who believe that angels are supernatural beings that should be revered, but are subordinate to God. It also mirrors in some regards, the Catholic belief in patron saints. Just as certain saints are held responsible for certain activities, certain Hindu gods are responsible for administering their own corner of creation. This modified form of monolatry is thus common to both Christianity and Hinduism.

Muslims condemn Christianity because they are "radical monotheists." They believe that any modification of monotheism contradicts it. For Muslims monotheism can only mean that there is one true God and that all other gods are false. "There is no God but Allah," meaning that no person can be a monotheist who posits the existence of more than one supernatural being (although most Muslims believe paradoxically in angels "*farishta,*" and angels play a significant role in the Qu'ran).

Muslims condemn Christianity as a polytheistic religion posing as monotheism. This is because Christians believe in the holy trinity, that God is three persons in one, God, Son, and Holy Spirit. To Muslims, there can be no such thing as a trinity, as God is eternally one united being. Likewise, there can be no "incarnation of God," as that would imply that God could separate into two beings, one inferior to the other. Therefore, for Muslims, Jesus Christ cannot be the "son of God." Thus, ironically, Muslims condemn Christians as polytheists, just as many Christians condemn Hindus as polytheists.

Another monotheistic concept of God is that of henotheism. This is the belief that there exists only one Supreme being, who appears in an unlimited variety of forms depending on the context. Therefore different people in different cultural contexts, perceive God in the way that best mirrors their culture, and God, because He loves His creation, is happy to oblige. Different people in different contexts choose which form of the Supreme to worship and venerate. God appears as Supreme to each of these individuals, although the form in which He/She is perceived is radically different.

In the henotheistic concept, God speaks to the individual personally and appears to each worshipper in the form he/she prefers, thus assisting and enabling a personal

89

relationship between the devotee and God. There is no such thing as a "one size fits all" God. In this concept, God, while one, appears in a variety of forms to enable each person to have access to their own personal God. Each individual's concept of God is of a Supreme Being, although different individuals worship different beings. This concept, is highly paradoxical, and is thus appealing to the Hindu mind, which we have seen, embraces paradox.

The Semitic faiths, (Christianity, Islam, and Judaism), reflect their Middle Eastern origins. The societies that gave birth to these three religions were patriarchal. Women played a subordinate role and were not allowed to occupy positions of leadership. The concept of God within these faiths reflects their patriarchal origins. God is a male. This restricts the appeal of these faiths, because God is not allowed to reflect "female" traits. Catholicism gets around this restriction by incorporating the concept of the Madonna, the Virgin Mary. She is the Mother of God, and is viewed by many Catholics as the mother of mankind, who like our own mothers, listens to our entreaties and responds with kindness and caring.

Hinduism, with its multifaceted view of divinity incorporates masculine, feminine and hermaphroditic concepts of God. In the Hindu pantheon we see gods and goddesses, and gods that incorporate both feminine and masculine traits. Many Hindus worship God as a female deity (the Goddess), and therefore use both masculine and feminine pronouns to address God. In addition, gods in the Hindu pantheon are almost always part of a pair, with a male deity and a female consort. Hindu philosophers assert that these couples are not to be viewed as mere extensions of the human husband and wife concept, but as essentially unitary deities incorporating the masculine and the feminine. By worshipping a god that incorporates a male and female personality, it is possible to conceive of God with both masculine and feminine attributes.

Hindu henotheism is encapsulated as the belief in an "*ishta devta*" (personal God). Most Hindus believe that each individual relates to God in his/her personal way and that God chooses His/Her worshipper, not the other way around. Technically, this is a qualified form of polytheism, as it posits the existence of multiple gods and does not make up a universal hierarchy with one God universally recognized as Supreme. Instead, this decision is left up to each individual, who picks and choose between many divine alternatives.

This reflects a Hindu belief in "live and let live." While a devotee may believe, for example, that Shiva is his/her own personal God and worship Shiva, as such. He/She does not believe that every person on the planet must worship only Shiva and that all other concepts of God are false. This is another example of paradoxical thought. It reflects the Hindu conclusion that the nature of the universe cannot be rationally comprehended because it is inherently paradoxical. This means that the universe is not to be "comprehended," but rather "experienced," as rational thought and concepts captured by words are inherently incapable of capturing the nature of reality, which transcends everything we think we know.

I would argue that the most common concept of divinity within modern Hinduism is Polymorphic Monotheism. This is the belief that there exists only one God, but that this one God incorporates a seemingly infinite variety of forms within His/Her one being. God is by definition omnipotent, meaning that God can do anything. Hindu metaphysics examine in great detail the concept of omnipotence and all its implications. It asserts that omnipotence, like most spiritual concepts, cannot adequately be described in words. Hinduism therefore relies on a vast panoply of metaphors to communicate the divine, most particularly a highly-developed iconographic system.

In the Hindu mind, since God is omnipotent, it makes perfect sense that He/She can appear to His/Her devotee in any form. Furthermore, Hindus believe that God interacts personally with every worshipper, and that God so loves each individual human being that He/She will do anything to bring that person back into a personal relationship. Since God is omnipotent, He/She is perfectly capable of entering into a personal relationship with an infinite number of beings, not only on the planet earth, but on planets found throughout an infinite universe.

This omnipotent God knows each individual personally and when that individual begins to awake from *maya* and seek a relationship with the divine, God knows what form will best appeal to the worshipper and make that relationship easy and attractive. God then appears to the worshipper in that form.

In the Indian context, the individual grows up in India, surrounded by all manner of worship (*puja*) and all kinds of different depictions of God. These depictions take the form of statues, pictures, and highly-developed characters in the Epics and Puranas, that are reproduced in books, posters, calendars, movies, plays, and television shows all over India. Over the course of his/her lifetime, the individual worshipper becomes attracted to one of these forms and enters into a personal relationship with it. This form then becomes the *ishta devta* for the individual worshipper.

The concept of polymorphic monotheism is elucidated in text 12, Chapter 11 of the *Bhagavad Gita*. Arjuna is aware that his charioteer Krishna, with whom he enjoys a deep personal relationship, is a human being, but that He is also an incarnation of God. Arjuna is so close to Krishna that he can ask for personal favors. He asks Krishna to reveal His true form. Krishna assents, and reveals the *Vishwa Rupa Darshana* (the view of the universal form) in which He is one being that incorporates all the forms of the God found in the Hindu world.

"Arjuna saw in that universal form unlimited mouths, unlimited eyes, unlimited wonderful visions. The form was decorated with many celestial ornaments and bore many divine upraised weapons. He wore celestial garlands and garments, and many divine scents were smeared over His body. All was wondrous, brilliant, unlimited, all-expanding."[12]

Arjuna is overcome by the majesty and power of this form, tells Krishna he cannot stand it, and asks Krishna to return to his human form. This means that for Arjuna, Krishna's form as his intimate friend is the best, the *ishta devta*, and Arjuna is content to worship God in that form.

Idolatry

The other modern Christian concept mistakenly attributed to Old Testament Jews is the belief that the worship of idols is false and that God cannot be depicted in a statue or picture. Islam has taken this concept to its ultimate extreme, banning any pictorial representation of the define as idolatrous. Many Protestant denominations occupy a middle realm, refusing to allow any statues within churches or on church altars, and condemning Catholic iconography as idolatrous.

The Jews believed their Supreme God transcended idols and that no statue or picture could encompass Him. An intermediate step in this developing belief was the period when the Jews (than nomadic) believed in the sacred "ark of the covenant." Eventually the ark disappeared, and the Jews came to conceive of God as an individual entity that could not be perceived by the earthly senses.

This did not mean, however, that the Jews did not believe that the idols worshipped by their neighbors were not real divine beings. One has only to read the story in the book of Exodus to see that the Jews were jealous of the faith of their neighbors and longed to copy that faith by believing in a god that could be encapsulated within an idol and worshipped. This leads the Jews to create a golden calf and worship it. The Jews that performed this act, so soundly condemned by the prophet Moses, sincerely believed that "idol worship" was a real possibility. That is why Moses incorporates a prescription against it in the ten commandments that he bring down from Mount Sinai.

When Christians encountered Hinduism in India, they found that statues played in intimate role in Hindu worship. They projected their religious views into a totally different cultural context. They equated this style of worship with the idolatry depicted in the Old Testament and condemned by the Ten Commandments, thus equating Hindus with the Old Testament idolaters. This is a principal reason why Hinduism has been so often vilified by Christians. However, scholarship shows that there are many problems with this projection exercise. It is based on an inaccurate representation of the religious beliefs and practices of the Hindus.

There is essential difference between the use of statues by worshippers in the ancient Middle East, as depicted in the Bible, and that found in India today. In the ancient Middle East (and the ancient Western world generally), it was believed that the statue and the god were one and the same thing. This is the common definition of idolatry accepted by Christians.

---

[12] *Bhagavad Gita as it is,* page 562

When European travelers encountered Hindu religious practice, they saw Hindus "worshipping statues." In India, statues are found in private home shrines, in temples, in neighborhood street corner shrines, on car, truck and bus dashboards, and on office desks and in shops and restaurants. Hindus (and to be quite frank, Indians of all faiths) perform worship "puja" in front of these statues, offering incense, water, and food. This process is called "*arotik.*" The food offered to the statue is shared with God, and is transformed from mundane food into "*prasad,*" (which literally means grace). This process mirrors the transubstantiation process of Catholic churches during which a priest transforms bread and wine into the body and blood of Jesus Christ during the mass.

In addition, in Hindu temples the priest and his helpers dress the statue in different outfits that are changed daily, and the temple is closed at different intervals to allow the statues to "sleep," and the statues are taken out on processions through the streets to allow humanity to get a glimpse "*darshan.*" Similar practices are found within Catholicism, with statues of the Virgin Mary, Jesus Christ and the saints, treated in a similar fashion.

However, do these practices mean that Hindus and Catholics are idolaters, as many Protestants assert? This is not the case. Hindus and Catholics do not believe that the statues are God. The Hindu concept of God is far more subtle and sophisticated than the relatively simplistic beliefs of the ancient residents of the Middle East. We already confirmed that for Hindus God is immanent and transcendent. This means that God is above and beyond the material world and inhabits a spiritual realm, and, at the same time permeates the material world. This is an essential paradox, meaning it is a concept that defies human understanding.

Since God is immanent and omnipotent, it is entirely logical that He/She can "inhabit" a statue or picture. To a Hindu, religious statues are not "idols" but "deities." Religious scholar Steven J. Rosen defines Hindu "deities" as "visible images of God, his incarnations, and divine associates, made of material elements such as stone, marble, metal, and so on."[13]

The Old Testament of the Bible clearly asserts that in the ancient Middle East, human beings simply created idols out of their imagination, claimed them to be God, and worshipped them. The Hindu concept is much different. Statues cannot be in any form, they must meet proscribed qualifications. They can only be in the recognized forms found in the Hindu scriptures and epics. When a statue meets these qualifications, God agrees to "inhabit" it. This is part of a religious worship process carried out by a qualified and recognized priest.

---

[13] Steven J. Rosen, *Essential Hinduism,* Praeger, Westport Connecticut, 2006, page 191

In the Catholic mass, there is a precise moment when bread and wine are transformed into the body and blood of Jesus Christ. It is usually signified by the ringing of a bell. Likewise, there is a precise moment in the Hindu religious ritual when the statue is transformed into a deity fit to be worshipped. Until that moment, the statue is just another statue, and no different from any other statue. When the process is complete, the stone statue is no longer simply a statue, but a divine form (*archa vigraha*).

It is only then that the statue is worshipped, because God is present within it. While God is present within that statue, this does not mean that the statue is God, for God is all pervasive and cannot be confined within any single statue or picture. God loves humankind, and out of this love wants to bring human beings into a loving relationship with Him/Her. To do this, He/She incarnates within a statue, thus providing a specific focal point of concentration and enabling the devotee to interact with God. Because we are still enmeshed in *maya*, we cannot see God with our own eyes. This makes the entire process of liberation from *maya* and the perception of the ultimate reality extremely difficult. However, God has made it possible to see Him/Her in the form of a statue, and with the right devotional attitude, it is possible to interact intimately with God through the medium of this statue. He/She is able to do this because He/She is omnipotent, meaning there is nothing He/She cannot do. To deny God this ability is to deny God's omnipotence. A God who is not omnipotent is not God. Hindus define this process as "grace," (*prasad*). This belies another common misperception of most Christians, namely that Christianity is the only religion ever found on Earth with the concept of divine grace.

Hindus view the temple as a gateway to the divine. Because God inhabits the temple, it is a point at which the spiritual and material worlds intersect. Worshippers in a temple can gain a glimpse of the divine. This is because God has agreed to inhabit that temple and spiritualize it. The statue lives at the heart of the temple (God's residence point inside the temple is indicated by a pointed steeple – *shikha*). God is the divine guest, who out of His/Her grace has agreed to reside in the temple and is therefore treated to a loving elaborate set of rituals throughout the day and into the night.

There are two types of worship of the deity, the public and the private. Deities are housed in elaborate temples, simple shrines, and almost anywhere, creating a plethora of sacred spaces. The most common form of worship is the *arathi*.

"*Arathi* is a ceremony replete with symbolism. The word *arathi*, for example, literally means 'before night,' and this is not only because the first of these ceremonies begins in predawn hours. The waving of the *arati* lamp as an offering to the deity implies an end to the 'night' of the practitioner's material sojourn."[14]

After the deity is awakened by the lamp, He/She is offered candles, incense, flowers, food, and is "cooled" with a fly whisk fan. In home temples the *arati* ceremony is usually performed early in the morning before departing for work or starting the household day, and sometimes late at night before going to bed. In temples, staffed by resident priests, *aratis* are performed on a regular schedule throughout the day.

Temples can be small village or neighborhood affairs, or large and elaborate. Large temples can house multiple deities on different altars. Individual Hindus maintain home temples, where they worship their personal *ishta devatas*.

---

[14] *Essential Hinduism*, page 196

Chapter VII

Gaudiya Vaishnavism and Mysticism

Sectarian Hinduism

The multi-faceted and highly-variegated world of Hinduism provides many different ways for individual worshippers to engage with the divine. Since divinity infuses the world, (the divine is both transcendental and immanent), it can be found anywhere and everywhere. It cannot be confined within specific places or buildings, and cannot be confined to specific concepts of God and divine personalities. Observers from other cultures have found this utterly paradoxical approach mystifying, stating that in India, it appears anything can be holy and sacred. They offer the rejoinder that if everything is sacred, then nothing is sacred, or so it appears to them.

We have already seen how polymorphic monotheism dominates the Hindu mind. Without being aware of this concept, Hindu religious practice would be difficult to penetrate or comprehend. The predominance of this concept allows individual worshippers to pick and choose who and/or what they will worship. Hinduism incorporates a large number of gods, who as a group are commonly called the "Hindu pantheon" by many Western writers. In addition, divine personalities occupy a middle rung between full-fledged gods and human beings.

For example, the character of Hanuman plays a significant role in the Hindu epic the *Ramayana*. This epic concerns the descent of God to the earth in the form of the King of Ayodha, Ram. Hanuman encounters Ram as the story unfolds, recognizes His divine status and accepts Him as his *ishta devta*. Hanuman exhibits incredible devotion to Ram throughout the story, and is subsequently upheld as the epitome of the ideal devotee. Although the *Ramayana* states that Hanuman is the son of the wind god Vayu and therefore has divine attributes, he is not himself a god.

Hanuman is popular because he represents the emotional outpouring of love for God exhibited by a true devotee. The *Ramayana* is particularly popular in North India, and North Indians like to keep pictures and statues of Hanuman around to remind them of Hanuman's example. Temples to Hanuman are found throughout India and most particularly in North India, and pictures and statues of Hanuman are found everywhere.

Another very popular divine personality of similar stature is Ganesh. Ganesh is not a member of the "Hindu pantheon" in his own right, but remains more popular than many Hindu gods. Ganesh is the son of Shiva and his consort Parvati, and therefore not fully a god. However, Ganesh blesses the beginnings of all undertakings and is beloved by Hindus. His image is found everywhere, as

Hindus like to seek his blessing at the start of any important activity. He is depicted in iconography as a boy with the head of an elephant:

When Western scholars first started to study Hinduism, they had trouble deciphering what it was all about. They often fell back on familiar metaphors from their own culture to help them make sense of something totally unfamiliar. For example, they talked of a "Hindu trinity" consisting of the gods Vishnu, Shiva, and Brahma. While the concept of a holy trinity makes perfect sense for Christians, it does not actually exist for Hindus. It is true that Vishnu is the most popular form of God, and Shiva the second most popular, but there is only one Brahma temple in all of India, located in the town of Pushkar in the state of Rajasthan.

The popularity of Vishnu as an object of devotion is of long standing. Vishnu is so popular because He is seen to be infused with love for all beings all over the universe.

Vishnu expresses His love for humanity by descending to Earth over and over again to intervene on behalf of troubled humanity. There is thus a plethora of stories involving Vishnu's ten *avatars* that appear in different forms in different *yugas*.

Krishna is commonly perceived as the most popular of these avatars. He plays a powerful role in India's longest epic, the *Mahabharata*, which relates the story of the successional battle between the Pandava and Kaurava families, with the Pandavas representing good and the Kauravas evil. Krishna descends to earth to help the Pandavas defeat the Kauravas and assure their ascent to the throne.

Krishna is important because just before the final battle between the two houses is set to commence on the battlefield of Kurekshetra, Krishna advises his friend and confidant Arjuna, one of the leading members of the Pandavas. This discourse is the *Bhagavad Gita*, the most popular and influential of Hindu scriptures.

Most scholars are well-aware of Krishna's role in this epic and the importance of his discourse. However, Krishna's entire incarnation is minutely described not only in the *Bhagavad Gita,* and the *Mahabharata*, but in the *Bhagavata Purana*, one of 18 Puranas that form an encyclopedic corpus dealing with all manner of topics and divine personalities.

The *Bhagavata Purana,* also called the *Srimad Bhagavatam,* is a lengthy multi-volume work. Within the work is Krishna's entire story from His advent in Mayapur to His departure in Gujarat. In the first phase of the story, Krishna is raised as a simple cowherd in the village of Vrindavan, where He exhibits His divine identity for the first time, and becomes an object of veneration and adoration. For devotees of Krishna, this is far and away the most important part of the story.

Although Krishna performs many miraculous acts while in Vrindavan, the most significant is his dance (the *rasa* dance) with the cowherd maidens (*gopis*). These simple women adore Krishna, and each wants to have Krishna to herself. As a response to their sincere devotion to Him, Krishna dances with each separately yet with all at the same time in the holy groves of Vrindavan. The *rasa* dance is a poignant example of how to communicate profound metaphysical concepts to the average person. One can be swept into the *rasa* dance and not be consciously aware of its significance. It is a perfect metaphor for the essential paradox of the universe, the simultaneous immanence and transcendence of the divine. Krishna devotees see this relationship between the gopis and Krishna as the epitome of divine love, and it is something they aspire to.

The second period of Krishna's life starts when he leaves Vrindavan never to return and assumes the throne of Dwarka, which is incorporated into the modern Indian state of Gujarat. As king, Krishna possesses powerful armies. When the Kaurava/Pandava war breaks out, Krishna tells the two warring factions they can have either his armies, or Himself as a humble charioteer. The greedy Kauravas see no value in Krishna as charioteer, and immediately demand Krishna's armies. By contrast, the humble and virtuous Pandavas are happy to have Krishna on their side, stating that where Krishna resides is victory. This again is another transmittal of a basic Vaishnava teaching, for it is relaying a universal truth, that Krishna's presence is necessary for genuine success, and wherever Krishna is present genuine success is guaranteed. Since Arjuna and Krishna are such close friends, Arjuna requests Krishna to drive his chariot, setting the scene for the narration that constitutes the *Bhagavad Gita*.

The third and final period of Krishna's incarnation takes place after the Pandava victory. Yudhisthira, the pre-eminent of the five Pandava brothers, takes the throne, but despite his attempts to rule with mercy and compassion, the world deteriorates and the kingdom is destroyed, and Krishna disappears. This entire episode signifies the downward shift from one yuga to another, and the role of God in this divine drama.

Hindus who accept Vishnu as their *ishta devta* are part of the Vaishnava sect of Hinduism. Vaishnavas believe Vishnu is Lord and that Krishna is one of Vishnu's ten incarnations. However, a different interpretation of Vaishnavism arose in the state of Bengal, in the Northeast of India. Bengal was originally known as Gaud, and incorporated the present Indian states of West Bengal and Bihar, and the modern country of Bangladesh. The Vaishnavas of Gaud embraced Krishna as their *ishta devta*. They believe Krishna is not an avatar of Vishnu, but rather the Lord Himself. This subset of Vaishnavas are called the Gaudiya Vaishnavas.

These Bengali devotees of Krishna practiced their faith undisturbed until the conquest of Gaud by the emerging Muslim rulers from the 12th to the 16th

Centuries. In the middle of the period of Muslim dominance and persecution, Sri Krishna Chaitanya was born in 1486 in the village of Navadwip in present-day West Bengal State. Sri Chaitanya would revolutionize Gaudiya Vaishnivism. Sri Chaitanya was a Brahmin, schooled in Sanskrit and the Hindu scriptures, and because of his innate intelligence and erudition, was expected to fulfill his *Varna Dharma* (caste duty), by becoming a priest/scholar/teacher. At a young age, he became an ecstatic devotee of Krishna. This led him to preach a radical new gospel, and adopt a totally different path.[15]

Sri Chaitanya espoused an intense devotionalism based on immersion in the study of Krishna, His attributes, philosophy, and role in the Epics/scriptures. He renounced his expected role as a Brahmin priest and teacher, gave up his formal religious studies and took the vows of *sannyasa* (renunciation), leaving his wife and family and traveling throughout India. Sri Chaitanya discouraged monasticism, and quietism, and intense study of yoga and the scriptures in favor. He preached that devotees should not renounce society but should immerse themselves in it, while engaging in ecstatic and emotional religious practice based on intense devotion to a personal God -- Krishna. Sri Chaitanya advocated public chanting of Krishna's name "in every town and village," the quiet repetition of Krishna's name (*japa*), and the ecstatic worship of Krishna in the temple, as the best way to attain liberation in this present age.

Sri Chaitanya eschewed the prejudices of orthodox Hindus, with their stress on ritual purity and pollution, and memorization of Sanskrit texts. He emphasized that religion should not be restricted to a chosen few, but should be free and open to all, and permeate daily life. Unlike orthodox Hindus, he did not emphasize caste, stating that Krishna loved everyone and everyone could love Krishna. As a *sanyasi*, Sri Chaitanya had no personal contact with women, but, unlike some contemporary Hindus, did not believe women should be excluded from religious life and kept secluded. Sri Chaitanya did not differentiate between people of different religious faiths. Although the Muslims occupied Bengal and ruled over the Bengalis, Sri Chaitanya welcomed Muslim converts into his inner circle.

The Gaudiya Vaishnavas concluded that Sri Chaitanya was more than a religious teacher and leader. In *Sri Caitanya-Caritamrta*, a reverential biography of Sri Chaitanya written by one of his followers, Sri Chaitanya reveals his true identity as Lord Krishna Himself, over the course of His life, by participating in a series of miraculous events. Gaudiya Vaishnavas believe that Lord Krishna incarnated as Sri Chaitanya to provide an example of true devotion to Krishna that devotees could aspire to.

---

[15] For a modern biography of Sri Chaitanya, I recommend *The Birth of Kirtan (The Life and Teachings of Chaitanya)*, by Ranchor Prima, Mandala Publications, San Rafael, California, 2012. The contemporary hagiographic biography is titled *Sri Caitanya-Caritamrta (The Pastimes of Lord Caitanya Mahaprabhu)*, by A.C. Bhaktivedanta Swami Prabhupad, Bhaktivedanta Book Trust, Los Angeles, 2012

During Sri Chaitanya's lifetime, Hinduism was immersed in a philosophical conflict between its personalist and impersonalist schools. It was not a bloody conflict such as that between the Catholics and Protestants in the Christian Reformation and Counter-Reformation. It was a peaceful conflict centered on philosophical differences. During this period, it was customary for learned scholars from these two schools to engage in public debates meant to convince Hindus of the rightness of their positions. Sri Chaitanya participated in several of these debates, and the Gaudiya Vaishnavas believed He handily defeated His opponents.

Sri Chaitanya set off a firestorm of religious devotion not only in Bengal, but all over India, opening up Hinduism to common people and providing them with the means to access the divine without reliance on Brahmin priests, ceremonialism, the Sanskrit language, the study of obscure texts, or the orthodox following of exhaustive rules and regulations.

Sri Siksastaka

Like Jesus Christ, Sri Chaitanya did not leave behind a significant literary legacy. As was the case with Jesus, Sri Chaitanya's life and teachings were recorded by his disciples. Sri Chaitanya's sole literary work is the eight Sanskrit shlokas of the Sri Siksastaka. They read as follows:

Shloka One

Let there be victory for the chanting of the holy name of Lord Krishna, which can cleanse the mirror of the heart and stop the miseries of the blazing fire of material existence. That chanting is the waxing moon that spreads the white lotus of good fortune for all living entities. It is the life and soul of all education. The chanting of the holy name of Krishna expands the blissful ocean of transcendental life. It gives a cooling effect to everyone and enables one to taste full nectar at every step.

Shloka Two

O My Lord, O Supreme Personality of Godhead, in Your holy name there is all good fortune for the living entity, and therefore You have many names, such as Krishna and Govinda, by which You expand Yourself. You have invested all Your potencies in those names, and there are no hard and fast rules for remembering them. My dear Lord, although You bestow such mercy on the fallen conditioned souls by liberally teaching them Your holy names, I am so unfortunate that I commit offenses while chanting the holy name, and therefore I do not achieve attachment for chanting.

Shloka Three

One who thinks himself lower than the grass, who is more tolerant than a tree, and who does not expect personal honor but is always prepared to give all respect to others, can very easily always chant the holy name of the Lord.

Shloka Four

O Lord of the universe, I do not desire material wealth, materialistic followers, a beautiful wife or fruitive activities described in flowery language. All I want, life after life, is unmotivated devotional service unto You.

Shloka Five

O My Lord, O Krishna, son of Maharaja Nanda, I am Your eternal servant, but because of My own fruitive acts, I have fallen in this horrible ocean of nescience. Now please be causelessly merciful to me; consider me a particle of dust at Your lotus feet.

Shloka Six

My dear Lord, when will My eyes be beautified by filling with tears that constantly glide down as I chant Your holy name? When will My voice falter and all the hairs on My body stand erect in transcendental happiness as I chant Your holy name?

Shloka Seven

My Lord Govinda, because of separation from You, I consider even a moment a great millennium. Tears flow from My eyes like torrents of rain, and I see the entire world as void.

Shloka Eight

Let Krishna tightly embrace this servant, who has fallen at His lotus feel. Or let Him trample Me, or break My heart by never being visible to Me. He is a debauchee, after all, and can do whatever He likes, but He is still no one other than the worshipable Lord of My heart.[16]

These eight shlokas encapsulate the essence of Sri Chaitanya's contribution to spirituality. The heart and soul of this contribution is Sri Chaitanya's doctrine of *Achintya-Bheda-Abheda*. Wikipedia describes this profound paradoxical idea as follows:

---

[16] *Sri Siksastaka (Eight Beautiful Instructions)*, by Sri Chaitanya, Harmonist Publications, New Delhi, 1991

Achintya-Bheda-Abheda is a school of Vedanta representing the philosophy of inconceivable one-ness and difference. In Sanskrit achintya means 'inconceivable,' bheda translates as 'difference,' and abheda translates as 'non-difference.' The Gaudiya Vaishnava religious tradition employs the term in to the relationship of creation and creator between God and his energies. It is believed this this philosophy was taught by the movement's theological founder Chaitanya Mahaprabhu (1486-1534) and differentiates the Gaudiya tradition from the other Vaishnava Sampradayas. It can be understood as an integration of the strict dualist (dvaita) theology of Madhvacharya and the qualified monism (vishishtadvaita) of Ramanuja.[17]

Sri Chaitanya explained this concept by using a metaphor. He said that Krishna was like the sun, with unlimited power and potency. The individual souls are like the sunlight. The nature of sunlight is the same as that of the sun, but sunlight is powerless compared to the vast power of the sun. Likewise, Krishna and the individual soul share the same spiritual nature, but Krishna is omnipotent. By contrast, the individual soul is impotent, and remains dependent upon Krishna for everything. This means that Krishna and the individual soul are inconceivably one and different.

Sri Chaitanya's other major emphasis was on the unlimited potency of God/Krishna, an expression of His omnipotence. Sri Chaitanya pointed out that just as a lifeless stone statue is transformed into a deity when it is inhabited by the Lord, the holy names of God, Krishna and Rama, are inhabited by the Lord. To Sri Chaitanya, this merciful and beneficent action by the Lord constitutes His greatest blessing. Krishna loves humankind so much that he tries everything to help the fallen souls living in the material world come back to Him. He therefore has provided humanity with the Hare Krishna mantra, "Hare Krishna, Hare Krishna, Krishna Krishna, Hare Hare. Hare Rama, Hare Rama, Rama Rama, Hare Hare."

We human beings have lived for so long in this material world that we have become too degraded to follow the recommended yogic methods of reuniting with God. Yoga requires discipline and focus and concentration. In this present age of Kali (the lowest of the four yugas), humankind is no longer capable of such rigorous activity. We are soft, undisciplined, and self-indulgent. Sri Chaitanya says that even is this age, Krishna longs for us and so has incarnated as His holy name, so we can become aware of His presence simply by chanting it.

Sri Chaitanya also stresses the need for humility, (see Shloka Two). He stresses that ego and its accompanying arrogance are the greatest impediments to awakening the spiritual nature. In *Sri Caitanya-Caritamrta* Sri Chaitanya is

---

[17] Wikipedia

humiliated again and again by ignorant and arrogant people. He humbly accepts this treatment, although he is the Lord incarnate.

By urging his followers to spread the public chanting of the holy name (*sankirtan*) to "every town and village," Sri Chaitanya emphasized a proselytizing mission for His followers. Hinduism was not then, and is not today a proselytizing religion. It does not have a concept of evangelism. We should not confuse Sri Chaitanya's concept of proselytization with the common Christian concept, however.

Sri Chaitanya is not calling on his followers to formally convert the world's population to Gaudiya Vaishnavism and is not saying that followers of other faiths are incapable of making spiritual progress or reuniting with God. Rather, Sri Chaitanya states that the chanting of the holy names of the Lord is so blissful that anyone can benefit from it. As a totally realized being, Sri Chaitanya does not differentiate between human beings.

As Krishna states in Chapter Five, Text 18 of the *Bhagavad Gita,*

"The humble sages, by virtue of true knowledge, see with equal vision a learned and gentle brahmana, a cow, an elephant, a dog and a dog-eater (outcaste)."[18]

The implication is that an enlightened individual no longer differentiates between Hindus, Muslims, or Christians, and recognizes any of the many and varied ways that humankind differentiates one human being from another.

Sri Chaitanya's emphasis here is on mercy and empathy, helping imprisoned souls gain liberation. It is not a question of "keeping score" or drawing false distinctions and claiming that "my religion" is going to be bigger than "your religion."

---

[18] *The Bhagavad Gita as it Is*, page 293

Chapter VIII

ISKCON and Mysticism

Sri Chaitanya's Followers

Sri Chaitanya disappeared in the environs of the city of Puri in Orissa state.

"After twelve years of this constant rapture of love, he could no longer sustain his body and mind. In 1534, at the age of forty-eight, he left this world. Some say he was carried out to sea; others, that he merged with the deity of Jagannath, or with Tota Gopinath, worshipped in Puri by his dearest friend, Gadadhar. Whatever the truth, he left no earthly remains."[19]

Sri Chaitanya dispatched a group of intimate disciples, the Six Goswamis, to Vrindavan. They remained there the rest of their lives. Over the course of the succeeding years, the Six Goswamis developed that tiny rural village into a pilgrimage town, building temples and ashrams, that were enlarged and beautified in subsequent centuries. During their lifetimes, the Goswamis wrote a huge corpus of literature dealing with Sri Chaitanya, his life, and most particularly, devotion to Sri Krishna.

Chaitanya's followers in Bengal were initially centered around Sri Chaitanya's birthplace in the city of Mayapur, but the sect spread throughout the region. While the dominant Hindu sect in Bengal was, and remains, that of devotion of the Goddess in her many forms, the Gaudiya Vaishnavas maintained a vibrant devotional tradition and passed on their teachings and practices from one generation to the next.

Largely restricted to Bengalis, the Gaudiya Vaishnava sect experienced a mini-revival starting in the late 19th Century. This was a period of turmoil not only in Bengal, but throughout the British colony of India. The Gaudiya Vaishnavas, their practices and attitudes were influenced by intensive interaction with British colonizers and the introduction of the English language. Bengal was one of the first footholds for British Colonialism and by the 19th Century, British administrators, soldiers, merchants, and educators had been living in Bengal for over a century.

The British introduced an English language education system in Bengal, meant to produce a race of "Brown Englishmen" to help the British administer their massive Indian colony. The Bengalis were well-known for their education and erudition, and took to this new type of education with great enthusiasm. A group of these English speaking Bengalis, belonging to the Gaudiya Vaishnava sect, began to see the English language as an effective means of spreading their

---

[19] *The Birth of Kirtan (The Life and Teachings of Chaitanya)*, page 162

philosophy throughout India and beyond. They began to take seriously Sri Chaitanya's admonition to spread the chanting of Hare Krishna to "every town and village" around the world.

The most prominent of these Vaishnavas was Srila Bhaktivinode Thakur, a career civil servant in the colonial government of Bengal, who upon retirement devoted himself exclusively to religious devotion. He created a Gaudiya Vaishnava organization called the Gaudiya Math. Thakur, "predicted that one day there would be Vaishnavas from every country of the world, but did not actively pursue creating such an international community, apart from sending copies of a brief Chaitanya biography to literary figures and educational institutions abroad."[20]

Upon the death of Thakur, his son, Bhaktisiddanta Saraswati became the new head of Gaudiya Math. He eagerly embraced modernism and was more determined than his father to spread Gaudiya Vaishnavism around the world. Saraswati sent Gaudiya Math disciples to Europe with hopes of establishing temples there and recruiting Western followers, but his efforts came to naught. The Bengali missionaries were like fish out of water wandering the streets of London. They did not have the skills or determination required to present their faith to skeptical Europeans.

In 1919 a Bengali gentleman named Abhay Charan De met Saraswati. De came from a devout Gaudiya Vaishnava family and was deeply religious. De was unhappy with his job in a pharmaceutical firm and longed to devote himself fulltime to devotion to Krishna, but had failed to find a genuine Vaishnava guru. His interactions with purported Vaishnava leaders had been disappointing, and he was deeply skeptical. Saraswati proved to be the exception to the rule. De became devoted to Saraswati, worked closely with him, and took formal initiation in 1932.

Saraswati was an ambitious guru committed to modernizing the somnolent Gaudiya Vaishnava sect and following Chaitanya's orders to convert it from a strictly Indian religious movement to an international one. Saraswati was particularly interested in the United States, and said that no international religious institution could be taken seriously unless it was accepted by Americans. He ordered his disciple to undertake the journey to America to provide Americans with their first exposure to Krishna devotion.

Abhay Charan De did not follow his guru's command immediately. In 1950, he gave up his job, left his family behind in Calcutta and moved to the Radha Damodara Temple in Vrindavan. On September 17, 1959 Srila Prabhupada

---

[20] *Swami in a Strange Land (How Krishna Came to the West),* Joshua M. Greene, Mandala Publishing Company, San Rafael, California, 2016

accepted the order of *sannyasa* from Sri Srimad Bhaktiprajnana Kesava Maharaja at the Kesavaji Math in Mathura. His new name was A.C. Bhaktivedanta Swami Prabhupad. During the nine years he lived in Vrindavan, Srila Prabhupad translated the first two cantos of the *Srimad Bhagavatam* into English, and tried to establish a League of Devotees that would supersede the ineffective Gaudiya Math and carry on the mission of his guru.

On August 13, 1965, at the age of 70, Srila Prabhupad boarded a Scindia Lines steamship to travel alone to New York. He had only a few dollars' worth of rupees, a steamer trunk containing some of his English translations of *Srimad Bhagavatam,* and a few articles of clothing. During his journey, he suffered a heart attack, but persisted, eventually settling into a converted storefront in New York City's East Village. The former tenants had run a small gift shop there and the sign, still read "Matchless Gifts."

While living in the East Village, Srila Prabhupad gathered around him a small group of earnest but naïve devotees. Knowing nothing about Krishna or Gaudiya Vaishnavism, they relied completely on their guru. Although he had established only a small storefront temple populated by a tiny group of ignorant followers, Srila Prabhupad had big plans. He legally incorporated this group as a formal society. He called the new group, "The International Society for Krishna Consciousness, (ISKCON)."

Chapter IX

ISKCON and Me

While living in Frankfurt, Germany, and attending the Frankfurt American High School, I began reading Srila Prabhupad's books and listening to the Radha Krishna Temple album recorded by the ISKCON devotees in London. I first encountered ISKCON in the flesh in 1968 in Amsterdam.[21]

I have never been one to act impulsively. I resist getting swept off my feet. It would certainly be dramatic to say that this Amsterdam encounter was a golden moment of realization, but that was far from the case. Even at this young and naïve age, I was not the type of person to run away from home and join the circus. Instead, my Amsterdam encounter consisted of a rather quiet afternoon event at the smallish ISKCON temple. My younger brother and I ate *prasad*, and talked with the devotees, before heading to the train station to get back to Frankfurt.

ISKCON was only three years old at this time, and had only been active in Europe a few years. The release of the "Radha Krishna Temple" LP, and its best-selling single "Hare Krishna," had put the movement on the map in Europe, however. ISKCON attracted lots of attention, which only increased after George Harrison released his single "My Sweet Lord," (featured on his first solo album "All Things Must Pass"). George's "My Sweet Lord," featured him alternating between "Hare Krishna," and "Hallelujah," joined by a small choir of enthusiastic female backup singers.

However, the ISKCON devotees I encountered were new to their professed faith and not very knowledgeable. They provided some insight into the type of life they were trying to establish in their nascent temples, but could provide little instruction about the actual faith they were propounding. They seemed young, insecure, and far from inspiring.

Later, while attending Schiller College in the small Swabian village of Boennigheim, I met more devotees trying to establish a temple in the nearby city of Stuttgart. I convinced them to come to our small campus on a balmy Spring afternoon and hold a Krishna festival, replete with food, singing, dancing, and, of course, lots of chanting Hare Krishna.[22]

These encounters remained intermittent. In between, I continued spiritual pursuits on my own. I listened to my inner voice and experienced no desire to sign up with

---

[21] You can read about this encounter in Volume One of *In the Clear Light of Day*, Jon Dorschner, 2018

[22] This encounter is also described in detail in *In the Clear Light of Day Volume One.*

ISKCON or any other religious group. I was convinced I would know the real thing when I encountered it, and no "real thing" had yet emerged.

I did see the nascent Krishna devotees as kindred souls, with whom I shared a connection. I was happy to sit down with devotees, talk philosophy, and share *prasad*. I viewed these encounters as learning opportunities, pointing me in a direction that remained unclear. Up to this point I had only encountered small rudimentary ISKCON temples in Stuttgart and Amsterdam. I had not yet been exposed to the elaborate and impressive deity worship ISKCON is noted for.

Nor had I encountered senior ISKCON devotees who had the benefit of extensive interaction with Srila Prabhupad, and his personal instruction. The common complaint about ISKCON devotees was their often robotic repetition of pat phrases they had memorized. To me, and most scholarly observers, this evidenced a flimsy knowledge of scripture, tradition, and precept. I longed to meet someone who could speak with calm self-assurance and authority and provide more detailed explanations and analysis.

Srila Prabhupad's guru, Bhaktisiddanta Saraswati firmly believed in the power of the printed word. Saraswati was determined to spread Gaudiya Vaishnavism through the writing, publication, and dissemination of books, especially books in the English language. Srila Prabhupad took his guru's admonitions to heart, and spent hours each day translating religious texts.

ISKCON insiders fondly say Prabhupad's books are a window into his teachings. This is certainly true. Although I never personally saw Prabhupad, heard him speak, or received any instruction from him, he has certainly revealed his deepest teachings to me in the extensive library of books he left behind.[23] This literary legacy makes it possible for anyone, anywhere in the world to study Prabhupad's message, and this is what I have done. As ISKCON devotees say, to read Prabhupad's books is like personal association. Since I am strong on self-study, I felt no imperative to take formal classes at an ISKCON temple.

After departing from Europe, I ended up in Washington DC. My friend William, his girlfriend, and I rented a small apartment in the Dupont Circle neighborhood. Now a thriving gay neighborhood, at that time it was a countercultural nexus. Social life centered around the Dupont Circle Park. Something was always happening there.

---

[23] When I visited Vrindavan for the first time as a teenager, I missed meeting Srila Prabhupad by a matter of minutes. This was the closest I ever came to personal association with him.

There was an active ISKCON temple in our neighborhood, and I often encountered devotees during my frequent walks. This was a low-pressure, casual opportunity to hang out at a temple, and an introduction to serious deity worship. ISKCON was well-integrated into the neighborhood and enjoyed a good relationship with local people.

When I walked into that temple, I was struck. I got it. The temple is supposed to be an intersection between the mundane and the divine, and this temple filled the bill. I did not take intoxicants, but the temple itself was intoxicating. Indians say that as soon as they smell real Indian incense, it doesn't matter where they are in the world, they are immediately transported to a Hindu temple. I understand what they mean. I fell in love with everything. I loved the iconography. I loved the deities on the altar. I loved the way they were worshipped. I loved participating in that worship. I loved the food. I loved gorging myself on Indian vegetarian food, while talking high philosophy with devotees. I loved the music. The singing and chanting was divine. In coming years, I experienced these sensations in temples all over the world, but most intensely in Indian temples.

After arriving in Tucson to study India at the University of Arizona in 1974, I had several opportunities to interact with ISKCON devotees. The thriving University was an active and vibrant place, where all manner of ideas were discussed and debated openly and continuously. Students experimented with anything and everything, and ISKCON was part of the mix. There was no temple in Tucson at that time, and devotees only passed through.[24]

At the end of my university studies, just before my departure to Rankhandi, I lived in a small student apartment by myself within walking distance of the University. I had almost no possessions and spent most of my time on campus. When not in class, I hung around on the University mall, went to the library, or hung out at the Student Union. I had no money for restaurants or night life, and did not drink alcohol. A big night out for me was to see a cheap movie at the Student Union theater and eat a cheap meal at a restaurant. I was particularly fond of Mexican food and ice cream, which I ate in abundance at Student Union eateries. The University campus is extremely beautiful and can be very peaceful, especially in the summer when most students have departed.

During a leisurely sojourn on the mall, I saw one of ISKCON's most famous and revered gurus of this period, Sri Visnujana Swami. This is another example of divine serendipity. It was totally unplanned. I was in the right place at the right time. It was meant to be. I did not know it at the time, but Visnujana Maharaj was (and remains) a legendary figure within ISKCON. He was famous for his outreach to young people based on enthusiastic *sankirtana* and preaching. Visnujana Swami epitomized the renunciate, interested in active religious joy.

---

[24] An ISKCON temple with a Govinda's restaurant was established in Tucson in 1987 and has thrived ever since. It is now a mainstay of the Tucson scene.

Possessing little interest in politics or administration, Visnujana Swami headed a travelling party of devotees that drove around the US holding public presentations. The University of Arizona in Tucson was one of his stops. I regret that I did not have the opportunity to personally interact with him. I could have learned a lot.

In retrospect, those writing about ISKCON, from both inside and outside the movement, point to Visnujana Swami and his fate as an indicator that the organization was headed for dark times. Srila Prabhupad died in Vrindavan in 1977. His departure marked a serious turning point for the organization he founded. Subsequent events revealed serious problems that threatened to eradicate ISKCON altogether.

The Gaudiya Vaishnava movement has a long history of such problems. They were rooted in the cultural and philosophical tenets of the sect, which, while extremely idealistic, were difficult to practically implement. This failure to meet expected standards destroyed the Gaudiya Math prior to Srila Prabhupad's departure for the US. A principal area of contention was the proper role of the guru and how to implement succession once the guru has departed.

The Vaishnavas have demonstrated a dedication to the concept of the guru, which is quite admirable in the abstract, but has had disastrous consequences in the real world. To Vaishnavas, the gurus are overwhelmingly important objects of veneration. ISKCON is no exception in this regard.

In his book *The Dark* Lord[25] Larry D. Shinn describes this attitude towards the guru. Shinn points out that Prabhupad was adamant that he, and all other gurus within Gaudiya Vaishnavism, were not incarnations of God. Prabhupad was quick to denounce any guru who claimed to be an incarnation of God or tried to make himself the object of worship. Srila Prabhupad had a deep abhorrence for what he called religious charlatans.

However, Prabhupad pointed out, the guru, in the Gaudiya Vaishnava tradition, is a personal representative of Krishna, and is authorized to take the initiated devotee home, "back to Godhead." Gaudiya Vaishnava treatment of the guru sometimes seems to contradict Srila Prabhupad's intent. To outside observers, it can appear that the guru himself, rather than Krishna, is the object of worship. Any guru too weak to resist, can fall prey to this veneration and let it slip into worship. Such a detour usually proves disastrous.

Shinn explains that:

---

[25] Larry D. Shinn, *The Dark Lord (Cult Images and the Hare Krishnas in America),* The Westminister Press, Philadelphia, PA, 1987

The Krishna tradition of Caitanya says that the tests of a true guru are that (1) he must be able to extinguish the seeker's anxiety; (2) he must always be engaged in chanting the names of God: (3) he must engage others in the worship of God; (4) he must encourage the distribution of God's "blessed food," or prasadam; and (5) he must always be thinking of the Lord Krishna and his lifetime on earth. ... The guru must be ordained in a disciplic line (guru succession, or *parampara*) in order to give formal initiation to others.[26]

Formal initiation in the Gaudiya Vaishnava tradition is seen as an essential prerequisite to liberation. It is not to be taken lightly, and any human being with the power to formally initiate disciples falls into a very special category. The guru's position as the representative of God on earth places an enormous burden on both the guru and his disciples. Not only must the guru meet all the requirements listed above, he must take on all the bad *karma* of his disciples, and do whatever he can to ensure they make spiritual progress. Many of the initiates into ISKCON during this period came from troubled backgrounds and had some very bad karma indeed.

In return, disciples are required to show a measure of respect for the guru incomprehensible to many Westerners. They shower the guru with admiration, praise, and devotion. They place the guru's picture on the altar with the deities, they prostrate themselves full length before the guru, and follow his every desire as a direct edict from God.

In India, the gurus are usually older and experienced men, who have been well-prepared and well-educated for their role. Despite this, many of them fall prey to temptation, let the veneration go to their heads, and betray their sannyasi vows, becoming involved with power, egotism, sex, intoxication, and the acquisition of wealth, reflected in a lavish lifestyle. It would prove impossible for Srila Prabhupad's much younger and less seasoned senior devotees not to fall prey to these temptations.

The Vaishnava concept of the guru and all its powerful implications, makes the succession issue very difficult. When the guru leaves the scene, there must be someone of equal stature available to step in. If there is no clearly identified successor, or if said successor does not enjoy universal respect and admiration, it opens the door to competition. After the departure of the guru, competing aspiring gurus can emerge, and the Vaishnava organization can split into warring factions and descend into chaos.

Srila Prabhupad was the *guru acharya* (founding guru) for ISKCON and its sole head. As ISKCON mushroomed in size through the 1970's, he created a Governing Body Commission (GBC) of his most senior and trusted disciples to handle day to day administration. Srila Prabhupad was trying to prepare for his

---

[26] *The Dark Lord*, page 32

imminent departure, ensure that the organization would function smoothly after he was gone, and free himself from administrative duties to focus on spiritual concerns.

After establishing the GBC, Prabhupad selected a group of these senior disciples to act as gurus after his departure. Each was given a "zone," a specific area of the world to oversee. As guru, they were authorized to accept disciples and initiate them. Although Srila Prabhupad never stated that these zonal gurus were to be viewed as his replacements or equals, they quickly asserted this position and demanded from their disciples the same veneration formerly provided to Prabhupad.

The ISKCON devotees selected for guru status were young, inexperienced and clearly not prepared for promotion to guru status. It is difficult to comprehend how it must feel to be a Vaishnava guru and subject to complete and total veneration 24 hours a day, while subject to strict sannyasi vows of poverty, celibacy, and non-intoxication. It is a lonely position and innately comes with powerful temptations.

The biggest temptation facing the new guru is to allow all the veneration to go to his head, and this is precisely what happened in ISKCON. Although the new gurus began to see themselves in a similar status as Srila Prabhupad, they did not have Prabhupad's qualifications to occupy this position. They were nowhere close. The veneration led to enormous egotism and arrogance. The gurus completely forgot Sri Chaitanya's admonition to be "as humble as a blade of grass." They craved ever more power, wealth, and veneration. Some began to think the rules did not apply to them and adopted a bizarre stunted ethical system that somehow justified any evil, wrong, or illegal act as long as it was done to benefit Krishna's ISKCON. They forgot their vows and sexually exploited female and male devotees, while indulging in intoxication and erratic behavior. One by one the gurus "fell down." Those that did not voluntarily abandon their posts as gurus, leave the sannyasi order and, in the most extreme cases, leave ISKCON, were expelled.

The collapse of the gurus left the initiated devotees in confusion and despair.[27] Frustration, disappointment, and a sense of betrayal became rampant. The rapid decline of the institution led to a mass exodus of initiated devotees. Writing in 1987, Larry Shinn's research confirmed that fully 95% of the devotees initiated by

---

[27] There is an entire genre of literature written by former devotees, often quite senior, in which they describe the frustration, disgust and sense of betrayal that caused their departure from ISKCON during this period. Two of the best are: *Betrayal of the Spirit (My Life Behind the Headlines of the Hare Krishna Movement)*, Nori Muster, University of Illinois Press, 2001, and *Killing for Krishna (The Danger of Deranged Devotion)*, Henry Doktorski, Createspace Independent Publishing Platform, 2018

Srila Prabhupad had left. In this new, post-Prabhupad dispensation, earnest and sincere devotees like Visnujana Swami found they had no place.[28]

During this chaotic and dark period, I interacted with some senior devotees (but none of the gurus, who were inaccessible).

In 1978, I was on my way to India but stuck in Germany waiting for my visa. Every day I took public transportation to the Taunus Mountains outside Frankfurt. There, at Schloss Rettershof, a palatial German residence taken over by ISKCON, I interacted with devotees, participated in the daily rituals and gained valuable insight.

ISKCON Germany had been under the leadership of Hamsadutta Swami, one of the initiating gurus, who would later leave ISKCON after a spectacular "fall down." Under Hamsadutta's leadership, ISKCON engaged in fraudulent fundraising, approaching Germans on the street and telling them they were collecting money for starving people in India, when in fact all collections went into Hamsadutta's coffers.[29] The German government initiated an investigation that confirmed numerous legal violations, culminating in a police raid and the confiscation of ISKCON's fraudulently collected assets.

In his book *Srila Prabhupada and His disciples in Germany* Vedavyasa Dasa writes,

Hamsaduta requested his godbrothers to relieve him from his responsibilities in Europe so that he would be free to preach in India, and they readily accepted his proposal. Jayatirtha, until then the Governing Body Commissioner (GBC) for California, became responsible for Germany...Those who remained at Schloss Rettershof were disheartened....The devotees were struggling and discouraged, there being only fifty-five left in the country. The German media and government had a campaign going to discredit ISKCON. ... The situation had been made worse by Hamsaduta's mismanagement.[30]

---

[28] There is an excellent two-volume biography of Visnujana Swami, *Radha-Damodar Vilasa (The Inner Life of Vishnujana Swami and Jayananda Prabhu)*, by Vaiyasaki das Adhikari. The third and final volume has not yet been released.

[29] Hamsadutta was not the only guru to engage in such practices. They were common throughout ISKCON during this period.

[30] Vedavyasa Dasa, *Srila Prabhupada and His Disciples in Germany*, The Mandir Media Group, Alicante, Spain, 1984, pages 369-70

This was the situation I discovered during my daytrips to Schloss Rettershof. The dispirited devotees carried out the "temple program," keeping to the worship schedule, but little productive activity was evident. The basement of the building was filled with ISKCON books, and LPs of music recorded by ISKCON bands. These had been part of Hamsaduta's aggressive fund raising, being offered to people on the streets of Germany for "donations." The devotees gave me some LPs, since they could no longer be sold because of German government legal rulings.

While I was on the floors below, Jayadvaita was upstairs in his private quarters wrestling with this grim situation. When I asked to see him, I was told he was too busy. Although I spent several days participating in the temple schedule, I never saw Jayadvaita. When I got back to Tucson, I wrote a paper about the travails of ISKCON Germany and my experiences at Schloss Rettershof and presented it at the annual conference of the American Association of Asian Studies, my first formal conference presentation.

Visnujana Maharaj was not the only senior ISKCON devotee to travel to Tucson. At one point I met Mukunda Goswami, one of Srila Prabhupad's first initiated disciples, who was then serving as the public affairs director for all of ISKCON. After earnest discussion, he came back with me to my sparse apartment. He was so humble I had no idea of his esteemed position and high status. We spoke informally. I still do not remember why this happened. Maybe he wanted to pick up a copy of my paper. This was before the days of the internet.

In the 1970's and 80's Tucson was a burgeoning center for the "deprogramming movement." It seems odd in the present context when mankind is facing imminent destruction from climate change, but during this period, many in the US were convinced that "cults" were one of the biggest threats facing the country.

While the definition of what constituted a "cult" always remained unclear and controversial, there were many groups active in this period that bore this designation. The Christian "cults" were known as "Jesus Freaks." Other "cults" were loosely Hindu, or Buddhist, while others were made up out of whole cloth. Many featured greedy "leaders" who exploited their followers, often young people, who were cut off and adrift during these tumultuous times.

It was common practice during this period to lump ISKCON into this group. There was some overlap. ISKCON was a high-demand, monastic organization. In retrospect, many observers of this period acknowledge that the recently initiated devotees were often exploited. ISKCON was going through a cash crunch. The devotees primarily resided in temples and relied on the organization for their upkeep. In return, they worked 24 hours per day for ISKCON.

Many post-Prabhupad gurus became quickly enamored with their new status and became infatuated with money. Some adopted a lavish lifestyle, while others wanted to build magnificent temples to increase their prestige. While the devotees were largely bereft of income, or possessions, (having donated their assets to ISKCON), they still had to be fed and clothed, and the bills had to be paid. ISKCON had no realistic economic plan to provide the economic basis for a sustainable and growing movement.

When the organization was still new, Prabhupad introduced the practice of *sankirtan* (public chanting) into the US. He was trying to import a cultural model that was commonly accepted in India, but was totally foreign and quite controversial in the US. Prabhupad instructed the devotees to regularly take to the streets and chant Hare Krishna. In India, these chanting parties regularly accept alms from the public, which is a longstanding culturally-sanctioned tradition. Prabhupad told his devotees to adopt the same practice, thinking that this, coupled with sales of his books, would support the temples, where virtually all ISKCON devotees lived during this period. Groups of devotees with drums and finger cymbals (*kartals*), wended their way through public thoroughfares loudly chanting Hare Krishna and attracting considerable attention. Once the crowds gathered around the chanting devotees, other devotees approached the curious people, engaged them in conversation and tried to convince them to accept a book or a magazine in return for a "donation."

Prabhupad had established ISKCON's publishing arm in Los Angeles, the Bhaktivedanta Book Trust. It published Prabhupad's translations of the *Bhagavad Gita, Srimad Bhagavatam*, and other works in the Gaudiya Vaishnava tradition. The *Bhagavad Gita*, was far and away the most popular of these books.[31] Prabhupad also prepared small pamphlets consisting of transcriptions of his lectures on topics such as reincarnation. These were aimed at Americans totally unfamiliar with Indian/Hindu religious tradition and concepts, and were meant to be cheap and available.

ISKCON initially (and naively) believed these book sales would support the movement, but this was not a viable economic basis for a large and growing movement, especially when initiates were all expected to work fulltime to ISKCON and not engage in outside employment. The new gurus became ever more obsessed with money collection, and quickly determined that this model was insufficient. Instead of restructuring ISKCON into a congregational rather than a monastic movement, they turned to fraud and illegal activities.

ISKCON guru Rameshwara Swami was famous for his money obsession. Based in Los Angeles, he emphasized book selling "marathons," during which devotees spent many hours on the streets selling books and convincing passersby to provide donations. He also initiated the ever more aggressive selling of books at airports, leading to a series of legal disputes. This culminated in legal orders banning ISKCON (and all other religious groups) from selling and proselytizing in airports.

[31] Srila Prabhupad's *Bhagavad Gita as it is*, is the largest selling of the many Gita translations available in English.

We have already examined the theological reasons why Hinduism stokes the ire of evangelical Christians. ISKCON was the most visible of the many Hindu groups active during this period. Unlike most others, it made no effort to downplay its Hindu identity. ISKCON devotees dressed in saffron robes, shaved their heads, and applied white clay markings to their foreheads (*tilak*), while female devotees dressed in saris. It all appeared odd and off-putting to many Americans.[32]

Perhaps the most egregious of ISKCON's faults in Christian evangelical eyes was its adoption of Hindu proselytization. Previous to ISKCON, Hindu groups had made no effort to convert those of other faiths. Earlier Hindu groups active in the US did not actively approach non-Hindus, but relied on gentle persuasion and word of mouth. No Indian gurus previously active in the US believed their message would appeal to large numbers of Americans. They were content to limit the size of their organizations to a select few.

ISKCON, by contrast, became more and more aggressive after Srila Prabhupad's departure. To conservative Christians that was a tremendous affront. They viewed religion as a competition for souls. When it came to Hindus, they had generally enjoyed a clear field. They saved Hindus by converting them to Christianity, which prevented them from spending eternity in hell. They now saw young Americans giving up their Christian faith to become Hindus, thus reversing the process.

For all these reasons, parents of young adults initiated into ISKCON were often deeply disturbed. They hired many of the same deprogrammers actively working against other "cults," to go after their children in ISKCON. The deprogrammers' standard procedure was to kidnap devotees, take them to another location, destroy their religious clothing, books, and paraphernalia, and work on them for days, often without access to proper food and water, until they agreed to renounce their new-found faith and return to the fold. The newly "deprogrammed" devotees were then returned to their families, which often tried to reintegrate them into their Jewish or Christian family traditions.

I learned that ISKCON devotees planned to picket one of these deprogramming organizations, demanding that the kidnapped devotees being held in Tucson be returned. I joined them. They were happy to give me a sign and have me join the picket line. This was not the first time I had participated in a demonstration. I knew the drill.

By this time, the tide had already begun to turn against the deprogrammers (who were charging the parents large sums of money and in some cases making a

---

[32] The sight of devotees on the street in their traditional garb set off such a negative reaction that the gurus began to disguise their fund-raisers, providing them with wigs and western clothes. These fund raisers did not identify themselves as ISKCON devotees but as members of charitable organizations.

handsome living). ISKCON had taken them to court and was starting to win court cases. They were being convicted of kidnapping and forced to pay settlements to ISKCON and kidnapped devotees.

The entire deprogramming phenomenon (as well as the cult phenomenon) largely disappeared just a few years after this. Public sentiment turned against the deprogrammers and parents became more and more reluctant to pay for their services. As the cults declined, so did the deprogrammers.

After our demonstration was over, the ISKCON team leader asked whether I would like to join them. He literally wanted me to give up everything right there on the spot, jump in their van and drive with them back to their temple in Washington State. The idea seemed absurd to me, and I declined.

US ISKCON was headquartered in Los Angeles, and ISKCON leaders invited me to come spend some time with them there. I took the train from the Tucson railway station downtown and got off in LA. ISKCON had an entire complex (it is still there), centered around a church that had been converted into a temple. It consisted of the temple, apartments for families, buildings for male and female single devotees and those aspiring for initiation, and buildings to house craft shops, and the Bhaktivedanta Book Trust.

I stayed for several days in the building housing the aspiring male devotees (the *bramacharyas ashram*). I was given total access and could go at will anywhere in the complex and could talk to anyone I wanted to. In the evening, I socialized with senior devotees. I remember with great fondness my pleasant and elucidating conversations with Achyutananda Dasa, Brahmananda Dasa, and Mukunda Dasa, members of the select group of Srila Prabhupad's original disciples. These were the quiet, relaxed, and knowledgeable devotees I enjoyed associating with in years to come, especially in India.

Achyutananda's short and snappy memoir *Blazing Sadhus (Never Trust a Holy Man who can't Dance)*[33] is a delightful spiritual romp that connects Achyutananda's beat past with his devotional present, and shows how the two can be homogeneously integrated. Sadly, Brahmananda Dasa is no longer with us, but ISKCON scholar Steven J. Rosen, has written an excellent reminiscence synopsizing his interviews with this devotee, *Swamiji (An Early Disciple, Brahmananda Remembers his Guru)*.[34]

I have two other vivid memories of my time at the LA temple. It was the most elaborate ISKCON temple I had visited up to that point. The temple hall and altar were very large and the worship ecstatic, involving hundreds of devotees at one

---

[33] CMB Books, Alachua, Florida, 2012

[34] Createspace Independent Publishing Platform, 2016

time. Part of the controversy surrounding the post-Prabhupad gurus centered around the use of *Vyasasanas*. These are elaborate seats at a height above the congregation and used exclusively by the guru. Prior to his departure, there were *Vyasasanas* in every major temple reserved for Srila Prabhupad. As part of their self-elevation, the post-Prabhupad gurus installed such seats for themselves in the temples within their zones. This move alienated and angered many devotees, who saw it as a self-appropriation of status by egotistical gurus and an insult to Srila Prabhupad. Devotees were particularly upset that these newly-declared gurus had their *Vyasasanas* installed at the same height as Prabhupad's. To ISKCON members this was evidence of glaring hubris and a cardinal sin.

As outrage grew, rebellious Temple Presidents throughout the United States unified under the leadership of Ravindra Svarupa dasa, the Temple President in Philadelphia. While living in New York, I visited Ravindra Svarupa and had extensive conversations with him. He was very accessible and quite humble and we spent the afternoon together. He was straightforward, describing his disappointment with the gurus and his hope for reform. By the time I arrived in LA, many gurus had already left ISKCON or renounced their guru status. Ravindra and the other Temple Presidents began a reform movement aimed at ending the abuses of the gurus. It resulted in an extensive overhaul that I will not go into here. One of the first things to go were the *Vyasasanas* installed by the pretentious gurus.

While in LA, I witnessed Rameswara, one of the most controversial of the gurus, preside over events in the temple from his *Vyasasana*. One by one, members of the book distribution groups reported to him with their total book sales. I was not impressed. The mood was not devotional. It seemed mercenary. While I had easy and seemingly unlimited access to many senior devotees, Rameswara remained inaccessible. This increasing inaccessibility of the senior leadership was another indicator that the gurus had become enamored of their own status and less concerned about listening to the concerns of others.

While sitting on the steps of the temple, I got into a conversation with a devotee. He began to talk about the possibility of violent attacks on the temple by opponents of ISKCON. He described efforts by ISKCON to create a force of *"Kshatriyas"* (members of the warrior caste) dedicated to the defense of ISKCON. The Kshatriyas have been armed, he said, and trained in the use of weapons.[35] This was another indication that things had gotten out of hand.

Then and Now

---

[35] Doktorski in his book *Killing for Krishna*, describes in detail the activities and mindset of these "kshatriyas," who acted as the strongarm men for the competing gurus during this period. Doktorski's book relates their descent into violence and murder, with killings taking place in the New Vrindavan Temple in West Virginia, and on the street not far from the LA temple.

Shinn's *The Dark Lord,* was written at the height of the deprogramming controversy and the obsession with dangerous cults. Shinn's research documented how and why ISKCON could not be lumped together with the cults of that era, most of which have totally disappeared. Shinn makes it clear that ISKCON was founded not by a deranged self-absorbed guru, but by Srila Prabhupad, a legitimate member of the Gaudiya Vaishnava sect, duly initiated as a disciple of Bhaktisiddanta Saraswati, a highly-respected guru recognized as the legitimate heir to the leadership of the Gaudiya Math.

Unlike the cult leaders of that era, Srila Prabhupad was never accused of duplicity or hypocrisy. No one could argue that the doctrines propounded by Prabhupad were not genuine Gaudiya Vaishnava. Scholars agree that Prabhupad epitomized the Gaudiya Vaishnava *sannyasi* and at all times lived up to the values he propounded. Prabhupad did not make anything up. He viewed himself not as a divine personality destined to bring a new dispensation into the world, but rather as a transmitter of eternal values that remain sacrosanct. He repeatedly stated that his intention was to transmit the Vaishnava message intact with no variation or addition. Despite its deep and troubling descent into chaos and fanaticism, ISKCON can therefore be legitimately viewed as an extension of the Gaudiya Vaishnava religious movement going back to Sri Chaitanya and earlier.

Shinn also addresses the accusation that ISKCON devotees were "brainwashed," deprived of their freedom and told to sever their ties with their friends, family, and former lives, something quite prevalent in many of the cults of this era. Shinn spent extensive periods in ISKCON temples in various locations, observed the behavior of the devotees residing there and conducted hundreds of interviews, some of which he quotes in his book.

The devotees Shinn interviewed clearly stated they were free to leave ISKCON any time they wanted. Shinn quotes former devotees, who simply walked out the door and left. This, says Shinn, is confirmed by the objective data. When the movement deteriorated and no longer lived up to its ideals in the eyes of the initiated devotes, those who had become disenchanted simply left.

From my personal point of view, I find it most interesting that Shinn documents that the devotees he interviewed did not join ISKCON at the spur of the moment. Shinn describes how the cults of this era quickly swept up converts with emotional appeals. These "cults" expected new converts to join quickly and without much prior thought or consideration. They were then quickly integrated into a highly-regimented environment based on compulsion and conformity that provided them with little opportunity to question the rightness of their snap decision.

By contrast, says Shinn, ISKCON devotees often spent years interacting with the organization before deciding to join. He also points out that ISKCON did not make it easy to become initiated. Formal initiation in ISKCON is a long process, similar to becoming a monk or a nun in the Christian tradition. The aspiring devotee must go through considerable training before being accepted for final initiation. At any point during this process, the aspiring devotee can leave.

Shinn discovered that a large majority of the devotees came from two religious traditions, the Roman Catholic and the Jewish. He found that there were fewer Protestants among the devotees. The formerly Jewish devotees often said that Reformed Judaism was too watered down and did not offer them sufficient opportunities to gain access to a personal God. The former Roman Catholic devotees, by contrast, were strong practicing Catholics prior to their initiation into ISKCON. Many stated that they did not feel they were renouncing their Catholic faith but building on it. They felt that there was considerable overlap between Catholicism and Gaudiya Vaishnavism. This is particularly true when it comes to the emphasis on the role of iconography and monasticism in religion.

I would argue that ISKCON appealed then and appeals now to practicing Christians, who, in former times, would have embraced Christian monasticism. The Protestant Church renounced monasticism as part of the Protestant Reformation, destroying monasteries and nunneries and "liberating" monks and nuns. The Protestant Church also introduced married clergy in place of the celibate clergy found in the Catholic Church. Within the modern Catholic Church in the US, monasticism and celibate clergy has fallen into disfavor. This is largely the result of recurring spectacular instances of sexual assault on children and nuns by Catholic priests. As a result, those growing up within the Catholic tradition are no longer encouraged to become nuns, monks, and priests. In the US, there is a drastic shortage of Priests, monks and nuns. Catholic parishes are struggling to find ordained clergy, while monasteries and convents are shutting down at a rapid pace. This trend discourages Catholics who in former times would have been attracted to a Catholic monastic life. Some young Catholics, who would formerly have embraced this alternative within their own families' tradition, have turned to ISKCON, as they readily recognize ISKCON's monastic emphasis.

ISKCON Today

The ISKCON of today is far different from the controversial ISKCON of the past. It has turned away from a strictly monastic model and embraced a more practical and relevant congregational model. Today, initiated devotees no longer are expected to reside in a temple. Most pursue their own careers and maintain their families. For them, the ISKCON temple is the center of worship and provides services such as religious instruction and the performance of rituals. The majority of the congregations are not initiated disciples, but rather families interested in actively pursuing the Hindu tradition and passing it on to their children. The majority of these non-initiated congregational members are Indian or Indian-American. These congregational devotees provide financial support to the temples. In addition to congregational support, ISKCON temples run highly successful vegetarian restaurants across the United States, and the Bhaktivedanta Book Trust publishes books by both Srila Prabhupad and his senior disciples, which provide other sources of income.

This switch to a congregational model and the establishment of viable temple-run businesses provided the much-needed economic basis that was previously lacking. ISKCON devotees are no longer expected to support themselves and their temples by approaching strangers on the streets and asking for donations.

The strictly monastic devotees who still live in temples are the priesthood, and serve functions similar to Catholic priests. They are the spiritual technicians trained to carry out complex rituals. They also serve as educators that socialize the children of congregants. Others live on ISKCON farms and rural retreats, which resemble Catholic monasteries. Hinduism and Indian culture dictate that marriage and motherhood are the rightful roles for women, and ISKCON has adopted this cultural model. There is therefore no ISKCON institution similar to a Catholic convent, although some single celibate women have acquired a revered status within ISKCON.[36]

American society has changed considerably from the 1960's when ISKCON arrived on US shores. There is a small corpus of American young people attracted to ISKCON and to Gaudiya Vaishnavism, but it no longer has the romantic appeal it enjoyed in the 60's. ISKCON has reached what may be its optimum level in the United States. Turnover of devotees remains high, but as devotees leave, they are replaced by new ones, and the absolute number remains constant.

The saving grace for ISKCON has been the increase in Indian immigration to the United States. The vast majority of Indian immigrants are practicing Hindus. They want their children to remain in the faith and have come to see ISKCON as a valid socialization agent. For these Indian Hindus, ISKCON provides their children, often born in the US and with little or no exposure to India, a pure Hindu environment and an opportunity to experience Hindu worship in a legitimate Hindu temple. The Indian-American community is the most affluent in the US and its donations to ISKCON temples provides a big component of the group's economic basis.

ISKCON has still not resolved its guru succession issue. It was an organization founded and led by Srila Prabhupad, and since his departure, no single personality has emerged to assume the mantle of the guru. As part of its earnest reform efforts, ISKCON has moved away from a set of powerful gurus into an initiation system based on more rather than less. Instead of eight or ten gurus, there are now over a hundred initiating gurus authorized to take on new disciples.

---

[36] Despite its strong patriarchal tradition, ISKCON has recently changed its leadership criteria. Unlike the Catholic church, ISKCON women have been accepted into the Governing Body Commission as senior leaders of the organization.

Fall downs of these gurus continues, but these are due to the same transgressions traditionally seen among *sannyasis*, namely the breaking of the vows. A modus vivendi seems to have emerged in which everyone has realized the fruitlessness of artificially building up a senior personality to a status he is not ready for. Senior devotees are now discouraged from seeking *Sannyas*, and householders with wives and children are no longer deemed incapable of being leaders. At one time, *Sannyasis* were viewed as the most legitimate devotees, and householders were ridiculed. As a result, ISKCON saw an enormous number of young men accepting *Sannyas* initiation. Most of them did not last very long. This was not in keeping with the Indian cultural model where young men are discouraged from becoming *sannyasins*. In India *sannyasins* are expected to be older and more mature. No one in ISKCON wants to see a repeat of the "guru wars" of the past. There appears to be no short term return to the standard model of one guru that heads the organization, and no indication when or if one will emerge.

Gaudiya Vaishnavism and ISKCON

There has been a concerted turn away from organized religion in Western countries and the United States is no exception. The fastest growing religious group in the US is the "nones." Those who profess no religious faith, or do not belong to any organized religious group. Hindus, including members of ISKCON, are not exempt from this development.

The turn away from organized religion should not be confused with a turn away from God, or a turn away from spirituality. Many nones state they are spiritual rather than religious. Much of this personal spirituality is channeled into Eastern religious practice, namely Buddhism and Hinduism. The post baby boom generations seek authenticity and have no patience for hypocrisy. They also attach no stigma to trying out different religious concepts and practices to see if they fit. This has resulted in "church shopping" or "guru shopping," in which the seeking individual goes from one religious group or faith to another in an effort to find the one that is genuinely his/hers.

Philosophically, earlier generations confused belonging to a religious group with being religious. Formerly in the US, it was all but mandatory for Americans to belong to a formal religious denomination and regularly attend religious services. During this earlier era, many that filled the church pews on Sunday were there out of a sense of compulsion and did not really believe. This is no longer the case. Americans are now free to pursue their own faith or no faith at all. As a result, those who are spiritual are genuinely spiritual, for they are engaging in religious practice out of a sense of deep personal urgency rather than social compulsion.

Many Americans have eschewed organized religion to pursue a personal religious path, a personal relationship with God or the divine. They are not tied to a particular dogma or clearly defined faith, but pick and choose from a variety of sources. This makes it difficult for social scientists to factually document religious belief and practice. Gaudiya Vaishnavism is one of the sources for those seeking religious truth.

Srila Prabhupad made an enormous contribution to American society. He introduced Gaudiya Vaishnavism, a love for Krishna as Lord, and the opportunity to establish a personal relationship with Krishna. Srila Prabhupad founded a religious organization, ISKCON, which provides many services, but it is not necessary to be a formal member of ISKCON to practice Gaudiya Vaishnavism.

We now see a variety of Gaudiya Vaishnavas in the US. Many devotees that left ISKCON in those turbulent early years remained personally devoted to Lord Krishna and established their own relationship with Him that remained after the relationship with ISKCON came to an end. Many devotees left ISKCON but continue to worship at ISKCON temples on an ad hoc informal basis. Some founded their own, less formal, Gaudiya Vaishnava groups. Some left ISKCON and joined other offshoots of the Gaudiya Math that have become established in the US.

Religion is a highly personal experience. It cannot be contained or limited to a relationship with any formally defined religious organization or doctrine. It is technically impossible to objectively determine who believes in what. In our present and rapidly changing religious environment, it would be impossible to conclude that spirituality is in decline or on the rise based on membership in formal religious organizations such as ISKCON.

Thanks to Srila Prabhupad, those looking for an authentic way to establish a relationship with God, now have another, viable alternative to pursue.

Chapter X

Vrindavan

Vrindavan is today a growing town located in the Braj Bhoomi region of Uttar Pradesh state in India. It is a pilgrimage center beloved by followers of Gaudiya Vaishnavism as the site of Lord Krishna's childhood and youth, and the scene of His many mystical pastimes. Today, there are more than 5,000 temples in Vrindavan and worship of Lord Krishna takes place 24 hours per day.

Vrindavan is 11 kilometers from the city of Mathura, South of Delhi on the railway line from the capital city to the popular tourist destination of Agra, home to the Taj Mahal. Western tourists making the popular "golden triangle" tour of India (Delhi, Agra, Jaipur) pass right by the Mathura Railway Station on their way to Agra. Most are unaware of Vrindavan and its significance. Vrindavan is no tourist attraction, but is visited by increasing numbers of Westerners nonetheless. These Western visitors are not tourists, however, but pilgrims. They are not interested in touring the sights associated with the Golden Triangle. They want to meet Krishna.

Sri Chaitanya Mahaprabhu was born in 1486 and left this planet in 1534. In the 16th Century, when Sri Chaitanya arrived at the site, Vrindavan was wild jungle populated primarily by animals. Despite its remoteness, Sri Chaitanya was determined to go there. With a small group of followers, he headed out from Bengal for the long journey across India. There was little infrastructure during this period. Most of the region through which Sri Chaitanya and his party passed was jungle. Any traveler making the trip had to contend with wild animals and violent bandits. Sri Chaitanya and his small entourage made their journey on foot, and arrived safely after many adventures.[37]

Sri Chaitanya was ecstatic when he reached Vrindavan. He and his small group of followers walked through the countryside and Sri Chaitanya stopped from time to time to identify places where Lord Krishna had been present and lived His miraculous life. Sri Chaitanya's followers documented that he was transported in ecstasy at spots that appeared no different from the surrounding countryside. He identified each as the location for one of Lord Krishna's mystical pastimes.

"He came to Govardhan Hill, once lifted by Krishna's hand. Beside the hill were the two ponds where Krishna and Radha used to meet and bathe. These ponds had been forgotten; people no longer knew what they were. He identified them as special to Krishna's memory and reestablished them as sacred places. They were

---

[37] You can read about this journey in, A.C. Bhaktivedanta Prabhupada, *Sri Chaitanya-Charitamrta*, KBI Reprint, Bhaktivedanta Book Trust, Los Angeles, 2014

later extended to become large stone-lined tanks, where pilgrims bathed and said their prayers to Radha and Krishna."[38]

After Sri Chaitanya departed from Vrindavan and returned to Bengal, he never returned. He sent six of his closest and most confidential disciples to Vrindavan to carry out his mission. He ordered them to re-establish the sacred sites that had been lost and forgotten for so long. These were the six Goswamis. They spent the rest of their lives in Vrindavan, living austere and simple lives devoted to Krishna. They built temples at the sacred sites, and oversaw the excavation of the sacred ponds (*kundas*). The temples and residencies of the six Goswamis remain in Vrindavan today, as well as the spot beside Radha Kunda where Sri Chaitanya stayed while in Vrindavan.

The six Goswamis were immersed in religious practice and ecstasy. They encountered Krishna on a daily basis while living in Vrindavan. They were literary devotees, leaving behind an extensive corpus of devotional literature dedicated to explaining the experience of God.

Vrindavan and Me

As recounted in Volume I of *In the Clear Light of Day*, I first came to India at the age of 20. Just below is a shot of me on this first trip. I am travelling through the Himalayas on my way to the shrine of the ice lingam in Kashmir.

By the time I travelled to India, I had been studying Hinduism and Gaudiya Vaishavism for about six years. I was well-aware of Vrindavan. I had read an original George Harrison printed edition of Srila Prabhupad's *Krishna Book*,[39] Srila Prabhupad's synopsis of the extensive and detailed *Srimad Bhagavatam* account of the life of Lord Krishna. Devotees of the Gaudiya Vaishnava sect view these stories of Lord Krishna to be the most intimate and potent of all devotional literature, most especially the accounts in Canto Ten of the *Srimad Bhagavatam*, which relate the relationship between the Lord and the *Gopis*, the cowherd girls of Vrindavan.

Although I had read the book from cover to cover several times and thoroughly enjoyed it, I did not fully comprehend what it was about. The stories of Lord Krishna as related in "the Krishna book" are difficult for non-Indians to understand when presented as is, with no explanation, and no cultural context.

---

[38] *The Birth of Kirtan (The Life and Teachings of Chaitanya)*, page 116

[39] "Krishna Book" is the affectionate name for this work written by Srila Prabhupad, which is actually titled, "Krishna (The Supreme Personality of Godhead)." My original copy has since disappeared, much to my regret. These original crude books, printed in Japan, were financed by George Harrison and are now extremely rare.

Srila Prabhupad had difficulty comprehending the level of ignorance in the West concerning these matters, for everyone in India, regardless of religious orientation, is familiar with Lord Krishna and the details of His life as described in the Hindu epics and the Puranas. Lacking this cultural background, I could not understand the subtle implications of the stories. While reading the book, I remained curious about Vrindavan and Braj (the region of the present-day state of Uttar Pradesh associated with Lord Krishna and his pastimes). It seemed amazing to me that God could descend to earth and live in a small village in the Indian countryside and herd cows with local boys.

It did not occur to me that Vrindavan was an actual physical place I could visit. While Western pilgrims are now visible all over Vrindavan, this was not something Americans did in the early 1970's when I traveled to India the first time. I travelled around India by myself, making my way in fits and stops from Nepal towards Delhi. I had arrived in Agra and was hanging around the Taj Mahal. I rode through the city in a rickshaw conversing with the rickshaw driver in a mixture of broken English and broken Hindi. He somehow determined I was a devotee of Krishna and told me I must go to Vrindavan. He told me it was nearby. It was because of him that I got on the train in Agra, boarding a slow local that stopped at the tiny Vrindavan Railway Station. The station was sleepy and deserted. I walked outside and caught a horse cart (*tonga*) into Vrindavan.

Perhaps this encounter was Krishna's mercy and that rickshaw wallah was more than he seemed. It seems mystical in retrospect. Mystically, God's hand is evident in everything. He intervenes in mysterious ways we cannot even fathom.

Over the years, between that day and now, I have been to Vrindavan many times. In preparation for writing this book, I sat at my desk and tried to list when I journeyed to Vrindavan and how many times I have been there. It was impossible for me to do so.

After I joined the US Foreign Service, I managed to get myself assigned to South Asian tours, twice in Islamabad, Pakistan, once in New Delhi, and once in Dhaka, Bangladesh, for a total of 10 years. These assignments provided plenty of opportunities to go to Vrindavan. In addition, I was assigned twice to South Asian jobs in Washington DC, which enabled me to fly to South Asian countries on temporary assignments (TDY). I took maximum advantage of these opportunities.

That first time I went to Vrindavan, I stayed for only one long day. I travelled in from the railway station and travelled out as the sun was setting. From Vrindavan I travelled about ten kilometers to Mathura, the birthplace of Lord Krishna, spending the night there in a local guesthouse before getting back on the train and travelling on to Delhi.

All my subsequent trips to Vrindavan involved residencies of various durations. I usually travelled alone, although I made separate trips with my son, my daughter, and my friend William Laray.

I have travelled to India many times since that first trip in 1973. India was a very different place in the 1970's. It was nothing like what it is today, and I have seen great changes in Vrindavan as well. Srila Prabhupad was adamant that ISKCON must build a temple in Vrindavan. Prior to Srila Prabhupad, Vrindavan was practically unknown to Westerners. Western visitors were unheard of. Most pilgrims were Bengali. There have long been homes in Vrindavan for Bengali widows, who spend their last days on earth in the holy dham (place of pilgrimage), assured of liberation upon their death. Although this custom is not as prevalent now as it once was, there are still group homes for Bengali widows in Vrindavan. They live spartan lives there, dependent on the charity of pilgrims.

While in Vrindavan I learned that during the period of British colonialism in the 1920's or 1930's a British serviceman got out of the military and retired in India. He was the first documented Westerner to live in Vrindavan, spending the rest of his life there. He left a very vivid account of his experiences in Vrindavan. He was very fond of Radha Kunda, and took a holy bath there every day. He wrote that while standing in the waters of Radha Kunda, he was transported to the realm of Lord Krishna and gained personal association with Krishna's consort Srimati Radharani. After he passed away, Vrindavan remained outside Western consciousness and unvisited by Western persons, until Srila Prabhupad's journey to the West.

After establishing ISKCON in the US, Srila Prabhupad returned to Vrindavan with a small group of his first disciples.[40] After establishing this initial presence, Srila Prabhupad sent a team of Western devotees to Vrindavan to build ISKCON's temple there. Vrindavan was little more than a village at this time and the living conditions were rudimentary. These devotees lived in Vrindavan for years and built a beautiful temple out of white marble designed by a Dutch devotee/architect, who personally oversaw its construction. It is now revered by Indian pilgrims coming to Vrindavan. Its beautiful and elaborate worship and ecstatic kirtans are legendary.

In his last years, Srila Prabhupad retired to Vrindavan to die, and lived in a small building adjoining the temple. He died in that building in 1977. Srila Prabhupad knew that Westerners would have a hard time staying in Vrindavan and would not be used to conditions there. When Prabhupad lived in Vrindavan at the Radha Damodara temple before his departure for the US, he stayed in a small room by himself, eating sparingly, devoted to Krishna and translating *Srimad Bhagavatam* from Sanskrit into English. He was convinced that Western readers would someday clamor to read this work, although it almost totally unknown outside India. Prabhupad was not famous in India. He was just one of many itinerant

---

[40] For a vivid account of what these initial Western devotees experienced, I recommend, *Vrindavan Days (Memories of an Indian Holy Town),* by Hayagriva Swami, Palace Publishing, New Vrindavan, West Virginia, 1990

Sannyasis, and many Indians dismissed his devotion to spreading Krishna devotion to the West as random ravings.

The summers in the Braj region of Uttar Pradesh can be unbearable. The heat is intense. There was no air conditioning in Vrindavan when Srila Prabhupad lived there and little electricity. Srila Prabhupad ensured ISKCON would build a comfortable, if spartan, guesthouse adjoining the temple, and that it would be affordable.

At this period, no one believed Westerners would ever come to Vrindavan for pilgrimage. Prabhupad's guesthouse was dismissed as a folly. Today, it is fully booked. The adjoining street has been renamed "Swami Bhaktivedanta Marg." This ISKCON guesthouse is where I usually stayed when in Vrindavan. While there, I followed the complete temple schedule.

In Hinduism, there is a "golden hour" called *Brahmamahurta.*

In Hinduism, Brahma muhurta (time of Brahma) is a period (muhurta) one and a half hours before sunrise and is 1Hr 36 Minutes (96 minutes) in duration.[41]

This period of time is most auspicious for any spiritual activity. This is why Hindu devotees awaken very early in the morning, take a bath and plunge into worship, meditation and religious study. Like the other inhabitants of Vrindavan, I awakened at around 4:00 AM. Vrindavan was absolutely still during the night. Devotees go to bed early, around 8:00 PM and silence prevails. In the morning, when I awoke, however, I was cascaded by bells. Temple bells were ringing all over Vrindavan, as each of the 5,000 temples performed morning aarti.

Aarti means something that removes *rātrī*, darkness (or light waved in darkness before an icon).[42]

The other sound was the cooing of peacocks. The peacock is an auspicious bird for Gaudiya Vaishnavas, as it is beloved by Lord Krishna, and He is depicted wearing a peacock feather.

Peacocks, monkeys, and cows roamed freely around Vrindavan, and peacock cries filled the auspicious air of *Brahmamahurta.*

After participating in *aarti* and eating *prasad*, I attended morning classes. The ISKCON temple in Vrindavan is devoted to Lord Krishna and his brother Balarama, and their images are featured on the altar along with those of Radha and Krishna.

---

[41] Wikipedia

[42] Wikipedia

After the morning *aarti*, the doors are closed and devotees gather on the steps to study the *Bhagavad Gita* and *Srimad Bhagavatam.* A senior devotee holds the class. He recites the passage in Sanskrit and we repeat it after him. We then read the English translation and the Prabhupad purport (I have attended these classes at various times in both Hindi and English). The senior devotee then provides his own commentary and explanation and takes questions from the students.

When not participating in the temple program, I visited holy places. These include the locations of Krishna's many pastimes, as identified by Sri Chaitanya. These locations are marked by temples, and shrines. The small temples are often manned by hereditary Brahmin priests. Their families have lived in Vrindavan, maintained the temples and performed the pujas for centuries. As is customary, I performed pujas at the temples, sometimes alone, and sometimes with Indian pilgrims. In the Vaishnava tradition, the worshipper performs "*dandavat*" before the sacred site or location. A danda is a stick, and to perform dandavat is to lie flat like a stick. The head faces the divine spot with the arms extended out in front. The worshipper never points his/her feet towards a divine spot or image.

As part of the *puja,* the priest extends a lighted lamp towards me. The wicks, immersed in *ghee* are burning bright. I place my hand over the heat, and move it over my head and forehead. When the priest proffers incense, I gently whisk the smoke towards my face and breathe in the special fragrance. At the end of the puja, the priest offers *prasad* (food shared with Krishna). It is usually sweets, almost totally made of sugar. Other times, I am offered water poured into my hands, which I then drink.

I have many beloved spots in Vrindavan where I have been transported and enlightened, but one of my most favorite is the Radha Kunda. This spot was little more than a country pond when discovered by Sri Chaitanya, but was subsequently developed into a brick lined "tank" filled with water and surrounded by temples, ashrams and other buildings. The devotee climbs down a series of steps to bathe in the water. This *Kunda* is sacred to Srimati Radharani and devotees believe Her to be present there and that she bathes in Her *Kunda* at certain times every day. Bathers commune with Her while bathing. Radha Kunda is a peaceful and very powerful spot. The *Bhajana Kutira* of Sri Chaitanya is marked by a small temple on the edge of Radha Kunda. A *Bhajana Kutira* is a spot where a holy personality resided, worshipped and meditated.[43]

---

[43] This is not the time and the place to catalog the many holy locations throughout Vrindavan and the surrounding countryside. These are described in great detail in authorized guidebooks written by esteemed devotees for pilgrims. I recommend, *Vrindavan Yatra with Radhanath Swami, Volume 1, The Six Goswamis of Vrindavan,* by Radhanath Swami, Tulsi Books, Mumbai, 2010, and *The Color Guide to Vrndavana (India's Most Holy City of Over 5,000 Temples*), by Rajasekhara dasa Brahmacari, Vedanta Vision Publications, 1994

I had one of my most powerful Vrindavan experiences in a tiny temple that does not even register among the most well-known pilgrimage spots in the city. It was a temple dedicated to Sri Narada Muni. He is one of my favorite saints. Of humble origins, he rose to prominence and became a direct associate of the Lord. He is depicted dressed in saffron, with long dark hair, and carrying a *vina* (an Indian musical instrument). Narada Muni travels from planet to planet throughout the universe spreading divine consciousness. I was told that the little temple I visited was a spot particularly beloved by Narada Muni and that he visits there frequently.

I had just been to Kusum Sarovar across the road from the temple. It is a medieval temple built by a Gujarati prince devoted to Krishna. It features gorgeous medieval architecture and a small manmade lake, with steps leading into the water. I had spent the afternoon there contemplating the peacefulness of the site, and then wandered across the road and down a small path and found myself in this temple.

I had no agenda and was not searching for anything in particular. I was led to this spot. Once I got there, I could tell it was someplace special. I sat down, leaned my head against the wall and slipped into a divine reverie. I felt transported to another place, and seemed to feel the presence of Narada Muni blessing me on my journey. I could envision him traveling throughout the universe.

On another visit to Vrindavan, I accompanied a female devotee on her rounds to the dying. Vrindavan is a sacred spot, the earthly version of the heavenly Goloka Vrindavana, the eternal residence of Lord Krishna. Those who die in the sacred precincts of Vrindavana are transported immediately to Goloka Vrindavana and do not have to endure rebirth on this earthly planet. For this reason, old devotees come to Vrindavan to die. They distribute their earthly possessions to their spouses and children and live simply in spare rooms.

One of the men we visited was lying flat on a cot in a small temple adjoining Kusam Sarovar. It was his last minutes on earth. He was very weak and quietly repeated the Hare Krishna Mantra while waiting for death to come. We did what we could to make him comfortable, and went on to a small room inhabited by a Vrindavan widow. The room had only a few articles of furniture, a string cot and a small table. We delivered a small sum of money to her to keep her going until the moment of her death arrives. She graciously offered us cookies that she removed from a small tin and gave to us with her own hands. We spent some time with her conversing in Hindi. She was very much at peace.

I do not have space here to recite all the events in the lives of Lord Krishna, Radharani, and Balarama that transpired in Vrindavan and are marked by shrines and temples. The BBT has reprinted the original "Krishna Book" many times since George Harrison sponsored the primitive (yet highly beloved) original version.[44] I also own a far more elaborate version with much more sophisticated

130

artwork and higher quality production. My current version is 844 pages long.[45] To understand the significance of Vrindavan and its sacred sites it would be best to read these books.

After seeing the sites associated with Lord Krishna, I visited those associated with the Six Goswamis, including their *Bhajana Kutiras*, and their tombs. In Hinduism the earthly remains of human beings are cremated after death and the ashes deposited in a holy river if possible. For most Hindus, the most auspicious spot to deposit the ashes of the deceased is the Holy Ganges, most particularly as it flows through the city of Varanasi.[46] For Gaudiya Vaishnavas the Yamuna River is considered the most sacred, because it was touched by the lotus feet of Lord Krishna. The Yamuna River runs through Vrindavan, and was the site of several of Krishna's pastimes.

In the Hindu tradition, the bodies of holy men (and women) are not cremated but buried. This indicates they are liberated and will not be born again in the material world. Hindu infants are also buried, as they are spotless and innocent and do not require cremation and the attending rituals. The tombs of the six Goswamis are among the most sacred sites in Vrindavan, and among my favorite spots to visit, linger and meditate. They are serene and holy places. I sat quietly there and absorbed the lingering spirits of the Gosvamis. Following this tradition, ISKCON buried the body of Srila Prabhupad within the grounds of its Krishna Balarama Temple in Vrindavan and erected a beautiful white marble tomb at the spot. Prabhupad's tomb then joined the list of sacred places in Vrindavan.

The Hindu tradition when visiting a holy spot is to circumambulate around it. The worshipper moves in a clockwise position around the spot, so that the pure side (the right side) of the body is always facing towards the spot and the impure side (the left side) is always facing away from it.

Because all of Vrindavan is a holy *dham*, it has long been traditional to circumambulate around the entire location. Likewise, the region containing Vrindavan (called Braj) is also holy and can also be circumambulated. These are called *parikramas*, or holy walks. The Vrindavan *parikrama* is done barefoot and takes about three hours to complete. When I first came to Vrindavan, the *parikrama* path was coated in a thick layer of soft dust. This was the sacred dust

---

[44] A.C. Bhaktivedanta Swami Prabhupad, *Krishna (The Supreme Personality of Godhead)*, Krishna Books, Incorporated, Authorized by the Bhaktivedanta Book Trust, Los Angeles, 2017, is the latest version.

[45] A.C. Bhaktivedanta Swami Prabhupad, *Krishna (The Supreme Personality of Godhead)*, Bhaktivedanta Book Trust, Los Angeles, 2003

[46] I visited this city during my first trip to India and took the first of many immersions in the Ganges there.

of Vrindavan. It was an offense to allow a shoe to touch this dust and auspicious for this dust to cover the bare feet. I have made this barefoot parikrama several times.

The parikrama path led through groves of trees populated by monkeys and past sacred sites too numerous to name here. At each site, I performed a puja, including *dandavats*. Afterwards, I often sat and meditated or performed a round of *japa* (108 repetitions of the Hare Krishna mantra), using *japa* beads. I shared the path with numerous pilgrims from all over India (there were practically no Westerners in Vrindavan during these early years).

In addition to the pilgrims, Vrindavan is inhabited by thousands of "babas," these are men (and women) who have become *sadhus* (renunciates) and retired to Vrindavan. In non-Vaishnava locales *Sadhus* can be surly and rude, but this is not the case in Vrindavan. The inhabitants of Braj are Brijabasis and are well-known for their kind and gentle nature. The Vrindavan babas are usually warm and friendly, and I became involved in long Hindi conversations with them.

In Vrindavan I lose the time pressure associated with Western life. I no longer keep track of time and live life in the moment, experiencing each second to the utmost. When I converse with fellow pilgrims, priests, and babas, I suffer from no time constraint. I allow conversation to go where it should and take as long as it likes. Needless to say, I wear no wristwatch while in Vrindavan.

On one occasion, I walked along a quiet path in the early morning behind the Krishna/Balarama temple when an aged baba approached me. He pulled a Hindi language letter out of his pocket and asked me to read it for him as he was illiterate. There was no reason for him to believe, that I, as a Westerner, could read or understand Hindi, but I was happy to read his letter for him.

The more devoted pilgrims perform a *dandavat parikrama* around the holy dham. He/she performs a *dandavat* and places a stone at the spot where the arms are extended. He/she then moves on to the next dandavat. The dandavat parikrama of the entire sacred city of Vrindavan requires an average of 17,300 dandavats to complete, and can take several weeks.

I spent hours at the *Kutira* of Srila Prabhupad at the Radha Damodara temple. It was a lonely and secluded spot then and there was usually no one around. Once, while leaving, I saw a young western devotee leaning against the wall of the *Kutira*. I sat next to him and spent the afternoon with him. We talked a little, but spent most of the afternoon in silence, sharing a special communion. He was trying to obtain maximum advantage of the spot, quietly chanting on his beads. We shared the quiet together.[47]

---

[47] Although I cannot say for certain, I have a distinct impression that this devotee was Mahanidhi Swami, an American from New York who has lived in Vrindavan

Vrindavan with my Children

I traveled to Vrindavan with my son and daughter separately on different occasions. For some reason I never went with both of them together. My son was a typical adolescent when we lived in India and preferred to spend his time with his own friends amidst his own circle. This was the phase in his life when he no longer was so eager to do things with his dad. My daughter, on the other hand, loved to have adventures with her dad and was up for anything.

My daughter and I stayed in the ISKCON guest house beside the temple and wandered around Vrindavan together. Devoutly religious, she was deeply respectful of the holy *dham* and all the people she met and was ever willing to learn. In her early teens, she was particularly delighted by the ever-present monkeys. Because of their connection to Hanuman and the key role they play in the *Ramayana*, monkeys are sacred and have unhindered access to pilgrimage spots like Vrindavan.

This does not mean that they are not exasperating, however. Indians, most particularly those who live in the holy dham, are well aware that living side by side with a huge monkey population can be trying. In Vrindavan, the monkeys clamber along the rooftops and observe pilgrims from overhead. If they spot an object they like, they swoop down, grab it and disappear. I learned quite early to keep track of my belongings and not give the monkeys an opportunity to snatch them. While my daughter and I were lingering in a temple courtyard, a monkey appeared from out of nowhere, grabbed my notebook, took it up to the rooftop, and started tearing it into pieces, raining the pieces down on our heads. The monkey found it quite amusing and laughed uproariously.

On another occasion, we walked through the town to the outskirts looking for a place to bathe in the Yamuna. It was a quiet and pleasant day with blue sky and cool breezes. We came upon some farmers working in the fields. I asked them where to find the river. They were amused by the odd foreigners and pointed out the way. We followed their directions and came to a spot where a tributary of the Yamuna flowed through farm fields. When we arrived at a suitable spot, we knelt down and splashed the holy water on our heads. This is another way of bathing in a holy river.

We both enjoyed eating Indian vegetarian food. By this point, a small bazaar had grown up across the street from the growing and popular ISKCON temple on Bhaktivedanta Swami Marg. We liked to sit there every day and enjoy large *dosas*. These are South Indian treats similar to enormous enchiladas filled with spicy vegetables. Like me, my daughter enjoyed being away from the stresses,

---

for over 40 years. During this period, he was overseeing Prabhupad's quarters for ISKCON.

strains, and noise of life in Delhi and immersing herself in a holy spot where all cares melt away.

Later, after moving to Ireland, my daughter went to the Dublin ISKCON restaurant to enjoy dosas and vegetarian food. Having grown up eating Indian food every day, she sometimes longed to experience the food she was used to. The ISKCON restaurant was one of the only Indian/vegetarian eateries in Dublin. The devotees liked to engage her in conversation and began to talk to her about Vrindavan. She amazed them when she said she had been to Vrindavan several times, and related her experiences there. The Irish devotees had never been to India, much less Vrindavan.

While the trips with my daughter were airy and light, those with my son were heavier. He was skeptical of the devotees and going through adolescence, questioning everything. He was at the stage of life where he was trying to make sense of things, and battling with shyness. He was wary of travelling with his dad. His experiences were not as pleasant as his sister's.

My son and I arrived in Vrindavan, checked into the guesthouse, and began wandering the streets. We sat at a table in front of a small shop to have a little food. A Vrindavan widow came to us and started begging aggressively. She implored us for food and money, and would not take no for an answer. This agitated the shopkeeper. She was interfering with his business and bothering his customers. The shopkeeper began to berate the begging widow in a loud voice, telling her in Hindi to go away. She would not. She kept begging, and my son became visibly troubled.

As an old South Asia hand, I was familiar with beggars. My policy is not to give money to them. Because of my white skin I attract attention wherever I go. Everyone assumes I am wealthy beyond belief. Beggars zero in on me. I know they are all watching me and if I give to one, a hundred more will descend on me, making my day miserable. Instead of giving money to beggars, who often work for organized crime and hand over the money to criminals at the end of each working day, I give to legitimate programs that take care of the poorest of the poor. That way I know that no money will be misused or fall into the wrong hands.

There are exceptions to this rule, however. There are exceptions to everything. Sometimes, when I am in a holy place such as Vrindavan I give money to the beggars lined up outside the entrances to temples and holy spots, as the spirit moves me. All the pilgrims carry small denomination notes to distribute to beggars and to give offerings at the various temples and shrines. This giving is considered part of the *dharma* of pilgrimage.

Eventually the shopkeeper emerged with a bucket of water and splashed it all over the widow, driving her away. My son was shocked and crestfallen.

Almost immediately after this jarring experience, we met up with a fake pundit (these rascals are called "*pandas*" in the local dialect) who prey on pilgrims. They descend on pilgrims and exploit their religiosity and devotion through various con games and schemes. As white skinned Westerners, we were marked as rich and exploitable. He admonished us to come to his "temple," for puja. We initially accompanied him, but when he led us to a simple room with a rudimentary deity and no particular puja, I quickly ascertained what he was up to. I refused to participate and started to leave, at which point he began to aggressively demand money from us. I ignored him and departed. While the encounter was of little significance to me, my son found it disturbing.

On this trip, we associated with some American ISKCON devotees who had been living in Vrindavan for many years. A very friendly woman devotee from Pennsylvania took the time to show us around. She took us to spots not well known to Western pilgrims. For example, my son and I visited the home village of Srimati Radharani, buried among low hills on the outskirts of Vrindavan. While walking up the narrow winding path to the village, we saw a set of Krishna's footprints outlined in the rocks in a remote spot outside the village.

ISKCON had recently purchased a small pilgrimage site associated with Srimati Radharani. It was a quiet and secluded spot far from the narrow and crowded alleyways of Vrindavan. It consisted of a small temple devoted to Radha, located next to a sacred pond. Our host explained to us that this spot is particularly beloved by Radharani, who visits it daily. We swam in the pond in the calm sunny warmth of the early afternoon. I thoroughly enjoyed the experience, but my son continued to feel awkward. He was not used to associating with devotees, especially in these circumstances. Not many American adolescents have such experiences, and perhaps he was not sure if this passed the coolness test and would meet with the approval of his friends.

Our host had teenaged children of her own, and suggested that my son hang out with them. They had grown up in Vrindavan and attended the ISKCON school (*gurukul*) there. My son was shy and reluctantly agreed. He hung out with the kids, who were exceedingly nice to him and invited him to come visit spots in Vrindavan and go swimming. He did not avail himself of this opportunity.

That night our host prepared a wonderful meal for us at her home. After we were thoroughly satiated, we socialized with senior devotees. One of them was Indradyumna Swami, who is famous within ISKCON for his charisma. He is a peripatetic swami, who travels the world preaching about Krishna. Indradyumna is the author of a series of books known as the *Diary of a Traveling Preacher.*[48] His official bio states:

---

[48] Published by Torchlight books

Delivering truckloads of vegetarian meals to impoverished Zulus in South Africa; journeying to the ancient Temple of Fire in Azerbaijan; leading kirtan with gypsies in sub-zero Siberia; chanting the Holy Names of the Lord at the massive Polish Woodstock; discussing philosophy with Amazonian village leaders; returning to his home in the sacred, mystical village of Vrindavan, India. These are just a sampling of the adventures of Indradyumna Swami--spiritual leader, traveling monk, Kirtan leader, public speaker, writer, and photographer.[49]

His adventures make Indradyumna Swami attractive to adolescents. He is not a dry, uptight person, but open to anything and everything. He made a special effort to connect with my son, but he continued to hold back. In my view, this was another missed opportunity. Encounters with spiritually enlightened individuals do not occur by chance, but are evidence of divine intervention, evidence that God is reaching out and trying to connect. These are golden opportunities and should not be easily cast aside.

Vraja Mandala Parikrama

During one of my Vrindavan stays, I ran into a senior devotee sitting at a table at the temple. He was signing up persons to take the Vraja Mandala Parikrama, an extended, one month walking circumambulation of the entire holy Braj region associated with Radha, Krishna, Balarama and their miraculous pastimes. It was scheduled to last from October 25 to November 25, 1996, and would be led by Lokanath Swami. His Wikipedia biography states that:

Lokanatha Swami. Lokanath Swami (born 1949) is an ISKCON guru from India. He is a senior disciple of A. C. Bhaktivedanta Swami Prabhupada (the founder of ISKCON). Lokanatha Swami oversees ISKCON activities and preaching in Maharashtra and Noida, and serves on the Governing Body Commission of ISKCON as a Minister of Padayatra.

I had been wanting to take such a trip for a long time. I knew it would be a great adventure, so I signed up immediately. The trip was to start at Lord Krishna's birthplace in Mathura, and then proceed to selected locations within Vrindavan proper before heading out to the countryside. I was to report back to Vrindavan several months later, meet up with Lokanath Swami and the Padayatra crew and begin the journey.

On the slated day for the beginning of the yatra I duly showed up at the bustling ISKCON temple in Vrindavan (The Krishna/Balarama Temple). The temple had morphed into something far larger than when I had first started going there. It was now a multifaceted affair, with numerous offices and its own bureaucracy. There were now shops selling all manner of devotional items, and an entire bazaar had come up directly across from the temple. When it was originally built, the Krishna

---

[49] Author's bio used on his books' dust jackets. Bhaktivedanta Book Trust.

Balarama temple was on the outskirts of Vrindavan. It was surrounded by groves of trees, and a short distance up the road was a small ashram. Past that was only countryside. Spurred by the growth of the temple, the city of Vrindavan grew to absorb it.

I met the administrators of the yatra and checked in. It was October, the very best time to be in Vrindavan, and the temple guest house was full. My hosts informed me I would be put up overnight in a local *dharmshala* (guest house for pilgrims), and that we would head out on the pilgrimage early the next morning.

When I arrived at the *dharmshala*, I found it to be a simple traditional arrangement, two lines of brick huts with a raised platform in the middle. Because of the pleasant weather, the *charpoys* were put outside in the space between the two lines of facing buildings. Next to me was an Indian family, part of the Indian diaspora. Ethnically Indian, the husband and wife were born and raised in Singapore. The wife seemed to be put off by the spartan surroundings. I suspect that they were part of the wealthy Indian community in Singapore, and that she had no experience of village India or the simple Indian life. I discovered in the morning when I awoke that they had withdrawn from the yatra and returned home.

I turned in early, as we would be getting up around 4 AM. I still have the guide book given to all the pilgrims. This was our daily schedule:

4:30 AM – Mangala Arati and Tulasi Puja

5:15 AM – Announcements

5:25 AM – Packing

6:00 AM – Departure

9:30 AM – Breakfast on the way

1:00 to 2:00 PM

Arrival at the parikrama camp

Announcements

Unloading of Luggage

Settling in accommodation

2:00 TO 3:30 PM

Free for resting, washing, bathing, studying, etc.

3:30 PM – Lunch

5:00 PM – Class

6:00 PM – Gaura arati

6:30 PM – Damodarastaka (worship of Krishna)

7:00 PM – Reading/class

8:00 PM – Personal Reading

8:30 PM – Rest

We adhered to the daily schedule without fail. I met my fellow *yatris* at the temple. They consisted of a mix of devotees from around the world. I became particularly close to a German devotee, and another from South Africa (of Indian descent), as well as several Americans. There were also several Bengali devotees. They were quite young and bristling with a particular immaturity that I have often witnessed among adolescent male Indians from a rural background. They did not quite know what to make of the Western devotees. They did not speak English, but rather Bengali and rudimentary Hindi. I tried to communicate with them in both languages, but they seemed shy and giggled a lot.

Our first stops were principal spots in Vrindavan proper. These included the Madan Ter, the Kaliya Ghat, the Madana Mohana Mandir, Sanatana Goswami's Samadhi, and Keshi Ghat. (I would become particular familiar with the Kaliya and Keshi Ghats over the coming years).

We were led by Lokanath Swami, who performed pujas at each of the sites and explained their religious significance to us. The custom was to make the entire padayatra barefoot, but I am afraid that I chickened out on that score. I feared for my feet and purchased a pair of Tevas. These contained no leather and would not pollute any of the sacred places, but it meant that I would have to take them off whenever I entered a sacred spot. Indians wear simple *"hawaii chappals,"*[50] thongs that can easily be slipped on and off. The Tevas, by contrast, had Velcro straps that had to be opened and closed. It meant that I had to sit down each time I took them off and put them on. I should have tried to make the yatra totally barefoot.

Lokanath Swami's explanations of the events that had transpired at each of the spots were riveting and quite moving. I found him to be a truly inspired individual who experienced the essence of the yatra and appreciated every spot we visited.

---

[50] The word "hawaii" in this context does not refer to the American state. In Hindi the word 'hawa' means air or wind, and chappals are simple shoes. This means shoes that are open to the wind. In most cases they are the same simple shoes Americans call "flip flops."

The following morning we resumed the schedule. I attended the daily *aratis* and classes. There were classes in English for the foreign devotees and classes in Hindi for the Indian devotees. I alternated between the two. The Indian devotees were amazed to see me there and further amazed that I had no trouble comprehending the readings and the lessons. Apparently, no foreigner had ever attended the Hindi classes before.

We started walking. Over the course of the next two weeks the party and I walked several hundred kilometers. Again, we stopped periodically at sacred spots to listen to addresses by Lokanath Maharaj. He knew every spot intimately and could speak authoritatively about everything connected with the Braj region.

Lokanath Maharaj spoke extemporaneously, with no notes or assistance. The distance to Mathura was around five kilometers, but we then walked through the town to the Yamuna River and the sacred Visrama Ghat. Mathura, like seemingly every town in India, was growing rapidly. When I returned to Mathura, years later, it had vastly expanded. Much of the simple countryside that I walked through on the *Yatra* had been swallowed up by the expanding town. I would encounter this phenomena is pilgrimage towns all over India. Every city in town in India continues to grow exponentially both to absorb the ever-growing population, and the exodus of villagers from the countryside, as India experiences rapid urbanization.

We were in the midst of an auspicious full-moon period (*Purnima*), which is the best time to perform religious rituals of all kinds. This made it the best time to bathe in the Yamuna River. As is the case all over India, steps led down from the riverbank into the water. In traditional India, villagers went to tanks and rivers to bathe every day and wash their clothes, and the steps made it easier to access the water.

But the site Lokanath Maharaj had picked was on the bank. There were no steps there and we could walk right into the river. We were dressed in our traveling clothes. I must have been wearing my traditional cotton kurta pajama. Maharaj told us to strip down to our undergarments to go into the river. He told us to leave everything on the shore and that no one would disturb our possessions. He was right. I descended with the pilgrims into the river water and immersed myself. The water was warm and the atmosphere filled with devotion, but it did not match the ecstasy of the previous night.

On day three of the yatra we visited 10 sacred spots in and around Mathura, but the most significant was the Janmabhumi Bhagavat Bhawan, the birthplace of Lord Krishna. During the reign of the Muslim Mughals, they had constructed a mosque over the birth site in their effort to persecute and stamp out the worship of Krishna, which they had determined to be idolatry. After the decline and fall of the Mughals, the Hindus had constructed a temple adjoining the mosque to demarcate the sacred spot, but the actual birthplace was now under the mosque.

We journeyed through a long passage to get to the spot. It was a small underground chamber with an altar and some iconography. Pilgrims were immersed in the spot and absorbing its significance. After we emerged from the chamber, we began an ecstatic *sankirtan*, that rose in intensity. It is among the most moving examples of *sankirtan* I have ever experienced. I lost all track of time and place and was simply absorbed into the experience, which seemed to become and more and more frenzied. We danced in circles and chanted loudly under the full moon. In the remaining days we visited many sacred spots. We arose while it was still dark. It was cold in the morning. We slept on the bare ground in sleeping bags, or on the porches of schools and other public buildings. After waking up we lined up at hand pumps for bathing in the cold water. I had taken such baths before in Rankhandi and other villages. They are very cold, but very stimulating. We ate simple food, usually vegetables with chapattis, similar to what any villager in North Indian would eat. And we walked for kilometer after kilometer.

At one of the locations, we were put up in a government guest house with no toilet facilities. The yatra administrators told us to avail ourselves of the Indian custom and to relieve ourselves in the nearby fields. Early in the morning I did as instructed, but when I ventured into a grove of sugar cane for my morning ablutions, the Indians sitting nearby inexplicably began to abuse me in Hindi, telling me to go away. I still do not know what it was all about, as we were not doing anything different from any rural Indian. I think they were trying to put a foreigner in his place and thought they would be clever, but I was not amused and gave it back to them in Hindi telling them off.

At that same spot an Italian devotee on the trip got on top of a car and began to lead us in kirtan. He had been traveling around India for some time and had picked up quite a repertoire of devotional chants and songs. He was very effective and we surrounded the car and began chanting with great gusto.

The Bengali devotees were very amused that I could communicate with them in their own language, but seemed a bit contemptuous. Perhaps they felt threatened by the Bengali speaking foreigner. We were resting at a quiet and secluded spot and they asked whether I wanted to forego *kurta pajama* and wear the traditional Bengali *dhoti*. I was game, and duly put on the garment. The *dhoti* is one of the most comfortable garments a man can wear and it felt natural. They then asked whether I wanted to apply the traditional clay *tilak* on my forehead, and I did that as well. That was the one and only time that I was dressed in traditional devotee garb from head to toe, including *tilak*.

On day seven of the yatra we went to the Radha Kunda. It was the most auspicious time to bathe in the Kunda. It was surrounded by thousands of chanting devotees, filling the air with the sound of drums, chanting, and finger cymbals. I stood on the steps leading into the water, standing next to Lokanath Maharaj. The clear sky was bathed in moonlight, with no clouds and thousands of stars. We waited for the conch shells to blow, signifying that the ultimate most auspicious moment had arrived. The stone steps were slippery and when the conches blew we started down into the water. Lokanath Swami slipped and started to fall. I grabbed him by the arm and held him up. We both descended into the warm water together, and immersed ourselves. This was an ecstatic moment that remains seared into my memory. This spot will always have a special attachment to me.

My South African devotee friend had determined that he must make a *dandavat parikrama* around the entire Radha Kunda. He asked me to be his assistant. My job was to look after him and ensure he made the entire parikrama without harm. We started at the *Kutira* of Sri Krishna Chaitanya. He laboriously took the rock and placed it at his head and then performed *dandavat* and kept repeating the process until he had completely circumambulated the entire Radha Kunda. I helped him as best I could and made sure he drank plenty of water. He was completely and utterly exhausted by the end of the several hour process. We both retired to the *Kutira* to rest. Despite his exhaustion, he was happy. He had felt a crying need to perform the *dandavat padayatra* and had succeeded.

On day 10 we performed the Govardhana Parikrama. Govardhana is a mountain sacred to Lord Krishna.[51] I was particularly attracted to Govardhana and everything associated with it. I had studied the Govardhana puja during one of my classes in graduate school. The devotees make a mountain of food inside the temple and at the auspicious time, devour the food in honor of Lord Krishna's lifting of the Govardhana hill. I had circumambulated Govardhana before during previous trips and it was always a moving experience for me.

The padayatra lasted one month, but I was able to complete only two weeks, not because I was tired or lacking in enthusiasm. It was only because my leave had expired and I could no longer stay. I could have easily kept on going for the remaining two weeks. I completed my stint of the Yatra at Kamyavana.

We had been walking steadily for two weeks in the direction of Rajasthan covering lots of ground, and were in the absolute middle of the countryside by the time my stint was over. I joined a car heading back to Vrindavan to retrieve supplies. I had left my luggage with a female devotee and looked her up to retrieve it. This was my first experience of the private rooms where the Vrindavan temple devotees live. As you would expect, the rooms are simple, windowless and spartan.

Before departing Vrindavan I took one last walk around the city. I inexplicably found myself in a room overlooking one of the sacred Kundas with Mahanidhi Swami. He was one of ISKCON's more colorful residents of the holy dham, and

---

[51] You can read all about the significance of Govardhana in Chapters 24-27, pages 189-209 of *Krishna, (The Supreme Personality of Godhead)*, 2003 Edition.

has lived there for over 40 years.[52] He was wearing traditional devotee garb and sitting cross-legged on a raised platform.

For some reason, he had several telephones sitting beside him. I remained in his domain for some time, but he was continually talking on the telephone (I cannot remember what he was talking about). On my way out the door I was accosted by an irate Indian man of some years. He started berating me (I believe he was speaking English), telling me in no uncertain terms that I was desecrating the holy dham. He pointed out that I was wearing jeans and holding them up with a leather belt. I had somehow inadvertently forgotten to leave the belt at home. After receiving such a humiliating tongue-lashing I was duly put in my place. I have never allowed myself to bring any leather item into Vrindavan since.

Vrindavan and President GW Bush

In 2006 I headed the internal politics unit at the political section, in the US Embassy in New Delhi. I was a man wearing many hats. In addition to domestic political affairs, I was in charge of Islamic affairs, and served as an informal religious advisor to Ambassador David Mulford, who served in that post from 2004 to 2009. The Ambassador and I worked quite closely together on a number of issues. He made it clear to me that he was not interested in handling religious affairs. This being India, his office was inundated with requests for meetings from religious leaders. They covered the spectrum of faiths, with, as expected, the majority being Hindu holy men. The Ambassador could not wrap his arms around the concept of a Hindu holy man and was happy to allow me to meet take these meetings for him.

The Embassy learned that we would be hosting President Bush, who would be in India on March 2-4, 2006. As is the practice, all work came to a stop, and everyone in the Embassy worked around the clock for the month prior to the visit. I was put in charge of a meeting between President Bush and a cross-section of Indian religious leaders of my choice. I worked with my staff to compile a list, and we arrived at a Christian, Muslim, and two Hindu leaders.

One of my Indian assistants suggested that I ask Srivatsa Goswami of Vrindavan to be one of the Hindu representatives at the meeting. Here is his official biography:

Shri Shrivatsa Goswami is a member of an eminent family of spiritual leaders and scholars at Sri Radharamana Mandir, Vrindavan. His writings on Vaishnavism, Krishna, Radha, and the Hare Krishna movement have been published by the university presses of Princeton, Berkeley, and others. He is the editor of the

---

[52] He has since been expelled from ISKCON after one of the group's colorful "fall-downs" of Sannyasis. I found his guidebook to Vrindavan to be quite useful, *Appreciating Sri Vrndavana* Dhama, self-published, ISKCON Vrindavan, 1991.

forthcoming volume on Chaitanya for the Encyclopedia of Indian Philosophy published by the American Institute of Indian Studies. Shri Goswami is Director of Sri Caitanya Prema Samsthana, an institute of Vaishnava culture and studies at Vrindavan, whose Vraja Research Project is sponsored by the Indira Gandhi National Centre for the Arts, Government of India. His recent book "Celebrating Krishna"[53] was received with much acclaim. Pope Benedict XVI invited him to represent Hindu tradition at the 25th anniversary of the World Day of Prayer at Assisi in October 2011. He is connected with several important international movements including World Council of Churches and Religions for Peace.[54]

His official biodata does not begin to capture who Shrivatsa Goswami is. He is the direct descendent of one of the disciples of Sri Chaitanya. His ancestor was the first of an unbroken line of priests to serve at the celebrated Sri Radharamana Mandir (temple) in Vrindavan. This temple was founded by Gopal Bhatt Goswami, one of the six original Goswamis of Vrindavan.

Gopal Bhatt Goswami, was from South India. When Sri Chaitanya was making his monumental pilgrimage through India, he stayed at the home of Gopal Bhatt Goswami's family. Gopal Bhatt was just a young boy at the time and waited on Sri Chaitanya and was totally devoted to Him. Sri Chaitanya initiated the boy and told him that it was his duty to go to Vrindavan and serve Krishna. Upon reaching adulthood, Gopal Bhatt left his South Indian home and made the long journey to Vrindavan, where he joined the Goswamis residing there.

In the Gaudiya Vaishnava tradition devotees travel to the Gandaki River in present-day Nepal to collect black stones called *Shaligram*. These are not collected casually because they are sacred manifestations of Vishnu/Krishna. The devotee is not to collect a stone from the riverbed unless it speaks to him personally. Gopal Bhatt undertook the long journey from Vrindavan to Nepal and personally collected 12 Shaligram stones that he brought back with him. He lived in very austere conditions in Vrindavan, sleeping under a tree and subsisting on food provided by local villagers. He kept his *Shaligram* stones in a basket suspended on a tree branch above his sleeping spot.

Gopal Bhatt was not satisfied with worshipping the stones alone. He wanted them to assume the form of his beloved Damodar, an aspect of the young Krishna in Vrindavan. He prayed earnestly to the Lord, and awoke one morning to find that one of the Shaligram had assumed the fort of Damodar.

---

[53] Shrivatsa Goswami, *Celebrating Krishna*, Sri Caitanya Prema Samsthana, Vrindavan, India, no publication date. The Goswamiji presented me with an autographed copy, which is among my most prized possessions.

[54] *World Interfaith Harmony Week, List of Speakers*

Sri Damodar is characterized by a series of distinctive marks on His back. When Gopal Bhatt Goswami examined the statue, he found the marks and fell down in ecstasy. This is an incidence of a "self-manifested deity," as it was not made by any person. The statue has been examined numerous times in the past 500 years since its advent, and there are no signs of human workmanship.

Gopal Bhatt Goswami built a temple at the site of his humble sleeping spot under the tree in the wilderness of Vrindavan, to serve as the residence of Sri Radharamana. The original six Goswamis were celibate monks and left no offspring. Gopal Bhatt Goswami ascertained that he would have to establish a line of married priests to serve the deity in the temple. He appointed Damador Dasa Goswami as the first of these priests. Their descendants are responsible for maintaining the elaborate worship of Sri Radharamana. Shrivatsa Goswami is one of these descendants.

My Indian assistant and I drove to his compound to establish contact and deliver the invitation to Shrivatsa Goswami to participate in the Presidential visit. The temple priests live in ancestral residences located around the temple. Shrivatsa and his family founded a religious organization, the Sri Caitanya Prema Samsthana to research and propagate the Vaishnava culture of Vrindavan. They built a compound/ashram on the banks of the sacred Yamuna River at the Chira ghat. A ghat is a series of steps that descend into a body of water, in this case, the Yamuna River. This is the spot where Lord Krishna performed one of his childhood pastimes, stealing the saris of the Gopis and hiding them in a tree. Lord Krishna sat in the branches of the tree and played his flute while the Gopis implored him to return their garments so they could emerge from the water. This tree, stands just meters away from the gate to the compound.

Shrivatsa Goswami was delighted to receive the invitation to the event and agreed instantly to participate. He graciously invited us into his home for tea. I made an instant connection with him, over the course of succeeding years, I would visit him several times and stay at his ashram.

Sri Kesava Bharati Dasa Goswami

While I was in Vrindavan, my Indian assistant took me to the ashram of Sri Kesava Bharati Dasa Goswami, located on the pilgrim path circumambulating the sacred Govardhan hill. Kesava Maharaj, an American ISKCON devotee, restored the derelict building that was once the personal palace of a Maharaja from Rajasthan. As was the case with Shrivatsa Goswami, Kesava Maharaj and I were instantly on the same wavelength. After our initial meeting, I asked Kesava Maharaj whether it would be possible for me to come visit him and stay in the ashram in the future. He immediately assented.

The Event

The President's visit was surrounded by airtight security. My inter-religious roundtable was scheduled to take place at the hotel where the President was staying. The Catholic Father representing Christianity was delayed and the event was about to begin. I drove to his residence in my car, picked him up, and drove with him through the security checkpoints ringing the hotel. I escorted the Padre past through the Secret Service and we climbing the hotel stairs to make it to the venue just in time.

The President was on a tight schedule. He had 45 minutes set aside for my event. Afterwards, he was scheduled to meet with Sonia Gandhi (then head of the Congress Party). He enjoyed his interaction with the religious figures so much that he insisted that he could not end the discussion. The meeting went on for an additional 45 minutes, and Mrs. Gandhi was kept waiting. The President said it was the most captivating and stimulating of his scheduled meetings in New Delhi.

Further Adventures with the Two Goswamis

My wife and I drove to Vrindavan to celebrate Holi with Shrivatsa Goswami and his family. Holi is a major Hindu festival to celebrate the advent of Spring. It involves a relaxation of traditional rules governing interactions between men and women, the rich and the poor, and the high and low castes. In addition, a special dispensation is provided to those abjuring intoxication for religious or caste reasons. Throughout much of India, Holi has grown into a stressful affair, as bands of men go through the streets harassing women and consuming *bhang sharbat*, an intoxicating mixture of yogurt, milk, sugar, and marijuana or hashish that can be quite potent.

The Holi tradition includes dumping buckets of water on others and throwing colored powder. Some of these exchanges can be quite raucous. We were happy to go celebrate with Shrivatsa Goswami and his family in Vrindavan. Holi is special in Vrindavan, which epitomizes the *Brijabasi* virtues of kindness and gentleness. It is not like Holi in other places.

We arrived at the compound and changed into our Holi outfits, old kurta/pajama that we did not mind getting stained by the colored powder and water. While driving through the streets of Vrindavan to the compound we were pleasantly impressed by the gentle nature of the "brijabasis" of Vrindavan. There was none of the tension and stress found on the streets of New Delhi. Everyone was happy and smiling, gentle, kind, and polite.

Shrivatsa Goswami had obtained organic natural Holi powder, whereas most of the powder in India was made of harsh artificial chemicals that could damage the skin or eyes. We had a wonderful time "playing Holi" on the lawns of the compound and afterwards retired to one of the ashram apartments to shower and change. We enjoyed wonderful food and conversation, with Shrivatsa Goswami, his wife and his sons (who in the Vaishnava tradition would inherit their father's position and serve as priests in the temple).

145

Shrivatsa Goswami introduced us to Robyn Beeche. She was an Australian photographer who had made her fortune as a fashion photographer in New York City. She was a disciple of Shrivatsa Goswami and the two of them had authored *Celebrating Krishna* together.

Robyn had her own apartment on the compound and traveled to Vrindavan on a regular basis, studying the many traditions associated with Krishna worship in Vrindavan and documenting religious practices with her photography. Her best pictures were included in the book she produced with Shrivatsa Goswami.

Shrivatsa Goswami is reviving and preserving the many artforms associated with Vrindavan's Vaishnava tradition, and has built an auditorium on the compound for the performance of traditional folk plays on devotional themes. We had the pleasure to witness a performance during that wonderful Holi day.

Later, when my wife was away, I traveled to Vrindavan alone to spend time at the ashram of Sri Kesava Bharati Dasa Goswami. It is not located in Vrindavan proper but on the Govardhana pilgrimage path. I traveled to Govardhan to celebrate the Hindu holiday of Diwali, the festival of lights. Diwali marks the return of Lord Ram to his kingdom of Ayodhya after rescuing his wife Sita from the clutches of the demon Ravana, who had kidnapped her. It is among the culminating events in the *Ramayana*. Ram and Sita returned to Ayodhya in a sky chariot that flew through the air. The people of *Bharat Varsha* (the ancient name for India) guided the holy couple back by setting out oil lamps. To commemorate this event, homes and public buildings are illuminated. City buildings are illuminated with electric lights, but traditionally homes were decorated with oil lamps made of clay. The clay lamps are open with a small space to hold ghee. A wick, usually made of white string is placed in the lamp and lit and it provides a warm, soft light.

I was given a small room at the top floor of the ashram. That Holi night, there were no electric lights anywhere. Every building in all directions was decorated with traditional oil lamps by the thousands. They were placed along the roof of our building. I walked outside my small room with it simple *charpoy*, and sat on the rooftop next to the softly burning oil lamps and took in the serenity and beauty of the scene. I felt like I was experiencing the timeless beauty of India itself, an experience becoming increasingly rare as modernization replaces these ancient traditions with the gaudy commercialism of modernization.

The next day I made the *Govardhan Parikrama* barefoot and alone. It was an ecstatic experience. I returned feeling elated. It so happened that much of the top leaders of ISKCON were meeting inside the ashram to discuss the worldwide affairs of the organization, and I was invited to attend. I was privileged to meet and interact with some momentous figures. During the course of the meeting, one of them turned to me and said, "Your feet are all cut up. You should go see a doctor and have that looked at." I had not even noticed.

When I returned to the Embassy I went to the medical unit and the doctor treated numerous cuts on my feet. It took several weeks for them to heal.

While at the Govardhan Ashram, I shadowed Sri Kesava Bharati Dasa Goswami. He was very humble and very gracious. Although he was a *sannyasi*, he did not stand on formality. At one point during the day, he sat in a chair and provided *darshan* to his Indian devotees. They touched his feet and presented him with money and sweets. The *Sannyasi* lived very simply in a single room at the ashram, sleeping on a mat on the floor. All funds provided by devotees were straight to the Ashram treasurer to maintain the Ashram. I acted as translator from Kesava Maharaj, allowing him to converse with the devotees. Afterwards he expressed his thanks.

Chapter XI

Vrindavan Tirtha Yatra (Govardhan)

Our 2014 Trip to Vrindavan[55]

Journal Entry #1

This year two friends traveled to India, me and William R. Laray. I stayed for the months of October, November and December, and part of January, but William was only with me for the first month. William and I have been friends since we went to high school together at a Department of Defense school in Frankfurt Germany.

While in Frankfurt, we acquired a Volkswagen van, and built a platform in the back to sleep on. I had been interested in India since I was a child in elementary school and knew I would be going there at some point. We were young and free and could go anywhere and do anything we wanted, although we had no money. We decided to take the van to India. It was possible in those days to start from Germany and drive cross-country to India and on to Nepal. It meant driving across Germany, Austria, Italy, Yugoslavia, Bulgaria, Greece, Turkey, Iraq, Iran, Afghanistan and Pakistan.

While it sounds preposterous today, people traveled from Europe to India overland in those days. The revolutions and wars that effectively closed this route had not yet happened. It was possible to catch a bus in Munich and take it all the way to India.

In his autobiography, *The Journey Home (Autobiography of an American Swami)*[56] Radhanath Swami describes the trip in detail and what he did when he arrived in

---

[55] This is excerpted from, Jon P. Dorschner, *My Indian Journey (Mera Bharatiya Yatra)*, CreateSpace Independent Publishing Platform (June 18, 2015)

India, and how it changed his life, leading him to eventually become a *sannyasi* (hence the name Radhanath Swami).

Radhanath Swami's book is perhaps the best current example of a genre I call "The White Sadhu Genre," in which an earnest young man travels to India and goes through a series of transformative experiences and emerges as a full-fledged sadhu (or swami). The other notable genre, which overlaps with that of the White Sadhu, is the Indian Literary Travelogue. While the protagonists in the White Sadhu genre go to India with the specific intent of exploring Indian spirituality and are open to its transformative powers, the protagonists in the Indian Literary Travelogue are literary figures with a different agenda. They are open-minded and willing to take India as it comes, but come to India to explore it and write about it rather than to adopt a new spiritual identity. The Most notable examples of this genre are *Indian Journals*, by Allen Ginsberg,[57] and *Passage Through India*, by Gary Snyder.[58]

I had always envisioned writing a work about my Indian travels that would incorporate elements from both of these genres, and now am actually attempting it. This account also includes elements of a guidebook to India, as readers will find in it practical advice to help them plan their own *Bharatiya Yatra*.

When William and I were living in Europe, people taking the overland route traveled all over India once they arrived. It was very cheap. Many traveled on to Kathmandu, Nepal. In Volume one of *In the Clear Light of Day*, I recount my own experiences in Nepal in India. While I eventually got to India, I was forced to fly rather than go overland. It was no longer possible when I was ready.

William and I had visions of doing the same things as the stream of hippies leaving Europe for the Kathmandu Trail. In the end, we did not go. There was never a moment when we decided to call off the trip. If simply did not happen. Our friend Eric was supposed to be part of a trio that made the trip. However, Eric was up for the draft and returned to the United States to straighten that out. This was the catalyst. In our minds, we felt we could not go without Eric. In any case, we were increasingly distracted by other things and drifted back to the US.

William and I parted company after Frankfurt. I went on to attend school at Schiller College in Boennigheim, Germany, while he remained in Frankfurt and had his own solitary adventures. We both journeyed to the US separately, but

---

[56] Radhanath Swami, *The Journey Home (Autobiography of an American Swami)*, Mandala Publishing, Rafael, California, 2008

[57] Allen Ginsberg, *Indian Journals (March 1962-May 1963)*. Grove Press, New York, 1979

[58] Gary Snyder, *Passage Through India*, Shoemaker and Hoard, 1972

eventually got together again. William and I shared a flat in the DuPont Circle neighborhood of Washington, DC, and then several houses in Tucson, Arizona, (where we both attended the University of Arizona). Then we drifted apart again.

William had wanted to go to India ever since the aborted 1971 trip. This was a chance for us to complete what we had set out to do those many years ago. I had lived in India in various capacities for years and had traveled all over the country and could show William around. He accepted.

Tirtha Yatra Begins

This is only William's second day in India, and he is going straight to Govardhana. My body clock is back on schedule and I got up in plenty of time to go downstairs for breakfast. My intention was to demonstrate my complete faith in Kesava Maharaj by not calling anyone regarding our pick-up. He had assured us that one of his disciples would meet up with us at the YMCA and drive us right to the ashram.

Having completed that task, I broke down and called Ananta Rupa Dasa, the disciple driving us to Govardhan. He confirmed the 1300 pickup. It seems old habits are hard to break. It is a Western expectation to have everything solid and confirmed and on time. It takes a long time for a Westerner to adapt to an Indian "lightly-planned, ever flexible" environment.

We were picked up by Ananta Rupa Dasa for the drive to Govardhan right on time. After driving through Delhi, we crossed over into Uttar Pradesh. It was an entirely different world than the India I had left just four years ago. We drove on a divided super highway, with hardly any cars on it at a high rate of speed. Massive construction projects were building high rises on both sides and went on for miles. It took us a long time to pass through all this construction, and find the remaining Indian countryside.

We turned off the highway and drove to Vrindavan. Although I had been to Vrindavan many times, I hardly recognized anything. It was as if the entire region, once so quiet and serene, had been filled with people. The wide open spaces of Braj seem to have been carpeted with buildings, and traffic and people. There were signs for new housing developments everywhere saying things like "invest in the land of the Lord." Many of the new high rises were for the middle class. It appears that many Indians want to live in Braj to be in that sacred land. Many Hindus want to die in a holy place and retire there to live out their last years. Developers are happy to oblige them.

Despite all the building, or perhaps because of it, there appeared to be a total lack of sanitation. For the first time, I saw liquor shops openly selling alcohol (intoxicants of any kind are not allowed in a pilgrimage area). I never dreamed such things would be allowed in Braj.

149

From Vrindavan we took the side road to Govardhan. There was so much traffic; congestion and noise that I failed to realize that we had arrived at the holy *dham* (pilgrimage site) until William pointed out Govardhan hill itself.[59]

We turned into the ashram and were affectionately greeted by Kesava Maharaj. He stated that he was at our disposal and that we could approach him any time. We settled into our room, a long two room suite with a bathroom at the edge of the building. It was directly across from Kesava Maharaj's *kutir* (residence of a renounced person or Sannyasi). We then explored the ashram and spent time with the small herd of cows in the courtyard. The ashram was built some 400 year ago, and had been rebuilt, refurbished and modernized by Kesava Maharaj. It therefore was a medieval sandstone building in the Rajput style, and appeared to be a miniature palace in many ways, although it was spartan throughout with no hint of ostentation. The ashram was a monastery. Only men could reside there. Women could visit during the day, but had to remain in the public areas and leave before they shut and locked the gates at night.

Kesava Maharaj then invited us into his *kutir* for a long discussion. The room was small. It contained a small bed on which he slept and a desk with a computer. It was lined with bookcases containing a large collection of books on Vaishnavism and contained his personal altar and deities. Several points emerged during our talk. William brought up the existence of suffering and pointed out that it is suffering which pushes us out of our material tendency towards complacency.

Two principal points of spiritual life emerged for me. Spiritual life is an experience of the divine. It is not philosophizing or conceptualizing. One does not imagine elaborate heavens and hope to experience them, one follows the spiritual path dictated by the inner voice of the spirit soul (the paramatma) and the experience follows as one grows in spiritual life. What is to come cannot be presaged through contemplation. Whatever comes will prove to be a surprise. Liberation always exceeds expectations.

Maharaj pointed out that our presence in Govardhan was no accident ("there are no coincidences"). There is no randomness to the universe. God (Krishna) oversees the movement of every atom. Our presence here at this ashram indicates that William and I engaged in numerous spiritual practices in previous lives. I had a strong image of Allen Ginsburg in my mind. Maharaj spoke of the great boon of seeing and interacting with Srila Prabhupad. Ginsberg personally associated with Prabhupad. The two men spent hours discussing Vaishnava philosophy, and chanted the Hare Krishna mantra repeatedly together. Despite all of this personal

---

[59] Govardhan is a mountain intimately associated with Lord Krishna and is considered a holy deity itself. For example, when Sri Chaitanya visited Govardhan, he refused to set foot on the hill, saying that it was non-different from Krishna Himself. To this day, vaishnavas do not set foot on the hill but confine themselves to walking around it.

association with a guru, at the time of his death, Allen Ginsburg denied everything he had been taught, saying that death was followed by emptiness. Ginsberg seemed to reject every opportunity he had been provided. I wanted to ask Maharaj about this, but saved the question for a future meeting.

After speaking for several hours, we returned to our rooms. We had not had food or drink for some time. We were about to break out William's "emergency rations," when we heard the *prasadam* bell. While residing at the ashram, we were to eat only *prasadam*, food offered to Krishna and shared with Him. The food met strict requirements to ensure it was in the mode of goodness (*sattva*). In the *Bhagavad Gita*, the Lord states that he will not accept offerings that are impure.

Except for Kesava Maharaj, we are the only non-Indians here. The others are the Indian temple residents, and some Indian devotees, who like us, are spending time in the ashram to work on their spirituality. The monks are dressed in the traditional dress of Vaishnava celibate renunciates (*brahmacaris*), saffron colored *dhotis* and *kurtas*. Kesava described them as "simple village boys." Several were from West Bengal, one from Odisha, and one from Assam, with the rest coming from the "Hindi belt" of Hindi speaking states. They communicated with each other in a combination of Hindi and Bengali.

As with many rural Indians from a village background, they were simple in a positive sense. They were open and affectionate and mutually supportive and incapable of guile or deceit. We would get to know them very well over the coming week and grow quite close. I communicated with them in a combination of Hindi and Bengali and translated for William. We ate traditional *prasad* with them. The *prasadam* hall is in front of our room. It is a long open air verandah in front of one of the ashram buildings. The food was *saddharan* (simple), containing no garlic, onions, or chilies. I have been conquering my tendency to overeat ever since entering India. The sparse, all vegetarian diet will do me good.

We told Kesava Maharaj that we would participate in the complete temple program, the same as all monks in the ashram. It consists of a series of pujas. The schedule was as follows:

Mangal Aarati – at 0430 – followed by Tulasi Puja

Pushpa Aarati - at 0830

Guru Puja – at 1230

Shaya Aarati – at 2030 – followed by Govardhan Puja

We retired to our room to sleep after Govardhan Puja. We slept on simple cots with no blankets or quilts. I used my yellow hare namer chaddar (devotional scarf) as a covering. We awoke at 0400 in the morning to prepare for Mangal

Aarati, taking a bucket bath, and thoroughly washing. It is still pitch black dark when we awake.

The temple is located upstairs across the courtyard. The ashram is an old Rajput retreat used by the nobility for pilgrimage to Govardhan. It is located right on the parikrama path. The temple houses around 10 devotees. Some are initiated and some are in the initiation process.

We cross the *prasadam* hall and the courtyard in the dark and climb the steep steps up to the temple. The stairs are enormous and it is almost like climbing a mountain. The temple is small and sits over the reception room. It has two altars; one contains Govardhan *shilas*, including the personal *shilas* of Kesava Maharaj. One of the *shilas* was found inside the building when ISKCON acquired the premises through donation. The other was found when the devotees were excavating a well during the renovation of the property. They are exact matches. It is obvious that they were once a set, but had become separated over the course of the centuries, only to be reunited when the temple was reactivated.

The Govardhan *shilas* are often painted with faces in simple primary colors that are highly evocative. The Shilas at our ashram are those of Krishna and his eternal consort, Srimati Radharani. Krishna wears a turban laced with pearls and capped with a peacock feather, the symbol of Lord Krishna, while Radharani wears a crown. They are also dressed in rich brocades. Under the Vaishnava *arcana* doctrine, statues and shilas are not idols or mere representations. Krishna and Radha have, out of their mercy agreed to be present in the *shilas* to provide an opportunity for the devotees to interact with them. To the Vaishnava devotee, the encounter with the *shilas* is a chance to interact with a physical manifestation of God.

The second altar has conventional statues of Gaura Nitai, Sri Chaitanya Mahaprabhu and his principal associate Sri Nityananda, which Gaudiya Vaishnavas equate with Krishna and his brother Balarama. When facing the altars, there is a life size statue of Srila Prabhupad sitting on a *vyasasana* against the right wall.

When I awoke at 0400 I remembered a vivid dream. I dreamed that I was awake and sitting at the foot of my bed on the floor. Suddenly, the door opened and a group of persons entered into the room. They were all Hispanics and could not use their legs and had to crawl across the floor. One of them was crawling into my bed. I was horrified. "This is my personal room," I thought. My inclination was to get upset. But a voice inside me said "Is this any way to behave? You need to show compassion and willingly share your room." They had told me that Kesava Maharaj had decided we would share this room.

The Mangala Aarati starts with the prayers of the spiritual masters, accompanied by *kartalas* and *mrdangam*[60] The prayers have been written by gurus in the line of disciplic succession (*guru parampara*) of ISKCON and are in both Sanskrit and Bengali. They are sung in a process known as *sawal/jawab* (question and answer). The leader sings the line and everyone else repeats it.

While we pray, the two pujaris at the altar complete the ritual. The two pujaris have special status. Both are Brahmins and wear the sacred thread (*jeneuu*). Lord Chaitanya taught that caste status should be based on merit rather than purely on birth. ISKCON has taken Lord Chaitanya's teachings to heart and provides opportunities for devotees not of "twice born" status to become Brahmins through Brahmin initiation after completing requisite training and examination and demonstrating commitment to Brahminical values.

Pujaris devote their lives to the deities on the altars. One is assigned to each altar. They spend their days dressing the deities, decorating the altar and performing the pujas. They must adhere to strict standards of cleanliness. They wear different clothing than the other devotees. They wear the same saffron colored dhoti, but do not wear a shirt. Instead, they drape their upper body in a single piece of saffron colored cloth. In addition to the *tilak* (clay markings of a Vaishnava) on the forehead, pujaris have *tilak* along their arms.

In our temple, the *pujaris* have an assistant, who was not of high caste. He cleaned all of the utensils used in the pujas, washing them with clay and water while the *pujas* were ongoing. He was from Assam and was particularly devoted. He was an enthusiastic participant in each *kirtan*. I asked him whether he was on the path to himself becoming a *pujari*, and he replied that he would always remain the lowly assistant, as he did not have the qualifications.

The *aarati* schedule is based around the day of the deities. The Mangala Aarati is meant to gently awaken the sleeping deities so they can start their day. In our temple the Pushpa Aarati represented the full-fledged revelation of the deities in their entire splendor, after they have been dressed in new outfits for the day. In large temples, the altars often have large doors that shut at the conclusion of the *aarati*. In these temples, this revelatory puja is particularly dramatic, as the doors are swung open to reveal the newly dressed deities on a newly decorated altar with their *pujaris* in attendance. The devotees, filled with anticipation await the moment in semi-darkness, when the doors open, the deities are bathed in light. Our temple was small and only had a curtain that was opened at the beginning of the puja.

In every ISKCON temple, this *aarati* opens with the song "Govindam adhi parusham" (You are Govinda the primal Lord), as recorded by British devotees in the late 1960's. The song was produced by George Harrison and he did the orchestration and arrangement and plays guitar. It is a particularly moving and

[60] Brass cymbals and a two headed drum that is strapped over the shoulder and played with both hands.

153

dramatic song. When Prabhupad heard the song, he liked it so much that he ordered it to be used in all ISKCON temples for this aarati and this has been the case ever since. This puja is particularly dramatic in a large temple with many devotees. As soon as the song begins, the altar doors are opened, and every devotee immediately performs *dandavat*. Our temple was small an intimate, with only five or six worshippers on average, but it was still a powerful experience.

Each *aarati* follows the same pattern. The pujaris offer the deities a series of devotional items while ringing a brass bell held in their left hand. The offerings include a fly whisk, incense, water, a flaming oil lamp and a handkerchief. The pujaris share the water by throwing drops into the assembled worshippers. They hand the oil lamp to one of the devotees and he walks among us holding it up to each worshipper. We share this heat with God by holding our hands over the lamp and running them across our head. This gives us an opportunity to share an intimate moment with Krishna. The fervor of the prayers increases as the ritual proceeds, and concludes with the Hare Krishna Maha Mantra. At the conclusion of the ritual, we lie flat on the floor in front of the deities, while the prayer leader recites Sanskrit *slokas* in praise of all the holy saints and holy places. Since we are in Govardhan, it is always mentioned.

After the Mangala Aarati, we perform the Tulasi Puja. The *pujari* moves a small table to the center of the temple. On top of the table is a pot decorated with embroidered cloth. It contains a *Tulasi* (or *Vrinda*), a basil plant. Tulasi is worshipped by vaishnavas who keep a plant in a special pot in their home. In the puja, we sing prayers to the goddess Tulasi, who is particularly beloved by Lord Krishna and circumambulate the plant, spinning around one time at the same spot to the right. We then take turns taking a small spoon and watering the plant. At the conclusion, worshippers often touch the plant and then touch their heads, asking Tulasi Devi to bless them.

With the conclusion of this puja we have greeted the day. We return to our rooms to perform *japa* until the start of classes. When Kesava Maharaj is present, he teaches the class in English, otherwise, the temple president Asita Krishna Prabhu teaches the class in Hindi. Sometimes Kesava Maharaj participates in the Mangala Aarati and Tulasi Puja as well. This morning he arrives in full sannyasi attire and carrying his *sannyasi danda*.[61]

He performs his prostrations and prayers before the altars and the statue of Srila Prabhupad while holding his danda straight up. He then performs a series of prayers in Sanskrit and Bengali. We participate in some of the prayers and merely listen to him recite the others. He then teaches a verse from the Srimad Bhagavatam using the traditional method. He recites the verse in Sanskrit. We

---

[61] Sannyasis carry a stick about two meters long wrapped in saffron cloth as a mark of their renunciate status.

then repeat the original words and their English meanings. He reads the Prabhupad purport and then preaches.

Today he was inspired. He spoke at length about the mercy of the Lord, and how the Lord incarnates again and again to save the fallen souls, and changes his form to please and attract the devotees at any stage of their spiritual development. Maharaj emphasizes the nature of the loving relationship between the devotee and Krishna. Krishna wants this relationship and the devotee aspires to please the Lord by acting in the way the Lord wants and providing the Lord what he requests in sacrifice.

After the class, we have morning *prasadam* in the prasadam hall. The *prasadam* is doled out by monks onto plates and bowls made of dried leaves and pinned together with thorns. These traditional plates and bowls are completely biodegradable. While the *prasadam* is being distributed, Asita Krishna Prabhu leads us in prayers culminating in the Hare Krishna Maha Mantra.

Asita Krishna Prabhu has been with this ashram since it was opened. As a child he had a dream in which Lord Krishna directed him to a certain spot and told him never to leave it. After attaining adulthood, he ran away from home to join ISKCON. The first time he saw the portion of Govardhana hill that is just in front of the ashram, he fell weeping to his knees. It was the exact spot that Lord Krishna had showed him in his dream. He immediately took a vow never to leave and has remained at the ashram ever since. He remains at the ashram year round, even during the summer when the temperatures average over 110 degrees Fahrenheit and there is no air conditioning.

Asita Krishna Prabhu is an intense devotee with his own particular charisma. He acts as the assistant to Kesava Maharaj in all matters and is the executive head of the ashram. When Kesava Maharaj is away on a preaching tour of the US or Europe, Kesava Maharaj is fully in charge. He is a man of few words. He epitomizes the classic depiction of the "stern sannyasi" Kesava Maharaj has complete trust in Asita Krishna Prabhu and works to "train him up," to greater accomplishments. Asita Krishna Prabhu is single and has no intention of leaving the *brahmacharya* order to marry and start a family (entering the *grihashta* or householder order). I found myself wondering whether Asita Krishna Prabhu would himself at some point take *Sannyas* initiation and become a *Sannyasi*, but felt this was too personal a question to ask. Technically, *sannyasis* are expected not to put down permanent roots in any one place, but to wander from one place to another. This would conflict with Asita Krishna Prabhu's vow to remain in the Govardhan Ashram his entire life.

After Asita Krishna Prabhu completes the prayers, as always, concluding with the Hare Krishna Maha Mantra, we all dig into our eating and conversation ends. We eat only with our hands. There are no utensils, even for rice and rice pudding (*khir*). By the end of the meal, our hands are covered with food and we lick our fingers to clean them off.

After prasadam we went to the *kutir* of Kesava Maharaj and he taught us how to perform *japa* properly and we recited a round together on our *japa* beads. He presented William with his own set of *japa* beads and an embroidered bag to keep them in. I had been reciting *japa* for decades, but never would experience it as intensely as during this *tirtha yatra*.

We were free for the rest of the day. We were very tired. We took a long nap. After the nap, we studied scripture. I had vowed to use this opportunity to seriously study the *Bhagavad Gita*, I would read the entire work by the end of my trip. Prabhupad said all ISKCON devotes had to seriously study the scriptures. He set up the *Bhakti Shastra* program to encourage this process, which awards certificates to those who study seriously and pass a series of examinations. The very first work to be studied under this program is the *Bhagavad Gita* and I am earnestly starting this process.

I studied the introduction by Prabhupad, in which he summarizes the Gita and applies it to Vaishnava philosophy. I learned many new things even though I had been reading the Gita for a long time.

Prabhupad described the Vaishnava metaphysical system in which God has three different forms, but remains the Supreme Personality of Godhead. Krishna is the *Brahman*, or the impersonal effulgence, the *Paramatma*, which is the individual residing in the heart of every individual, and the Supreme Personality of Godhead, which is Krishna in his original form. When we live in the material world, we feel threatened by *asat* (non-existence). This anxiety is not necessary, as we are all eternal spirit souls who have never been created and will never die. We are *jiva* conscious, when we are aware only of our own bodies. The Lord is *Isvara* and is conscious of all bodies. As *paramatma*, He gives direction to all willing to listen about the right path, but each *jiva* has free will to accept or reject these directions, and the covered *jiva* may have no perception of the *paramatma* or His instructions.

There are three modes or categories of material nature – the *sattvic* (goodness), the *tamasic* (ignorance) and passion (*rajasic*). Only within the mode of sattva can one change his activities to perceive the absolute truth and make spiritual progress. Initially this process is meant to reverse evil practices and generate good karma. However, once a devotee makes sufficient spiritual progress, he purifies his consciousness and transcends the inferior modes of material nature altogether, and reflects only the *sattvic*. As this point, the devotee has transcended material nature and is free from karma. This is one of the essential teachings of the *Bhagavad Gita*. Happiness is not to be found in enjoying the things of this world, but by participating in the eternal enjoyment of the Supreme Lord by providing service. The Lord is perpetually happy and we can share in this happiness.

Empowered *jivas* are avatars or incarnations of the Lord. They are not full avatars of Krishna but a soul from the spiritual world who descends to Earth to fulfill a specific purpose. Such souls include Mohammed, Buddha, and Jesus. Since Prabhupad left this world, his devotees have suggested that he falls in this category

156

as well. Prabhupad emphasizes that when one takes shelter of the Supreme Lord, he has nothing to fear, even in the midst of the greatest calamity.

After studying scripture, we walked to the bazaar along the *parikrama* path. Emerging from the ashram was like walking from serenity into noisy confusion. The *parikrama* path was lined with beggars, who live on the ground by the side of the road and collect alms. Many are elderly. Others are in poor health. Cows and dogs were everywhere. The air was filled with a foul odor from the open sewage and there was continuous noise from honking horns. India is a perpetual traffic jam, and the Indian solution is to keep honking the horn and muscling your way through. We found a shop and purchased some bottled water. We stuck meticulously to the temple program and never ate any outside food, but had to drink about four liters of water a day to remain hydrated.

In the evening we performed Guru Puja before the statue of Srila Prabhupad and the evening *aarati*. The guru puja is similar to those offered to the deities, but prayers are sung in praise of the guru and the elements are offered to him. In the Vaishnava tradition, no one believes that any guru is as good as God, but he must be revered like God because he brings the message of Krishna and delivers the fallen souls.

After the puja, we went for evening *prasad* and sat next to Kesava Maharaj. We discussed the worship of the demigods and Prabhupad's instructions. Prabhupad said that no Vaishnava should show disrespect to the demigods (Shiva, the Goddess and the other non-Vaishnava deities commonly worshipped in India), but he should not worship them. He explained that there are different types of worship determined by the worshippers' level of spiritual development. The demigods are totally dependent on Krishna, who has tasked them with providing material goods to the general population and performing specific functions. As such, they are little more than administrators. Those who are in the mode of ignorance (*tamas*) worship the demigods because they are not interested in spiritual progress but only in approaching God to fulfill material wishes.

Each night concludes with the final puja at 2030. At the end of this *aarati*, the curtains are closed and we go to the porch outside the temple doors facing Govardhan hill. There we perform another puja to Govardhan that concludes with the most enthusiastic kirtan of the day. Our Assamese friend is always particularly enlivened for this kirtan, jumping, dancing and spinning enthusiastically. We then perform our final *dandavats* facing Govardhan hill. At the conclusion of each *aarati*, the *pujari* blows a conch shell (*shank*), which makes a loud noise that carries very far. For me, the sound of the conch evoked the high point of the *aarati* and signaled the conclusion of the ritual.

While we were living in the ashram the moon was full, which is considered particularly auspicious. It bathed the environment in a soft light. The air was filled with stars that William and I could not see in our brightly lit environments in the United States. The air reverberated with the sound of similar pujas going on in temples all around us. Govardhan hill loomed in front of us. It was our spiritual focus.

I started staying on the porch after the conclusion of the day's *aaratis* to soak in this spiritual atmosphere. By this point, my consciousness was permeated with devotional practice and the Hare Krishna Maha Mantra seemed to be a constant presence.

The First Aside – Krishna and Jesus

My conversations with Kesava Maharaj and my initial study of the *Bhagavad Gita (as it is)*, by His Divine Grace A.C. Bhaktivedanta Prabhupad, revealed an interesting facet of Vaishnava philosophy that is not often publicly discussed or acknowledged. Vaishnavas believe that there are two types of *avatars* (incarnations of God). When Krishna descends to Earth as an *avatar*, this is called a "full *avatar*." There is a second category of *avatar*, however. This is the "empowered *jiva*." Empowered *jivas* are realized souls who reside eternally with Krishna. They are sent by Krishna to this planet to fulfill specific tasks, all intended to awaken dormant love of God in souls living in ignorance *(maya)*, separated from the Lord, and incapable of comprehending their situation. Empowered *jivas* are not incarnations of Krishna, but rather incarnations of close associates of Krishna who are "realized souls." Vaishnavas put Jesus in this category.

As a person raised in the Christian faith, it was readily apparent to me that this doctrine contradicts and rejects the Christian interpretation of Christ's divinity, as least on a formal theological level. Unlike the Vaishnavas, Christians believe that there has been only one incarnation of God in the entire history of this planet, Jesus Christ. They believe Jesus Christ is one aspect of a triune God and cannot be differentiated from God in any way shape or form, and that his incarnation is nothing less than the descent of God to man to demonstrate his love by dying on the cross. Christians deny the validity of the Hindu doctrine of multiple incarnations. Furthermore, as a traditionally exclusivist religion, Christian doctrine has long asserted that Jesus Christ is the one true son of God and that all other alleged incarnations are false.

Christians would look askance at the Vaishnava doctrine that Jesus Christ is anything less than a full incarnation of God, viewing it as an attempt to denigrate Christ's significance and belittle him. I myself was surprised to learn of this doctrine. I had always assumed that there was no essential contradiction between the incarnation of Jesus and that of other *avatars* and was not aware that there are two different types of avatars. Although I have read much of Prabhupad's writings, this was the first time that I saw this doctrine clearly spelled out.

Prabhupad himself always demonstrated profound respect for Christians and stated that there is no competition between religious faiths. He never expressed any desire to supplant or replace the Christian faith in the West with Vaishnavism and always asserted that the Christian faith is as valid as the Vaishnava one. His principal criticism regarded the Christian tendency to approve of meat eating. He was adamant that this practice contradicts one of the ten commandments, "thou shalt not kill." In his talks with Christians, Prabhupad quoted the Ten Commandments, with its rule against killing, and said it should be extended to include the killing and eating of animals. While expressing profound reverence for Jesus Christ, he kept silent when speaking in public regarding the doctrine of empowered *jivas*.

Prabhupad urged his disciples to respect the sensitivities of Christians and not say anything that could be seen as disparaging Jesus Christ. It appears that this is why this doctrine of empowered *jivas* was not actively propounded by ISKCON. In Prabhupad's view, Jesus Christ was sent to Earth by Krishna to bring the human race closer to God, to emphasize the love of God for the human race, and to change the character of biblical religion from the angry God of the Old Testament to the God of love found in the New Testament. Thus Jesus was "empowered" to carry out these specific tasks, and should be venerated as a divine being.

While many Christians would be rightfully angered by this doctrine, it should be placed in context. Vaishnavism is not an exclusivist faith. It recognizes the divine essence of all world faiths and does not denigrate or deny the essential divinity of religious figures, including Lord Buddha, the Prophet Muhammad, and Jesus Christ. Contrast this essentially liberal doctrine with the attitude of many Christians, who decry all religions except Christianity as "false faiths," and calls for the conversion of non-Christians to Christianity to save them from worshipping "false Gods."

It would not take long for me to come up with numerous statements by Christians and Christian missionaries, in which they unleash a torrent of invective against Krishna, and Sri Chaitanya. This was very popular in the 19th and early 20th centuries, when both the United States and the United Kingdom were undergoing evangelical revivals and has largely faded away in a more enlightened and tolerant age. The appearance of Prabhupad's saffron-clad followers on the streets of major American cities has revived this tendency among some, more conservative, Christians. To read attacks on Vaishnavas by contemporary American Christians, one need only go to select Christian bookshops and page through the selection attacking "cults," which are viewed as non-Christian threats to the Christian faith.

Tirtha Yatra Continues

We did not follow the temple program today. Instead, we undertook padayatra. As instructed by Kesava Maharaj, we awoke at 0300, bathed and put on fresh clothes. We walked out into the dark night but the ashram gate was locked. We roused the *chowkidar*, but he did not have the key. He had to search for the man with the key. While we waited, I sat in a chair and appreciated the night. In Govardhan there are few lights at night, you can see many more stars. The

159

constellations are clearly visible, as are shooting stars. One fell across the sky as the *Chowkidar* opened the gate and we started.

We walked for many kilometers along the parikrama path. Sadly, it is no longer a path, but has been transformed into an ordinary street, with rapid, unplanned construction on both sides. Whereas the night is supposed to be quiet and peaceful, we occasionally had to dodge trucks and other vehicles driving at great speed with their horns blaring even at this peaceful period in the middle of the night.

In addition, businesses selling bottled drinks and snacks were open even then. Each featured a TV or DVD player, playing Hindi movies with the volume turned up all of the way. There are signs of deterioration is this age of Kali.

Govardhan hill was on our right as we walked. The Hill is the focus of our *parikrama* and must always remain on our right side. This is why the *parikrama* can only be made in one direction. As the sun rose, we made out the Hill looming off to the side. We stopped at a village *kund* (pond or tank). It was a trip back in time. Women drew water from a well, put it into metal pots and carried it home on their heads. Others bathed in the *kund*. Children put on their uniforms after their morning baths and headed off to school.

We were getting tired of the noise, the filth, and dodging speeding vehicles, when we noticed an interior path running alongside Govardhan Hill. We took a right turn off of the road and headed into the interior of the forest (*van*) surrounding Govardhan Hill. We got on to the path I originally spied and went further in to another path. We saw the gentle slopes of Govardhan Hill just 50 meters ahead of us.

We found an old well covered with concrete and surrounded by grazing cows and bulls and monkeys chattering in the trees. I was spontaneously moved, lit a joss stick (*agarbatti*) and completed one round of *japa*. We went even closer to Govardhan Hill and found a platform with an installed *shila*. I was very moved at this spot. It felt right. The genuine devotional mode was there. We lingered and took some pictures. I lit more joss sticks and completed my own *puja*, and we head back to the path, being careful not to commit an offense by stepping on Govardhan Hill.

This quiet, peaceful, tree-lined path came to an end, and we were back on the street. We quickly came to a town. The parikrama path disappeared. We asked some schoolboys for directions and they gave us the wrong advice. We walked in the wrong direction for some time, through the heart of the noisy bazaar, dodging huge trucks bearing down on us and blaring air horns into our ears, as well as pigs, dogs, rickshaws, and lots of pedestrians. It did not feel right, so I asked another man, who gave us the correct route. We quickly returned to the *parikrama* path, headed in the direction of Radha Kund.

It was a nine kilometer walk to the kund, but the area was no longer so densely populated and there was little traffic. Most buildings were ashrams and *goshallas* (cow sanctuaries) and sidewalk shops selling drinks to pilgrims. We walked side by side with our fellow pilgrims, many of whom were sadhus.

We arrived at Radha Kund with big temples lining the road. We stopped and ate a samosa and walked on until we arrived at the gate of Radha Kunda. This spot is among the most sacred for vaishnavas, who believe it was established by Radha Herself. For many vaishnavas, the water of the kund is seen as a direct gateway to the spiritual world and bathing in the kund is seen as more than merely an auspicious experience, but rather the epitome of all auspicious experiences, as it provides a personal experience of Radha's presence.

Pandas met us at the gate. They descended on us and began their work with great gusto. Before we had a chance to think, they started their "puja." I am no Sanskrit scholar or Brahmin priest, but can tell the difference between legitimate *slokas* and made-up mumbo jumbo. They merely repeated meaningless syllables and the names of random deities and personalities. At one point, they asked for my *japa* beads. I removed them from the bag and they immersed them into Radha Kunda, while saying one of their "*mantras*." Although we were well aware that the entire thing was a con job, we felt compelled to pay them. They insisted we were not paying them a fee, but merely providing a "donation" to help them feed the sadhus (another con). I negotiated with them to bring down the sum as much as possible and limit the damage.

After they left, we found a shady spot on the steps leading into the *kund*. The tank is surrounded by buildings on all sides, with a platform running alongside and steps leading into the water. I was inspired by the *kund* and lit another joss stick and performed another round of *japa*.

We were then approached by a sannyasi from the Philippines. He was from the Narain sect (a non ISKCON Gaudiya Vaishnava sect). He expressed great admiration for Prabhupad. He oversees a project to beautify and restore Radha Kund. His sect had refinished several walls around the Kund, and removed the commercial advertising painted there, replacing it with devotional paintings. We sat with him and had a friendly discussion. He asked whether he could sing a famous bhajan (devotional song) dedicated to Radha, and we eagerly accepted and sang along with him, as he had provided us with sheets containing the lyrics and the English translation. William and I had provided the sannyasi with our e-mail addresses. Months later, after we had returned to the US, he sent us photographs of all their work around the *kund*, and asked for a donation. We gladly did so.

While leaving the *kund* through the same gate and bargaining with the girl there on how much to pay her for watching our shoes, another *panda* approached us. He took us across the street to an ISKCON temple containing the *Samadhi* (tomb) of Sri Damodar, one of Srila Prabhupad's original Indian disciples. We therefore assumed he was with ISKCON and legitimate.

He then took us to the *Samadhi* of Raghunatha das Goswami, (one of the six goswamis of Vrindavan), as well as other *samadhis*, and Raghunatha das Goswami's *Kutir*. He then took us to the adjoining Shyam Kund (the tank created by Lord Krishna), and to a spot containing three large old trees. The five Pandavas of the *Mahabharata* epic are said to have requested to be reincarnated as these trees and perpetually remain at Shyam Kund. He insisted we do a puja there and ran off to procure some incense. By this time we realized that we had encountered another *panda*. As expected, his "puja" was totally bogus, and I was again forced to bargain hard to cut our losses. While his services as a pujari were not required, he had been a good guide and a friendly soul, and we parted company in a mood of mutual respect.

It was then getting late and quite hot. We stopped for food and walked passed Kusuma Sarovara, Narada Vana and Manasi Ganga and back to our Ashram. Even though we had started in the dead of night, it was now late afternoon. There were hardly any people on the streets, as the local population and all the pilgrims retired for afternoon naps. The sun was high in the sky and we were tired, hot and hungry. We walked from one shade tree to the next, cooling off under each one before resuming our journey, while continuing to drink lots of water. We bought numerous bottles of water and drained them dry. We walked past the beggars outside our ashram and into the gates. We had been gone for 14 hours. The back of one of my feet was blistered. We took bucket baths, bathed, changed into clean clothes and collapsed into bed.

We had dinner *prasad* with Kesava Maharaj. He explained that the holy *dham* is being covered by illusion in this age of greed. He said, however, that the spiritually advanced can still sense the real *dham* under its covering of *maya*. I thought this was an apt analogy, as I remember the original *padayatra* path in Vrindavan I first encountered in 1972, when it consisted of fine dust cool to the touch of bare feet, which was now literally covered by pavement. This is the story of the holy *dham*. It is repeatedly lost and rediscovered. Tomorrow we go back to Kusama Sarovar, Narada Kund, Sri Chaitanya's *baitak* at Radha Kund, and Manasi Ganga, to spend some more time in these holy places.

Tirtha Yatra Continues

Today was a good day. We were still recovering from our *padayatra*, but participated in the full temple program, awakening the deities with Mangal Arati at 0400, continuing with Tulasi Puja and settling in for class. Kesava Maharaj is not going to class, so Temple President Asiti Krishna Das conducted it in Hindi. He spoke on a verse from *Srimad Bhagavatam* dealing with the heavenly and hellish planets.

Asking the question, "Why does the human soul wander from the heavenly to the hellish plants?" Asiti Krishna Das provided a number of answers. Man has free will. He becomes confused. He beings to convince himself that bad is good and good is bad. In earlier ages, morality was maintained by society. Everyone had a clear idea of what was sinful and the negative consequences of sinful behavior. But in this present age, society no longer teaches moral behavior. Many are confused. They do not know what is sinful and some do not even know sin exists. In this confusion, they develop a taste for bad things and convince themselves that the bad things are good. When someone comes to them and tells them the truth, he is ridiculed.

Because there is a law of karma, this evil behavior results in hellish consequences, and the soul descends to the hellish planets. He mentioned that Srila Prabhupad was riding a Korean Air flight and the stewardesses began handing out slabs of raw meat to the Korean passengers. Naturally, Prabhupad was disgusted, saying that this shows how confused people cannot discern good from evil. Asita Krishna Das then stated that in Thailand, people place meat every day in a pot and let it rot and during a big festival take the rotten mean out of the pot and eat it with great fanfare and delight.

He then described a group of female fish sellers who carried baskets of salted fish on their heads and sold it from village to village. As a result, they were surrounded by a strong fishy smell that permeated their hair, clothing, and skin. They were selling one night in a village and it was too late to return, so they found lodging at the home of a gardener surrounded by plots filled with beautiful fragrant flowers. In the middle of the night, the women woke up and could not get back to sleep. They could not deal with what they thought was the nauseating smell coming from the flower gardens, so they grabbed the old rags from the bottom of their fish baskets and put them over their faces. They then felt relieved, because they smelled a "normal" smell again, and went right back to sleep.

At lunch I discussed reincarnation with Kesava Maharaj. He pointed out that Christians believe they are reunited with their loved ones in heaven after death, but Indians believe in reincarnation, which means they are unlikely to see their loved ones again after they die. This must be very painful for Indians, I noted, as they place such a strong stress on family connections.

Kesava Maharaj replied that it is possible to be in Goloka Vrindavana (the abode of Lord Krishna) with a loved one, but it is not that important to liberated souls. They see such things as reminders of their life in the material world.

I continued with my reading of the *Bhagavad Gita* and it touched on this same topic. Arjuna did not want to fight because he did not want to fight against members of his own family. Krishna tells Arjuna that a liberated soul cultivates detachments and is not disturbed by family ties.

After lunch we took a motor rickshaw back to Radha Kunda. It was a wonderful experience. There were no pandas today. We left our shoes in front of the ISKCON temple at Radha Kunda and made a complete *parikrama* of Shyam Kund. We spent a powerful hour at the *baitak* (sitting place) of Sri Chaitanya Mahaprabhu. At first it was just us, the Brahmin priest who maintains the small temple at the site and two widows. I then sat down for a round of *japa*. While my eyes were closed, the widows left and when I opened my eyes, there was only an Indian devotee and myself performing *japa*. We circumambulated the *baitak* seven times as required.

We then returned to Shyam Kund and were the only persons there. This is an example of something meant to be. This was the precise spot at which we were meant to be at this precise moment. Krishna controls every atom and there are no coincidences. It was serene and peaceful. This the experience meant for Shyam Kund.

While at the two sacred *kunds*, we took ceremonial baths, going down the steps to the edge of the kund and sprinkling the water on our heads. I told William that Srila Prabhupad had been disgusted when he received reports that some Western ISKCON devotees had behaved improperly at Radha Kunda. The devotees had viewed their puja at Radha Kund as an ordinary swimming expedition and had begun to play and splash in the water, disturbing the other worshippers. Prabhupad then moved to prevent such alarming behavior. He ordered that ISKCON devotees no longer wade into the water, but sit on the steps and splash the water over their heads. I insisted that we follow these orders. In retrospect, I have concluded that since we were in the proper devotional mindset, we would have gotten greater benefit from our experience had we gone in the water, and immersed our heads, in the traditional fashion. I will make sure to do this next time I am in Vrindavan.

We walked back to the ashram. On the way, we passed a grove of trees. Inside was a large tile containing two footprints. This marked a spot visited by Sri Chaitanya Mahaprabhu while in Vrindavan.

When we got back, we took a nap. I studied *Bhagavad Gita* and performed *japa*. We went around the ashram taking pictures. We took a picture with one of the *pujaris* and his assistants and they allowed us to take some wonderful pictures of the deities.

We went to the roof of the ashram and saw all of Govardhan.

We went to evening *aarati* and participated in a lively *kirtan*, concluding the evening with the beautiful Govardhan Puja under the moonlight.

At dinner, Kesava Maharaj said it was time for us to read the entire *Srimad Bhagavatam*. He said we could skip the entire Sanskrit, and if we read 41 pages per day, we could complete the entire work in one year. The *Srimad Bhagavatam* is monumental in scope. It consists of 10 Cantos (or volumes). Each of the 10 Cantos consists of at least two large books. If fills an entire shelf in my office. I have been reading the *Srimad Bhagavatam* intermittently since my return, but have failed to fulfill the Guru's request of 41 pages every day. As a result, I am still reading Canto Three.

The next day was special. We got up as usual and went to morning *aarati*. There were fewer devotees present because many were conducting programs elsewhere.

Yesterday, Kesava Maharaj had told us to set aside time for a final meeting with him. He is leaving at 0300 to go to Kanpur to open a new temple and will not return until an hour after our departure for Vrindavan.

He sent for us this morning to come to his *kutir*. We had a very long and intimate discussion with him that continued through breakfast, and on into the morning hours. We provided Maharaj with our donations. He arranged for us to meet with Dharamatma Das, the assistant to the ISKCON Temple President while in Vrindavan, and arranged to take pictures with us later in the day.

After taking leave from Kesava Maharaj, we drove in a motor rickshaw to Kusum Sarovar, a huge structure built on a sacred lake in 1765 by a Jat King. This was my third trip to this location, and each time I come, there is no one around and the area is peaceful and serene.

The lake is a scene of Radha Krishna pastimes and there is a Shiva *Lingam* at the spot where a famous sage died while performing austerities. The lake has always been full of water. It is surrounded by steps leading into the water (bathing *ghats*) and small piers topped by houses that jut out into the lake. On previous visits, it was possible to jump off the piers directly into the water. Sadly, the lake is at a very low level, not deep enough for swimming. There are piles of garbage at the corners and pieces of trash floating on the lake. A trio of white swans swims peacefully across the water, and water birds stand on its edges.

Behind the lake are a series of buildings built in a classic Rajasthani style out of red sandstone. The buildings on either side were built as pleasure palaces for the king, his family, and his retinue. There are two buildings in the center. One is the tomb of the king. The other is the tomb of his wives. The tombs are decorated with beautiful wall and ceiling paintings depicting the pastimes of Krishna and Radha and the King's victories in battle.

We spend a long time at the site enjoying the peaceful atmosphere. We wandered to the edge of a pavilion on the rear wall and looked into the peaceful countryside of Braj. Water buffaloes sat in a pool of water, with water birds perched on their backs, and the countryside slept. It was the time when villagers take their afternoon naps and everything is peaceful.

On the way out, I recognized the temple on the right. It is the Sri Sri Radha Bana Bihari Mandir, which commemorates a pastime in which Krishna brushed Radha's hair while she looked into a mirror. I remembered it as a special temple. During a previous visit, I accompanied ISKCON devotees who took care of elderly people who were terminally ill. One of them was inside this temple lying on a cot. He was very weak. His death was approaching rapidly. Although he had very little strength, he kept repeating the Hare Krishna mantra softly. He was under the care of a young female devotee, who made him comfortable in his last moments.

We approached the door, but it was closed and it appeared we would not be able to gain entrance. However, a British ISKCON devotee opened the door. He said he was just about to put the deities to bed, but we had come just in time. The deities are two *shilas* reenacting the pastime of Sri Krishna combing Radha's hair. The temple atmosphere was tranquil and we had a great conversation with the *pujari*. He said the temple priest had died, leaving his wife to take care of the temple. However, she was elderly herself and could not do this singlehanded. The former priest was a personal friend of Srila Prabhupad and had spent many hours with him in the past. His wife requested ISKCON to provide devotees to take over management. Every place has its own atmosphere (vibration). The atmosphere at this temple was very good.

We then went to Narada Kund. I had fond memories of this location. During a previous visit, I had crossed over to Narada Kund on foot from Kusama Sarovar and spent a long time in quiet contemplation. The temple commemorates the sage Narada Muni. He is a powerful Vaishnava sage cursed to wander the universe from place to place. He plays a crucial role in many episodes of the Srimad Bhagavatam. Krishna allowed Narada Muni to come to Narada Kund to rest from his eternal wanderings. I nurture a special affection for this personality. During the previous visit, I found a spot against a pillar within the small temple and meditated on Narada Muni.

This time I could not find the temple. I was forced to ask a cycle rickshaw wallah to take us there, which he did in short order. He turned off the main road onto a small path and I then remembered the location and realized why I could not find this temple. There was now a large apartment block on the right side of the path and various businesses on the main road blocking the view into Narada Kund.

The rickshaw *wallah* left us at the gate and we removed our shoes. Several men sat on a raised platform above the *kund*, which was covered by green algae. This phenomenon is caused by the extensive use of chemical fertilizer. The fertilizer drains into the *kund* and feeds the algae, which grows out of control. There was a two-story building in front of the *kund*, and a large single story building to its left. Before, there were no buildings for miles in any direction except for small temples.

We went to the kund and took pictures. We visited the standard Hanuman and Shiva temples, but there was no sign of the Narada Muni temple. A sadhu sat in a small building repeating mantras while playing on a drum. The room was adorned with the picture of Narada Muni that I recognized from my earlier trip. I asked the pujari guiding us where the temple was. He took us to a large single story building that looked like a warehouse and contained stacked grain and several cars. In the back was a shoddy makeshift temple covered by a curtain. This was an example of a place with bad vibrations. I did not want to remain there and did not want to perform puja as they recommended.

The altar contained a disparate collection of random religious objects and seemed to serve no purpose.

Before we left, the pujari told us the original temple had simply collapsed into ruin and a new temple was coming up on the site. During the interim, when the construction was in progress. The local people had erected this makeshift temple within the precincts of this warehouse/garage. The impression I received was bad. This appeared to be an example of someone taking over a renowned temple and trying to turn it into a profit making enterprise. I was disappointed and had a strong urge to leave the scene. We quickly boarded a waiting rickshaw and left.

When we returned to the ashram, Kesava Maharaj was waiting for us. We shot some pictures with Maharaj.

Afterward, we discovered that a feast was being served in the *prasadam* hall. It was a gift to the ashram devotees from a generous donor. It was delicious. We ate parathas, pakoras, sweet rice, gulab jamun and almond barfi. Everything was made with plenty of ghee.

We then met with the temple devotees and took group photos. It was ecstatic. We took photos all over the ashram, including a series of photos with the ashram cows. The devotees particularly enjoyed seeing William interacting with the cows and calves. After evening *aarati*, we ate our meal and said final goodbyes to Kesava Maharaj.

Govardhan Tirtha Yatra Comes to an End

Today was a quiet day. We woke up at the usual time. I was a little early, around 0330. At around 0400 we heard Kesava Maharaj's car pull out, Asita Krishna Prabhu was with him. With Guru Maharaj and the Temple President gone, there was a noticeable decline in energy. The morning *kirtan/aarati* was lackluster. There were only five of us there and the *pujaris* were short-staffed. One of the pujaris had disappeared during the night. He had found life at the ashram to be too demanding. He packed up his belongings and moved into another ashram run by another sect that was less rigorous.

The Guru Puja was even less intense. We quietly ate our breakfast and departed for Manasi Ganga, the last stop on our Govardhan tirtha yatra. Manasi Ganga was created by Lord Krishna as part of one of his pastimes. Radha had demanded that He bathe in the Ganges. He replied that He did not want to leave his beloved braj. He therefore created this lake out of his own mind (*man*) which was filled with the waters of the Ganges and bathed at this spot. From that time, bathing at Manasi Ganga has been viewed by Vaishnavas as more auspicious than bathing in the Ganges.

The lake is also the site of one of Krishna's pastimes with Radha and the Gopis, in which he rowed them across the lake in disguise, and played various tricks on them. We took a motor rickshaw, which let us off in front of the gate.

The temple was of a low standard. There was a man on a loudspeaker urging the pilgrims to spend money, frequent the shops inside and pay for expensive pujas. This is what Lord Jesus Christ faced when he went to the temple in Jerusalem. It made him angry, and it made me angry.

The pandas descended on us trying to compel us to pay for expensive and useless pujas. We ignored them, walked through the temple without stopping, and headed for the walkway around the lake. It is actually a giant tank, with walkways leading into the water, and surrounded by walls and houses. There is a small island not far from the temple. The lake is located in the middle of the town of Govardhan.

It struck me that we have beautiful deities at our little temple at the ashram, and our *pujaris* are our personal friends. Why should we pay greedy pandas to perform insincere and empty rituals?

In addition, we can perform *pujas* with heartfelt sincerity and communicate our devotion directly to the Lord. For Vaishnavas, it is the heartfelt devotion that matters, not empty rituals, especially when they are purely for monetary gain and insincere.

We started walking around the edge of the lake. There was a quasi-*parikrama* path, but it came to an end at a temple. We then entered a warren of small alleys, with small temples located at various places. We fended off various pandas and beggars as we walked. The path ended at a large old tree with small shrines underneath.

There exist here little islands of calm and serenity in the middle of an ocean of chaos and pandemonium. While walking, it is possible to be surrounded by noise and bad smells one minute and be in the middle of a quiet interlude the next. We wound our way through small dark alleys back to the lake and found a quiet spot on the steps leading into the water. There was no one around except for two *dhobis* doing laundry.

We walked down the steps to the water's edge. We took turns taking our ceremonial dip (*snan*), putting drops of water on our heads. It was a joy to perform in a serene and holy setting. I then sat quietly on the steps and performed a round of *japa*.

We tried to complete a *parikrama* of the lake, but there was no *parikrama* path. It looks like one may have existed, but houses were built over portions of it, making the parikrama impossible. This forced us to retrace our steps and return to the noisy temple.

The next stop was the Hari Deva Temple, which overlooks the lake from a hill. In Vaishnava tradition, pilgrims are supposed to complete a puja at the Hari Deva Temple before starting the Govardhan parikrama. The temple and the neighborhood were very old. There were only neighborhood people about, no pilgrims, as it was getting late in the afternoon when all the temples close and everyone takes a nap.

This has always been one of my favorite temples. I visited Hari Deva when I made the Braj *parikrama* with Lokanath Swami some years ago. At that time we visited the temple at dusk. It is square and blockish. Pilgrims climb steep steps to enter. Unlike most Hindu temples, it has a lot of space inside. Two long empty rooms lead up to the altar. It looked grey in the fading light. There was no electricity inside and as we entered, the only light was from the altar while the rest of the temple was bathed in darkness. It was a powerful experience. This time was different.

It was the early afternoon when we arrived, and the priest was closing the altar doors. He offered to reopen them but only if we agreed to pay for an expensive puja. We refused. This made him angry. He scowled at us and closed the doors with great relish. The only *darshan* I had of the deities was brief and took place while I was walking through the two long rooms leading to the altar.

When we got outside, one of William's shoes was missing. I thought it must have been taken by a monkey. A neighborhood boy on a bicycle asked what had happened. I said a shoe was missing. He said the neighborhood boys would conduct a search. We agreed and started looking on our own. We headed off to check behind the temple. No sooner were we out of sight when one of the boys called for us to come back. He said they had found the missing shoe in the shrine to Hanuman located in front of the temple. We were grateful for their help. They asked William to donate money to Hanuman. He put down 10 rupees before the Hanuman status. They then said that we should give them 50 rupees as a reward.

We then figured out what was going on. The boys had arranged the whole thing, taking William's shoe, hiding it, arranging to meet with us as we left the temple, and asking to help, all in hopes of obtaining a reward from us. Despite their best efforts, they would get only the money lying before the Hanuman statue. We told them we had no money to give. Despite the prank, the boys were smiling *brijabasis* and quite nice. It struck me as we left, that their playful prank resembled the pastimes of Lord Krishna that took place at this very location.

We walked back to the ashram.

That evening one of the devotees, Rangana Giridhari das, stopped by to say farewell and we conversed. He said he came to seek our blessing. I told him that we should seek his blessing, as we were uncultured *mlecchas* (dog eaters), and he was a devotee of the Lord. We told him we hoped he could become a *Brahmana* and a pujari, but he said he only cleaned puja implements, and would never be anything else. He said he was of low caste but after initiation was no longer concerned with caste, as all Vaishnavas are equal. We told him he should work hard and Krishna would reward him. He seemed to suffer from a sense of inferiority because of his background, his village origins in remote Assam, and lack of a formal education. We wish him well, as he is a sincere devotee.

Tonight the devotees had me lead the kirtan for Govardhan Puja. This was our last night time Govardhan Puja under the stars.

Chapter XII

Vrindavan Tirtha Yatra

Govardhan Ends – Vrindavan Begins

We woke up at the usual time (0400), performed Mangal Aarati and returned to our room. It was still dark, with the stars all out and the moon bright. After performing japa I laid on the cot and went to sleep to awake with the dawn. As the sun rose, I studied the *Bhagavad Gita*, reading the Sanskrit, then the meanings of the individual words, the verse and the purport. I have been reading the Sanskrit out loud, and learning new words. As I progress, I understand more and more.

We then went to the temple for our final puja. It was Guru Puja. There was no class again today, as Asiti Krishna and Kesava Maharaj were still in Kanpur.

After puja, we rested for a bit, and were called into the prasadam hall for our final prasad. It was delicious.

We had both packed up our back packs and were ready to go. We headed for the car, saying goodbye to the devotees on the way. One devotee, Manohar, was going with us to Vrindavan. The temple administrator did the driving.

We came to the edge of Govardhan and turned right onto the Vrindavan road. We were very quickly in the countryside. The road was broken and rutted and the ride bouncy. We drove through several villages. They all looked unchanged from when I first came to India 42 years ago. We shared the road with young men on motorcycles (three to a motorcycle) and motor rickshaws filled to capacity (I counted 12 people in one).

Our hosts were going to the ISKCON Krishna Balaram Temple. When they arrived we got out, grabbed our luggage, and said our final *pranams*. We were headed to Jai Singh Ghera, the headquarters of Srivatsa Goswami and his family at Chir Ghat. We found a rickshaw almost immediately. The street (Bhaktivedanta Marg) was totally congested. Traffic was barely moving, and horns honked everywhere.

The rickshaw turned off the main street into the warren of alleys constituting the old original Vrindavan. We moved slowly through alleys clogged with pedestrians. We then reached the parikrama path, and turned into a normal street congested with traffic. This is where the rickshaw wallah dropped us off. He said he could go no further because of the congestion.

We walked along the Yamuna, with the river on our left, holding our luggage. Then the street stopped and turned into a rutted path strewn with rocks and clogged with people, rickshaws, and motorcycles. We slowly moved up the path into an old neighborhood of narrow streets surrounded by very old buildings, many in severe disrepair. We reached the Jai Singh Ghera entrance, a massive medieval gate made of wood and studded with metal bands. A narrow pedestrian door was cut into the gate. We knocked and the chowkidar let us in. We were met by Srivatsaji's assistant Sri Upadhyaya, who took us to our room. We appeared to be the only guests in the compound. It is square with buildings on all four sides. The buildings are relatively new and appear somewhat modern, the square, cinderblock and cement construction found all over India.

In the center of the compound is a lovely green lawn ringed by trees and shrubs. A driveway leads from the gate to the main building, which is five stories tall. This is the center of the ashram. Here, on the bottom floor is the auditorium where Ras Lila plays are performed. In the back are the prasadam hall, kitchen and servants' quarters. This being India, there are no seats in the theatre, as everyone sits on the floor. The administrative offices, including Sri Upadhyaya's office is up a staircase to the right of the stage on the second floor.

The kitchen is traditional Indian. When the ashram is full, cooks make large pots of vegetarian food over cooking fires. This is where we would take our meals during our stay. Since we were the only two guests in this entire huge compound, we had the servants to ourselves. The cook made us as much prasad as we wanted, and we were waited on by a local woman, who was quite talkative. While this is an active ashram, it is not in session and there are no activities scheduled. There are therefore no prayers before the meal.

On the left is an old temple in a sad state of disrepair. It is not part of our property, but is separated by a high wall from the compound. On the right are a high wall and the personal gardens of the Goswami family. The back wall of the compound is made up of the family residence, about three stories tall, and more residential rooms. Our room was in that building. There were easily 70 rooms in the compound, which are usually occupied by groups from all over the world who come to study Bhakti yoga in the holy dham.

The Hindu month of Kartik is the most auspicious time to come to Vrindavan. Pilgrims flood into Vrindavan during Kartik to make their pilgrimage at the most auspicious time. We had arrived just before the beginning of Kartik. The weather was pleasant enough, although it was still hot in the afternoons. Everything in Vrindavan shuts down in the heat of the afternoon. Everyone stops where they are and takes a nap, with shopkeepers sound asleep on the floor of their stalls. The streets are empty.

We were given room number 108, the most auspicious number to Vaishnavas. I never learned if this is something that Srivatsa Goswami had done intentionally or it was a matter of serendipity. I suspect that it was the latter. Nevertheless, my mind harkened back to what Kesava Maharaj had said, "There are no coincidences." We unpacked our luggage and rested in our room. It was hot and humid. A temple servant came and delivered a bottle of water, which we eagerly consumed. We would continue to drink at least four liters of water per day.

Goswamiji then knocked on the door. It was great to see him again. He looked the same as ever, with a broad smile on his face. He explained that he was unable to meet with us earlier, as it was dussehra (a major Hindu holiday) and he was conducting pujas. This explained why the town was so full of people. Goswamiji had to leave us again, so we went to the local bazaar just around the corner from Jai Singh Ghera to complete some errands.

At 2100, a servant took us to the prasadam hall for dinner. It was similar to the fare at Govardhan, except we ate out of a metal tray and were allowed to use a spoon. Jai Singh Ghera is not a temple or a monastery. There is no temple program. This means we will not wake up at 0400 unless we want to, but will have to conduct pujas in some of the 5,000 temples of Vrindavan. I determine to construct my own temple program.

Vrindavan Tirtha Yatra

I felt guilty today because I got up late (0530). William wanted to go to the banks of the Yamuna to take pictures. The sun was already up. We joked with the boatmen. Their boats were tethered at the bank while they were off looking for customers. They insisted we hire them for rides along the river. They were gentle but insistent in a brijabasi way. While we were eager to take a traditional Vrindavan boat ride, we told them we would look them up later.

William had worn his glasses. A monkey jumped on him and grabbed them from his face. William was going to chase the monkey, who had jumped onto a nearby shrine with the glasses in his hand. Immediately, a group of young men ran to William and offered to retrieve his glasses for 1,000 rupees ($16.70). They told him it would be fruitless for him to try. William agreed and handed them the money. One lad took a bag of snacks, opened it, and handed it to the monkey. The others climbed up on the roof of the building. When the monkey dropped the glasses to eat the snacks, the boys quickly grabbed them and gave them back to William.

William was convinced that the monkey was in cahoots with the young men and shared in the profits. I laughed and said this was just one episode of the William Laray pastimes in Vrindavan.

We had very simple breakfast prasadam, *cholle* (chickpeas) with tea. The rule regarding conduct in the holy dham states that any intoxicant is forbidden, including tea, coffee, and coke. In ISKCON parlance, to drink tea while in the holy dham would be considered an "offense" (*aparadh*). The doctrine is that any pious act committed inside the holy dham is magnified 1,000 times, but the same is true for offenses. While drinking tea is a relatively minor offense, having sex while in the holy dham is the most offensive. Srivatsa Goswami told us he did not agree with the ruling against tea drinking and that he, as our Goswami, gave his permission for us to drink tea in Vrindavan without any ill effects. I could tell that we were not inside an ISKCON ashram any longer.

After *prasadam*, we walked to the bazaar so William could buy some plastic chappals. He needed them, as he could not wear expensive American Tevas that could be stolen while he was inside temples, and they took far too long to take on and off. He had another Indian shopping experience. We found the shop of the *chappal wallah*, and it was open. It was just a narrow space five or six feet wide, with a small bench to try on the shoes. Boxes of *chappals* were stacked against the opposite wall. We negotiated at length, and William tried on several pairs before he found the ones he liked. As he departed India, William gave them to me. They are blue with the word "flite" written along the side. I used them for the remainder of my India trip. They are extremely practical and I now wear them when I go swimming. He must have spent around $1.50 for them.

I tried to get cash at the ATM, but the machine was empty. Others in line said it was the same at every ATM in town. This was because the town was full of people celebrating dussehra. I would realize later that Vrindavan is not just a Vaishnava pilgrimage site; it is a tourist attraction (at least for Indians). Indians who have no interest in Vaishnavism and are not part of the tradition come to do a puja, eat, and buy souvenirs on three day weekends. The increasing numbers of private automobiles and new highways make it possible for tourists to drive here for a day trip and get back to their homes in Delhi, or Haryana the same day.

Our first stop was the Radha Madana Mohan temple built by Sanatan Goswami. He was one of the six Goswamis of Vrindavan, one of the most senior, and one of the most austere. Among the first Goswamis to arrive in Vrindavan, he came at a time when there were no temples. He lived simply under a tree and cared for his personal deity. He continually prayed to Lord Krishna to provide a temple for his deity so he could be worshipped properly.

One day, a barge loaded with salt beached on the bank beneath the hill and could not be moved. The rich merchant transporting the salt said his entire fortune was invested in the shipment. He begged Sanatan Goswami to help him. Sanatan Goswami implored Krishna to intervene, the water level rose and the barge was freed from the sand bank. The merchant was so grateful that he promised to provide Sanatan Goswami with a large donation after he had gone to Agra and sold the shipment. He was true to his word and Sanatan Goswami used that money to start construction of the Madana Mohan Temple.

We travelled through the narrow streets and alleyways and up a long flight of steps to the top of the hill and the temple entrance. It provides an expansive vista of the Yamuna River and the countryside on the opposite bank from Vrindavan. The temple has two spires (*shikaras*). The old temple on the right is completely shut. The new temple is under the larger spire on the left. It is a simple altar with an installed deity and priest. Both the priest and the devotees were Bengali (as were the deities) and were engrossed in a lively Bengali conversation. I waited patiently until the talk concluded so I could receive proper *darshan* of the deities and do my *pranams* with *dandavat*.

We walked around the temple to the back. There, off to the side on a lower plateau hidden within a growth of old trees was the actual *kutir* of Sanatan Goswami. This was where the Goswamiji lived out his austere life. It was far more spiritually powerful than the temple. It was a quiet, serene location befitting one of the greatest Goswamis. The *kutirs* of the Goswamis are shrines in their own right and similar to temples, although the buildings themselves are most humble. The structures are square huts with grills that can be opened. They often contain simple items commemorating the Goswami and a picture of him. Sometimes the room contains a yellow shawls emblazoned with the Hare Krishna Mantra (*Hare Namer Chaddar*) symbolizing the presence of the Goswami.

Many holy sites prohibit photography. This is entirely understandable, as the priests want to preserve the sanctity of the location. William and I respected such prohibitions and did not take pictures. This was one such site.

From the Goswami's kutir, I could see his Samadhi (tomb) below, adjoining the parikrama path. We walked through more alleys to get to the entrance.

It was a pleasant surprise. The samadhi was being restored, with workmen working at the site. There was such restoration work going on all over Vrindavan. India's new prosperity and the donations from Western devotees were being put to good use. When Vrindavan was relatively unknown, it was difficult to find funds for much-needed maintenance. The work of Srila Prabhupad and his contemporaries have put Vrindavan back on the map, renewing Indian interest in this pilgrimage center. Middle class Indians who formerly would have ignored places like Vrindavan in their rush to embrace modernity, were now proudly returning to their culture, coming to Vrindavan and making donations for restoration of holy sites.

We were the only people at the Samadhi, except for one other devotee. The restoration job was beautifully done and the building immaculate and pristine. The pujari was kindly and gentle, and let us take as many pictures as we liked.

We then tried to see the Banke Bihari Temple, but as we got closer, the crowds grew larger, and the narrow streets were jammed with people. We had to squeeze through crowds to make slow progress. The temple was so crowded that we decided to come back after the dussehra crowds depart. The city will empty out on Monday (the day after tomorrow).

We took a cycle rickshaw back to Jai Singh Ghera. The rickshaw wallah took us through the crowds, then through the traffic on the parikrama path. At the spot where the street ends and becomes a rocky path, we bounced in the rickshaw. We told the driver to stop and we walked the rest of the way.

We ate noon prasad, took a nap, and ventured out again as the sun was setting. We went back to the Yamuna banks. The sun was a beautiful orange disk in the hazy sky.

175

While William took pictures, I talked to an Italian devotee. He told me he joined ISKCON as a young man in Switzerland, but was never initiated, dropped out of ISKCON, and was initiated into the Gaudiya Math sect. But said he became disenchanted with the Gaudiya Math, as it suffers from "skin disease."[62] This Gaudiya Vaishnava sect, he complained, repeatedly states that only Indians can be true Vaishnavas, and treat Western devotees like himself as second class citizens.

The man was a great admirer of the Pope and Radhanath Swami, an ISKCON guru, who resides in Mumbai and is in charge of the enormous ISKCON temple there. My Italian friend told me that he goes to Mumbai for two weeks every year for association with Radhanath Swami, and acts as Radhanath's translator whenever he comes to Italy. The devotee was effusive in his praise for Radhanath Swami, saying he was the "real deal," and a "genuine saint." Radhanath loves me," he said, "and I love him."

Sadly, the Italian cannot take initiation from Radhanath, as two initiations are not allowed. He described Prabhupad as the crown jewel of Vaishnava acharyas, and asserted that Radhanath enjoys a growing reputation for saintliness. He noted that Radhanath has assembled a group of Brahmacaris around him that are the essence of goodness, and called Radhanath the personification of humility. While my informant was enamored with Radhanath, the ISKCON leader has plenty of enemies who attack him on the internet, accusing him of all manner of *aparadh*. I have never met Radhanath. I have only read his two books and read about him in others, but I have no reason to be judgmental, and scrupulously avoid ISKCON's political squabbles.

After leaving the beach, we tried to visit several more temples, but they were packed with people. We located the Radha Ramana Temple, our "home temple." Srivatsa Goswami is a member of the extended Goswami family that has administered the Radha Ramana Temple, taken care of the deity and performed pujas there for five centuries. Only the Brahmin members of this extended family can serve as pujaris in the Radha Ramana Temple and come into direct contact with the Radha Ramana deity. As guests of Srivatsa Goswami, we are attached to him, his family and the temple.

With night descending, we visited two neighborhood temples. These were built for the local people and had no particular religious or historical significance. They were both quiet and friendly. They had the special brijabasi atmosphere. They were totally integrated into their communities, and people from the neighborhood came to spend time there and make spiritual progress. Both the pujaris and the worshippers were kind and friendly. We were free to sit quietly on the floor,

---

[62] This is a phrase used by Srila Prabhupad. He said that those who differentiate between people because of their outward appearance, rather than considering everyone as spirit soul, were suffering from "skin disease."

perform our worship as we wished, and spend as long as we like. Neighbors sat in the temple conversing in low voices.

When in the holy *dham*, one should attend a minimum of two *aaratis* per day. Since we are surrounded by 5,000 temples, including the temples of the six Goswamis, and are directly associated with the Radha Ramana Temple, we plan to take advantage of this opportunity to fulfill our duty.

Dream Diary Interval

I thought there was a possibility that I would have dreams of a spiritual nature on this *yatra*. However, this has not proved to be the case so far. I had a quasi-spiritual dream involving Kesava Maharaj on my first night. Since then, I have drawn a blank.

Last night I had a very vivid dream. I was living "back East." It could have been Highland falls, that nondescript town outside the United States Military Academy at West Point. I had a nondescript office job, the kind with ill-defined duties and few accomplishments, but I was desperate to hold on to it. I had taken the job to resolve some issues regarding my daughter, which had long concluded. It was a temporary job, but was always being extended. We had a new boss and held an office party for him. He came in. Three of us were standing in a line. He went down the line. "We are taking back your medal," he said to the man standing next to me, who appeared to be mentally defective. He then turned to me and said, "Your training course has been cancelled," and laughed. "Don't you have a job of your own?" Then I realized that yes, I did have a job of my own. "I work for the University of Arizona," I replied, and started making plans to return.

At first, upon awakening, I thought this was a standard post-retirement dream about adjusting to changed circumstances, and longing for the previous reliability of a nine to five job. But now, I realize that this dream has a spiritual aspect.

I am reading the *Bhagavad Gita*. In it Sri Krishna tells Arjuna about detachment. He says that without the acquisition and practice of detachment, it is impossible to make spiritual progress. This dream is a sign of a lack of detachment. When true detachment is achieved, all such dreams disappear.

The very next day, I awakened from a similar dream. I had the same type of job in a different locale. This time I was cheerful and helpful and free of anxiety. I was friendly and popular with the others in the office.

Does this mean that my *sadhana* (spiritual practice) is having an effect, and that I am absorbing the lesson of the *Bhagavad Gita* regarding detachment?

At first I said "yes," but on second thought, in the dream I still have the job, and I am still having the dreams. To bring this series of dreams to closure, I need to quit the job while still in the dream. That is true detachment.

Vrindavan Tirtha Yatra

Vrindavan is still crowded and I feel our access to important temples is being denied by the crowds. Luckily, we will be living here for some time and can take advantage of that to select proper times for visits. This allows us to spend time at temples and other sacred spots when there are not hordes of people there. Luckily, William has fun ideas about what to do until the crowds depart.

This morning we got up early and went back to the Yamuna banks while the sun was still rising and the world was wrapped in a hazy light. We witnessed the wake-up routines going on all around us. People dressing, and bathing and farmers crossing the river in ferries with big baskets of produce on their heads to take to market.

At my suggestion, we took to the parikrama path in the proper clockwise position. Large groups of *parikramis* set off along the path with us. It wound through a series of old abandoned buildings built during the Mughul period. These were built to house pilgrims who had come to the Yamuna for their *snans* (holy baths). They contained long steps leading into the Yamuna. However, the river had since shifted and the steps now just led down into mud. Sadhus camped out on various ledges, begging from the *parikramis*. Makeshift temples were set up in some abandoned rooms. A large population of monkeys trailed the people on the path, hoping for scraps or a chance to snatch a morsel from the hand of some unaware pilgrim. The monkeys are a parallel society that lives beside us and interacts with us but has its own rules, hierarchies and concerns.

The buildings came to an abrupt end where a small temple had been erected with a signboard that read in English "Yamuna Tample." An ever present loudspeaker boomed in the background, and the sand plain along the river stretched out before us.

Boats were parked along the riverbank, with ferries going back and forth carrying people to their jobs and to market. Along the bank the usual assortment of sadhus were begging. Some were applying *tilak* (clay) markings along their body to get ready for the day.

A large group of bathers, both male and female were in various stages of undress. They were taking a holy dip in the Yamuna and getting clean (although the water was totally polluted). A woman stood in the river brushing her teeth. Although this is a puritanical society, very condemning of public nudity, especially female, women bathed topless and changed their clothes openly (but discretely). Everyone, especially males, politely averted their eyes.

We walked back along the parikrama path, but were swimming against the current of oncoming *padayatris*. We thus took a detour into the narrow alleys lined with buildings hundreds of years old in Mughul/Rajasthani style.

We came to a spot where water was falling off of a roof onto the street below in a steady stream. The water made a lonely sound as it fell on the stones of the pavement. The roof sported a family of green parrots.

This building faced a perfectly preserved temple over 400 years old. It was shut up and there was no indication how long it had been closed. Neighbors lounging on a charpoy in front of the temple, told us it was totally empty. Built entirely of sandstone, it had beautifully carved decorative motifs along its walls.

The narrow alleys were quiet and serene after the hubbub of the parikrama path, and we returned to Jai Singh Ghera quickly.

After a short rest, we set off to visit the Nidhivan. This is a grove of Tulsi trees surrounded by a high wall. It is a site of the rasa dance performed by Lord Krishna, Radharani, and the Gopis. Since the dance takes place every night, the walls are shut and the gates locked and no one is allowed inside. The Nidhivan is surrounded by high walls. Anyone who ventures into the Nidhivan at night hoping to join Lord Krishna and the Gopis in the Rasa dance, will quickly go mad and die. Although this is common knowledge, priests and locals told me that several men scale the walls and venture inside every year, and are always found dead in the morning.

Usually this spot is peaceful, but today it too is filled with day trippers from Haryana, and Delhi. They were not in a devotional mood, and were loudly laughing, joking, and shouting, and taking endless selfies and family shots with their cellphones. While William got the general idea, the *rasa* (devotional mood) was spoiled by the tourists. Some religious group conducted a raucous kirtan in a building constructed at the site since my last visit. They used a loudspeaker turned to maximum volume. The high volume distorted the sound and flooded the enclosed space with high decibel noise. We planned to return when Nidhivan was less crowded and more peaceful.

After lunch, we took a nap, waiting for the sun to begin to descend and the temperature to drop. We walked along the parikrama path to Radha Madana Mohana Temple to take pictures in the special light of dusk.

It was a quiet walk. The crowds of the previous day were absent, and we made it to Sanatan Goswami's Samadhi very quickly. A family was singing *bhajan* (religious songs) in front of the Samadhi. The sound of the bhajan, allowed me to more readily focus on my *japa* and gain the benefit of spiritual practice in a holy place.

Afterwards, we went to the Madana Mohana Temple, paid our obsceiences to the deities, and William started snapping pictures. I went to the *kutir* of Sanatan Goswami, a particularly spiritual spot, to perform more japa, but the priests had a speaker outside and were playing Bengali bhajans. I decided it would be better to perform japa while doing parikrama around the *kutir*. I started to do so and a

179

priest noticed I was holding the japa bag incorrectly. He stopped me and showed me the proper method. I yelled "Hari Bol!" and thanked him in Bengali.

When several groups of Bengali pilgrims arrived for darshan, it became too crowded. I retired to the lawns outside to continue. I completed one round, but towards the end, noticed a loud cacophony of blowing car horns emanating from the street at the bottom of the hill. I went to the pavilion overlooking the street to see what was happening. William was snapping pictures. A traffic jam stretched several blocks in both directions. "It seems all the tourists have decided to leave town at once," said William.

The sunset was beautiful, an orange ring in the hazy sky that slowly sunk beneath the horizon. It outlined the *shikaras* of the nearby temples and reflected off the water of the holy Yamuna. As the sun went down, the moon came up between the two *shikaras* of the Madana Mohana Temple, and increased in brightness as the sky grew dark.

We determined that the only viable way back to Jai Singh Ghera was through the traffic jam, as all paths were blocked by mobs of people. A rickshaw was out of the question. We began our walk through the throngs of people. After a few blocks, the jam disappeared, and the parikrama path was quiet and normal again. The jam was caused by crowds of tourists rushing to the Banke Bihari Temple to attend the evening *aarati* before departing back home.

Vrindavan Tirtha Yatra

Today was packed with activity. As we get adjusted to our surroundings and learn to navigate around Vrindavan, it becomes easier to reach the holy sites. We are beginning to get our bearings and determine where everything is. We got up at 0530 and made a pre-breakfast exploratory venture. We had been going to the river bank. Now we began to explore the interior of the town.

Our plan was to go to the Radharaman Temple for a morning puja and on to Nidhivan. The temple was closed and would not open until 0900. Nidhivan was open. We hoped to experience it in quiet, but there were loudspeakers blaring and was still crowded. At the Rang Mahal, (the spot where Radha prepares for Her nightly rasa dance with Lord Krishna and retires to rest), the priest tried to explain the daily miracle. Every night, he and other priests leave jewelry and cosmetics for Radharani on the bed inside the Rang Mahal. These are for Radharani's use during her rest after performing the rasa dance. Each night the priests lock the five locks on the door of the Rang Mahal. The priest swung the door open and showed the locks to us. Each night, the priests ensure that the Rang Mahal is sealed and all five locks locked before departing for the night. Nidhivan itself is surrounded by a high wall and the gates are closed and locked. Every morning when they open the door, the priests find the cosmetics have been used and the clothing worn.

We leave Nidhivan and move on to our 1100 appointment at ISKCON's Krishna Balarama temple. Upon arrival, we were guided to Dharamatma's office. He was very embarrassed because he had forgotten our appointment. He invited us to come tomorrow to Prabhupad's residence for a private tour of the museum. In the evening, he said, they move Prabhupad's statue to his garden, with mahaprasad afterwards.

Since we were already in the temple premises, we attended aarati. The temple is clad in white marble and open to the sky, with three huge altars. Krishna Balarama Temple is famous for its beautiful altars and deities and high standard of worship. A party performed *kirtan* in front of the altars. Each altar had its own *pujari* conducting the worship. Instead of the melodic prayers we sang in Govardhan, the devotees conducted ecstatic Hare Krishna *sankirtana*. The space in front of the altars was packed, so the *pujaris* could not share the *aarati* elements with us.

It was far too raucous for me, as I am currently in a contemplative devotional mood. This does not mean that I am not capable of enjoying this type of *kirtan* and fully participating in it. I have fond memories of such kirtans during my stay at the ISKCON temple in Mayapur, West Bengal, and during the Braj Padayatra.

After finishing the *aarati*, we took a motor rickshaw back to Kesi Ghat, and walked to our Radharaman temple for the evening aarati. We waited about 30 minutes for the *aarati* to begin. A pundit asked us and a family from Kanpur to sit with him in the raised alcove at the rear of the temple. I was performing japa, but the pundit wanted to talk. He could not believe I was not Indian (we were conversing in Hindi). He thought I was a Non Resident Indian (NRI) from Delhi temporarily resident in the USA. The girl from Kanpur tried to set him straight, telling him several times I was 100% American, but he could not accept it.

The curtains opened giving us darshan of the Radha Ramana deity. This self-manifested deity appeared to Gopala Bhatta Goswami. The deity is very small, about 18 inches in height. He is usually kept on a silver multi-tiered altar that can be moved. He is alone. There has never been a Radha deity to accompany him. Instead, Radha is represented by a small crown kept beside the deity. Unlike most other temples, there is nothing present on the altar, and Radha Ramana is the sole focus of attention. He is made of jet black stone, with mischievous eyes and a grin on his face.

There were few worshippers present. I was in front with a clear view of the deity. The worshipper beside me was the same woman from the Kanpur family who failed to convince the pundit that I was not Indian. She stood totally enraptured by Radha Ramana. I could tell she had a strong relationship with Him and was making a heartfelt request.

The *aarati* was short, only 15 minutes, and the curtains were closed. We then went around the corner to the Samadhi of Gopala Bhatta Goswami. There were only three or four other worshippers there. We paid our obsceiences, and conducted *parikrama*. A side window provided a clear view of the inside of the *Samadhi*. In the rear of the room was an altar containing *shilas*, Jagannath deities, and a small set of Radha Krishna deities.

With evening approaching, we went to the Yamuna riverbank and contracted with a boatman to take a ride on the river. He was pleasant and we had good conversations with him. While we drifted down the Yamuna, the sun began to go down and the moon came out. The boatman propelled the boat with a pole. At several points, he allowed the boat to drift. During these intervals, there was no sound except the water lapping the sides of the boat as it drifted slowly down the river. We drifted by water buffalo bathing. A teenage girl herded cattle into the river. She was taking the herd back home after spending the day grazing them on the other side of the Yamuna. I thought she could be a Gopi that sported with Lord Krishna. Vaishnava literature asserts that the cowherd girls of Braj can be the original Gopis, the eternal companions of Krishna and Radharani, who have descended from the spiritual sky to spend time in the earthly Vrindavan.

After it got dark, we encountered several boats conducting *"diwa puja."* They released 108 clay lamps into the water. The lamps flickered against the dark water as we drifted slowly back to conclude our ride.

Vrindavana Tirtha Yatra

This morning I was on the porch performing japa when Srivatsaji and his wife came by on their morning walk. He stopped, greeted us and asked if we could join him for breakfast at 0900. Upon our arrival, Goswamiji took us to the front verandah for conversation and breakfast. I then asked whether we could extend our stay, saying I did not want to impose. He laughed and said, "You can stay as long as you like, and you don't even have to ask."

William, Goswamiji and I spoke for about three hours on a variety of subjects. He spoke about the significance of Lord Krishna from a scientific/modern perspective. He pointed out that Krishna may have saved Hinduism from dying out. The Brahminical faith had become tyrannical and obsessed with wealth and exploitation. The priestly class was using the faith to exploit believers.

Krishna introduced the concept of Bhakti, which has three elements:

A) Everyone has a need to serve something or someone (*dasya*)

B) Relationships are what provide meaning to life and allow us to survive.

C) Service should be selfless. The reason it is selfless is that it is based on love.

This breathed new life into Hinduism, by providing the common man with a hopeful and solid way to deal with the world. Sri Chaitanya then later spread

Bhakti and further enlivened Hinduism by stating that everyone could freely participate in the love of God regardless of their caste or religion (both low caste Hindus, and Muslims joined the Chaitanya movement and rose to become intimate associates of Sri Chaitanya, including several of the six Goswamis).

The *Krishna Lila*[63] reflects the inter-relatedness between man and God in the light of Bhakti. Instead of fruitive pujas to Vedic gods, Krishna told the brijabasis to worship nature (especially when he told them to stop performing the puja to Indra and worship Govardhan Hill instead). This made the Govardhana story the most significant of Krishna's Lila.

Likewise, the series of demons Krishna defeats in His Lila represents the polluting forces making life unbearable in Braj. Krishna demonstrated that man could reverse environmental degradation to maintain and sustain a naturally pure environment on earth (transporting Goloka Vrindavana to Earth).

Srivatsaji said that the Vaishnava literature (and religious literature in general) is suffused with hyperbole. That is because there are no restraints on religious writing. Goloka Vrindavana, as described in the scriptures, represents the profound desires of poor, agrarian people, when all limits are removed. The emphases are agrarian, on the number of cows owned by Lord Krishna (He was responding to my question as to how we should react when we read the statement in the Vaishnava scriptures that Lord Krishna as a cowherd boy took 900,000 cattle out to graze every day).

Srivatsaji did not address the relationship between Lord Krishna and Radha, the rasa dance, or the significance of conjugal love, as defined and expanded by Sri Chaitanya. This just as well, as I prefer to follow Srila Prabhupad's dictates and avoid such topics until I feel ready to discuss them.

In response to my question regarding proper behavior in the holy dham and my mention of our previous lesson in Govardhan regarding the hellish planets and the results of immoral conduct, Srivatsaji stated that the concept of the 27 hellish plants (as expounded in the *Srimad Bhagavatam*), is a narrow minded one. He laughed, saying, "ISKCON wants to send me to hell for drinking tea in the holy dham."

In the evening, we went back to the ISKCON temple for our rescheduled appointment with Dharamatma das. He showed us Prabhupad's rooms (one of Dharamatma's duties is to manage the museum). He took us to the spot where Prabhupad left his body. There was a bed there, but it was not the original one which Prabhupad used. Dharamatma then took us to the garden in which

---

[63] The Sanskrit word "lila" literally means "play," for God is playful and has a good sense of humor. It is sometimes translated at "pastime," such as an amusing way to spend the day.

Prabhupad sat and chanted japa. It was moving to see everything and remember Prabhupad. I felt particularly moved to see his *sannyasi danda*.

Vrindavan Tirtha Yatra

Today was devoted to Sri Damodara Mandir and Seva Kunja. We did not have breakfast this morning. Instead, we set out early in the soft light of the dawning day. We went to our own Radha Ramana Mandir for early morning *aarati* at 0800. I stopped afterwards at the room where the Radha Ramana deity self-manifested. There is a wonderful little altar there and a masonry column (*sthala*) decorated with elaborate carvings. We took some pictures outside the Samadhi of Sri Gopala Bhatta Goswami. While shooting the pictures, monkeys grabbed Prasad from my hand.

Afterwards, we walked through Vrindavan to Seva Kunja. This and Nidhivan are the sites of the Radha Krishna Ras Lila, the rasa dance between Sri Krishna, Srimati Radharani, and the Gopis. Seva Kunj, like Nidhi Van, is a grove of Tulasi trees surrounded by a high wall and/or buildings. It has the appearance of an urban park. The Tulasi is a scrub tree that clings to the ground, more like a bush than a tree, so the area gives the appearance of a field covered by bushes. Various shrines are built among the Tulasi trees. The focal point of the Seva Kunj is a platform made of white stone with a small bench/altar on one side. Vaishnavas believe this is the spot where Sri Krishna, Srimati Radharani and the Gopis dance the rasa dance every night.

There is a parikrama path around the edge of the entire Seva Kunj. Due to the monkey menace, it is covered by chain link fencing and a roof. Our Bengali guide was named Putara. He was mentally handicapped and only capable of limited conversation in Hindi or Bengali, but totally devoted to Radha and Krishna. He carried a short stick to protect us from monkey attacks. He opened the gates for us, allowing us to wander out amidst the Tulasi grove and visit the sacred sites scattered there.

Kunja means grove, and at intervals there were water pipes set in marble that watered the plants. The atmosphere at Seva Kunja was different than at Nidhi Van. There were far fewer people. When we visited a location with few visitors, they were invariably Bengali. Vrindavan is the most sacred pilgrimage city to members of the Bengali Gaudiya Vaishnava sects, and they take Vrindavan more seriously than many Hindi speaking pilgrims/tourists. Bengali pilgrims are also more knowledgeable. Our hosts told us that Bengali pilgrims take many weeks to visit every sacred location in Vrindavan and spend time there in contemplation and performing japa.

Putara was too simple to tell us more than a few words about each place we stopped, although I tried speaking to him in both Hindi and Bengali.

184

We first had darshan of the Radha Krishna deities at the Ranga Mahal. This small temple is built on the spot where Krishna braided flowers into Radharani's hair while they rested after completing the Rasa Dance.

We walked through Tulasi trees in our bare feet to the white marble platform marking the precise spot where the Rasa Dance takes place. The Seva Kunj is covered with fine dust that massages our bare feet. The entire Vrindavan parikrama once consisted of this wonderful "dust of Vrindavan," making it heavenly to perform parikrama. In those now bygone days, it would have been possible to spend the entire pilgrimage barefoot. We paid our obsceiences at the spot. A monkey sat on the steps of the empty altar. He put a washcloth over his head. It was appeared to be imitating the Gopis resting after the Rasa Dance. Maybe he was imitating the actions of the Gopis that he witnesses dancing in the holy grove every night when no human beings are present.

Other monkey dived off the bushes into pools of water and splashed like children playing in a swimming pool.

Our final stop was a building we thought was a Samadhi. It was not. It marked the spot where Sri Chaitanya Mahaprabhu stopped to appreciate Seva Kunj during his tour of Vrindavan. Inside the small white marble building was a block of marble marked with simple carved footprints, signifying the footprints of Sri Chaitanya. Putara opened the gate and allowed us inside to pay our respects.

We then moved to the Radha Damodara Temple just around the corner. We arrived just as aarati was concluding. Worshippers crowded in front of the deities for darshan. There are six separate deities on the altar – five pairs of Radha/Krishna, one statue of Lalita Sakhi (one of the Gopis closest to Srimati Radharani), and a Govardhana Shila that once belonged to Sri Chaitanya Mahaprabhu, and contains his thumbprint. We could not stand long enough at the darshan railing to get an adequate impression of the various deities, which belonged to various Goswamis and other holy personalities. I had to rely on a picture of the altar in the ISKCON guidebook to understand the deities and their meanings.

After the priests closed the curtains, we visited the samadhis within the temple grounds and paid our respects. We particularly wanted to see samadhis of famous persons known intimately to us. To the left of the altar are the Samadhis of Jiva Goswami and Krishna Kaviraj (the author of *Chaitanya Charitamrta* – the spiritual biography of Srila Chaitanya Mahaprabhu). There is a parikrama path that takes the worshipper behind the altar and through the samadhis on both sides. It is traditional to make this parikrama five times after the conclusion of the *aarati*.

For years I have been coming to this temple, but the physical structure has changed. This is because the temple courtyard has been covered with a concrete building. Previously it had been open. This inhibits the spiritual atmosphere. I remember how powerful it was to come to this temple at night and sit in front of the samadhis in the moonlight, with a blanket of stars overhead. Now, the scene is dominated by ugly concrete and bright electric lights. This decision was taken not in malice, but rather to protect worshippers from the growing monkey menace. There is a stark contrast between the Samadhi of Sanatan Goswami at Madana Mohan and these Samadhis because Madana Mohan retains its traditional openness.

When facing the altar, off to the right is the kutir and Samadhi of Rupa Goswami, one of the initial founding Goswamis of Vrindavan. The six Goswamis of Vrindavan were intimate disciples of Sri Chaitanya Mahaprabhu and were instructed by Chaitanya to establish the holy dham in Vrindavan and compile the essential scriptures of Gaudiya Vaishnavism. They were exceptional in every way, as they were ascetic devotees and great scholars. The six Goswamis include:

Rupa Goswami – Associated with the Radha Damodara Temple

His brother – Sanatan Goswami – founder of the Madana Mohan Temple

Their Nephew Jiva Goswami – Associated with the Radha Damodara Temple

Raghunatha Bhatta – The founder of the Radha Govinda Temple, renowned for his scholarship

Raghunatha dasa Goswami - who established his kutir at Radha Kunda

Gopala Bhatta Goswami – the founder of Radha Ramana Temple

All were Bengalis except for Gopal Bhatta Goswami, who came from South India. All were from aristocratic backgrounds and highly educated. They renounced their wealth and status to live in Vrindavan at a time when it was a virtual jungle. Originally, Rupa and Sanatan Goswami were accompanied by their brother Anupama, but after he died during the long a perilous journey from Bengal to Vrindavan, his son took his place. Anupama's son later became Jiva Goswami.

Directly off to the right of the altar are the rooms of Srila Prabhupad. Prabhupad took sannyasi in 1959 while living in Vrindavan. He remained in Vrindavan for the next six years, until he departed for the United States in 1964. He lived in two rooms at Radha Damodara Temple. He used one for his study and kutir and the other as his kitchen. He stayed in the same rooms when he returned to Vrindavan with western disciples in 1967.

ISKCON and the Temple administration now maintain both rooms as shrines to Srila Prabhupad. Prasad is prepared in the kitchen, so it was closed to visitors. Prabhupad's kutir is a simple room, with a string cot (*charpoy*) and Indian furniture. The walls are decorated with pictures of the room as it looked then, showing Prabhupad interacting with friends and fellow devotees. It was quiet and still. Various devotees from around the world sat quietly in the room soaking up the atmosphere. We did the same for some time before departing.

We then walked back to Jai Singh Ghera through Loi Bazaar, Vrindaban's principal bazaar and the principal location for buying goods used in worship and devotion. Our caretakers at Jai Singh Ghera were Sri Upadhayaji, who manages the facility for the Goswami family, and Arvind Kumar Verma, who has only recently been taken on to help Upadhayaji. Arvind is a young man just learning the ropes. He is not from Vrindavan, not familiar with the city and its traditions, and cannot speak the local dialect. He comes from Ghaziabad, a district of Uttar Pradesh with a large Muslim population, where Hindustani and Urdu are common, rather than the Brijabasi dialect and pure Hindi preferred in the overwhelmingly Hindu braj region.

William suggested we ask our hosts to find us a taxi, rather than running from pillar to post looking all over Vrindavan. I asked them about this. They took down all the details regarding our departure for Agra on October 15, and said they would arrange for us to go at 0800.

After our naps, we returned to Radha Damodara for the complete aarati. It was a loud and raucous affair, with lots of clanging bells, cymbals, drums, a loudspeaker, flaming wicks, and fire. It went on for about 30 minutes, ending with an ecstatic kirtan. It was joyous. After the aarati, we circumambulated the altar area three times, passing through the rows of Samadhis. I paid final respects at the Samadhi of Rupa Goswami before departing.

Vrindavan Tirtha Yatra

Although William was sick today, and unable to participate in the morning, I got a lot done. We are just about finished with our darshan of the major temples of Vrindavan. There are seven temples in this category, six associated with the six Goswamis and one with the Vaishnava Saint Prabhu Sri Sri Shyamananda.

William stayed in our room to recover. I set off to see Shahji Temple, Mirabai Temple, and the Radha Shyam Sundar Temple. Shahji was my first stop. I arrived several minutes before the temple gates opened and sat in the courtyard to perform japa, but a monkey started tugging at my *hare naamer chador*, so I got up and stood in the middle of the courtyard, far away from any spot where monkeys could get to me. Despite my caution, a monkey leapt over my shoulder, grabbed my chador and jumped on a nearby roof. There, he slowly tore the garment to shreds. This was a simple cotton chador in a traditional style. Unlike chadors sold in Loi Bazaar, it was not mass-produced in a factory, but made by hand by devotees in Mayapur, West Bengal. I had picked up this chador during my stay there and had used it ever since.

Its destruction put me in a bad mood. But then I thought about detachment and the *Bhagavad Gita.* Maybe I was getting too attached to that chador (its monetary value was probably $4), and the Lord used the monkey to teach me a lesson.

I then went to the temple for aarati. The priest insisted I buy a garland from them for the puja and became angry when I declined. When I tried to snap a picture, he yelled at me like I was one of the monkeys. The temple looked more like a home puja room than a proper temple. There were only a small set of Radha/Krishna deities on a tiny altar, and a single priest.

This temple is not particularly old. It was built in the 19th Century by a wealthy businessman from Lucknow and reflects the tastes of the time (garish). It is one of the only Vrindavan temples to be all white. It is a long, single story temple built on a raised platform over a courtyard. It is decorated along the rooftop with odd sculptures that apparently were some Indian sculptor's idea of classical Greek depictions of Indian themes. The sculptures are so poorly done, that the building is embarrassing.

I left and went around the corner to the Mirabai temple. Although not part of the Gaudiya Vaishnava tradition, Mirabai (1498-1557) was a contemporary of Sri Chaitanya Mahaprabhu and a devotee of Lord Krishna, who resided for a time in Vrindavan. She is part of the Bhakti revival that swept India during this period, and is of both literary and religious significance. She composed a series of songs expressing her love for Lord Krishna that had a significant impact on the development of Hindi as a language and on Hindi literature.

The temple is built on the spot where Mirabai resided while in Vrindavan. Her Rajput husband tried to kill her after she refused to renounce Krishna and adopt his preferred deities. After she had departed from her husband's home to settle permanently in Vrindavan, his family sent a poisonous snake in a basket to her, but when she opened the basket, the snake turned into a garland of flowers, which she placed on the altar with the deity of Lord Krishna.

The temple was small and located at the confluence of two narrow alleys. It looks more like a private home than a temple. It had its own peaceful atmosphere. When I arrived, the priest was sitting against the wall in front of the altar telling stories of Mirabai to a small group of housewives. The altar contained an unusual set of deities. Krishna was in the center. On His right was Radha, and Mirabai was on Krishna's left. Below that was Mirabai's shila.

Temples, like people, come in all sizes and shapes. There are temples that are totally fraudulent, with a money-grubbing greedy atmosphere, and there are temples that are spiritual oases in the material world. The priests and management determine this. I have seen priests that epitomize spirituality and others that are pure rascals and little more than criminals.

My next top was the Sri Sri Radha Shyam Sundar Temple, but it proved difficult to find. Vrindavan streets are not marked in any way and temple signs are usually only in Hindi and/or Bengali. While I can read both languages, the signs are often so old and beat up as to be totally illegible. I had to ask half a dozen people before I found it. It was off of a side street.

The temple was built around the kutir of Prabhu Sri Sri Shyama Sundara to house his deity. Although a learned man from a good family and a high caste, he preferred to do *seva* for Radharani. He swept a wild area of the forest as part of his *seva* every day. One day, while sweeping, he found an ankle bracelet belonging to Radharani. He kept the bracelet in hopes Radharani would come for it. An old lady approached him and asked for the bracelet, saying it belonged to her daughter. Shyama Sundara did not believe this lady was really who she said she was. He asked the old lady to send her daughter in person to claim the anklet. The old lady then revealed her true identity as Lalita, one of the trusted Gopi confidants of Srimati Radharani. Shyama Sundara demanded that Radha come to him in person to retrieve the jewelry. When he met Srimati Radharani, he told Her he would not give the anklet back until she transported him to Goloka Vrindavana to see the rasa dance. Radharani complied with Shyama Sundara's request and presented him with the deity now housed at the temple.

This deity falls into a special category, as it is not made by the hands of men, nor was it self-manifested. Radharani produced it from her heart.

I first saw the kutir, which was different from others in Vrindavan in that it is a cave. Shyama Sundara dug the cave so he would not be disturbed and lived in it for 12 years. I took an extended darshan of the deity, which is unique in appearance. It has a different texture and appears shinier than other deities.

I then hoped to visit the spot where Shyam Sundara found Radha's anklet and was given darshan by Her, but try as I may, I could not find it. I gave up and returned to Jai Singh Ghera. Before returning, I bought a new chaddar. It cost me 150 rupees (about $2.75). As it turns out, I discovered when I got back home that I have an extensive collection of these distinctive yellow and red chaddars that I have picked up at holy spots all over India. None of these compare with the one taken from me by a monkey in Vrindavan. Perhaps another one will come to me when the time is right.

William said he was feeling a little better and could go out with me if we took a rickshaw. We went straight to the Govindaji Temple, one of the most spectacular in Vrindavan. Rupa Goswami built the Radha Govindaji Temple to house his special deity of Govindaji. The deity was originally installed in Vrindavan 5,000 years ago by the grandson of Lord Krishna, but was lost over time. Rupa rediscovered it when he spotted a cow dripping her milk on a spot on top of a hill in Vrindavan (which was then largely jungle).

Rupa Goswami and the villagers excavated this deity. Built to house the Govindaji deity of Rupa Goswami, the temple had a height of seven stories and was the tallest building in North India. When the Mughul Emperor and Islamic iconoclast Aurangzeb learned of this, he was angry. Declaring that no Hindu structure could be taller than a Muslim one, Aurangzeb ordered troops to Vrindavan to destroy the temple. It was so well built, however, that they could not. They were only able to remove several stories from the *shikaras* and damaged some of the outside carving. Given prior warning, the priests moved the Govindaji deity to the Amber palace in Rajasthan, where it continues to be worshipped today.

The temple is a long structure with the sanctum sanctorum beneath the *shikara*. While there is a deity in place, there is no regular worship or temple program. The inside of the temple is bare of decoration. It is a massive sandstone edifice on top of a hill with a magnificent view of the surrounding area and it can likewise be seen from almost anywhere in Vrindavan. The architecture and the construction are truly wonderful, with beautifully executed carving. On the left side of the temple is the "Yoga Pith," a room built into the temple itself, marking the spot where Rupa Goswami discovered and unearthed the Govindaji deity.

After viewing the temple and taking plenty of pictures, we went into the "new" temple built to house the replacement (*pratibha*) deity carved after the original deity was sent to Rajasthan for safekeeping. This temple was built in the mid 19th Century. It was not spectacular, but was a good example of 19th Century temple architecture, with beautiful painted bas reliefs around the walls. The altar was also unusual. In addition to the Radha/Krishna deities, there were a set of 8 principal Gopis and eight principal *manjaris* (prepubescent attendants) on both sides of the steps leading to the simple yet elegant altar. We have no pictures of this, as photography was not allowed inside the temple.

Afterwards, we walked down the hill and about 500 meters to the Rangaji temple. This is a copy of the original Rangaji temple in Trichey in Tamil Nadu. It is the only South Indian temple in the city and, according to our guidebook, the only one in Vrindavan that does not allow foreigners to enter (although some locals told us that this policy has been changed since the guidebook was published). Unwilling to test the no foreigners policy, we walked around the perimeter and took pictures, but did not go into the sanctum sanctorum in the center of the massive complex. We were lucky to find a small temple in the perimeter containing traditional South Indian versions of Radha and Krishna. The priest was friendly and not only allowed us darshan of the deities, but to take pictures. Although there were many worshippers in other areas, we were the only two people in this temple, so our darshan was extensive.

Dream Diary Reprise

I have not been monitoring my dreams, at least not consciously, but had a very vivid dream last night. I was getting ready for an appointment and talking to my daughter Kristl. "Time is going by so quickly," I said, "and I have been so blessed. Time is passing quickly because my life is filled, and I get to live in this wonderful, exciting city." Then I woke up and realized that it was the breakthrough.

For several years, I have had repeated dreams about being trapped in a meaningless job, but seeking desperately to hold on to it. These were dreams of judgment and attachment. It was negativity mixed with attachment. Now, thanks to the blessings of the Lord, and my presence here in the holy Dham, I have been freed of this negativity and attachment. I will not have those dreams any more, and my heart will be filled with gratitude for the blessed life that the Lord has provided to me.

Vrindavan Tirtha Yatra

I awoke at 0430 when it was still dark, bathed, dressed, and performed japa until sunrise. We thought we were going to see the last two remaining Goswami temples today. However, while coming out of breakfast, we encountered Srivatsaji, who invited us to his residence at 1000 to attend a puja in honor of his birthday.

It was an elaborate Sanskrit puja, with many different elements. It lasted for almost 30 minutes. The family priest recited Sanskrit throughout. I recognized a number of words. At several points Srivatsaji corrected the pundit on points of Sanskrit or ritual, and his wife also intervened to demonstrate how to perform aspects of the ritual.

At the end, the pundit tied red thread (*raksha bandhan*) on the wrists of the onlookers. Srivatsaji had me sit next to the pundit. When the time came, he put the red vermillion on my forehead, and pointed at me to indicate that I should extend my arm for the red thread. I inadvertently lifted up my left arm, and one of the onlookers quickly corrected me. Srivatsaji laughed.

After the puja, we set out for the parikrama. We had already done part of the path. Since I last took the parikrama, the path has been completely eradicated, and much of the stretches that once passed through isolated countryside are now paved streets lined with buildings and filled with traffic. The first part of the parikrama was quiet and unchanged from my previous walks. There was no traffic and we passed various babas in differing colorful attire and local villagers going about their everyday business.

Parts of the path that were totally immersed in forest are now lined with dubious "temples, ashrams, and goshallas," many of which appear to have been built overnight. Most, if not all, did not exist when I last performed parikrama during previous Vrindavan visits. They are emblazoned with large signs advertising their particular "babas."

191

Traditionally, the parikrama is made only in bare feet. However, since much of the parikrama path has been paved over and made into a street, many Indians have stopped taking parikrama with bare feet. I specifically asked Srivatsaji about this. He confirmed that he used to make the parikrama every single day, but has now stopped. Likewise, he tells his followers to wear shoes, as it is now too dangerous to walk on paved streets in bare feet.

We stopped at the small store of a local bead seller who ran a small temple behind his stall. He said he was an initiated disciple of Srila Prabhupad. He took us back into the temple and showed us the altar. Prabhupad's picture was prominently displayed, along with the ISKCON parampara.

I found much of the parikrama to be inherently uninteresting, as it was no different from walking down an ordinary street anywhere in North India. The formerly quiet stretches have now been filled in with random buildings of all types. After walking for some hours, we began to reenter Vrindavan.

The Krishna Balarama Temple was on the parikrama path, and we stopped to see the Samadhi of Srila Prabhupad. The temple was quiet. This was the first time we had seen the temple so still with no visitors present. We had the Samadhi to ourselves. It is a beautiful building. Made entirely of white marble, inside and out, the Samadhi structure is inside its own building and rises for two stories. There is a separate entry on the second floor, reached by walking up a long stairway.

The Samadhi structure features a small room with a life size statue of Srila Prabhupad. This is the site of regularly scheduled Guru Pujas. There was none scheduled while we were there, and the doors to this room were closed. Even so, it was a spiritually charged atmosphere. The floor extending out from the Samadhi structure is made of black and white marble. There is a parikrama path around the structure, and on the wall behind the Samadhi are two beautiful bas reliefs in brass showing Srila Prabhupad leading the Vaishnavas, and Srila Prabhupad on the Jagannath Rath during the first ISKCON Ratha Yatra (festival of the Jagannath carts).

After leaving the ISKCON temple, we passed a section of the path framed by the small portion of forest remaining in its original state. These are all held by private owners or by ISKCON, which has pledged to prevent destruction of its portion. We passed the ISKCON *goshalla*, which was also in a natural state, with large numbers of trees.

Our next stop was the site of the Kaliya pastimes of Lord Krishna. The Lord swung from a tree onto the back of the Kaliya serpent, a demon that had polluted the Yamuna River. When implored by his wives to spare him, Lord Krishna exiled Kaliya to the Pacific Ocean. This is the only instance in the Krishna Lila in which Lord Krishna spared a demon and did not kill him. It was a lovely site. The priest welcomed us and opened the Kaliya temple for us. It contained a set of deities depicting this pastime that were quite beautiful and evocative. Sadly, we have no photos, as photography was not allowed.

The priest was quite cooperative, however, complimenting me on my Hindi, and allowing us to photograph anything on the site except for the deities. The site also contains the tree from which Lord Krishna jumped to the back of the Kaliya demon. The actually spot is commemorated with a statue of Krishna performing his Kaliya dance on his back while the two wives stand to each side and implore the Lord to spare their husband.

Vrindavan Tirtha Yatra

Today was filled with experiences. We woke up determined to complete our darshan of the last two "Goswami – must see" temples that will complete our Vrindavan experience. I awoke at 0430 and retired to the verandah to complete two rounds of japa. It was dark, silent, and still. I shut my eyes to concentrate on the japa. It is indeed very difficult to concentrate the mind and to stop if from wildly wandering. When I had finished, the sky was turning a mild yellow and the sun was rising. It was truly the *Brahmamahurta* (the golden hours for religious practice).

William and I were then drawn to the ashram gardens overlooking the Yamuna by raucous shouting, chanting and singing. A huge procession was entering the parikrama, with hundreds of men, women, and children, many in devotional clothing, slowly walking along the parikrama path. Many chanted "Hare Krishna!" and it was a loud spectacle.

After breakfast we went to the first temple, the Radha Gopinatha Temple, founded by Madha Pandita Goswami in 1559. This temple is in two sections, the old and new temples. We went to the old temple first. Like many in Vrindavan, it had been desecrated and damaged by the troops of the Mughul Emperor Aurangzeb during his campaign of organized iconoclasm. It appeared very old and still damaged several centuries later. We reached the temple by walking up a small street and into an entryway. The original temple consisted solely of a small temple room under a shikara with beautiful deities and no priest present.

The "new" temple, built to replace the one damaged by Aurangzeb, had the traditional courtyard and the walk up the steps to the raised platform in front of the alcove containing the deities. We conversed with the priest sitting there. He spoke excellent English. Like many in Vrindavan, he asked if we were Russian and seemed relieved when we said we were Americans (this was also the reaction of most brijabasis we encountered).

This temple is run by Bengali priestly families. The priest complained to us about Hindi speaking worshippers from outside braj, saying many were merely on outings and did not even know who Radha was, or anything about Gaudiya Vaishnavism. The only other visitors we saw were Bengali. For them, Vrindavan is the most holy of pilgrimage sites and they spend weeks here meticulously visiting every temple and performing specific pujas with great devotion. At many sites, Bengalis are the only people we see.

We took the short walk to the Radha Gokulananda Temple, founded by Lokanatha Goswami. Not one of the original six Goswamis sent to Vrindavan by Sri Chaitanya Mahaprabhu, Lokanatha Goswami is often called "the Seventh Goswami" for his close association with them. The temple is managed by the Chaitanya Math, one of the offshoots of the Gaudiya Math; this group was founded by Bhaktisiddanta Goswami, the guru of Srila Prabhupad, and part of the ISKCON parampara.

The temple is clean and well maintained. It contains the Samadhi of Lokanath Swami and a Pushpa Samadhi of Narrottama dasa Thakura, one of the greats of Gaudiya Vaishnavism, who wrote many beautiful songs and prayers used in temple worship today.

We first went to the Samadhis and paid our obsceiences. These Samadhis were originally in an open courtyard. Worshippers could formerly visit them at night and meditate there under the stars. Because of the "monkey menace," the Samadhis have been covered over by a concrete enclosure, which detracts from the white marble Samadhis and undermines the devotional atmosphere.

We then went to the temple. An exhibit inside on the life and work of Bhaktisiddanta Goswami included many old photographs of him and his associates, including photos of him posing with British colonial officials wearing pith helmets. All are standing under a banner that reads, "God Save the King!" The exhibit also included photographs of some beautiful Gaudiya Math temples in Mayapur and elsewhere in West Bengal.

The altars of the Goswami temples feature several kinds of deities. These include deities found/discovered by Goswamis while excavating Vrindavan and locating the lost sacred sites. According to Gaudiya Vaishnava doctrine, the found deities were installed by Vajranaba, the grandson of Krishna, who first established Vrindavan as a religious site. Over the course of time, and long periods of Buddhist and Muslim rule, the sites were abandoned and covered over and the deities buried. The Goswamis were led to these deities by Lord Krishna through dreams or appearances.

The second category of deities is the self-manifested. These deities are not carved or constructed by men, but appear miraculously of their own accord. The most famous deity in this category is the Radha Ramana deity in our home temple. The deity in the Radha Shyam Sundar temple falls into its own category, as it was given to Shyam Sundar directly by Radha, who manifested it directly out of her own body.

The third category of deities is carved specifically for installation in Vrindavan temples. Through the *arcana* process, a Brahmin priest performs the ceremony that changes the carved image into a manifestation of Krishna. The most famous of the carved deities is in the Radha Damodar Temple and was carved by Sanatan Goswami himself and presented to his nephew Jiva Goswami, the founder of the temple.

The fourth category of deities is the *shaligrams*, the rocks, usually from Govardhan Hill, but sometimes from the Gandaki River in Nepal. Many of the shilas on the Goswami altars were presented to the Goswamis by Sri Chaitanya Mahaprabhu; several have the thumbprint of Sri Chaitanya, which he miraculously impressed upon them before presentation. These are particularly venerated. Usually the altars are crowded with a mix of these deities. This is also the case at Gokulananda.

We did not participate in aarati ceremonies at these two temples, as none were scheduled during our visit. We received darshan of the temple deities, however, approaching the rail in front of the recess in which the deities are placed on the altar. When visiting temples, worshippers are free to make a donation, and the priest provides *charanamrit* (water that has been poured over the deity) or *prasad* (food shared with the deities through offering). In the Gaudiya Vaishnava tradition, the worshipper usually pays obsceiences to the deity when approaching. He can do this in two ways – by getting on his knees and bringing his head to the floor, or performing *dandavat* – lying fully flat on the floor with the arms extended and the bead bag held off of the floor with the right hand. The bead bag is a religious object, and like all religious objects, is not allowed to touch the floor. In Indian culture, this proscription applies to all books, as knowledge is sacred.

As part of the darshan process, the worship repeats his/her personal prayers, followed by the performance of japa while sitting quietly on the floor of the temple or the temple courtyard. Some temples feature musicians or priests performing bhajans during the darshan hours and worshippers are free to sing along. Others feature priests telling stories of Lord Krishna and his pastimes (*Krishna katha*), usually from the *Srimad Bhagavatam*. Worshippers can sit for hours raptly listening to these stories.

Sometimes the priest will sit quietly with a small group of worshippers, and perform *katha* from memory. I find these occasions to be more spiritual as they are done without a microphone and loudspeaker. Many observers have complained about the "microphone menace," in that loudspeakers are often turned to maximum volume, creating a noisy atmosphere that disrupts japa and contemplation.

After a break for lunch and rest, we set out around 1700, first visiting a small courtyard at Jai Singh Ghera that contained a small building overlooking the Yamuna. In 1994, this garden was the site of a miraculous appearance of Lord Krishna documented in the academic work, "Seeing Krishna."[64] William is currently reading this work and wanted to see the site. This is also a site of one of the Radha/Krishna pastimes. William pointed out the two ghats attached to the garden. One is the Krishna Ghat, and one is the Radha ghat. Radha and Krishna arrived separately at this site from the other side of the Yamuna and used their own ghat to ascend the riverbank. They were greeted by their *sakhis* (associates), including the eight principal Gopis and the eight principal *manjaris*. The associates then dressed them in special clothes before uniting them in the garden to spend affectionate time together.

From this site, it is possible to take the back path to the Radha Ramana temple. This is where we go to find a rickshaw for our next adventure. We take it to the Rangaji temple, where we get off and walk through the old neighborhood surrounding the temple until we find the site of the 64 samadhis. This site was originally a forest containing a pond (*venu*). Several prominent Vaishnavas had their kutirs there. The site is also the location of a temple dedicated to the goddess Kalyayani. The Gopis worshipped this goddess at the temple.

After the deaths of the Vaishnavas resident in this grove, their kutirs were closed and it became the site for the Samadhis of sannyasis and Goswamis. The most prominent Samadhi is that of Radhunatha Bhatta Goswami, one of the original Six Goswamis. We discovered, however, that many more Samadhis, including the Samadhis of women devotees, have been added to this site and it is now quite jumbled and confused, making it almost impossible to find specific Samadhis.

The Samadhis are usually marked in Bengali and no other language. It would be incredibly difficult for me to go through the hundreds of Samadhis to find those of specific individuals. My failure to find several significant, yet small sites has convinced me that it would be impossible to find everything without the services of a local guide familiar with all of the sacred sites of Vrindavan. This is the method used by the Bengali families during their weeks in Vrindavan. The guides not only take the worshipper to often obscure sites, they provide explanations in Bengali. It was with such a guide that I and a pilgrim family toured Vrindavan during my first visit. Next time I go to Vrindavan, I should procure the services of such a learned soul.

The 64 Samadhis site is also home to several enormous banyan trees, which appear ancient and spread over hundreds of meters. This adds a particularly mystical aura to the site. In addition, parties of Bengali devotees were paying their respects by singing *bhajans* and playing *kartalas* (brass cymbals).

From the Samadhi garden, we took a rickshaw to the Jagannath Ghat on the parikrama path. We wanted to visit the Jagannath Temple there and pay our respects to the Jagannath deities. This temple was established in the 19th Century,

---

[64] Margaret H. Case, *Seeing Krishna (The Religious World of a Brahman Family in Vrindavan)*, Oxford University Press, Oxford, UK, 2000

when a Punjabi Vaishnava named Haridasa journeyed all the way to the Jagannath Puri Temple in Odisha. He had been told by Jagannath in a dream that he should bring the deities to Vrindavan. The Jagannath deities of the Puri Temple are replaced periodically and Haridasa convinced the temple authorities to hand the old deities over to him for installation in Vrindavan. He and his followers laboriously hauled the original deities across India to this location and installed them.

When we arrived, the aarati was going on. It was a beautiful temple, clean and well-maintained by a reputable Swami with an efficient organization. The aarati was wonderfully conducted, with the loud ringing of bells and the playing of musical instruments. The priests were very good and presented the entire aarati in authentic fashion. There were only a few devotees present and we were able to receive lengthy darshan.

The aarati was followed by lengthy prayers to Jagannath led by an older priest. He had a beautiful voice and the small congregation repeated the prayers he led with great passion and enthusiasm. They attained a unique harmony, which resounded around the temple. It was a particularly ecstatic experience. We participated as we could, yelling "Jai" at the appropriate points. We took time to explore the beautiful temple grounds and the buildings surrounding the temple, including the goshalla and guest house.

We rode the rickshaw back into Vrindavan as night fell. It was particularly peaceful and the road almost deserted. We turned off into town. It was largely dark, with spots of light at various food and tea stalls. Local people and pilgrims congregated, drank tea, and socialized.

I had spontaneously paid the rickshaw wallah 100 rupees for the first leg of the trip. We got off of the rickshaw at Radha Ramana and William paid him another 100 rupees. He face lit up and seemed to glow (because we had deliberately paid him several times the going rate for such a trip). We were also delighted that we could make a fellow human being so happy, at so little expense (around $3.50).

We then entered our temple for another evening aarati. It was filled with worshippers, with a group playing instruments and singing bhajans in the alcove. Everyone was in a happy mood. The curtain blocking the altar was open and people taking darshan of Radha Ramana.

The gong sounded signifying the beginning of aarati. The lights flickered and went out. Many worshippers held lighted diwa. A lovely young lady holding a tray of lighted diwas (lamps) gave each of us one. We held it before the deity, and like the other worshippers, put it on the ledge running to the altar. The temple was brightly decorated, probably in anticipation of Diwali, coming up in 13 days. After aarati, we returned to Jai Singh Ghera.

While waiting for dinner, the electricity in our room went out. We informed Upadhayaji, who sent a servant to check it out. The servant was unable to correct the problem. Only our air conditioner was functioning. At 0300, it too went out.

Mathura Tirtha Yatra

This morning there is still no power anywhere in the neighborhood (As it turned out, there was no power anywhere in the region, with power out in both Vrindavan and Mathura). Upadhayaji tells me electric company officials are demanding large bribes to have power restored.

Today is Sunday. We have set aside the day for a trip to Mathura. Although I had researched Mathura, I was still vague as to what to do there. One of Srivatsaji's sons told me Indian museums are all open on Sunday and closed on Monday, and Goswamiji had told us all about the Mathura museum and its collection of Hindu and Buddhist antiquities.

I therefore decided to see the museum first and then get our bearings and see the church constructed by F.S. Grouse, the 19th Century District Commissioner and gazetteer of Mathura. As it turned out, none of it was to be, and we went in a totally different direction. Something else was meant to be. There are no coincidences.

After breakfast we went to Keshi ghat to hire our motor rickshaw. Upadhayaji had told us not to use the Hindi word for museum, as all rickshaw wallahs only understood the English word. None of them understood either word. We finally contracted a driver who was convinced that a museum was a library. He turned out to be foolish and childish, constantly laughing, smiling, and singing, and speaking in unintelligible Pidgin English, which he was convinced, was evidence of his fluency. He also drove quite recklessly, making the trip through Indian traffic seem even more harrowing than usual.

We arrived at the museum and were greeted by the usual curious boys (who often want to practice their English). They informed us that the museum was closed on Sundays. We then contracted our driver to take us to look for the church, but first looked at the park across the street.

We were in what was known in colonial times at the "European Quarter." The park was probably the Queen Victoria Park or the Prince of Wales Park during that time and could have been closed to Indians.

Any English statues of royalty had long since been removed and replaced by a crude statue of the Rani of Jhansi, a hero of the First War of Indian Independence (or the Sepoy Mutiny). The park had been renamed Bhagat Singh Park, after a nationalist hero who assassinated a British official and was hanged by the colonial government.

We then set out for the church. We later learned that this church recommended by Grouse in his Mathura gazette was the Church of Saint Francis, the Catholic chapel on the Cantonment. It is a Christian church built in "oriental style." Our driver instead took us to an ordinary concrete structure built in the 1990's. It was not on the cantonment and had no redeeming features of any kind. It was a local Methodist Church. Services were going on as we arrived.

Having driven so far, we decided to look at the much older buildings behind the church. I had spotted a signboard which read, "Blackstone Intercollege for Girls," and it had sparked my curiosity. The buildings were classic Raj architecture from the 19th Century, although dilapidated and not maintained. We walked around the grounds until we found a stone plaque set into a wall which read:

Training School and Deaconers Home Memorial

Andrew Blackstone and Sarah His Wife of Adams New York

Erected by his Son W. E. Blackstone

Chicago, Illinois, USA, March 28, 1889

As we turned to leave, a lady leaving the church service introduced herself. Her name was Mrs. R. Greene, the wife of the Reverend Jonathan Paul Greene. Despite their names, the couple was 100 percent Indian in every regard. Mrs. Greene, the principal of the school, invited us into her house (in one of the old buildings occupied by the Blackstones in the 19th Century).

Mrs. Greene told us a tale of woe I have often heard from Christians in South Asia. Christian missionaries like the Blackstones devoted their lives to India. They collected contributions from American congregations and built schools, hospitals, churches, and orphanages all over the country. When the British departed, this property, of considerable value, was turned over to the Indian church, which often failed to maintain many of the buildings and grounds which suffered considerable deterioration.

As the Indian population mushroomed, doubling, and then doubling again, these properties vastly increased in value in a country hungry for space. Corrupt church officials then began selling off the property and pocketing much of the money. This is also the case with the Blackstone School. Muslim interests want to obtain the property, likely to tear down the buildings, and erect "modern" concrete box structures in their place. The Greenes are trying to save this property, and accused the Bishop of engineering the proposed sale to enrich himself. Mrs. Greene also asked if we could locate the Blackstone family descendants, as they still get mail addressed to the Blackstones. I made inquiries when I returned to the USA, and found references to Blackstone descendants in California, but it seems they have all passed on.

After chatting, drinking tea, and sharing some of Mrs. Greene's son's birthday cake, she gave our driver directions to the "old church" in the cantonment and we drove to the gate. The soldiers on duty were fully armed with automatic weapons. They asked what we wanted on the cantonment. We told them we only wanted to see the church. At first they refused us entry, but allowed us in after William told them he was a Captain in the US Navy and showed them his US military ID card. We drove through the cantonment to the church. It was a stark contrast to the noisy, dirty, Mathura outside the gate. As expected, the cantonment was immaculately clean, quiet, with good roads. The military personnel we spoke with were polite, well-dressed, and exhibited "suitable military bearing," as they would say at West Point. Everyone was in excellent physical condition.

The church we arrived at was also not the one we were supposed to see, (which we learned later was only a few hundred meters away on the campus of the Catholic school). Instead, we went to the old Anglican Church, which grouse describes as:

"The English Church, consecrated by Bishop Daltrey in December 1856, is in a non-descript style of architecture, but has a not inelegant Italian campanile, which is visible from a long distance. The interior had been lately enriched by stained-glass windows in memory of a young officer of the 16th Hussars, who met his death by an accident while out pig sticking."[65]

The small congregation was just concluding its service in pews set up outdoors under a tree. They were happy to talk to us. They explained that the church was very old and undergoing complete renovation starting with the roof. They opened it up for us to see. The pews were absent, and the floor covered with wood removed from the roof, which had completely deteriorated. As is often the case, the most interesting items were the plaques in the wall, mementos and memorials from the British regiments (always cavalry) which were stationed there during the long period of British rule.

We met the pastor and posed for pictures with some teenagers before setting out for the birthplace of Lord Krishna. We drove through Mathura until we reached the spot. We could not park directly in front of the birthplace, which had been fenced off. No vehicles were allowed. We parked some distance away and walked to the site. It became immediately apparent that the birth site is embroiled in unfortunate communal politics, with a high potential for violence.

Police barricades blocked the road. No traffic was allowed. CRPF (Central Reserve Police Force) soldiers with automatic weapons kept an eagle eye on everything. We had to check in our bags, cell phones and cameras and were only allowed to keep our wallets and watches. We then passed through a security checkpoint with two pat-down checks.

[65] Mathura District Memoir, F.S. Grouse, Asian Educational Services, New Delhi, 1993, page 161

Once inside, we removed our shoes. There was a *pandal* (tent) program going on. A large audience was seated before the huge stage under the tent. *Mahants* (Hindu holy men) were on stage reading from the *Ramayana*. They were accompanied by the unfortunate and irritating sound effects often used in such productions in India. The loudspeaker system was deafeningly loud. Since the loudspeakers were aimed straight at the next door mosque (built directly over the birth site in the 16ᵗʰ Century by Emperor Aurangzeb), I suspect that this was part of the ongoing culture war at this site. The Muslims have extra loud *azans* (call to prayer) and *Juma* (Friday) sermons aimed at the temple and broadcast through their own powerful loudspeakers, while the Hindus broadcast readings of Hindu scripture at maximum volume. It made for an unpleasant atmosphere.

We walked towards the birthplace location and passed shop after shop filled with cheap trinkets, both religious and secular. We came to a temple, which was closed. There were large signboards there in Hindi and English describing how Hindus had built temples at this site three times, only to have them destroyed by the Muslims.

We entered the site and went through a short tunnel. The way I previously took when some years ago was blocked by multiple locked barricades. Instead of walking through the long tunnel to the birth site directly under the mosque, we walked a short distance to another room. I was confused and asked the priest there if this was the birth site. He insisted it was. The room was plain, with a small altar featuring a few pictures of the birth narrative and some simple statues. The priest did not perform a religious ceremony. Instead, he tapped us gently on the head with a bundle of peacock feathers.

We left and went upstairs into a room where a group of bored singers performed a perfunctory kirtan. There is a large structure at the site with an enormous *shikara*. It is beside the birth place, (the mosque) and looms over it. Access to the higher levels of the building is denied to the public for security reasons. This temple purportedly marks the spot of "Kamsa's palace." Kamsa had imprisoned Lord Krishna's parents in a cell next to his palace just prior to the birth.[66] This temple had deliberately been built higher than the mosque to upstage the Muslims and send them a clear message.

On the way out, we bought a ticket to a diorama displaying the pastimes of Lord Krishna. It was built inside a concrete replica of Govardhan Hill. It consisted of scenes in a simple folk art style, with lots of flashing colored lights and a deafening sound track that consisted of a woman screaming repeatedly and what sounded like industrial machinery. There was no indication as to how the random noises related to the subject matter. It was so loud that it was impossible to

---

[66] You can read the entire story of Krishna's advent in Mathura in Srila Prabhupad's Krishna book.

converse. All legends on the dioramas were written only in Hindi. Hindu chauvinism and Hindi chauvinism go hand in hand.

We took another harrowing ride back to Vrindavan, with our singing/smiling driver, to find that there was still no electricity. Nothing to do, we sat outside in the garden until 1900, when the power came back on. We retired to our room to read, and the power went off again. It would go off and on three more times in the course of the night.

Vrindavan Tirtha Yatra – The Ageless Baba

We decided to try to see the Banke Bihari Temple and call an end to our temple yatra. We preceded the temple visit with a morning walk along the Yamuna. There was no sign of breakfast in the prasadam hall and no person to be found either, so we headed out on our morning trip without it.

We walked along the parikrama path, heading for the Jagannath Ghat. I hoped to pay my respects at a spot where Sri Chaitanya had performed kirtan. We also wanted to complete our Yamuna *snan*. One of my books contained the mantra Lord Chaitanya used when he bathed in the Yamuna. I brought to book along to recite the mantra before the *snan*.

I had my eye out for a good spot along the Yamuna.

Just before arriving at the Jagannath Temple, I found a road leading to the Yamuna, but it quickly turned from a road to a path. We arrived at a junction. Paths led in all directions through the fields. Workers were scattered throughout the fields performing fieldwork. One of them provided directions to the right path and soon the river was in sight.

When we arrived at the riverbank, there were no people visible in any direction. A low sandbar led into the river, with the Yamuna on both sides. Water birds ran along the sandbar looking for bugs to eat. We spotted a temple on the other side of the river, and walked along the sandbar enjoyed the serenity provided by the respite from crowds of people. I still had not found the right spot for our Yamuna *snan*. Groups of dragonflies glided over the surface of the sand.

A baba stood on the bank of the river overlooking the sandbar. He was rubbing plants between his hands. We did not know what he was doing. We later learned he was one of a group of babas harvesting wild *ganja,* which the babas would smoke later while sitting on the banks of the Yamuna.

We decided to take the ferry across the river to see the temple we had spotted. We had no idea what it was or its significance. We descended the bank and stood by a group of boats. A young farmhand doubled as the ferryman. He emerged from the fields and took us across. While he was poling the boat across the river, he provided some details regarding the temple we were about to visit. It was the ashram of Dev Raha Baba, and, said the ferryman, was very beautiful.

After leaving the ferry, we ascended the other bank and walked through the gate of the ashram. It was an extensive collection of buildings. It included quarters for devotees, several temples, and a stage with room for an audience to sit in front, and a large house set aside for the presiding guru. Everything was beautifully landscaped. A grassy garden stood in the middle of the complex, laid out around a lotus pool.

A priest quietly chanted in front of the altar of the Shiva Temple. We ended our tour of the complex at the lovely riverside building we had seen from the other side of the Yamuna. A young Russian female devotee sat on the ground in front of an altar there quietly chanting on japa beads.

Although we thought this building was a temple, it was actually the *Pushpa Samadhi*[67] of Dev Raha Baba. Inside the samadhi, his actual hut was mounted high on a pedestal, with his life sized statue peering out from within. Dev Raha Baba was an "ageless baba," living to a grand age while retaining his youth and vitality. Upon his death, his followers immersed his body in the Yamuna at this spot and erected his Pushpa Samadhi here. The ashram came later, as his followers built a complex of buildings around the Samadhi.

In the attached temple, we saw several photos of the baba. He looked old, but of indeterminate age, with long matted tresses in the Himalayan baba style. He was missing teeth and sported a long grey beard. Some pictures showed devotees carrying his body on a palanquin and immersing it in the river.

While waiting for the ferry back across the Yamuna, I struck up a conversation with an Indian devotee of the baba. He confirmed that Dev Raha Baba resided in this spot for many years and that his exact age was unknown, with some saying he could be as old as 500 years. The baba did not die, affirmed the devotee, but simply entered into Samadhi while meditating and left his body. When the body was immersed in the river, it disappeared. The Samadhi site now attracts pilgrims from around the world and a guru has taken over the Baba's mission. This guru recently led a group of 40 foreign devotees into the Himalayas for meditation. It included Germans, Russians, and others.

We arrived back at the other shore, found an appropriate spot along the sandbar and knelt down for our Yamuna *snan*. I pulled the book from my *jholla*, repeated the mantra, and we both sprinkled Yamuna water on our heads. Afterwards, we took the main road through the *dhobi ghat* to the Jagannath Temple. At the ghat

---

[67] When there is no body of a holy figure to be buried, for whatever reason. His followers erect a "pushpa samadhi" (pushpa means flower). A flower is buried in the grave in lieu of a body, and the tomb is erected over the site.

we spotted our own *dhobi* washing our clothes. He grinned at us and gave us a big wave. We toured the ground of the extensive Jagannath temple and ashram and took pictures.

We had not eaten since the previous night and had walked extensively along the parikrama path and the Yamuna River, so stopped for some lunch and took a nap. When I awoke, I was still drowsy. William suggested we go on the roof of the ashram, one of the highest points in Vrindavan, with a beautiful view of the city. We went upstairs and had just started walking across the roof, when a monkey quickly jumped on William's back, grabbed his glasses and bounded to a nearby roof.

William tried to entice the money to drop the glasses, but he refused. William then tried to distract the monkey by throwing his japa beads in front of him, but to no avail. William went downstairs to grab some food to distract the monkey, but by the time he returned, the monkey had climbed along a perimeter wall and disappeared. Upadhayaji mobilized the servant boys to conduct a search and everyone looked around the compound, but there was no sign of the monkey or the glasses.[68]

William determined that he would have to buy a pair of Indian reading glasses. That evening, we walked through Loi bazaar to a local optometrist. He was very busy with many customers. He addressed us in excellent English, and other customers in Hindi and Bengali. The optometrist determined that William could not wear readymade reading glasses, and would need an eye test and have prescription glasses made. While William was in the other room taking his eye test, I sat and watched the parade of customers. It was a cross-section of ordinary Indians in a tableau of daily life. In due course, William emerged with his prescription and ordered his glasses. He wanted to pick them up the next day. The optometrist said that would be no problem, provided there was electricity. The eye exam cost William 50 rupees (70 cents), and the glasses and frames with 250 rupees ($4.50).

We then went to the Banke Bihari temple. Although nothing I had heard or read recommended this temple to me, we had to see why it was always so crowded and listed among the most popular temples in India. It appears to have little connection to Gaudiya Vaishnavism and no connection whatsoever to the Six Goswamis of Vrindavan.

Critics of Hinduism decry the Hindu temple experience as mere exploitation by priests of the common man's religious sentiments. This trip confirmed that this

---

[68] After his return to the US, William was watching a travel program on television that featured Vrindavan. The host panned across the famous tree at Jai Singh Ghera, and there in the limbs was a big old male monkey wearing William's glasses.

does take place, and is more common that Hinduism's apologists would like to admit.

Banke Bihari is about making money from start to finish. While there, we confirmed that the temple management urged worshippers to spend money and lots of it. Religion was reduced to a commercial transaction. There was little sign of meaningful worship taking place. Priests sat next to a curtain in front of the deities. Worshippers gave the priests money and they opened the curtain for a brief darshan of the deities. Special prasad was on sale, made on the premises, for use in the expensive pujas.

Side Trip – "On Vrindavan"

"The ordinary man visiting Vrindavan can't see beyond the skinny dogs, open sewers, mischievous monkeys, salty water, underfed cows, all-pervading overfed pigs, opportunistic merchants, loudspeakers blaring from all directions, cacophonous concert of decibel-deafening diesel-powered buses, scooters, trucks, autos, cycles and Tempos. He will see a dry, dusty land, dotted with stubby thorn trees. Then there are carts driven by horses buffalo, bulls, or camels; horrifically hot summers, chased away by chest-chilling cold winters, and kids passing stool on the street as a regular daily function.

Externally, Vrndavana appears dilapidated, neglected and nothing like a celestial paradise. It may degrade even more with the advance of Kali-yuga. Prabhupada said that because of impiety, Vrndavana was becoming like a desert and would become more so in the future. 'This is Krishna's land, Vrndavana,' said Srila Prabhupada, 'and they are doing sinful things here. And they are being punished directly by Krishna.'[69]

I have witnessed that Prabhupada's prophetic statement, uttered decades ago, is coming true. I have been coming to Vrindavan for 42 years and has seen it slowly degrade. In recent years, the pace of degradation, both spiritual and material, has picked up rapidly.

This has been largely the result of conscious decisions taken by the area's political, economic, and religious leaders. This was substantiated during my conversations with both Srila Kesava Bharati das Goswami, and Srila Srivatsa Goswami. Both have considerable experience with these leaders.

For Gaudiya Vaishnavas, Vrindavan is the most holy dham. It is nothing less than a direct connection to Goloka Vrindavana, the spiritual sky, the eternal residence of Sri Krishna Bhagavan and Srimati Radharani. Krishna is always present here. There are 10 offenses to be avoided in the Holy Dham. Among them is:

---

[69] *Appreciating Vrndavana Dhama*, Mahanidhi Swami, self-published, Vrindavan, India, 1991, page 10

"Earning money by and making a business of deity worship and changing the holy name."[70]

Vaishnavas believe that any devotional act committed in the holy dham is magnified 1,000 times, and that likewise, any offense (*aparadh*) committed in Vrindavana is magnified 1,000 times. This is far and away the most common of the 10 offenses committed in Vrindavan today, and the impact has been devastating. During my stay in the holy dham, I saw and experienced everything described in the opening quote, and much more. The sanctity of the dham has been desecrated by greed and avarice.

India's massive population increases is causing a growing land shortage. The population is already densely packed and continues to grow by the day. Economic development has increased the size of the Indian middle class, while aspires to a "middle class lifestyle," replete with all modern amenities. This has increased the demand on scarce resources, including land. Vrindavan has been for five centuries a small pilgrimage town, surrounded by forests and farmland. This is now coming to an end. Vrindavan is growing into a bustling city.

The land shortage and frenetic economic development have pushed up land prices and fueled a real estate boom. "Land mafias" use violence and corruption to gain control of valuable property. They suborn the local leadership, gain access to Vrindavan's forests, and chop them down to erect high-rise apartment blocks. This incessant development has vastly increased the size of the local population, overloading the area's rudimentary infrastructure, placing a strain on resources, and causing unprecedented environmental despoliation.

In Vrindavan itself, the space between the Yamuna River bank and the parikrama path, formerly empty, is filling up with a motley assortment of crude illegal structures, and both sides of the parikrama path have been lined with hastily erected illegal businesses. During our Vrindavan stay, we heard many Indians complain that these land grabs take place with the collaboration of local leaders, who receive large bribes and guaranteed vote banks in exchange.

Vrindavan has become home to "temples" and "ashrams" of what Prabhupad called the "bogey yogis." The "ashrams" are most often purely moneymaking schemes, erected with the intention of fleecing pilgrims and making their founders rich. They are also usually erected illegally on land grabbed from others. Local Indians told us that many of these "bogey yogis" are actually criminals who have gone into the mahatma business to make easy money. These buildings crowd the road and fill the air with the sound of loudspeakers.

---

[70] *The Color Guide to Vrndavana*, Rajesekhara dasa Brahmacarya, Vedanta Vision Publications, Vrindavan, India, 1994, page 21

The pervasive corruption, coupled with ever-present illegal construction, and vast increases in population, have clogged the roads with traffic. The sanitation system in Vrindavan dates back to the 16th Century and was never adequate. It cannot keep pace with the vast amount of sewage and garbage generated by a growing population, and the burgeoning 21st Century lifestyle. This problem has been compounded by the introduction of vast numbers of plastic bags and processed snack foods, packed in indestructible packaging.

The absence of a modern sewage system means that sewage flows directly into the Yamuna River. In the old city, open sewers line the streets. These are now permanently clogged with trash, despite the constant efforts of sweepers to keep them clean.

Vrindavan has traditionally been home to a large animal population. This population has also increased exponentially along with the human population. Illegal settlers bring their livestock with them. The cows and buffaloes clog the narrow streets. The ever-increasing trash encourages the growth of the feral dog and pig populations.

The biggest impact has been on the monkey population. Monkeys have always been a part of Vrindavan life. In the past, their habitat was the forests surrounding the city. A limited number came into Vrindavan in search of food, providing amusement by occasionally stealing food from the hands of pilgrims.

As developers level their forest habitat, monkeys are being forced into the city, where they feed off of garbage dumps. As their population increases and their habitat declines, the monkeys become more desperate and more aggressive. They have become bolder and now do not hesitate to attack and bite small children and women. Unable to combat this "monkey menace," the local population must erect metal grills over their courtyards and verandahs. Most sadly, the principal temples, housing the Samadhis of the Six Goswamis, have been forced to encase their temple courtyards in ugly concrete to keep out the monkeys. This is most noticeable in the courtyards containing the Samadhis of Jiva Goswami at Radha Damodara, and Lokanath Goswami at Radha Gokulananda.

Srila Prabhupada predicted decades ago that Braj would turn into a desert as a result of massive impiety during the Kali Yuga. This was decades before climate change was openly discussed. Prabhupad was particularly prescient.

The mushrooming population has vastly increased the demand for water. The water table is sinking fast, forcing deeper and deeper drilling. Combined with the long-term implications of climate change, Braj could well revert to desert in our lifetimes.

The BJP government of Narendra Modi has launched a nationwide campaign to clean up India. He argues that there is no reason why India cannot be as clean and healthy as any developed country. Currently, only 30% of the Indian population has access to toilets. Modi has committed billions of dollars to make toilets universally available by 2019, the hundred year birth anniversary of Mahatma Gandhi. This campaign is sorely needed in Vrindavan, but is unlikely to succeed unless corruption is tackled and laws enforced.

Prabhupad urged his disciples to purify their senses to truly appreciate Vrindavan, as the holy dham. There remain plenty of earnest devotees who continue to view Vrindavan in this way. They are trying hard to take on the forces of Kali Yuga and serve Vrindavan. Signs of their activities are apparent everywhere in Vrindavan.

Here are some examples:

--Motor rickshaws are being phased out and replaced by small electric vehicles that resemble golf carts. They do not pollute the air and are silent and therefore do not contribute to noise pollution.

--Plastic bags are being phased out and replaced by reusable bags.

--Renovation and restoration of historic and spiritually significant buildings is ongoing all over the city. Several significant buildings have been completely restored.

--Religious organizations are creating spiritual oases in the midst of the chaos. Examples include our own Jai Singh Ghera, the Narain sect of Gaudiya Math's "ladies ashram," which is a totally restored Mughul era building on the Yamuna waterfront, and the Krishna Balaram temple of ISKCON, which is always immaculately clean and beautifully landscaped. ISKCON also has adopted the streets around the temple and ensures they are always clean.

--New temples are being built to replace older ones. The most notable is the Imlitala Temple, at the site of one of Lord Krishna's principal pastimes. The site of the Kaliya pastime has also been restored with beautiful sandstone sculptures added.

--A consortium of environmental and religious organizations is campaigning for a cleaner and greener Vrindavan. They have sponsored wall paintings all over town in Hindi urging everyone to be clean, not pollute the environment, most particularly the Yamuna, and to plant new trees while protecting the old ones. This consortium will have to tackle those responsible for some of the more deleterious ongoing trends.

There are some initial signs that the government cleanliness campaign is beginning. I saw schoolchildren going through the bazaar at Manasi Ganga, and picking up trash. They were organized by their schools, carried school banners, and were accompanied by their teachers. In addition, the government is introducing a cleanliness and sanitation curriculum in all schools, from primary through high school, and the message is being broadcast through all media 24 hours per day every day.

It is not impossible to conceive that this could result in a paradigm shift in values among the younger generation. Many westerners fail to appreciate that it was not very long ago that our own cities were once as filthy as those in India, and this was not reversed without a concerted long-term campaign to shift values that took decades and relied on universal education to impart the message. Despite this, there are many places in the United States that are blighted and filthy today, and plenty of Americans who do not care about their environment.

Srila Prabhupad said that the devotees see "so much contamination in Vrindavana...because your senses are impure, but when your eyes are smeared with the salve of love, they you can see Vrndavana. Don't judge Vrndavana by the external manifestation."[71]

We should never forget that Vrindavan is the most sacred place on earth for the Gaudiya Vaishnava. It is where the Supreme Lord descended to Earth in His true form, along with all His associates and the divine space of Goloka Vrindavana, and enacted his pastimes with Srimati Radharani.

It is for this reason that Sri Chaitanya Mahaprabhu traveled across the country to Vrindavan. When he arrived, he was swept away in ecstasy. Pilgrims who come to Vrindavan today, can go to the same spots where Sri Chaitanya chanted with thousands of people. Lord Chaitanya wept upon discovering the sites of Sri Krishna's pastimes in Vrindavan.

Sri Chaitanya dispatched the six Goswamis to Vrindavan, and you can see their bhajan kutirs, their samadhis, and their magnificent temples there. By worshipping in these same temples, you can participate in an unbroken chain going all the way back to Sri Chaitanya, Himself.

The Goswamis were exemplary spiritual beings. Their spirituality was so powerful that it permeates their sites scattered throughout Vrindavan 500 years later.

Vrindavan, India, October 14, 2014

On Srila Prabhupada and ISKCON

---

[71] *The Color Guide to Vrndavana*, Rajesekhara dasa Brahmacarya, Vedanta Vision Publications, Vrindavan, India, 1994, page 21

Srila Prabhupad is a universally recognized saint among Vaishnavas. His character is spotless. He was a man immersed in Krishna prem, personally in the presence of Sri Krishna 24 hours per day.

I am grateful to Srila Prabhupad, for he had a profound impact on my life. Srila Prabhupad presented me with Gaudiya Vaishnavism, "as it is," with no attempts to sugarcoat the message. He made it clear that the spiritual path is not the cheap and easy path, but requires time, dedication, devotion, and discipline. He made it clear that this path was not for the masses, but for those who could stick with it.

Through his books and his personal example, Prabhupad presented the essence of the profound philosophy of Gaudiya Vaishnavism. Because of Prabhupad, I was able to make my way through the minefield of competing scriptures and spiritual practices and make sense of this life and this world.

Prabhupad presented me with the gift of Acintya Bhedabheda-tattva, and Sri Siksastakam. I learned that we are inconceivably the same as the Lord, yet different, that we are eternal in the true sense, in that we have always existed and always will. I learned that Krishna created this material world for us out of love, because we wanted to be independent and live apart from Him. We live in this material world and sleep. We do not realize that our eternal position is to love and serve the Lord and be loved by Him in return.

Srila Prabhupad introduced me to the Hare Krishna mantra of Sri Chaitanya, which for over 40 years; I have heard, chanted and sung in countless variations, bringing me untold joy and ecstasy.

Srila Prabhupad introduced me to a spiritualized culture that transported me to ecstasy time and time again.

I am profoundly grateful to Srila Prabhupad. I feel I am personally communicating with him every time I read his books, and that he is personally taking time to guide me through the intricacies of the philosophy, and the perils of life here in the material world.

Sri Prabhupad founded ISKCON to realize Sri Chaitanya's prophecy that the Hare Krishna Maha Mantra would be heard in every town and village on earth. I have been associating with ISKCON and ISKCON devotees since I was in high school. One of my profound memories is the first time I picked up Prabhupad's "*Krishna Book*," in high school (the original one printed in Japan and underwritten by George Harrison). Over the years, I have met ISKCON leaders at the highest levels all over the world.

Some were very impressive and were true gurus and sannyasis. Others failed to impress at all, appearing merely petulant, power hungry, or puffed up.

I still remember the day in 1977 when I heard that Srila Prabhupada had left his body. I listen to my own inner voice. I cannot commit to any organization or guru unless my inner voice guides me there. Despite this, my association with some ISKCON devotees and gurus has been deeply moving. The one credible voice is that of Srila Prabhupad, as elucidated in his books. This is my guide and principal focus.

Vrindavan, India, October 14, 2014

Our Final Day in Vrindavan

We spent our final day in Vrindavan resting. After morning japa, bathing, dressing and breakfast, I spent several hours collecting my thoughts and getting them down on paper. The result was the two previous essays, "On Vrindavan," and "On Srila Prabhupada and ISKCON."

We had two appointments. At 1100, we went to the bazaar and picked up William's new Indian glasses. It was serendipitous. We walked all the way through the marketplace and the shop was free of customers as we arrived. The optician was just finishing the glasses. Since they were already paid for, William simply tried them on to see how they worked. He read from the booklet provided, and confirmed that they worked perfectly. It was inconceivable to us that fully functional prescription glasses could be had for $4.50.

At home, I had two small sets of figures of Radha Krishna in brass and one set of Gaura Nitai figures. I had purchased these at the Loi Bazaar in Vrindavan on previous trips. They had moved with me all over the world over the course of my travels. I kept them in a "Jai Govardhan" shoulder bag (jholla) also purchased in Vrindavan. The statues themselves are sturdy brass and difficult to damage. However, their eyes are made of shell and are glued in with a weak paste and fall out over time. Likewise, the small brass flutes that fit into the hands of Lord Krishna invariably become bent.

I went to Loi Bazaar and purchased new flutes for the Krishna murtis, new sets of eyes for all of the statues, earrings, and garlands, and new clothes. I also purchased small pictures encased in plastic. These are meant for a home altar and are similar to the pictures found on ISKCON temple altars. One was a standard devotional picture of the six Goswamis (seen in the introduction). This could easily go on my desk and serve to inspire me as I work. Another was of the guru parampara, ending with Srila Prabhupad.

While at the "ladies' Ashram" of the Narain Sect, I went to the bookstore and saw beautiful devotional prints. They are made from original paintings by an artist in the sect. I purchased two of these prints as well. One is of Gaura Nitai, and the other is of Sri Radha experiencing separation from Sri Krishna. I plan to frame these when I return and put them in my devotional space.

William is attracted to Jagannath deities, and should have a set where he can see them every day. There is no need to purchase these in Vrindavan and carry them in his bag all over India. These deities originate in Assam and are made there.

211

While revered and worshipped in Vrindavan, they are not produced there. A set crafted in Assam can easily be obtained from the Assam Emporium in New Delhi.[72]

At 1800 we had an appointment with Ahbinav, one of Srivatsaji's two sons. He met us at the Goswami residence and graciously made time for us, although he was very busy. We gave him our donations and 2,000 rupees for the servants, and thanked him and his family for everything they had done for us. Goswamiji was in Kolkatta and his wife in Mumbai, so Ahbinav will convey our feelings to them upon their return.

In the course of our conversation, Ahbinav answered several of my questions. He explained that the Banke-Bihari Temple was established by wealthy Marwaris (a business caste from Rajasthan) to accommodate their sense of worship. Being businessmen, they view worship not as an act of devotion, but a bargain with the Lord. They did not want protracted aarati or rasa, as found in the other temples; they want to make an offering in expectation of material reward. This is what Srila Prabhupad called "fruitive worship." The Marwaris thus built a temple that reduced puja to a transaction. Worshippers lay expensive offerings on the altar and provide money to the priests, who carry out hardly any ritual function. The Worshipper makes a specific request and expects the Lord to answer that request. Ahbinav said that the temple is held in low regard by devotee Vaishnavas, who consider it to be of a low devotional standard.

In addition to the Marwaris, this temple is patronized by Punjabi Hindus, who Ahbinav characterized as a cheap class interested in eating rich foods and shopping. Both groups flock to Banke Bihari in droves, while avoiding the other temples in Vrindavan. Likewise, the devotees in Vrindavan avoid Banke Bihari.

Ahbinav then described how difficult it is to be a priest at Radha Ramana. There are 40 families in the Goswami extended clan that administers the temple and carries out the pujas. These are all descended from Damodara, the original Goswami. This extended family has served the temple since it was founded. The Brahmin priests in each family serve the deity in turn in three month stints. While in service, as per Sri Chaitanya's instruction, the priests are considered equal in stature to Sri Gopal Bhatta Goswami, the original founder of the temple, and the person to whom the Radha Ramana deity manifested Himself.

When serving, the priest's work day is 18 hours long. He must get up at 0300 and walk in bare feet in priestly garb (the only clothing allowed is a dhoti and a shawl wrapped over the bare upper body), to open the temple. He must stay ritually pure and take numerous baths throughout the day and wash his hands 300 times before touching the Radha Ramana deity. While in the inner sanctum of the temple with the deity, he must be totally focused and not do anything but serve the Lord. His

---

[72] Upon our return, William duly went to the emporium and purchased a set, which grace his home today.

duties include dressing and feeding the deity and performing all the aaratis throughout the day.

Only the priest is allowed to move the deity from the altar to the throne set up in front of it, and he must do it by himself. He must be silent and absolutely focused during this act, as he is in sole charge of the deity. Ahbinav confirmed that this is a terrifying duty, for to drop or damage the deity would be catastrophic.

Radha Ramana is the only temple with the hereditary priesthood established by Sri Chaitanya himself and stretching back to the original priest. By the 18th Century, other Goswami temples were falling into disarray because they had no systematic means of recruiting and retaining priests. The priests were a series of babas, were not regulated and often fell down.

The king of Rajasthan intervened to save the temples and forced the other temples to adopt the hereditary system. However, these temples often retain only a single priestly family or a small group, instead of the 40 priests found at Radha Ramana. As a result, they are not as strictly regulated as the Radha Ramana Temple. Ahbinav then confirmed that Radha Ramana was the first temple to initiate westerners. The first western initiate was a British Royal Air Force pilot, who was initiated in the 1920's as Krishna Prem.

After our meeting concluded, we walked to Radha Ramana Temple for a final darshan. It was serene and peaceful there. As musicians played and sang bhajans, I collected my thoughts. There was no aarati, simply darshan. After the curtains opened, I stood in front of Radha Ramana for a long time looking at Him. I remembered that He is a self-manifested deity and God manifesting Himself before us. My heart was filled with great love and affection for Him. I gave Him my heartfelt obsceiences and departed for Jai Singh Ghera.

The servants have been expressing growing affection for us. A *chowkidar* stopped me and said, "Just as a rudraksha bead appears with the miraculous letter AUM on it, your appearance is as miraculous. I have seen many foreigners come here and none know India as well as you."

Vrindavan and Western Devotees

Much has been written about the presence of Western devotees in Vrindavan. I will not spend much time on this subject, as it was not our focus. We came to Vrindavan to live with Indians and spent our time almost exclusively with Indians. I went to the ISKCON Temple three times for various reasons while staying in Vrindavan, but the only devotees I associated with there were also Indian (principally Dharamatma Das).

There are three large groups of Western devotees in the city – ISKCON, the Narain sect, and the Chaitanya Math. There are independent Western devotees as well. Formerly the subject of considerable attention and controversy, especially among curious Indian pilgrims, Westerners no longer attract much attention in

Vrindavan. Many dress exactly like their Indian counterparts and behave no differently. Others are less well-integrated, but appear earnest and try their best. I was aware of no controversy surrounding them. The Indians seem accepting, if not terribly excited or very interested, when it came to the ever-present Western devotees. This is understandable. There is often a huge cultural and language gap between Indian and Western devotees.

The businessmen of the city appreciate the infusion of funds the westerners bring, as do the beggars, and rickshaw wallahs. Brijabasis are happy to shout "Hari Bol!!" or "Radhe Radhe!!" at passing Western devotees, just as they do with Indian pilgrims.

There are now, for some reason, large numbers of Russian, mostly female, devotees (or possibly just tourists) in Vrindavan. "Why Vrindavan?" It appeared to me that the preaching of some Gaudiya Vaishnava groups is having some impact in Russia and that large numbers of Russians had become interested in coming to India to pursue this new faith they had heard about. This was confirmed by a conversation we had with a British devotee at the Chaitanya Math. He said that his organization is privileged to have a Russian leader who is a charismatic preacher. His events attract thousands of Russians, who then become interested in Gaudiya Vaishnavism. This phenomenon, of course, also reflects the spiritual vacuum left in Russia after the collapse of the Soviet Union and its official espousal of atheism.

Some Russians seemed to be the epitome of spiritual dilettantes – with little idea of what they are doing. Others seemed no different from other Western devotees from a wide variety of countries. I suspect that this will sort itself out over time, and that the number of Russians will decline as serious devotees separate out from those spiritual seekers who move on to something else.

Western devotees from a wide variety of countries live in Vrindavan permanently or come on a yearly basis. The city fills up with Westerners during the holy month of Kartik, when it is most auspicious to worship in Vrindavan and the weather is more pleasant. It is not unusual to encounter these devotees during pilgrimage. Vrindavan is not an easy place to live and to live there for any length of time is difficult for Westerners used to all the comforts of life. Life in Vrindavan can be austere. A small group of devotees with sufficient dedication tough it out. Radha Kund has its own unique attraction as an epicenter of devotion, and attracts its own Western devotees, who live there permanently and are dedicated to the Kund and its environs.

During our stay in Vrindavan, we struck up conversations with devotees from Italy, the Philippines, and the Netherlands. Each has spent long years pursuing the Vaishnava faith and their personal sadhana in Vrindavan. They are a special subset of devotees with their own stories to tell.

Since we were not in Vrindavan to "hang out" with devotees from the West, we were polite and friendly but did not devote a lot of time to these encounters.

This inherent austerity is its own winnowing out process. It determines who sticks with this lifestyle, and who moves on to something else.

Departure from Vrindavan – Tirtha Yatra's End

I awoke at the usual time 0430 and performed japa while sitting in a chair outside my room. This is the time Vrindavan comes awake, as thousands of temples perform Mangala aaratis. The air fills with the sound of bells and gongs and chanting. The wife of one of the servants was walking around the same floor of the ashram at the same time I was performing japa. (The servants' quarters are just next door). We quietly said "Radhe Radhe," and do not disturb each other. She has her bead bag in her hand and performs her japa at the same time as me. For me, this somehow epitomized the spiritual essence of Vrindavan.

After japa, I took my bucket bath and dressed. As part of my transition out of Vrindavan, I removed the *kanthi mala* from around my neck, and cut the red thread from my right hand. I am leaving the holy dham and will soon become anonymous again. Nothing should distinguish me from the average man on the street and attract undue attention. After I leave the holy dham, I will no longer be a pilgrim (*tirthi*), but just another western tourist. I keep a larger *kanthi mala* loosely draped around my neck under my shirt, where no one can see it.

I then dressed in a complete set of Western clothes, including shoes and socks. This was the first time I had worn Western shoes in over three weeks, and the first time I was not wearing kurta and pajama. I took my wristwatch out of my backpack and kept it, with its leather wrist band, in my pants pocket. I would put it on after leaving the holy dham.

We finished packing our luggage and took it downstairs. The musicians were planning and singing "Hare Krishna." One played a harmonium, one played the mrdangam, and one sang. They played in the same spot at the ashram every day from 0700 to 1100. During this time at Jai Singh Ghera, I had several times removed my chappals, sat down on the carpet, and sang with them. We had never exchanged one word of conversation. Rather, they gave me deep looks welcoming me into their fraternity. They performed the Hare Krishna Maha mantra in many variations.

As usual, they wordlessly nodded to acknowledge my presence and we were joyful together. We communicated through the music and the Hare Krishna mantra. This was the last time I would sing with them during this trip.

Perhaps we would sing together again during another tirtha yatra.

We ate a dish of cholle from leaf bowls and drank some chai. This was our last Vrindavan breakfast.

Upadhayaji and Arvind bid us farewell. I thought I saw Arvind wipe a small tear from his eye. We bid "Radhe Radhe" to the other servants.

The taxi was right on time. We put our luggage in the trunk. Upadhayaji and Arvind waved to us as the car pulled out of the drive and down the small alley to Keshi Ghat and the street running along the Yamuna.

We saw all the sights of Vrindavan drift past the window of the car and then transitioned on to the highway. Of course it was more than a simple transition from a country road to an expressway; it was a transition from a timeless Holy Dham to a modern, fast-moving society. They are two worlds that do not overlap.

We were now back in that everyday India, sharing that space with 1.3 billion people.

Chapter XIII

The Himalayas

I am not a beach person. I am a mountain and desert person. As a child growing up in land locked New Mexico, we did not take beach vacations. We headed into the Rocky Mountains. I grew up camping in the mountains with the Boy Scouts and my family.

I fell in love with the Himalayan mountain chain as soon as I encountered it. The Himalayas are the world's greatest mountains. The Himalayan chain stretches across the northern edge of the South Asian subcontinent. Its mountain ranges cross the countries of India, Pakistan, Bhutan, and Nepal, and into Tibet and China. It includes some of the highest peaks in the world. I have been lucky enough to have traveled through the Hindu Kush Mountain Range of Pakistan, and the Himalayas of India and Nepal. By the time I finish, I hope to travel the length of the Himalayas, from one end to the other.

I encountered the Himalayas on my very first trip to India.[73] I have been coming back ever since. This mountain range has particular religious significance for Hindus. *"Him"* means "snow" in Sanskrit, and the Himalayas is "the land of snow."

Until recently, when advances in technology made travel much easier, it was difficult to get to the Himalayas. They were a remote and pristine place. As such, the Himalayas are home to both sadhus and the gods, and the site of many holy places. They were the place that the ordinary person could not go and where

---

[73] You can read about this trip in Volume One of *In the Clear Light of Day*

he/she could not stay. Hinduism has a strong renunciate tradition. Those truly devoted to a spiritual path are free to renounce everything, go to a secluded place and devote themselves to spirituality. The Himalayas is a traditional destination for such sadhus. It has therefore been traditionally home to holy men who have attained higher states of spiritual awareness. This often comes with spiritual powers (*siddhi*) and long life spans. I call such individuals "ageless babas." They are the stuff of legend and profound reverence in Hindu culture.

Hinduism embraces geomancy. This term is defined simply in most dictionaries as, "divination by means of figures or lines or geographic features,"[74] However, like many philosophical and theological terms, it cannot be adequately encompassed within such a simple definition. Scholars have written entire books on the meaning and implication of this word.

In the Hindu context, geomancy is the concept of "sacred geography." Hindus do not just believe in the abstract that there are sacred places that transcend the mundane and put the worshipper in direct contact with the spiritual world, they accept this as an everyday fact.

Many Hindus experience this reality during a "*tirtha yatra*" or pilgrimage. Diana L. Eck, in her excellent book *India (A Sacred Geography)*[75] makes clear what pilgrimage means to a Hindu. A *tirtha* is literally a ford, a place where one crosses a river. A *yatra* is a trip. A pilgrimage is therefore a journey undertaken to a sacred spot which serves as a ford or crossing between the material world and the spiritual world. This is not some theoretical formulation but an actual experience. The pilgrim goes on pilgrimage expecting to encounter and experience the spiritual world, which ordinarily would beyond perception. Likewise, a *dham* is a dwelling. Eck points out that for Hindus the holy *dham* is not just a place where pilgrims gain insight into the divine, it is a place where the divine descends to earth, and where the pilgrim, looking through eyes of devotion, can, for a time live in the spiritual world. He/she gains an experience of the eternal spiritual experience that is liberation (*moksha*), that is the pilgrim's ultimate goal.

My first Himalayan trip was in Kashmir. At age 20 in 1972, I journeyed to the Amarnath cave (elevation 3,888 meters) that houses the "ice lingam." In those days, it was a long and difficult trip. This is not the case today.

---

[74] This definition is from Merriam Webster, but you can find similar succinct definitions in other dictionaries.

[75] Harmony Books, New York, New York, 2012

Upon joining the Foreign Service, I was assigned to South Asia multiple times: Islamabad, Pakistan – 1985-1987, Dhaka Bangladesh – 1990-1992, Islamabad – 1995-1997, New Delhi, India – 2003-2007. I took advantage of these assignments to take repeated trips to the Himalayas.

The Himalayas are filled with sacred sites and it would be impossible to visit them all in one lifetime. However, for Hindus, the most sacred sites are the *Char Dham* (four holy places). These are Yamunotri, Gangotri, Kedarnath and Badrinath.

A typical Indian pilgrimage website[76] describes them as follows:

Yamunotri Temple: Maharani Gularia of Jaipur built the temple in the 19th Century. It was destroyed twice in the present century and rebuilt again. At Yamunotri, One can cook rice by packing it in a cloth and dipping it in the hot water of the Tapt kund. Pilgrims take this cooked rice home as "Prasad". Here near the temple "Pooja" can be offered to Divya Shila. (Altitude 3235 meters)

Gangotri Temple: The temple was constructed by the Gorkha General Amar Singh Thapa in the 18th Century, is situated on the right bank of Bhagirathi. (Altitude 3048 meters)

Kedarnath: The Kedarnath shrine, one of the 12 jyotirlingas of Lord Shiva, is a scenic spot situated, against the backdrop of the majestic Kedarnath range. Kedar is another name of Lord Shiva. According to legend, the Pandavas after having won over the Kaurava in the Kurukshetra war, felt guilty of having killed their own brothers and sought the blessings of Lord Shiva for redemption. He eluded them repeatedly and while fleeing took refuge at Kedarnath in the form of a bull. On being followed he dived into the ground, leaving his hump on the surface. The remaining portions of Lord Shiva appeared at four other places and are worshipped there as his manifestations. The arms appeared at Tungnath, the face at Rudranath, the belly at Madhmaheshwar and his locks (hair) with head at Kalpeshwar. Kedarnath and the four above-mentioned shrines are treated as Panch Kedar. (altitude 3384 meters)

Badrinath is one of the most celebrated pilgrimage spots of the country and is situated at an elevation of 3,133 meters, guarded on either side by the two mountain ranges known as Nar & Narayan with the towering Neelkanth Peak providing a splendid backdrop. This revered spot was once carpeted with wild berries. Thus the place got the name "Badri van", meaning "forest of berries." (altitude 3133 meters)

I made the pilgrimage to the *char dham* with my brother in law Ranu. He also traveled with me in 2014 from Delhi to Bihar, with a side trip to my home village

[76] Global Connect Hospitality, website

in Rankhandi, described in an earlier chapter. Ranu and I made this trip when I was assigned to Islamabad. I flew into Delhi from Pakistan and met him there. To travel to the *char dham* you must pass through the "gateway," which is the city of Hardwar. The Sanskrit word *dwar*, literally means "gate" or "doorway." To get from Delhi to Hardwar, pilgrims travel by train. The rail line ends at Hardwar. There are no railways in the Himalayas. Hardwar is at the very early foothills of the Himalayas. The holy Ganges River (*Ganga Mai*) emerges from the mountains at Hardwar and runs through the city. As the Ganges makes its way through the Gangetic Plain to join the Indian Ocean at the Bay of Bengal in far-off Kolkatta, it passes through town after town. Each town and city dumps its sewage and refuse, and industrial pollutants into the river. This has left Indians, and most particularly Hindu Indians, with a major crisis, that must be resolved. Efforts to clean-up the Ganges have been launched repeatedly by successive Indian governments, but with limited success.

At its midpoint, the Ganges passes through the sacred city of Benares. Hindus revere the Ganges as the most sacred of the many sacred rivers in India. They therefore journey to Benares for two principal reasons. Hindus take holy baths in sacred bodies of water to cleanse themselves and sanctify their efforts at obtaining liberation. A sacred bath in the Ganges is considered absolutely essential. To take a holy bath at the holy ghats in Benares is considered the most auspicious event of a lifetime. Upon death, Hindus aspire to be cremated on the banks of the Ganges and have their ashes interred in the sacred river. Many believe that death and cremation on the banks of the Ganges in Benares ensures liberation from further rebirth. Benares is therefore a principal pilgrimage spot.[77]

The Ganges is a glacier fed river. Its water comes from giant glaciers in the high reaches of the Himalayas. The water emerges from the glacier at the sacred spot of *gau mukh* (cow's mouth), in the high Himalayas. Global warming has, however, caused the glacier to recede, and it is no longer visible at gau mukh. Scientists warn that unless global warming is contained, warming will dry up the glaciers feeding the Ganges. This would precipitate a disaster in India, as a large portion of Indian agriculture relies on the Ganges for irrigation of crops.

The water at the source of the Ganges is totally pure. It is untouched by human hands. It remains so until it reaches Hardwar. This enables the pilgrim to take a pure and auspicious dip in the Ganges in Hardwar without journeying high into the Himalayas. Pilgrims collect this pure Ganges water in bottles and take it home

---

[77] You can read about my first visit to Benares and my first holy dip in the Ganges in Volume One of *In the Clear Light of Day*. The best book to read about the role of the Ganges and the meaning of Benares is: *Banaras (City of Light)*, Diana L. Eck. My edition is published by Penguin, Random House, India, Gurgaon, Haryana, India, 2015. This seminal work established Dr. Eck's reputation as one of the premier American scholars of Hinduism.

with them for use in pujas. I have carried such bottles of *"Ganga jhol"* (Ganges water) down from the high Himalayas myself.

Ranu and I travelled simply, as ordinary Hindu pilgrims. We got off the train in Hardwar and toured the city. Much has changed since I was first in Hardwar. Everything in India is changing rapidly. The once remote and inaccessible places are increasingly accessible, as roads, railroads, and airports open up once-secluded areas. As a result, many sacred spots within India that were once quiet and secluded, have been inundated with pilgrims and tourists. This easy access has opened the Himalayas to commercial development, with hotels, restaurants, and souvenir shops proliferating in areas that were once pristine wilderness.

This was not the case when Ranu and I arrived there. The city still retained much of its ancient character. The sacred sites within Hardwar are centered around the ghats, the steps that descend into the Ganges. The river is channeled between the ghats and flows quickly. Above the ghats are small temples manned by Brahmin priests, who perform sacred rituals, and read horoscopes.

Every evening there is an enormous "fire puja" at this site. In Hindu temples, priests use brass lamps with oil wicks as part of the puja. The worshipper places his/her hand above the flame and moves it over the face and forehead. In Hardwar the priests use massive lamps similar to torches. The reflection from these lamps illuminates the night and reflects off of the flowing Ganges water and the many bathers within. We strolled along the ghats observing everything going on and I took a holy dip. I have been to Hardwar on numerous occasions. I never leave the city without bathing in the Ganges.

The other spot that I usually go is the Manasi Devi temple. Wikipedia describes it thus:

Mansa Devi Temple, Haridwar is a Hindu temple dedicated to a goddess Manasa Devi in the holy city of Haridwar in the Uttarakhand state of India. The temple is located atop the Bilwa Parwat on the Sivalik Hills, the southernmost mountain chain of the Himalayas. The temple, also known as Bilwa Tirth, is one of the Panch Tirth (Five Pilgrimages) within Haridwar.

The temple is known for being the holy above of Manasa Devi, a form of Shakti, and is said to have emerged from the mind of Lord Shiva.[78]

This temple sits on a hill overlooking Hardwar and is reached by riding a cable car. Many villagers who make the Hardwar pilgrimage have never ridden a cable car. The temple experience therefore allows them to combine tourism with pilgrimage. I did not find going to the temple a particularly spiritual experience.

---

[78]Wikipedia

It was crowded with people and was in many ways more of a pleasure trip than a pilgrimage. There was a good view from the temple of the city laid out below, with the mighty Ganges coursing through it, and the throngs of worshippers at its banks.

Ranu and I spent several weeks in the Himalayas making our way to all four of the Char Dham. Once we arrived in the mountains we took local busses. Life in the Himalayas is much simpler than in Delhi. There was no meat or alcohol anywhere. The fare consisted of roti an dal, very similar to what I ate when I resided in Rankhandi. The air was free of pollution and had a sharp cool tang, that I associate with mountains. We stayed in basic Indian lodging, small guest houses that were incredibly cheap, sleeping on string cots (*charpoy*) and wrapping ourselves in quilts (*rezaaii*) to escape the cold mountain air at night.

Once we left Hardwar, it became incredibly quiet. We ate our simple vegetarian meals, chatted a little bit and went to bed early. The people were also simple and easy to get along with. No one spoke English. The mountain people (*pahardi*) speak their own dialects with each other, but speak Hindi with outsiders. There was none of the cynicism of the big city and no one tried to defraud me. They did not display the obsession with money so evident in Delhi. To our jaded urban eyes they appeared to be people satisfied with the simple things of life. There was a general innocence. I relished being there and relished the experience. It was profoundly peaceful.

From Hardwar, we moved on to Rishikesh.[79] This is one of my favorite spots in India. When we were there, it was a small town separated from Hardwar by deep forests populated by tribes of monkeys. There was a small one lane road connecting the two entities. I carried a backpack with my few changes of clothing and walked on the forest path to Rishikesh. Since those days, the forest has been completely swallowed-up by urban growth, and the two towns are no longer separated.

The *Rishis* were the ancient sages, spiritually realized beings. The Sanskrit word *kesh* means "field or place." Rishikesh is the place of the Rishis, the place where the sages reside. When we arrived on the path from Hardwar we saw the spires of the many Rishikesh temples arising from the opposite bank of the Ganges. In

---

[79] To people of my generation and background, Rishikesh will always be associated with the Beatles, as that is where they stayed at the Ashram of Maharishi Mahesh Yogi. The best book on this subject is: *The Beatles in India,* by Paul Saltzman, Insight Editions, San Rafael, California, 2018. Another book on the same subject by an Indian Author is: *Across The Universe (The Beatles in India)*, by Ajoy Bose, Penguin/Viking India, Gurgaon, India, 2018.

addition, there were ashrams and temples scattered throughout the hills behind Rishikesh, with their spires rising through the forest cover.

The bridge was a one lane footbridge and quite long, as the Ganges is very broad at this point. Along both sides of the Ganges are "beaches" of soft sand broken up by rocks. It is possible to cross the bridge, wander down to the sand and sit quietly and listen to the Ganges flow by. I have spent many happy hours in this spot. As it the wont of the mountains, everything changes throughout the day, as the sun takes a long time to enter the mountain valleys. It must rise above the surrounding hills. Until then, there is the long mountain morning. There is a distinct chill in the air until the sun's heat arrives, and everyone bundles up in sweaters and huddles around fires to keep warm. When I got up early and wandered down to the riverbank, the air was chilly and everything was bathed in half-light. The chilly air can be invigorating and there is an all-pervasive stillness that encourages spiritual practice.

Locals, pilgrims and residents of the many ashrams in Rishikesh go to the river bank, burn incense, meditate, and engage in myriad spiritual practices. Everyone gets up early, when it is still dark. They start small fires in the clay hearths (*chullas*) to brew up morning tea. Since Indian tea is black and boiled rather than steeped, it can be very strong and highly caffeinated. When in the Himalayas, we drank spiced herbal tea mixed with milk that was noncaffeinated. Caffeine is viewed as an intoxicant, and the consumption of all intoxicants is forbidden in holy *dhams*. This is the origin of the "yogi tea" sold in health stores across America.

It is easy to simply stroll around Rishikesh and visit the many temples and ashrams. There are many gardens attached to the religious establishments. When I first arrived, there were few motorized vehicles, if any. The streets were narrow lanes. I relish the food in the Himalayas. It somehow tastes different. Everything is vegetarian. There was a large "pure vegetarian" (*shudh shakihari*) restaurant in the center of Rishikesh. It was possible to buy a huge "*thalli*" (plate) of vegetarian food for only a few rupees. Everything tasted delicious.

After staying in Rishikesh for some time, Ranu and I went to the bus station and caught a local bus. It was similar to my train experience in that seats were at a premium. If lucky enough to procure seats, we did not leave them for any reason. The roads were winding and narrow and the busses old and underpowered and overloaded. They moved slowly. We spent many hours in our seats looking out the window at the passing scenery. As we climbed in altitude, the view from the window changed. The vegetation became sparser and we could spot snow-capped Himalayan peaks in the distance. The locals were totally dependent on the busses to get from one place to another. They lived in small far-flung villages and walked many kilometers to get to the road and catch the bus. This meant that the bus stopped frequently with villagers getting on and off. This meant that the bus trips were slow and long in duration, requiring the cultivation of the patience essential to successfully living in India.

We went to the Char Dham in the proper order, starting at Yamunotri and ending at Badrinath. Some temples were easy to access, as they were not far from the road. It was possible to get off the bus, find lodging, and then walk to the temples. They were not crowded. They were quiet. The temples themselves were sometimes relatively new, but they were built on timeless sacred spots that had probably housed a succession of different temples over the years.

Other temples were not so easy to get to. The most difficult was Kedarnath. At 3384 meters elevation, and in a remote location, there was no road leading to it. We got off the bus and were directed to a mountain path that wound its way into the clouds. We had no special gear of any kind, and the climb was quite steep and rocky. I wore aged hiking boots and wore them throughout the trip, (I have completely worn through several pairs of hiking boots in my travels) but Ranu had only street shoes. The hike was around 15 kilometers, moving ever upward on a steeply inclined mountain path that never flattened out and left no easy stretches for rest. We hiked silently, joining with other pilgrims. Some were taking a walking pilgrimage into the Himalayas, meaning they started from their home on the plains and walked all the way. Others were sadhus, wearing white or saffron dhotis and kurtas, with holy scarves around their necks. Some of them had matted hair in long dreadlocks going all the way to their feet. Others wore saffron turbans. Some carried pitchforks with three points (*trishul*) denoting their sadhu status. Periodically, we had to hug the sides of the trail to allow mountain ponies to pass. They carried wealthy and/or unhealthy Indians who wanted to make the pilgrimage but were unwilling or incapable of making the trek. The ponies were sure-footed, finding their way among the rocks on the path, and were led by their *pahardi* owners. Life in India's mountain villages is hardscrabble at best, and the *pahardis* supplement their meagre income by providing all manner of services to the pilgrims.

Since the climb was so arduous, there was little of the conversation one usually finds in India. There was a wide variation in personality among the sadhus. Some were quite friendly and outgoing, while others were silent. Here on the high mountain path, with the air thin and total concentration required to put one foot in front of the other, and to avoid slipping and falling on the rocks, we were all united in our silence.

Ranu and I were in the midst of our climb when it started to rain. It continued to rain throughout the rest of our hike. We had no raingear and were quickly and completely soaked. Our feet were also soaked. With our socks wet, our feet were swimming in water collected in our shoes The rocks grew slippery and the footing treacherous. Sunset comes early in the mountains and the temperature drops rapidly. We were wet, cold, and hungry when we arrived at the small village surrounding the temple.

While wandering through the narrow alleys looking for a place to stay, we encountered a villager who noticed our state and asked what he could do to help. He directed us to a humble dwelling and said we could stay there. It was one room with a fire in the center. We changed into dry clothes from our backpacks and removed our wet shoes and socks and placed them close to the fire to dry out. They literally smoked as the fire evaporated the water saturating them. We were barefoot and still shivering when our host arrived. It turned out he was a priest at the Kedarnath Temple. He was concerned about us and made sure we were able to dry our wet clothes and got some cooked food.

We lingered in that room with the priest and spoke into the night. In the mountains, once it gets dark, there is little or no entertainment. The options are to go to bed early or stay up and talk. This is particularly true when there is no electricity. The priest determined that we were earnest individuals with no guile. He offered to take us into the inner sanctum of the temple early in the morning at the most auspicious hour and perform a puja for us. We thanked him profusely and readily accepted his kind offer.

We awoke when it was still dark and cold. As is the custom, we were not allowed to wear any footwear in the temple compound. When we arrived at the gate, we immediately removed our shoes and socks. Our feet froze almost instantly. This is the *tapasya* (renunciation) needed for religious progress.

The temple was a square structure, not very large. It was made of stone blocks and set in a courtyard paved with large flat stones. The mountains rose above us into the darkness in all directions. We circumambulated the temple as is the custom, walking in our bare feet on the cold stone blocks. After completing the circumambulation, the priest took us into the temple. It was closed and there was no one else around. It was quite dark inside, lit only by small oil lamps. He took us through the section open to the public and into the inner sanctum in the back. We walked around a large stone brazier with burning coals inside while he performed a fire sacrifice, repeating Sanskrit shlokas and throwing various substances into the hot coals. They fizzled and burned up, glowing in the dim light. When he had concluded the ceremony, the priest led us from the temple. The sun had risen. The scene was bathed in light. We both felt like we had experienced something very special. It was serendipity that we had met the priest's family the night before and they had taken us in. As Keshava Bharati Goswami iterated to William and I in Vrindavan, "there are no coincidences."

After completing the puja experience, we bade farewell to the priest and hiked back down the mountain. Although the trail was still wet from the rain of the day before, there was no further rain. We hiked back to the highway and caught a local bus to our next destination.

At one point, we arrived at bus stop and pilgrims were getting out to trek to the Hemkund Sahib. This is a Sikh shrine in the "valley of the flowers," a heavenly mountain valley carpeted with flowers. Pilgrims walk on a narrow path through the idyllic valley to arrive at the Sikh Gurdwara at the pilgrimage site.

This is how Wikipedia describes the site:

Hemkund Sahib (also spelled Hemkunt), formally known as Gurdwara Shri Hemkund Sahib Ji, is a Sikh place of worship and pilgrimage site in Uttarakhand, India. It is devoted to Guru Gobind Singh (1666-1708), the tenth Sikh Guru, and finds mention in Dasam Granth, a work dictated by Guruji himself. Its setting is a glacial lake surrounded by seven mountain peaks. It is at an elevation of 4,632 meters (15,197 feet).[80]

I immediately wanted to get off the bus and take the trek to Hemkund. It would have involved another day long hike to a much higher elevation. Hemkund was beloved by Guru Gobind Singh, who had a religious vision at this spot. It is the highest elevation Sikh Gurdwara in the world, and is set at the edge of a pristine lake filled with freshly melted snow.

After hiking in, we would have stayed at the Gurdwara itself. Paid our respects and hiked out the next day. The hike is through the absolutely overwhelming "valley of flowers," a Himalayan valley surrounded by snow-capped peaks and carpeted in wild flowers. Ranu decided that we did not have time to make the *char dham* and visit Hemkund Sahib. This is one of the Himalayan spots I have yet to visit. I intend to make another pilgrimage and visit the char dham once again, and hike to Hemkunt Sahib.

I have vivid memories of another hike to another temple. I am not sure which one it is. Perhaps it is Badrinath. We hiked for several hours to reach it. It was perched on the top of a mountain, but higher mountain peaks rose high above it on all sides. It was a small temple, with a series of steps leading to its only entrance. We removed our shoes and went inside to perform our puja.

When we emerged, we were literally in the clouds. We stood on the steps and our feet were immersed in clouds. We could not see anything but clouds in all directions. It was as if the temple were built on a giant cloud. This temple is so far up in the Himalayas that it is physically impossible to remain there in the

[80] Wikipedia

winter. Every fall, the priests light lamps inside the temple and trek down to the towns to spend the winter. When they return in the Spring, the lamps are still lit, even though the oil only lasts for several days at best.

Gau Mukh

I had long wanted to make the trip to Gau Mukh. It was described in the texts as the sheer wall of a glacier. Pure glacial water was said to flow from an opening in the glacier wall. The opening was said to resemble a cow's mouth, thus the name *gau mukh*. According to my reading, it was impossible to hike all the way to the site in one day. There was said to be a spot not far from the site where it was possible to rent blankets from a woman who provided services to the pilgrims. The books stated that it was necessary to spend the night at that spot, and perform the puja the next day. For some reason, perhaps my active imagination, I got the impression that this overnight stay would be in a cave.

When assigned to Delhi, I decided it was time to make the trip. I went with my son. This time, we decided to charter a car and driver rather than take local busses. We started in Delhi and drove to Hardwar. We stayed at a guesthouse in Hardwar that was formerly a hostel for pilgrims. It was an old building not far from the Ganges. It was not cheap by Indian standards, and was restored and furnished with original furniture from the 19th Century. My son and I both love Hardwar. He is visibly changed when he goes there. His excitement is palpable. We ate a wonderful vegetarian meal, had a night of deep sleep that seems to only come in the mountains, and awoke early in the morning to walk to the banks of the Ganges to pay our respects.

We then packed into the car and drove to Rishikesh, where we paid our respects at all the spots and enjoyed the wonderful food and yogi chai before heading out into the mountains. To visit Gau Mukh it was necessary to first go to the holy dham of Gangotri, and our car headed higher and higher into the mountains. It took several days to reach, and we stayed in simple Indian guest houses.

I awoke early in one such rest house. We were staying on the second floor. I wandered out of the building alone. It was in a small village next to a raging mountain stream, with the usual high peaks and steep mountains on all sides. Someone had built a devotional garden next to the guest house. I went there and sat on a bench. There was a statue of Shiva at the head of the garden. I ruminated and contemplated the scene and felt at peace and glad to be alive.

The car parked at Gangotri and we put on our packs and started walking. We followed a path along the Bhagirathi river which pours from Gau Mukh and joins with other Himalayan rivers to constitute the Ganges. We arrived at the edge of the town and entered a shed-like building that covered the roaring river. This was a spot especially constructed for pilgrims to take baths in the flowing water and

226

collect *ganga jhol* to take home with them. My son was so moved by this moment that he could not walk any further. He put down his pack and went to the edge and sat at the edge of the raging water for a long time taking in the scene. He could not get over the power of the rushing water, the overwhelming sound it produced, and the sacred environs.

Gau Mukh is located at 4,023 meters elevation. The air is quite thin. As we walked along the river, we crossed the tree line and vegetation melted away. It became more and more difficult to breathe. There were rocky cliffs on either side and boulders dotted the landscape. We were accompanied by the roaring sound of the river rushing beside us throughout our walk.

We encountered very few people. Only the most dedicated pilgrims go to sites such as Gau Mukh, which require strenuous hikes. After hours of walking, we encountered a small band of sadhus, all dressed in white. Unlike us, they did not have any backpacks or warm clothes. It is said that the more advanced of the Himalayan sadhus can endure extreme cold without discomfort and eat practically nothing. They were in a happy mood and greeted us with ebullient warmth. As soon as we entered the mountains, the English language disappeared. We were in a monolingual environment. Hindi was the only language. It thus came as no surprise to me when they addressed me in Hindi and started joking, laughing and making conversation.

They said they were heading deep into the Himalayas on a religious quest, and asked whether my son would like to join them and become a sadhu. When I translated for him, my son was chagrined and laughed. "It is tempting," he said. "How often do you get an offer like that." However, he quickly determined that it was not to be and politely declined. We came to a fork in the trail, and the sadhus departed on their way.

We hiked the entire day and were increasingly short of breath. We came to a valley strewn with large rocks. There was a simple tarpaulin structure built over some flat rocks. This was the break point. The sun was already setting and it would soon get quite cold. We walked under the flap of the tent-like structure and arranged for our stay for the night. This was definitely not the cave I was expecting. The only other guests were a group of traders, who took pack animals filled with goods to remote locations in the Himalayas. We paid to rent some warm woolen blankets. We would wrap ourselves in these thick woolen blankets to keep warm and reduce the hardness of the rocks we would be sleeping on. We bought some simple cooked food. We laid our blankets on flat rocks and drifted off to sleep. The sound of the river was ringing in my ears in my half-waking state. I also heard the horsemen joking and laughing. Although I was sleeping on a flat rock during a long and cold mountain night, I slept soundly. I had very vivid dreams and awoke with the dawn.

After eating a simple breakfast and drinking some yogi chai, we started out for Gau Mukh. There was no longer a trail. There was only rocks, with water flowing through the walks. It was a difficult hike, but we made it to our destination.

We were disappointed to discover that the sheer wall of the glacier was no longer there. The Gangotri Glacier had broken off and receded. Although we were unaware of it at the time, this was the impact of global warming. We were later told that it would be another 25 kilometer hike to actually see the glacier. We were told not to attempt it. It was too difficult. We were also approaching the Chinese border and were told not to get too close, as we could stray into Chinese territory.

Once we had gotten over our disappointment, we explored the site. It was a field of rocks, they were of different sizes, but were generally about the size of a brick. They were rounded. Ice cold water from the glacier flowed between the rocks. I knelt down and performed a puja, sprinkling the holy water of the Ganges on my head and praying. This locale would be similar to the Himalayan valley in Nepal where vaishnavas go to procure their personal shilas. In that locale, the pilgrim would walk through the rocks, all round and smooth from the glacial water and wait for one to speak to him.

My son wandered around the site and his eyes strayed to the ground where he spotted a brand new 500 rupee note. It looked like it had gone straight from the printing press to the rock in the Himalayas. It was almost miraculous. I told my son that this event could be interpreted two ways. It was possibly a miracle in that God had made this appear to him as a an auspicious sign, or someone had performed a puja on this spot and left this brand new note as an offering. In either case, I told him, you should treat the note with respect. If you are planning to take the note away and not leave it as an offering to Ganga Mai, I said, you should hold on to the note and not part with it under any circumstance. He ignored my advice and spent the rupees when he returned to Delhi.

Having completed our pilgrimage to the holy site, we hiked back. I do not recall whether we spent another night on the flat rocks, or determined that we would hike all the way back to Gangotri (around 25 kilometers). I think it was the latter.

I had foolishly packed too many things, including sleeping bags that we never used. As the hike progressed, I began to tire. My lungs were becoming strained from hiking with a loaded pack at such a high altitude. We had been breathing very thin air for several days and carrying overly heavy loads. My son was much younger than me and was doing well. As we hiked, we encountered a group of *pahardi* horsemen. They asked whether they could give me a ride for a small fee. I agreed and climbed onto the back of a horse behind the rider and rode for the last few kilometers.

Hardwar and Rishikesh Redux

Just as Vrindavan became like a second home to me, I, over the course of time began to feel very much at home in Hardwar and Rishikesh. I do not think of them as different places, but rather different sides to the same place. This is because I always travel to both places together, at the same time. I particularly enjoyed the walk through the jungle from Hardwar to Rishikesh, which, sad to say, has now been eradicated. I experienced some of the same regrets regarding Vrindavan. When you return to places over a forty year span, you notice changes that take place over the course of time. This is particularly true when the pace of that change is rapid. These changes are not always for the better.

Hardwar/Rishikesh differs from Vrindavan in that it is a place that I journeyed to with my family. I traveled to Vrindavan with each of my children, separately, and with my wife, separately, but never as a family together. This was not the case with Hardwar/Rishikesh.

I already described how my daughter and I took a trip together to Hardwar/Rishikesh. It was a glorious trip and one of our fondest memories. We gloried in the special atmosphere. We spied a shikha (spire) of a religious building sticking out of the forest covering the foothills leading up to the Himalayas. We, on the spur of the moment, decided we would hike to the spot. I have no idea what we expected to find at the end of our hike. We walked through the low trees and bushes along country paths, moving ever-upward. We relished the peace, the quiet, and the feeling that we were connected to India's Vedic times. Of course, when we made it to the end, we had arrived at a small Himalayan ashram surrounded by trees. We lingered for a while, took in the moment, and headed back.

Once, while walking through some ashram grounds, I got the urge to reread *Autobiography of a Yogi,* by Paramhansa Yogananda. This is a spiritual classic, and one of the most widely-read books by young Westerners moved to study Hindu spirituality. I retraced my steps back to the Ashram bookstall and bought a copy and read it again while traveling. It was an Indian version and extremely cheap. I still have the book in my library.

I must have felt protective of my daughter, for I did something in Rishikesh that I would not have done ordinarily. I love the Himalayas, and feel comfortable there, and generally when traveling in India, I go with the flow. In the Indian fashion I go to the bus stand and find a bus going where I want to go and get on. For some reason, when it was time for us to return, I was unable to do that when traveling with my daughter. Instead, I took the totally superfluous step of buying bus tickets from the young men who keep a stall in the bazaar. I had to pay extra money for this service, and they themselves seemed surprised that I was willing to do so. I bought the tickets the day before, and when it was time to go, we went to their stall and they walked us to the bus stand and put us on our bus. I felt embarrassed that as an old India hand, I had to rely on the lads in the bazaar. It was something inexplicable that has not happened since.

When we were on the bus heading back to Delhi, it was a long trip. There was a young American woman sitting in the seat behind us. She was traveling alone on a mega trip throughout India. It is always puzzling to me when I meet young Western women traveling alone in India. The country is extremely dangerous for women. Indian women must be very careful, lest they find themselves victimized by misogynistic Indian men. Delhi is called the rape capital of India, and Indian women living there must be careful everywhere they go, conscious of how they are dressed and how they deal with strangers, and how they act, especially when taking public transportation. Yet, this woman, who as a white Westerner, attracts lots of attention wherever she goes, takes her life in her hands and travels alone.

She explained to us that she worked on a fishing boat in Alaska, and as a single person, saved up her money and used it to take adventurous trips around the world. This was her year to go to India.

When I traveled to Hardwar/Rishikesh with my wife, she was as entranced as I was, most particularly with Rishikesh. We walked across the long footbridge over the Ganges to the bank opposite from Rishikesh. We walked into a small building. Someone sat there on the floor in Indian fashion, selling all manner of religious paraphernalia. My wife had never exhibited much interest in such things, but from time to time, her innate Indian heritage comes forth in her. She gets into conversations with Indians regarding innately Indians things, such as the magical properties of gemstones. She will, for example, buy a gemstone and put it under her pillow to see what kinds of dreams she will have. If she has pleasant dreams, she will take the stone to the jeweler to have it set into a piece of jewelry. Should she ever experience bad dreams, she would take it as a sign that the jewel is not meant for her, and she would get rid of it.

Once in the shop, my wife got into a long conversation with the person seated there regarding all manner of Indian esoterica. This is not the kind of conversation she would typically have, especially in Delhi. After conversing for some time, she purchased a copper vessel (lotha), when she got home, she placed water in the lotha, kept it by her bedside, and drank it every morning for its medicinal benefits. I have found that Indians of all religious and ethnic and socio-economic backgrounds engage in such practices. It is a pan-Indian phenomena not limited to Hindus. My wife also purchased a bracelet made of rudraksha beads. I cannot recall what my wife did with these beads upon our return to Delhi, or where they are now.

We traveled to Hardwar/Rishikesh as a family, wife, children, and myself. Kristian fell under Hardwar's spell during this trip. It was evening and we were attending the fire sacrifice. The Brahmin priests stood at the edge of the ghat in traditional priestly attire, saffron dhotis, shirtless, wrapped in shawls over their bare torsos, with the sacred thread (jeneuu) clearly visible strung over the shoulder and across the chest. The sun was sinking into the Himalayas, and the particular inky darkness associated with the mountains was descending over the city. They waved their giant diwas over the rushing Ganga, while reciting melodic Sanskrit shlokas.

The water was filled with devotees from all walks of life, and from all over India. This was an example of the ultimate democracy of Hindu worship. Although India is a caste-bound society with deep social and ethnic divides, everyone is equal when in the Ganges. It is no questions asked. No one cares who you are. There is no question of a religious requirement. This is not something restricted to Hindus, or restricted to Indians, although, we were the only apparent non-Indians present. My son was so moved, that he spontaneously removed his shirt, pants, and shoes, and like other male devotees, descended into the Ganges in his underwear. India is a puritanical society with very strict dress codes, and standards of "decent" attire, especially for women, but when it comes to taking the holy dip, all such restrictions are lifted. It is a transcendental experience not bound by the rigid codes of the secular world. My son remained in the water for a long time. When he finally emerged and dried off and put his clothes back on, he was bathed in an effusive glow. It was obvious that he had just undergone a deeply-moving spiritual experience.

We had not booked any place to stay in Hardwar, and made enquiries and were directed to an ashram not far from the Ganges. It was a quiet place. It was the real deal. India is replete with stories of religious charlatans who take example of earnest religious seekers at the holy places. Our experience at the ashram was the opposite. They asked for a tiny amount of money from us and provided us with a clean, spartan room. The ashram was so close to the Ganges, that we could hear the sound of the rushing water throughout our stay.

We retired to our room for the night and were relaxing. Outside of our window, a Brahmin priest was performing a family puja for a group staying at the ashram. The sound of the shlokas wafted through the air into our room, along with the smells of Indian incense, and the ringing of small bells. It transported us immediately to another spot. Indians often say that whenever they smell real Indian incense they are transported to an Indian temple, or a sacred spot. This is certainly the case with us.

When we woke up in the morning, the ashram provided us with simple vegetarian fare. This food, despite its utter simplicity, tastes better than the most expensive gourmet meal consumed at the fanciest restaurant. I can say this from experience, for I have dined in gourmet restaurants all over the world.

After our meal, we changed into suitable attire. I cannot recall whether my son and I wore swimming suits. I probably wore a kurta pajama of simple cotton, in one color, probably white, with no designs. This is part of the simplicity of Indian life that I cannot get enough of, and to me represents the heart and soul of India. The women would not wear inappropriate attire, and probably wore a simple cotton shalwar kameez (pant-shirt) outfit.

The ashram had its own bathing ghat and the entire family took a holy dip together. The rushing Ganges water (ganga jhol) was crystal clear and was emerging out of the holy Himalayas. It had its origin in Himalayan glaciers and was still icy cold. The water was rushing by so quickly that we had to hold on to thick iron chains firmly grounded into the stone wall of the ghat. We descended into the water down the steps of the ghat holding tightly to our individual chains. Once we were up to our necks in the Ganges, we held on to the chains and immersed ourselves into the cold water. We emerged from the Ganges and simply held on to the changes and felt the rushing water. We stayed like that for some time. It was an inexplicable shared ecstatic experience. We all agreed that everything about the ashram was special and that this was an experience we were meant to have, and that we were guided to this ashram.

Another vivid memory for this trip concerns our emerging as a group from some eatery, where we had just consumed another pilgrim vegetarian feast. The street was filled with people from end to end. This is not an unusual experience in India. In Delhi, we often encountered such streets. In Delhi, the experience was aggravating, and we resented the inevitable pushing and shoving and could not wait to get out of the crowd. This was not our experience in Hardwar. For some reason the experience was pleasant. It was as if we were all sharing a special experience.

Chapter XIV

Non-Himalayan India

While the Himalayas are sacred territory and dotted with numerous pilgrimage destinations, this does not mean that the rest of India is devoid of tirthas. In *India (A Sacred Geography)* Diana L. Eck provides a useful map as a scene-setter before she even gets into the text.[81] When I glance over the map, I see that I have traveled to almost all the spots in the Himalayas, and everything associated with Lord Krishna in Vrindavan (for some reason, she does not include Mayapur on the map).

I have traveled all over India and have visited many non-Himalayan spots she mentions. For example, she lists the following notable North Indian tirthas I have visited:

Kurukshetra

This is the site of the final battle of the *Mahabharata*, and the site of the narration of the *Bhagavad Gita* by Lord Krishna to Arjuna. I visited this site while residing in Rankhandi. ISKCON had opened a temple there, and I spent a quiet afternoon conversing with its President. Kurukshetra is in rural Haryana state, surrounded by farm fields. There is a statue of Krishna and Arjuna on the spot where the *Bhagavad Gita* narration took place. They are both standing inside the chariot. I have seen pictures of this scene all over India. It is found in almost every Hindu home. It felt humbling to be standing on the actual spot.

Delhi

Delhi is a vast historic panoply and contains religious sites sacred to both Hindus and Muslims. Over the course of this narrative, I have described Delhi and environs in some detail, most particularly in Volume One. I will discuss Delhi in greater detail in a subsequent chapter dealing with Islam.

Ajmer

While many Hindus take pilgrimages to Ajmer, it is technically a Sufi Muslim religious site, and I will deal with my experiences there in my subsequent Islam chapter.

Pushkara

---

[81] Page XII

Pushkara is located in the state of Rajasthan. It is ordinarily a small village, which swells in size during the annual Pushkar camel fair. My wife and I attended this fair during which Rajasthanis from villages all over the state converge on Pushkar. It is not only an event during which thousands of camels change hands, it is truly a fair, replete with temporary bazaars, and lots of cultural programs, music, and food consumption.

Pushkar is the site of the only temple in India in which Lord Brahma is worshipped. Lord Brahma plays a big role in Hinduism. I have spent years reading the *Srimad Bhagavatam*. In this monumental work, Lord Brahma plays a crucial role as the father of the creation of the material universe. The *Bhagavatam* describes Lord Brahma's role in this creation process in great detail. The Gaudiya Vaishnava Sampradaya, to which ISKCON and most other groups in this tradition subscribe, traces its origin back to Lord Brahma.

Western textbooks on Hinduism used to teach the doctrine of a "Hindu Trinity," which purportedly consisted of Lords Brahma (creation), Vishnu (maintenance), and Shiva (destruction). This simplistic concept was imposed on Hinduism in an effort to make this complex religion more intelligible, especially for Christian audiences brought up with the concept of a holy trinity. I have not heard Indians make any reference to this concept, and it seems to have fallen out of favor in Western curricula as well.

Despite his importance, the worship of Lord Brahma, which was likely common in earlier eras, has largely stopped. We thus find only the one remaining Brahma temple in Pushkar.

After taking in the camel fair, my wife and I wandered into the village. The temple is in a quiet location in Pushkar, located on the edge of a large "tank" (manmade pond). It is a small one story affair and was quite sleepy when we visited. We spent some time there taking it in, and there was no one else around. Eventually a Rajasthani peasant family entered the temple courtyard, and were quite surprised to see foreigners for the first time. They appeared much more interested in us than in the temple. They were gracious and hospitable in the rustic fashion of rural India and totally free of guile. They walked up to us and asked to be in a photograph. We duly took the picture, and they had an exciting story to tell of their strange encounter when they returned to their village.

Mount Abu

Mount Abu is more famous in India as a "hill station" than a pilgrimage site. It is the only hill station in Rajasthan. I have been to Rajasthan many times for both business and pleasure. It is one of my favorite places in India, and the ancestral home of the Rajput caste in which I was inducted. My wife and I took one grand trip in which we hired a car and driver and spent weeks traveling from one end of

Rajasthan to the other, taking in all manner of religious, historical, and cultural sites, as well as scenery. For example, we journeyed to the Thar Desert, which is an actual desert like the Sahara Desert, and we perched on the edge of tall sand dunes, and rolled down.

Our Rajastani trip culminated at Mount Abu, where we stayed in a "chummery" left over from the Raj. When British civil servants, and military officers served in colonial India, they often went in together on a house, called a "chummery." The building we stayed in appeared unchanged from the day the British left, and was still furnished with the original furniture and pictures. I have often had this experience in India, Pakistan, Bangladesh and Sri Lanka, finding British buildings unchanged since the departure of the British, often including the interiors, which still boast the original furniture. Handmade Indian furniture can be quite sturdy and last forever. Indian furniture makers are incredibly skilled and can copy any style, often with only a picture from a book or magazine for a guide. For the British, they made the clunky Victorian furniture everyone in the UK was familiar with. I know this from experience, as much of the furniture in my Tucson home was made in India, Pakistan, and Bangladesh.

Mount Abu was a lovely site. The British built hill stations in locations where they could escape from the heat in the era before air conditioning. As expected, the climate was delightful, and the greenery refreshing. It was great to see green pine trees, as Rajasthan is a desert state very similar to Southern Arizona where I live.

There was a temple not far from our "chummery." which is the pilgrimage site. Eck states that describes it as a place "on a steep forested hillside of Mount Abu in Rajasthan, thick with ferns, moss, and fan palms. There Gomukh Kund, a square, stone bathing tank, is filled with water that flows through the mouth of a white marble cow's head protruding from one side, fresh marigolds tucked behind its ears."[82] It was a sleepy rural temple and not very busy.

Ayodhya

Ayodhya is the site of the birthplace of Lord Rama, the principal character in the Hindu epic, *the Ramayana*. Lord Rama is a much-beloved incarnation of Lord Vishnu (especially in North India). He is depicted in iconography as a handsome young man of the Kshatriya caste, often carrying his bow and accompanied by his consort Sita. In *the Ramayana*, Lord Rama is portrayed as the ideal devotee, the ideal ruler, and the ideal husband. He represents the aspirational role model that all good Hindus should aspire too. His picture can be found everywhere in North India, as well as temples dedicated to him.

---

[82] *India (A Sacred Geography)*, page 135

There is some contention regarding the location of Lord Rama's birthplace and the birth site has become a political and communal football, with Hindu nationalists saying that the Muslims tore down the Ram birth site temple and constructed a mosque (the Babri Mosque) over it. In December 1992, Hindu militants descended on the mosque and destroyed it. In my previous discussion of the ISKCON temple in Dhaka, I described the aftermath of this event, which set off communal rioting in India, Pakistan, and Bangladesh. Muslims in Pakistan and Bangladesh destroyed numerous Hindu temples in retaliation for the destruction of the Babri Masjid.

When assigned to the US Embassy in Delhi, I traveled to the temple site as part of my duties. Indian archeologists took me to the area they had excavated beneath the destroyed mosque to show me what they said were the remains of the destroyed Ram temple. The Hindu nationalist BJP government said this was definitive proof that Muslims had destroyed this sacred site and erected a mosque over it. They have demanded that the Hindu temple be rebuilt, although the site is in dispute, with both Muslims and Hindus claiming it. I was also shown a new disassembled Ram temple. It was made of massive stone blocks. Each block was numbered. BJP activists told me it could be erected at the site in a matter of hours.

While we were at the hotel, we encountered a group of gunmen from the Samajwadi Party, notorious for violence and corruption. This was not the first such encounter for me. During the period of Samajwadi rule, its gunmen were found all over Uttar Pradesh. They drove four wheel drive vehicles and carried sawed-off shotguns, and terrorized those deemed enemies of the party. They were eyeing my wife. The hotel was quite rudimentary and security non-existent. Fearing a late-night attack by the gunmen, my Indian assistant called the Maharajah of Ayodhya and asked whether he could take us in, as our location was not secure. He was happy to do so, and we spent a pleasant evening in his palace and dined with his family.

Prayag

Diana Eck writes:

"The great site of the meeting rivers in north India is the *sangam*, the confluence, of the Ganga and Yamuna at Prayaga, which the city now called Allahabad, stands...According to the Puranas, there is also a third river, the Sarasvati, that joins the confluence at Prayaga, flowing in from underground. The Saraswati was clearly one of the great rivers of Vedic India, so impressive that it is mentioned some fifty times in the Vedic Hymns."[83] Eck uses Vedic texts to confirm that this

---

[83] *India (A Sacred Geography)*, page 145

confluence of three holy rivers is one of the most auspicious places in India to bathe and has been so since the Vedic times.

The two mighty rivers flow together. They are both very broad and the confluence creates a wide expanse of water. As the pilgrims do, I rode out into the center of this expanse in a boat and took my holy dip.

Varanasi

I have traveled to Varanasi numerous times for both business and pleasure. I described my first visit to Varanasi and my first holy dip into the Ganges in Volume One of *In the Clear Light of Day*.

Kolkatta

As described earlier, Kolkatta has been a central location for me. I have been to the city numerous times and have explored its environs quite thoroughly. It is a fascinating city replete with religious sites, and places cultural, historical, and political significance.

During one of our trips to Kolkatta, my wife and I visited the only temple in India that still performs animal sacrifices, located on the banks of the Ganges River. We saw the location where goats are placed into a stock-like device that keeps them steady, so that temple personnel can decapitate them with a large knife. We did not witness a sacrifice, however.

Kolkatta is also known for its association with Ramakrishna, a 19th Century Hindu saint and reformer and the founder of the Ramakrishna Mission, one of the oldest Hindu organizations to make forays into the West. We were also able to see sites associated with Ramakrishna and his successor Swami Vivekananda.

The notable places I have yet to visit are located primarily in the states of Gujarat (Ahmedabad, Girnar, Somnath, and Dvarka), and Orissa (Bhubaneswara, Puri/Jagannatha Temple). Of these spots, Somnath, and Dwarka are associated with Lord Krishna. After He defeated the evil *raksha* (demon) Kamsa in his birthplace of Mathura, Krishna's true identity was revealed. He had been living in Vrindavan as a cowherd boy (of the vaisha caste) to escape death at the hands of Kamsa (although as God incarnate, no demon could kill Him).

This was part of Krishna's holy lila. In reality, Krishna was born of aristocratic parents and was of the Kshatriya (warrior caste), just below the priestly Brahmin caste. After his true identity was revealed, Krishna became the Prince of Dwarka in present day Gujarat, where he played out his princely role in the cosmic story. As Prince of Dwarka, Krishna brought about the defeat of the Kauravas by the

Pandavas, related in the epic *Mahabharata*. This signifies the end of one period in the cosmic cycle (*yuga*) and the beginning of another.

Likewise, the sites of Puri, Bhubaneshwar and Kolkatta are associated with Sri Krishna Chaitanya, the 15th Century incarnation of Krishna. The Jagannath Deities located in the Jagannath Temple in Puri were much loved by Sri Chaitanya, and Puri is the site of many "pastimes" of Sri Chaitanya and the place of His disappearance. I plan to travel throughout Gujarat and Orissa in future trips. The Jagannath Temple is one of the few in India that refuse to admit "non-Hindus." The temple authorities define a "non-Hindu" as anyone who is not Indian. Since there is no way to determine for sure whether an Indian is a Hindu or not, this means that Indians who are not Hindu are easily admitted, while non-Indians, who may be practicing Hindus, are not. While my wife will be able to enter, I will be left standing outside.

Khajaraho

I have travelled to Khajaraho twice. I went there for the first time during my 1972 trip, which is related in volume one of *In the Clear Light of Day*. My second journey to Khajaraho took place in 2015, when I traveled there with Ranu. Here is what happened.[84]

The Khajaraho temple complex dates back to the 11th Century and was completed over several centuries. Rulers of the Chandela dynasty, a powerful kingdom in central India, built them. Over the course of time, the Chandelas declined in power and prosperity and were superseded by other dynasties. The temples were abandoned and covered over by the jungle. Khajaraho was a remote and inaccessible location (and remains so today). This is what saved the temples from desecration. During the height of Muslim iconoclasm, the temples would most surely have been destroyed. However, the Muslims did not know about the existence of the temples because of their remoteness. They had literally been swallowed up by the jungle and forgotten.

In the 19th Century, the temples were "discovered" by a British Civil servant conducting an administrative tour of the region. Local villagers must have provided him with accounts of the forgotten temples and their locations. He had the undergrowth cut back to reveal exquisitely carved temples, which stand today among the greatest examples of Indo Aryan architecture.

---

[84] This episode is excerpted from: Jon Dorschner, *My Indian Journey (Mera Bharatiya Yatra), Phase Three,* Clearspace Publishing, San Bernadino, California, 2016

What sets these temples apart from many others in India is the carving. The temples are covered in carvings depicting not only divinities, but also the everyday activities of people during the Chandelan era.

The aspect of the carvings that gets the most attention is the explicit sexual and erotic sculpture. The carvings depict three types of sensual women, the surasundaris (heavenly nymphs), apsaras (dancing surasundaris), and nayikas (mortal surasundaris). The Chandelas were obviously great admirers of feminine beauty and sensuality and there were sculptors in the kingdom capable of capturing this feminine ideal. The women are depicted in various stages of nudity or semi-nudity and the beauty of their bodies is captured remarkably. The anonymous sculptors were able to make the stone live and breathe.

The openly sexual carvings attract the most attention. They depict men, women (and it at least one case horses) engaging in a wide variety of sexual acts in all possible combinations. Several of the carvings show women looking on and holding a hand to their mouth in embarrassment.

It is not clear why the Chandelas included the eroticism in the temple decoration. These carvings elicited a powerful response when the British discovered the temples at the height of the Victorian era. They were deemed to be so pornographic that tours of the site were separated by gender and Victorian women were known to faint at the site of the carvings. The erotic carvings have been mistakenly linked to the Kama Sutra, that famous Indian manual of sexual practices, and the tourist gift shops in Khajaraho often sell the Kama Sutra, illustrated with photos of the erotic carvings to unknowing tourists.

Although people in Khajaraho, including a guide and an archeologist, put forth various theories to us as to why the carvings are on the temples, no one really knows for certain the reasoning behind it. The explanations include: the Chandelas were very sensual and virile people. The rulers wanted to demonstrate their virility by showing their sexual exploits on the temples. India was obviously not as puritanical in the 11th Century as it is today, and these carvings may not have caused the uproar then that is associated with them today (or especially in the 19th Century). The archeologist claimed that the Chandela rulers were concerned because the population of the kingdom was declining. He stated that the rulers determined that they would encourage more sexual activity, and more children, by depicting sexual activities on their temples, to show that it was approved and encouraged by the ruling establishment.

When I was in Nepal, I saw temples with similar carvings. The Nepalis told me that the purpose of the carvings was to so embarrass the lightening that it would not strike the temple. There are other documented instances of erotic carvings placed on Hindu temples both in Nepal and India for this purpose.

I did not find the explicitly sexual carvings all that erotic. They seemed absurd in a quaint way. The sexual positions displayed were closer to gymnastics than lovemaking. Some positions were so complicated that assistants had to hold the participants in place (sometime upside down) to complete the act.

The carvings of the surasundaris, apsaras, and nayakas, were far more erotic and sensual, even though these beautiful young women were not engaged in any sexual acts. These carvings were genuinely beautiful and tasteful, and could be appreciated and admired in the 21st Century.

Khajaraho was never more than a tiny village and then a provincial town. It is quite small, with a few main roads. The hotel was on the Jhansi Road, which led straight to the Western group of temples. This is the site of the principal temples. Most are contained in a walled compound. The site is administered by the Archeological Survey of India, which charges foreigners 250 rupees to enter. There are a few temples located outside the enclosure, including the Matangesvara Temple, which is the only temple in the group which is still active.

All other temples in the Khajaraho area are free. These include the temples in the Eastern Group. One set of temples in this group called the "old village temples," is set in a garden along a river in a quiet rural setting. Other Eastern Group temples are located in the Jain enclosure, attached to an active Jain Temple from the 19th Century.

The remaining temples are in the Southern group. These are placed randomly along the countryside, including some ruins that are hard to access. Most tourists concentrate of the Western group of temples. The others are not nearly so well visited and are much quieter. Over the course of the day, we saw all the temples in Khajaraho, and spent time in the "Old Village," a picturesque site located between the temple complexes, which is home to Brahmin families that have resided there for centuries.

After breakfast at the hotel, we walked up Jhansi Road to the Western Group of temples. We bought tickets, but did not immediately go inside. Instead, we walked down a tree-lined path to the Matangesvara Temple. A festival involving worship of Lord Shiva was going on at this temple. It involved only women. They had come from neighboring villages in great numbers to perform their puja and were dressed in colorful saris encompassing every color in the spectrum.

The women carried trays containing their offerings of fruit, nuts, and sweets, and lined up outside the temple to go inside. On the pathway to the temple stood a sacred tree, as can be found all over India. It was wrapped with red thread and beneath it was a small shrine. A sadhu sat beneath the tree. Women performed puja there and tied threads to the branches to register their requests to the divine. Burning joss sticks filled the air with fragrance.

As the festival was going on, we could not get inside the temple or even close to it. We satisfied ourselves with taking lots of pictures. It was amazing to see an active religious festival in such an old temple.

We then walked through the gate into the compound. It incorporated a beautiful garden, with lawns, trees and flower beds, with temples rising out of the greenery. The temples seemed to float above the grass with an otherworldly air, like something out of an immense science fiction epic. There were ten temples of various sizes at the site. Some were actually shrines attached to the larger temples. The first impression of the site is overwhelming. It is similar to seeing the Taj Mahal for the first time.

We had to remove our shoes at every temple and shrine. I was wearing Western clothes with lace up shoes, and had to take them off at each site. I was not expecting to remove my shoes, as this was not required the first time I visited. The complex looked nothing like what I remembered from my 1972 trip. Then there were no tourist hotels. I stayed at a small guest house across the street from the Western group. Then, everything was free. There were no guides or guidebooks and the temples stood in the middle of the countryside, with no walled enclosure. Then I was the only non-Indian present. I sat under a big tree in front of the hotel in the evening chatting with local villagers. A mentally disabled man from the village (every Indian village seems to contain at least one such person), walked up and began chatting in his own language that was only intelligible to him. The villagers found him quite amusing.

The guest house was still there. It is quite old and rustic. No longer used as a hotel, it contained several small shops. In 1972, I walked around the temples at will and never had to remove my shoes. Although only the Matangesvara Temple is still actively used, the Indian government concluded that the remaining temples retain their holy status. All holy buildings in India, regardless of religion, cannot be entered with shoes.

Our first stop was the shrine of Lord Varaha, the boar incarnation, one of the ten incarnations of Vishnu. When the earth had been cast into a cosmic sea by demons, Varaha speared it on his tusks and saved it from destruction. There are several shrines at the site devoted to Vishnu incarnations. Each contains an animal incarnation or vehicle (the animals upon which Hindu gods ride are called vehicles). The other shrines feathered Garuda, the bird that is Lord Vishnu's vehicle, and Nandi, the bull that is the vehicle of Lord Shiva. The statues were beautifully carved and in wonderful condition. They looked new, although they were 1,000 years old. They were covered with carvings, giving them a wonderful texture.

241

The main temples were dedicated to various deities, including Lord Vishnu and Lord Shiva and several goddesses. The temples vary in size and construction. Some are monumental and others smaller and more subtle. All feature the same architectural features. They are built on raised platforms and approached by walking up steep steps. The space at the front of the temple is kept empty, with more steps leading up to the sanctum sanctorum containing the deity. Some temples contained the deity statues, while others were empty. The space for each deity is surrounded by a parikrama (circumambulation) path, as is the case with modern Hindu temples. The interiors of the temples were not that amazing. The spaces were small the carvings not as spectacular as those on the exterior. The temples were generally dark inside (there was no interior lighting), making it difficult to make out detail.

We spent most of our time walking around the outsides of the temples admiring the ornate carving. Every surface is covered, and it is hard to comprehend how much time and effort went into these projects. It is not difficult to understand that it actually took centuries to complete the entire temple complex. The carvings show royal processions with elephants, which could be victory processions to demonstrate the military prowess of the Chandelas. There are depictions of people performing pujas, including figures with big bellies that could be Brahmin priests. Other statues depict people performing hatha yoga or meditating and such mundane activities as women combing their hair, applying makeup and getting dressed. The carvings provide a tableau of life during this period.

Carvings of divine and semi-divine beings supplement those depicting everyday life. These become repetitious, as they are repeated incessantly. One very common motif depicted a creature resembling a dragon, with a woman kneeling down in front of him. It appeared to be a metaphor for divine power and majesty. Ganesha was also shown at every temple, as he is the god that blesses all activities and renders them auspicious. As is still the case today, his presence ensures that the completed temple project will enjoy success.

It took us approximately four hours to see all the temples. By the end, we were tired, hungry, and thirsty. We left the compound and crossed the street to eat lunch at the same site where I had stayed so many years before. We ate in a South Indian coffee house. The food was delicious and the proprietor chatted with us. He told us to contract with a motor rickshaw driver to see the rest of the temples. He explained that his family came to Khajaraho over a century before to open a South Indian restaurant and was close to the ruling family. Khajaraho had been the site of a petty kingdom of no import. The proprietor pointed out the Maharajah's "palace" across the street. The building was so non-descript and non-imposing that we would never have recognized it as a palace.

By this time, the puja in the temple had ended. Large crowds of women and children gathered in the open space in front of the restaurant and loudly ate the lunches they had brought from home. As peasants from surrounding villages, they had no money to eat in restaurants, but were excited to enjoy an outing away from their villages. To them, Khajaraho was the big city.

The restaurant was located in a complex of buildings surrounding an old tomb. After lunch we walked through the gate into the center of the courtyard contained the tomb. It was a large building with a big dome and contained the body of a previous maharajah. The building was only from the 19th Century but was in bad shape. It looked like no one had bothered to keep it up. The Maharaja's family had established a small school along the wall of the complex. The schoolchildren sat in their uniforms on the ground inside low buildings repeating their lessons, while the schoolmaster walked among them.

We left the complex and walked down the road until we encountered a motor rickshaw. We contracted with the driver to take us to the remaining temples in the Khajaraho area. He first took us to the Eastern group temples within the Jain Enclosure. On the way, we drove through town and noticed lots of signs for guest houses and restaurants for European tourists. These included restaurants serving "genuine" Italian food and espresso. When we got to the Jain Enclosure a line of handicraft shops outside the gate featured signs written in Italian.

We walked through the gate into the Jain Temple compound. Jainism is an offshoot of Buddhism. The two faiths originated as a reaction against the excesses of Brahmanical Hinduism. Jainism takes an absolutist position regarding karma and non-violence. Jains are very abstemious vegetarians and limited in their choice of professions by their commitment not to kill any living being, even by accident.

The Jain temple was an ordinary 19th Century temple with nothing unique to recommend it. It had an attached book shop selling books on Jainism in various languages, but no one was inside. The temple had strict requirements to enter. We had to remove both socks and shoes and could not carry any object made of leather. We decided to pass on the temple and went straight to the ancient temples located beside it. This was the real reason why we had come after all.

The ancient temples were Jain as well, dating from the same period as the temples in the Western group. They were all but indistinguishable from the Hindu temples we visited earlier. The only appreciable difference was the presence of carvings of Jain Mahatmas (saints) along the outside. These were carved in a distinctive Jain style. The temples were smaller and less impressive than those of the Western Group, but it was a pleasant setting. The virtual absence of tourists made it possible to relax, sit, and enjoy the quiet ambiance, while surrounded by 1,000 year old temples.

The driver then took us to the old village temples, driving us through the old village to get there. I had been all over India, but had not seen anything like it before. In some ways, it appeared more Mediterranean than South Asian. The streets were completely paved. There was no dirt anywhere inside the village. The houses were painted in subtle pastels in a variety of colors. Each house featured a flat wall in front, and enclosed small gardens, with plants growing over the walls.

I told the driver to stop and let us take pictures. I walked up and down the village's main street. Villagers sat in front of their houses and small village shops conversing. I plan to use my photographs as a basis for an art project. I hope to use the photos as subjects and draw them in pastel colors on paper.

We jumped back on the motor rickshaw and drove through the village to a remote spot surrounded by a wall. Inside was a garden containing green lawns, some flowerbeds and massive old trees. The trees dominating the landscape appeared centuries old.

There was hardly anyone around. Several beggars sat in front of the gate plying their trade. In the rear were two nondescript temples. After the spectacular temples we had been looking at, these appeared anti-climactic. The temples were in bad shape. The roofs had caved in at some point and the Archeological Survey of India had done a poor job of reconstructing them. Random stones were placed over the temples to keep water out, but the congruity of the temples was lost. Two local men sat on the steps basking in the sun and relaxing. They said the temples were not much to look at, but agreed with us that the old trees were spectacular.

By now it was around 4 PM. The driver wanted to take us back to the hotel. I told him I had noticed a sign pointing to another temple and we headed off to see it. At first the driver did not want to go, saying the road was too rough. He eventually relented and turned off the paved road onto a narrow dirt track. It was muddy and rocky and led deep into the countryside. We drove over a narrow country bridge. Local boys sat on the edge playing cards and gambling. There was nothing but farm fields and trees and in all directions.

The motor rickshaw rounded a bend and we spotted a large mound and some sheds ahead. Getting out of the rickshaw, we approached the sheds, where several men lounged about. These included a *chowkidar* and several archeologists. They seemed bored and welcomed us, seeing our visit as an opportunity to break their monotony. The site, which appeared so unimpressive at first, turned out to be quite interesting.

A display showed how the site had been excavated. When first discovered, it was only a gravel-covered mound. As dirt was removed, it revealed the carved platform upon which the temple had stood. The rubble of the temple was on top of the platform. The archeologists took us around the site and demonstrated how they had stabilized it with plastic netting and were reassembling the stones. The local maharajah had placed a Shiva lingam on top of the site, where the original deity must have been situated. I took of my shoes and posed for several pictures at the lingam site. They turned out to be some of my better shots.

The site was covered with wild grass and wild flowers. We were able to get very close to the carvings and take close-up shots. The combination of the close-ups and the wild plants with their purple flowers gave the shots a surreal effect. In the photos, the statues seem almost fairy like possessing a life of their own. The statues seem to be interacting with the plants.

Orcha

The next day we rode the local train to Jhansi. The Jamshedpur train would not depart until night, so we had time on our hands. I had read in my guidebook that the town of Orcha, just over the Madhya Pradesh border was a must see location. We jumped in a cab.

When the taxi arrived in Orcha we were not disappointed. The town was the seat of the Rajput state of Bundela in the medieval era and the Rajputs had erected the enormous Chaturbhuj temple (dedicated to Lord Vishnu) in Orcha, as well as a large palace.

We took turns wandering the town, as one person had to stay in the cab with our luggage. It is part of the wonder of Madhya Pradesh that towns like Orcha sit almost abandoned in the countryside. I walked up the hill to the palace. There was a small hotel inside the palace, but no sign of serious tourism and no fees or guides.

I wandered back down the hill to the temple site and explored the inside of the temple. There was no artificial light and it was growing dim inside. The ceiling was already bathed in darkness. I walked through the enormous rear door and into the winding medieval alleyways leading back to the car.

South India

There are two distinct cultural zones in India. The Vindhya mountain, chain, which stretches across the middle of the country, divides North and South India. The two regions are vastly different. North India is dominated by one lingua franca, Hindi, spoken by the majority of people, regardless of their mother tongue. A Hindi speaker can travel throughout North India and converse with almost anyone. When I travel in North India, I am in a linguistic home region, where I never feel out of place. I can converse with a Gujarati, or a Punjabi, for example, whose mother tongue is not Hindi, but nine times out of ten, they will speak it.

While there are multiple languages in North India, they share many commonalities, and there is considerable overlap.

When living with Italians in my Italian provincial reconstruction team in Iraq, it became apparent to me that a European who speaks a romance language, Italian, Spanish, Portuguese, French, can understand much of what the speaker of another romance language is saying. I could freely use Spanish words with my Italian hosts, and they readily understood them. This is similar to the experience in North India.

This is not the case in South India. After independence, India created linguistic states. Each South Indian state has its own language, which is the language used for everything in that state. The South Indian languages are not mutually intelligible. Hindi is supposed to be India's national language, but the South Indians, the Bengalis, and others have resisted learning the language of the North Indians. This is one reason why English persists as an Indian lingua franca. This is particularly true in South India, where English remains more common than Hindi.

Language is not the only thing separating North and South India. While South Indians do not share a lingua franca, they share considerable cultural affinity. There is a distinct South Indian cultural pattern. South Indians feel at home traveling around their region, but feel out of place traveling or residing in North India. The same is true when North Indians venture South of the Vindhyas.

The map of India in Eck's *India (A Sacred Geography)*, shows that the Southern part of India contains a large number of sacred pilgrimage spots. My wife and I have spent considerable time in this region. We have traveled to all its major cities and traversed the countryside by train, bus, and cab. Over the course of our travels we visited many important South Indian temple complexes. I cannot remember the names of any of them. South Indian languages are known for their long, multisyllable words. It can be quite intimidating to pronounce and remember place names. In addition, no South Indian language uses the devanagri alphabet. Hindi speakers cannot decipher even one word.

While I cannot remember specific places, I retain powerful impressions. Most Indian temples are stand-alone affairs. While they can be located within their own landscaped compounds surrounded by walls, they are usually by themselves. South Indian temples are often enclosed in "temple-complexes" that can resemble cities in their size and scope. Within the complexes all kinds of activities are going on. Without the language, unable to read anything, and without a guide, it can be difficult to decipher what is happening. South Indian iconography can also be totally different. The pictures and statues of divine beings often bear no resemblance to those found in North India. I found it difficult to determine which deity I was looking at.

The temple architecture can be monumental in scope, with buildings of enormous size and antiquity. They rise up into the sky, and are covered in elaborate carvings, which are often painted in multiple colors, presenting a vivid tableau to the eye. Material aimed at educating Westerners about Hinduism, often features photographs and footage of these complexes, giving the false impression that massive Indian temples are found throughout India. North Indian temples can appear simple in comparison.

I often found the interiors of the South Indian temples to be very dim, almost to the point of darkness. I vividly recall standing in one temple that was so dark as to be close to pitch black, although it was the middle of the afternoon and the sun was brightly shining. There were no windows to let in natural light, and the only illumination was from small oil lamps. The lamps consisted of round clay saucers with space for ghee. A wick lay within the ghee, saturated with clarified butter. A short spout extends from the saucer making a space for the wick. This lighted wick provides the flame. The ghee was very pungent and the air smelled like old butter.

It appeared to me that the South Indian Hindus were very devout, at least compared to their North Indian brethren. Entire families spent the day participating in extensive rituals that could be quite expensive. There was no rush to be in and out. South Indian temple complexes are noted for their great wealth, the result of generous giving by the devotees.

I also felt that the South Indian worshippers were more devoted to performing the proper rituals at the proper time. For example, one ritual requires the male child's head to be shaved prior to his journey to the temple (and sometimes at the barber shop within the temple complex itself). Within the temple, it was very common to see young boys with shaved heads, and even on the streets. This sight is less common in North India.

Temples devoted to Shiva often feature a statue of his bull vehicle Nandi. His statue is found outside the entrance to the temple, and perhaps even outside the gate of the temple complex. Nandi serves as a guardian. Like Ganesh, he is much beloved. This was one temple feature common to both North and South India. Like most Indians, I felt a special affinity and affection for Nandi. Perhaps this was a reflection of homesickness. Perhaps I was longing for something more familiar, more comprehensible, something more comfortable.

Beyond Hinduism

This is the end of my musings regarding Hinduism, and the experience of Hinduism.

Hinduism is not the sole religion of India, it is merely the principal religion and the bedrock of Indian culture. All religions are present in the South Asian subcontinent, including the Semitic religions originating in the Middle East, the religions of East Asia, and pantheistic religion that stretches back millennia and practiced not only by India's tribal population, but, mixed with Hinduism, is practiced by many rural Indians.

I cannot emphasize enough that the strict dividing lines found in the West between religious faiths and religious practice are much more elastic in South Asia. Hinduism absorbed many elements of the pantheistic religion practiced by the region's aboriginal inhabitants, and went on to borrow heavily from the faiths of others they encountered, including the imperialist conquerors.

Hindus see this as quite normal and are not averse or ashamed to borrow from others. Worship at sites not associated with one's faith is common in India. Sacred sites are sacred sites. They do not have to be strictly ascribed to one faith or another. Hindus worship at Islamic sacred sites, and pay homage at the tombs of Muslim holy men. They can be found in Sikh Gurdwaras and Christian churches. For all but the most closed-minded, this is no cause for rebuke or concern. It is somewhat of a cliché, but it is often repeated that Hindus can find almost anything to be sacred. The same thing can be said regarding the Hindu attitude towards religious personalities. There is no need to draw a line and say that Hindus cannot pay homage to Sikh, Muslim, Buddhist, and Christian "holy men."

There is often no strict dividing line between faiths, with worshippers "crossing over" for a an hour, or an afternoon, or a few days into the environs of another religious faith and participating in that faith with genuine enthusiasm and reverence. This is not to say that these distinctive faiths do not exist. Religions are more than sets of prescribed beliefs. Religions are all-encompassing cultures that define every aspect of existence from birth until death, and are usually the principal determinants of personal identity. While Religion is a principal source of identity for people all over the world, this is particularly true in South Asia.

Chapter XV

Buddhism

In volume one of this work, I talked about my youthful infatuation with Zen Buddhism. My little group of aspiring intellectuals wanted desperately to be cool and bohemian. It is a rite of passage for American adolescents to latch on to the beats when they are trying to break free of their bourgeoise boundaries and establish their own identities (that is unless the parents are themselves beats, in which case their offspring must take a totally different route).

The beats were the 1950's incarnation of American bohemianism, but were part of a long tradition going back to the early origins of the United States. This tradition is characterized by its openness to new and different ideas. It attracts persons not comfortable with assumptions. Not willing to accept verbatim established truths and ways of living, they postulate new avenues and open themselves to new things.

The beats were far from a unified movement. They were divided and subdivided into many different groups, that espoused and believed many different things. When open to all kinds of influences and willing to examine disapproved ideas, it can open the floodgates to all manner of experiences and concepts. People infatuated with free expression and exploration head off in many different directions.

While it is not fair to the many brilliant people encompassed within the beat movement, it is often centered in the popular imagination in the group surrounding Jack Kerouac. He was the most famous of the beats because he wrote the book "On the Road," which is among the most widely-read beat literary works. His associates included the most well-known beat authors, most especially Allen Ginsberg. Kerouac's "On the Road" describes Jack's travels all over the United States. In subsequent novels, he would write about his travels to Europe and North Africa. Jack and Allen met at Columbia University, where they were both studying. Both dropped out to pursue travel, sensation, and literary pursuits. Over the course of their travels, they picked-up Neal Cassady, who was not a New Yorker, but rather a denizen of Denver, Colorado, and they made their way to the San Francisco Area on the West Coast.

There, these Eastern Beats met another set of Beats with a different orientation. On the West Coast, the Beats were into more than sensation for its own sake. Some of the West Coast beats became obsessed with Buddhism in general and Zen Buddhism in particular. This was primarily because of the powerful influence of Gary Snyder and Alan Watts. Gary was part of a circle of students at Portland Oregon's Reed College, who were seriously studying all things Japanese. Alan

Watts, based in San Francisco, was a former Anglican Priest, who gave up his vocation to serious study Zen.

These West Coast Zen devotees had a serious impact on Jack Kerouac. He admired Gary Snyder immensely and made him the central subject of his novel, "the Dharma Bums." Jack wanted to be a Buddhist in the worst way. He wanted to meditate like Gary Snyder and immerse himself in Zen. Jack had high aspirations in this area and made immense efforts to become a serious Zen student. Jack wrote about these efforts in his novels, poems, and essays. But Jack was never able to fully emulate Gary Snyder. This was because Jack was too lazy, too undisciplined, and too fond of drinking alcohol to excess.

American adolescents attracted to the Beats generally break up into these two camps. Jack Kerouac had his feet in both camps. Those who see the message as one of freedom from convention and the drive to sensation, go one way. Those attracted to Buddhism go another. For example, Gary Snyder was no slouch. He learned to read, write, and speak Japanese, and internalized the finely-tuned subtleties of Japanese culture. Gary was a bona-fide Zen monk, and had incredible self-discipline and will-power.

Because I had fallen into this pattern of embracing the beats as an adolescent, it tainted my perception of Buddhism. Our group was entranced by Zazen (meditation), Koans (Zen riddles), and the unorthodox and unconventional way Zen masters reflect their experience and interact with the world. In our immaturity, we determined that Zen Buddhism was the essence of Buddhism, and that the myriads of schools and cultures encompassed with the Buddhist religion were not as relevant.

Zen is the essence of Japanese culture. It was studied intensely by the Samurai, the Japanese warrior elites. Within Japan, Zen is considered difficult to comprehend and practice, and perhaps too tied in with the old ways. Modern Japanese prefer a more accessible "pure land" Buddhism, mixed with their Shinto heritage. The heart and soul of Zen is the ancient city of Kyoto, home to Zen Buddhist monasteries and other aspects of traditional Japan. When Western people start studying Zen, they invariably read books containing many photographs of the Kyoto Zen monasteries, for they epitomize the subtle Japanese esthetic. While it is not advisable to generalize, Zen Buddhism embraces a vacuum. It loves empty space. By contrast, Hindu culture abhors a vacuum. Hindus want to see a picture with every empty space filled in.

Zen art emphasizes subtle brush strokes, pastel colors, and figures separated by empty space. The Buddhist pilgrim walks along the mountain path. He is just a small figure dwarfed by high mountains wreathed in fog. The colors are pastel, the brush strokes subtle and light, and the picture is never filled-up, but contains lots of empty space. In Zen this is a reflection of the nature of existence, and is seen as supremely comforting. Hindu pictures are "busy," with every space filled with bright colors. Hindu pictures can overwhelm the senses, and point to a reality that transcends the everyday.

When my son was in high school in New Delhi, his sister was a Western Religion major at Pomona College in California, and met a wide variety of religious figures from various traditions, including the Abbot of a Zen Monastery in Kyoto, willing to take in American students. My son signed up for a trial run as a Zen monk.

My wife and I took him to Kyoto to drop him off. We explored the crowded environs of Tokyo, and boarded the bullet train to Kyoto. I had lived in Japan as a three-year-old child, but had only vague memories of my stay there. It was a challenging experience. Nothing was familiar. There was no language in common. I was unable to read anything, talk to anyone, or understand the television or radio. In addition, Tokyo was very crowded.

I was delighted to be on the bullet train travelling at unbelievable speed through the Japanese countryside. For a person from Arizona, Japan seemed unbelievably crowded. Even the countryside was filled with structures, and people. We got off of the train at the Kyoto railway station and had no way of asking for directions or getting around. Luckily, an English-speaking Japanese person had a small table in the station set-up to provide assistance to wayward tourists like ourselves.

The monastery was everything it was cracked-up to be. It was everything I had seen in the Zen photo books. The ancient, yet delicate, wooden structures with the pitched tile roofs, and, of course, the Zen rock gardens, just a few plants placed among the rocks, raked daily by the monks. Zen is all about the indescribable and attempting to communicate what is impossible to communicate. Thus, Zen things often appear random, for they are not meant to subscribe to delineation. This is why there are rock gardens.

The abbot spoke excellent English. He welcomed my son into the community of monks and reassured us that he would be alright. We dropped him off and went to our traditional Japanese inn, with paper doors, and a large communal bath. We dressed in Japanese robes, took a bath together in the warm water, washing each other with sponges. Wore the soft Japanese shoes as we walked across the mats on the floor. We slept on tatami mats covered by soft silken quilts with a wooden pillow.

The exchange rate was brutal. Our American money did not go very far. This meant that we had little choice but to subsist primarily on udon (noodles) from friendly noodle shops. We splurged on only one meal in a traditional restaurant. It was unbelievably expensive. The portions were small. We ate at a low table in a small room with paper walls. Our waitress got on her knees to serve us. We left almost as hungry as when we arrived.

We spent our days wandering the streets. We never saw another non-Japanese person. We visited the Buddhist temples, saw the sacred sites, and a palace of the emperor, and ate udon. While walking along a narrow street between traditional Japanese buildings in a quiet residential area, we encountered a group of geisha in traditional garb. Although we could not talk to them, we were able to take pictures with them.

When we met up with our son after his stint as a Zen monk, it was clear that it was an experience he will never forget. He lived in an environment for weeks in which he could not converse with anyone. He was the only non-Japanese monk. He ate very little food, and in true Zen fashion, engaged in menial work (lots of sweeping). Since Zen is the Buddhism of meditation, he spent his days in Zazen. He was not allowed to move a muscle, even when bugs landed on him and his muscles were aching. As per Zen training, he met periodically with the Abbot who provided him with his koans to solve. My son did not elaborate on how the koan process unfolded for him, also part of the Zen tradition.

Mahayana and Theravada

Zen is part of the Mahayana Buddhist tradition. Mahayana means the "great vehicle." It is called this because it emphasizes liberation for the layman rather than for monks (and nuns). The Theravada, or small vehicle, tradition is much more centered around monasticism. Lay people are expected to support the monks and pay them deference, as they are much closer to liberation.

My life was centered around India, the place of origin of Buddhism. Lord Buddha was himself a monk and founded a monastic faith, so the countries surrounding India are largely of the Theravada school. Over the course of my time in South Asia, I travelled several times to Thailand, for example, where the population practices Theravada Buddhism. Monks were visible everywhere, as were Buddhist temples and monasteries. It quickly became evident to me while in Thailand, that their Buddhism retains elements of its Hindu heritage. While wandering around Bangkok, I went to a market located under a highway overpass. Families were selling all manner of goods from low tables. I spotted a brass statue that was clearly of Lord Brahma, evident from his four-headed form. I bought the statue and it remains with me today. I also saw iconography of Garuda, the bird vehicle of Lord Vishnu, and references to the Hindu epics, *Ramayana* and *Mahabharata*.

When Buddhism began in India, it was originally viewed as a rebellion against the Brahminical orthodoxy of the Hindu priests and their obsession with ritual purity and the caste system. Just as Jesus was a Jew before becoming the founder of

Christianity, Buddha was a Hindu before starting a new faith. It is not clear that Buddha intended to found a totally different religion. He may have been principally concerned with communicating his particular message.

The Buddha was primarily concerned with suffering. He had come to realize that human existence was identified with suffering. As a Hindu, he believed in reincarnation, and saw humanity as trapped within the "wheel of samsara," a seemingly unending cycle of rebirth and suffering. When he had his realization under the Bodhi Tree in Bodh Gaya in the Indian state of Bihar, he realized that the goal of existence was to break free of this cycle of suffering, by obtain Moksha (enlightenment). That, not the founding of any religion, was his principal concern. When he experienced enlightenment, he merely wanted to share this knowledge and provide suffering human beings with the means to obtain liberation.

In this, the Buddha was similar to Martin Luther. Martin Luther was a Catholic monk immersed in the monastic tradition. He came to realize that the Christian faith was about obtaining salvation (liberation), not by paying money to the church or buying "indulgences," but by taking advantage of the grace freely offered by God. When he nailed his theses on the door of the church in Wittenberg, he had no intention of breaking away from the Catholic church. He merely wanted to right some wrongs.

My wife and I also traveled throughout Myanmar (Burma). When we made the trip, the country was still closed to the outside world and there was little organized tourism there. It was a world dominated by Theravada Buddhism. Monks are everywhere and are paid all due deference by the population of laypersons. Buddhism permeated Myanmar. Driving along muddy roads in the rain, coming out into the sunlit afternoon, we spied a hilltop monastery silhouetted against the afternoon sun. Our guide explained that families from hundreds of kilometers around hiked up the hill together to obtain the blessings of the place. One incredibly rainy day, we walked out a long pier to a sacred Buddhist site. The day felt like a Buddhist painting, with clouds closing in, and heavy rain drops falling rhythmically on the slight roof of the long quay. At the end, we stood with the roiling water lapping up around us and took in the stillness. Some of the temples featured stupas crowned with gold leaf. As the pilgrims came each day, they bought squares of flattened gold leaf. At the end of the day, the monks pounded it onto the stupa dome. Some appeared to be covered with many centimeters of gold, ever accumulating, every day.

Sri Lanka

Sri Lanka was perhaps the most Theravada Buddhist country of all.

We experienced a protracted journey from our guest house in Colombo to our new residence in Kandy. We were going to the most sacred spot in all Sri Lanka, the epicenter of Buddhism, the home of the sacred tooth of Lord Buddha.

The car picked us up early. We awoke around 0530, the tropical world around us was just coming to life. It was still dark. It had rained steadily during the night and the air was fresh. Night birds sang a variety of songs.

When we descended the stairs for an early breakfast prior to departure, the servants were in the midst of their morning devotions. Offering flowers and fruit to Lord Buddha and repeating their prayers silently. Our hostess "aunty" departed before us. Before leaving, she said good bye to the three servants. The cook knelt before her and touched her feet.

A small car picked us up and we drove all the way through Colombo before hitting the countryside. We were headed to the center of the country from the seacoast. We drove mostly in silence and I used this opportunity to think about Buddhism.

What was so profound about Lord Buddha's message? He identified the essential problem of human existence as the experience of suffering. However, thousands of books have been written about what Lord Buddha meant by "suffering."

He, like Hindu philosophers, stated the plain fact that suffering is an inherent component of human existence. Every human being experiences the four essentials of suffering. No amount of wealth, power, or good health can shield anyone from these experiences; the experiences of birth, disease, old age, and death.

But the Buddha did not confine suffering to these four events. Life is a series of negative and positive events, suffering, broken by periods of "happiness" and elation. The common philosophy of modern man, particularly in the West, is that the way to lead your life is to maximize the periods of happiness and minimize the periods of pain.

The Buddha said that this is Maya (delusion). He said he had received the enlightening message that one does not have to be buffeted by these positive and negative experiences, that it is possible to obtain a state beyond the fray.

When you are under water, you are not aware of the storms battering the sea above. The lotus flower blooms magnificently, no matter how dirty the water it is floating in.

Buddha said that rather than being buffeted in your journey across this ocean of births and deaths, you can cultivate "detachment." Again, thousands of books have been written in an attempt to discern what Lord Buddha meant by this term.

I believe he said that a liberated person experiences the same suffering as any other human being. It is an innate component of the human condition. However, he is detached. His experience of that suffering is essentially different from that of a person trapped by the chains of maya.

By following the noble eightfold path, propounded and described by Lord Buddha, it is possible to obtain such a state.

Our car dropped us off at a rural train station. It was a small station with two platforms, located in a small provincial town in the Sinhalese heartland. I sat on the platform for two hours until the train arrived, listening to the cawing of the crows and enjoying the moment.

The ticket to Kandy cost 70 rupees, about 45 cents. The trains are always full. There is never an empty seat. I stood the entire time, as the packed train moved slowly into the Sri Lankan highlands. I stood by the open door watching the green jungle roll by. The train never moved very fast and the procession of greenness was slow. I held on to my bag to keep it from rolling away by applying pressure with my foot. The train passed through many tunnels and stopped for long periods at tiny stations surrounded by jungle, with jungle-covered peaks off in the distance.

Although we are crowded together for hours on end, standing in the humidity and covered by sweat, we are all composed. Sri Lankans are soft-spoken, gentle, and polite, regardless of the circumstances. It reflects their internalization of the Buddhist values of compassion and humility.

That night, I walked down the hill from my hotel to the lake in front of the Kandy Temple. As the sun went down, I entered the park-like grounds surrounding the temple. The chants of the Buddhist monks were amplified. The sounds permeated the air. As the sun disappeared, I was immersed in a sea of temple lights, incense, and the soft light and smell given off by hundreds of oil wicks.

I walked from shrine to shrine. As is the custom, I removed my shoes and entered a Hindu temple. Although Kandy is the most holy of Sinhalese Buddhist shrines, it is ringed by Hindu temples. I carried my shoes and socks and walked through the grounds.

My feet hurt. My body ached. I was dehydrated and hungry. It had been a long day, with a long car ride, followed by an afternoon looking at 88 elephants in their natural habitat, followed by a long train ride. All I had imbibed since breakfast had been a few *vada* (south Indian donuts), and a cup of tea. But I was content and at peace.

The next day I returned to the temple complex. This time I would go inside to the inner sanctum. This time I did not war shoes but plastic *"hawai chappals"* (flip flops). I checked them in with the "shoe wallah) and passed through the gate into the temple compound, walking around the grounds in my bare feet. I can now enter any holy spot I wish with no difficulty.

I wend my way through the huge temple complex, getting ever-closer to the raised pavilion housing the casket containing the tooth of the Buddha.

The jeweled conical casket containing the tooth of the Buddha is rarely opened. It was brought to Kandy in the 4th Century AD. Three times per day the doors of the shrine room are opened, and pilgrims allowed to file past and look at the casket. We attended the evening viewing. It takes place every night at 1830.

We arrived early to get at the head of the line. The area in front of the shrine is filled with worshippers. A young girl suffering from lichen planis, a common skin disease in South Asia, is seated at the head of the line. It is not apparent how long she has been there. The disease discolors the skin, leaving pale patches. She is praying intently and appears as if in a trance. Her lips move as she silently intones the Buddhist prayers.

The pilgrims packed against the wall are all seated with the their palms together in front of their bodies deep in prayer. The long line of worshippers moves slowly past the metal table in front of the shrine railing. Each worshipper leaves an offering. Some leave flowers on top of the table. Others put money into the slotted openings of offering boxes. The falling coins make a mechanical, rattling sound as they fall into the boxes.

A much respected *Bhikku* (Theravada Holy Man) comes and stands at the railing opposite us. He is accompanied by three young monks who are part of his retinue. Temple personnel kneel and touch his feet as they pass in front of him. He goes into the small enclosure in front of the closed door to the shrine room, says his prayers and kneels to perform his oblations.

I immediately sense his presence. He has a calm look on his face, and our eyes meet. He bears a strong physical resemblance to Radhanath Swami. It strikes me that for beings at his spiritual level, there is no longer any question of the myriad divisions that perplex us members of the unenlightened masses.

The calm and gentle temple guard opens the gate. For many minutes the drummers downstairs have been beating a hypnotic beat. After some time they are joined by a reed instrument similar to the Indian shennai. I have been expecting monks to start chanting, but there is no chanting.

The praying girl at the head of the line has quietly gotten up from the spot where she has been seated for so many hours. After getting her glimpse of the casket she has disappeared. Perhaps she comes here every night and implores Lord Buddha to cure her disease so she can resume a normal life. Perhaps her prayers have nothing to do with her affliction at all.

The family ahead of us consists of three women and a baby. I suspect it is a young mother accompanied by her mother and her aunt. Like practically everyone in Sri Lanka, they are calm and radiate friendliness. I wonder if this is another indicator of the pervasive influence of Lord Buddha. He teaches a specific outlook centering on compassionate interaction with all beings, and the cultivation of a calm sense of detachment. Perhaps this is why the usual aggression and excitement found in other South Asian countries is absent. People here seem to accept the difficulties of life without rancor and resentment.

When we ride the local trains, they are packed with passengers. But there is no pushing or shoving. Everyone is on the journey and looks out for each other. Everyone eats the food sold by the vendors making their way slowly through the aisles. No one eats packaged junk food made by the local affiliates of US-based multi-national corporations and served in non-biodegradable packaging. Instead, we all eat traditional natural snacks, fresh fruit, and "vadas" of all shapes and sizes, and lots of nuts.

Although everything is wrapped in newspaper, nothing finds its way to the floor. The passengers hold on to their trash and deposit it in trash cans, (marked by color for recycling), found at every station.

These train journeys stand as a metaphor for life itself.

The three women pick up the baby and start on their way through the narrow fenced passage that will take us by the now open shrine door. There are many family groups in this expansive temple room. The many children are quiet, obedient, and reverently absorbed in the transcendental experience. They are learning how to be full participants in their faith, by following the example presented by their elders.

I follow the worshippers to the viewing window. Each looks with reverence and awe into the inner sanctum, puts their palms together and bows his/her head. I follow their example.

Tibetan – Mahayana Buddhism

Although Buddhism originated in India, there is only a remnant remaining. Most of the original Indian Buddhists were reabsorbed into Hinduism. Before this happened, the word of the Buddha spread throughout Asia. Monks from many countries came to India to visit the holy sites and learn about Buddhism, they departed and spread the faith.

Today in India, there are two types of Indian Buddhists. The followers of the Dalit Leader Dr. Ambedkar converted to neo-Buddhism. They did this to escape the horrors of untouchability, just like the dalits who had converted to Christianity, Islam, and Sikhism in the centuries before them. I have read about dalit neo-Buddhism in textbooks, but have seen little evidence of its presence. I never had an opportunity to interact with India's neo-Buddhists.

The other major group consists of followers of Tibetan Buddhism. These fall into two groups, Indians of Tibetan descent and Tibetan refugees who have escaped Chinese repression in their home country and found refuge in India. These two groups are virtually indistinguishable.

Today, devotees of Tibetan Buddhism travel to Ladakh in occupied Tibet in hopes of experiencing Tibetan Buddhism in its completeness. It appears many are disappointed, finding that the Chinese have so suppressed the free practice of religion in Tibet and so interfered with Buddhist institutions there, that they no longer fully-reflect the essence of Tibetan Buddhism. Informants, Indian, international, and Tibetan, have told me that the Tibetan Buddhism followed in India is closer to the real thing that what is presently found in occupied Tibet.

The native Indian followers of Tibetan Buddhism are found in the Himalayas, scattered throughout Nepal, Sikkim, and the Indian localities of Ladakh, and Leh, which are incorporated in the state of Jammu and Kashmir. Most are Tibetan by heredity and heritage.

The Tibetan refugees are clustered in Delhi and other urban centers, and in the Tibetan capital in exile in Dharamshala. The Tibetan government in exile is headed by the Dalai Lama, who is acknowledged by Tibetan Buddhists everywhere as their spiritual leader, although the Chinese have forbidden any public acknowledgement of the Dalai Lama in occupied Tibet. The Chinese have already selected their own successor to the Dalai Lama, who they hope to seat upon the death of the Dalai Lama. Tibetans do not acknowledge this Chinese usurper.

In book one, I described my stay in Nepal and my interaction with Tibetan Buddhists there. Since then I have had the good fortune to visit Dharamshala multiple times, interact with the Dalai Lama's family, attend a lecture on

Buddhism given by the Dalai Lama to Tibetan monks in New Delhi, and spend time in Ladakh and Leh.

Whenever I am in Delhi I try to go to visit Manju-ka-Tila (Little Lhasa). The following is a description of my 2014 visit.[85]

I am still determined to go to Manju-ka-Tila inhabited by members of Delhi's Tibetan refugee community. This is the same location that William and I tried to see earlier, but were unable to locate. This time, we flagged down a motor rickshaw right in front of the YMCA, our home away from home in New Delhi. The driver took us right to Manju-ka-Tila, letting us out across the busy street in front of the enclave. I was intent on eating Tibetan food and buying a small Tibetan Buddha (about 15 centimeters tall) made of several different metals, with a pale painted face and Tibetan features.

We crossed a long pedestrian bridge over the ring road to enter the community. At first, it did not appear distinctive, but then everything changed very quickly. There were stalls all along the perimeter wall where Tibetans sell ordinary clothes and shoes. Many of these items are originally from China. We then went around a corner and found a table filled with Tibetan items, many emblazoned with the Tibetan flag. They are always a big hit, as everyone loves these items. Young Tibetans, living in exile in India, are devoted to their occupied country and determined to regain their independence. All these hopes, dreams, and aspirations are symbolized by the Tibetan flag, which turns up all over Delhi. We bought key chains, decals that read, "Tibet for Tibetans" and "Chinese out of Tibet," and postcards featuring the Dalai Lama and his most cogent sayings. His picture is everywhere in the enclave. I bought extras of everything for my daughter, who was President of her school's chapter of "Students for Free Tibet" while in high school.

The lampposts were festooned with posters featuring cartoons lampooning the leader of China (as a devil and a scorpion), grabbing Indian territory. The banners read, "Tibetan Independence for Indian security."

We then ventured deeper into Little Lhasa. The streets are narrow alleys between overhanging buildings, and lined with small shops. We weaved and turned through the alleys until we arrived at a small square, a bit of openness among the congestion, a spot where sunlight broke through.

---

[85] This account is excerpted from *My Indian Journey (Mera Bharatiya Yatra), phase two,* CreateSpace Independent Publishing Platform (June 18, 2015), San Bernadino, California

On one side was a Tibetan Buddhist temple, on the other a Tibetan cultural center that looked like a temple, but was used to educate monks and other Tibetans in the fine points of their language and culture.

Old men sat at low tables teaching young men lessons from the long books that are the repositories of traditional Tibetan knowledge. They are long pieces of paper bound between slats of wood and hand-lettered in the Tibetan script.

I took off my shoes and entered the temple. It could have been in Tibet, as it seemed I had been transported out of India entirely. Although I have not yet been to Tibet, I have been to Ladakh and Leh, the Buddhist regions of India high in the Himalayas. I have also spent quite a bit of time in Dharamshala, the capital of the Tibetan government in exile and the home of the Dalai Lama. The temple in Little Lhasa mirrored the many Tibetan temples in these locations.

A young monk was lighting many yak oil lamps set in big holders in the alcove. Inside the temple room, a large statue of Lord Buddha and a large picture of the Dalai Lama dominated the front wall.

One a sidewall was a large altar covered with food items (including liter bottles of Coca Cola). It reminded me of the Native American ceremonials in Arizona and New Mexico, which featured lots of food sharing, and lots of liter bottles of Coca Cola. Scriptures bound in the long Tibetan books filled various alcoves. During worship, the congregation sits on the floor and reads from the books in the alcoves. I spent some time soaking up the ambience before returning to the square and taking more pictures. The cultural center had traditional Tibetan decorations on the rook, including a large Tibetan flag.

We then noticed a store on the square selling brand new Tibetan *thankas* (Tibetan religious pictures on cloth rollers) and Tibetan clothes. Although the collection of thankas on sale was extensive, I had no need to buy one. Several thankas already reside in my Tucson home, including one purchased in Dharamshala and hand painted by a Tibetan monk (who spent a year on the project), and another in my study presented to me by the Dalai Lama, who signed it on the lower right corner. The shop also sold many Tibetan clothes, including traditional Tibetan dresses.

We left the shop and wandered through more dark alleys. We rounded a corner to find a shop filled will all manner of Tibetan metalwork. It was closed, but a note posted on the door said to call the proprietor and he would come open the shop. Ranu did so. Within five minutes, a teenage boy came and opened the shop. Like almost all Tibetans, he was quiet, polite, and good-humored. Unlike many of their Indian counterparts, Tibetan shopkeepers do not engage in high pressure sales tactics, but are content to let the customer make up his own mind. The Tibetans generally do not seem particularly concerned whether they make a sale or not.

The shopkeeper found the exact Buddha statue I was looking for on one of his shelves. After I paid him, the boy wrapped the statue in bubble wrap and plastic tape for its trip back to Tucson. It now sits on my desk in my study right next to my computer.

We ducked into a narrow covered passageway inside a building with shops on both sides. Inside, Tibetan workers were packing up all manner of Tibetan items for shipment. These included special Tibetan cookware, Tibetan rosaries, lamps, carpets, wall hangings, and decorations.

We were hungry so we walked straight through the alleys, ignoring the many shops on all sides and found a restaurant for our Tibetan lunch.

We ordered three items:

Chuna – mutton sausage

Tingno – steamed buns

Thenthuk – fried noodles with chicken

Although I had eaten Tibetan food before in the course of my travels, this was the first time I had eaten these particular items. When staying in Nepal, as a teenager, I had subsisted on Tibetan food. I ate in a large Tibetan restaurant on the main square of Kathmandu every day. I ate lots of soup and noodles, but no Chuna, Tingno, or Thenthuk. I arrived at my Tibetan restaurant every day and calmly watched the colorful tableau unfold on the square outside. The square was filled with vans that had been driven to Kathmandu overland from Europe. The occupants lived in them for months, and then sold them to purchase air tickets to head back home.

Our lunch wrapped up our stay in "little Lhasa." We emerged well-fed from the maze of alleys and found a motor rickshaw to take us to the Red Fort.

Dharamshala

When I first arrived at my post in the Political Section of US Embassy New Delhi, I requested permission to take an official visit to Dharamshala. My request was greeted with incredulity by the powers that be. I received a sense from them that there was no point, that the Tibetans were not important, that they were outside the purview of our interest. I went anyway, and when I returned no one was particularly interested in what I did there.

My headquarters for trips in this region of the Himalayas was the old British hill station of Dalhousie. During the Raj, it was the summer getaway for British civil servants and military officers posted to the Punjab province. To get there, we take a long train journey from New Delhi to the Punjabi city of Pathankot, not far from the Pakistan border. For Pakistani forces attempting to capture Indian held Kashmir, Pathankot is a gateway providing relatively easy access. For this reason, after independence and the repeated Indo/Pakistan wars over Kashmir, Pathankot has become a military center.

When we exit the train at the Pathankot railway station, we bicker with the jeep drivers who will be taking us into the mountains. After we settle on the price, we load into the jeeps for the ride. The jeeps take us up twisty and narrow roads, including many hairpin turns. When I took one of my brothers-in-law on a Dalhousie trip, he got so car sick that we had to stop the jeeps so he could throw up.

As the jeeps climb, crossing from Punjab into Himachal Pradesh state, the vegetation changes from scrub bushes to pine forests. I usually stay at a Christian retreat in Dalhousie, located in one of the old summer homes. Dalhousie is a pleasant and quiet place where time has stood still. It is full of old British houses that have not changed one iota since the British departed. There is a small "mall" with old British shops, the bakery, the grocers, shops selling handicrafts. Everything is on hills and connected by small roads and narrow paths. We walked everywhere. The center of Dalhousie is a small square bordered on one side by the old British hotel, and on the other by the entrance to the military base. Dalhousie has been home to a regiment since the 19th Century.

The busses all stop in the square in front of the hotel, which retains its stately grandeur, although it is no longer as full as it was back then. It is a short bus ride from Dalhousie to Dharamshala. When the Dalai Lama and his retainers and guardians escaped from occupied Tibet, the Indian government offered them refuge. They made Dharamshala the capital of their government in exile. Ever since, Tibetans have made the long trip over the mountains to India, escaping Chinese border guards and soldiers. They usually arrive with only the clothes on their back. The Dalai Lama's administration takes care of them, sending them to refugee centers in Dharamshala, where they are provided with job training and processing before moving on to one of the Tibetan communities scattered around India.

When my wife and I arrived in Dharamshala, we were met by a government representative who looked after us and showed us around. He took us to the refugee center and introduced us to the new arrivals. We also toured the orphanage where child arrivals with no parents are looked after, and the monastery, where monks are being trained. Daily the monks engage in heated debates over points of Buddhist teaching. The debates are overseen by the senior monks who determine the winners. We were able to watch such a debate and go inside the monastery to view one of the largest Tibetan temples in India.

The monks wear Ochre robes and can be quite young. Tibetan Buddhism is technically part of the Mahayana tradition, but it heavily influenced by the Indian tantric tradition. It has a strong emphasis on monasticism and monks are revered. The monks cause no end of problems for the Chinese authorities in occupied Tibet. This is because the Chinese want to eradicate Tibetan traditions, Tibetan religion, and the monasteries. The monks are strong followers of the Dalai Lama and work with the Tibetan people to keep their culture and traditions alive. In the past few years, Tibetan monks have committed suicide to protest Chinese oppression, and the Chinese authorities use all measures possible to suppress news coming out of occupied Tibet.

Although Dharamshala is in India, it feels like Tibet. Indian tourists, primarily Punjabis, come to gawk at the Tibetans, especially the monks. The Indians generally stay in their own areas of the city, while the Tibetans keep their distance. There is a Tibetan market in Dharamshala, where it is possible to buy all manner of Tibetan handicrafts, rugs, furniture, clothing, wall hangings, lamps, and most particularly Tibetan statues and thankas.

We stayed in the same hotel in the traditional Tibetan part of the city where Richard Gere stays during his frequent visits to Dharamshala. Our hosts led us to the shop where Gere purchases many Tibetan items for his home and home temple. It was there that I was able to buy the splendid thanka hand painted by the Buddhist monk.

I met with the leaders of the government in exile and was briefed on all of their activities. They took me to the home of the Dalai Lama, which is on a small hill overlooking the monastery. His assistant enquired as to whether he was free for a meeting. The Dalai Lama was tied up and unable to meet with us. The assistant did present us with a thanka and book signed by the Dalai Lama, however.

Later in Delhi, I was able to interact with the Dalai Lama and his family. His sister and her husband took my daughter and I out to lunch. They had heard that my daughter was an activist in Students for a Free Tibet. The four of us spent a wonderful afternoon together. She regaled us with stories about the Dalai Lama and his childhood in Tibet. I questioned her about the book *Seven Years in Tibet*.[86] She graciously described those years in to Potala Palace that Harrer wrote about in the book and the subsequent experience of being driven from Tibet by the Chinese invasion. After lunch, they gave us a tour of the Tibet house in New Delhi. I spotted a picture on the wall of the just-arrived Dalai Lama and his group, taken

---

[86] By Heinrich Harrer, Penguin Putnam, New York, 1997

just after their arrival in India. She pointed herself out in the picture, standing not far from the Dalai Lama.

I was subsequently able to meet the Dalai Lama when I attended one of his lectures in Delhi. It was actually a lecture for Buddhist monks, given in Tibetan with an English translation. Since the lecture was for practitioners and mendicants, much of it was over my head. It dealt with the meditative experience and how it relates to Buddhist realization. I may have been the only non-Tibetan in the audience. I sat quietly with monks on either side of me. We all sat in reserved silence throughout the long address. In Asian fashion, we were sitting cross-legged on the ground. I have had participated in these Asian events many times. I realize that many Westerners are used to a fast-paced life. They expect to be massaged and entertained at all times and do not like to sit for long periods "doing nothing." They often lack the ability to focus. In the Western world we are strongly aware of the presence of time. We all have persistent clocks ticking inside our heads. We are always thinking of the next place we have to be. By contrast, in South Asia, I was often in environments where there was no time pressure at all, where the events were simply allowed to unfold, without any sense that something else was going to happen "afterwards." The monks and I were fine with the entire experience.

Afterwards, I congregated with other monks around the Dalai Lama. He graciously said hello to everyone who approached him. Despite his high position in the world, he was in no hurry to move on to another appointment. In my job as a diplomat, I often interacted with powerful and wealthy personages, and they often made it apparent that their time was valuable and that they did not have time to waste talking to the "little people." This was not the case with the Dalai Lama. There was no sense of pressure whatsoever. I do not remember what I said to him. I was probably overawed by the experience.

Ladakh and Leh

While in India, my wife and I traveled to the Buddhist areas of Ladakh and Leh. These remote mountain areas are administratively attached to the Indian state of Jammu and Kashmir. However, there are three distinct cultural areas within this state, the Muslim majority Vale of Kashmir, the Hindu majority Jammu, and Buddhist majority Ladakh and Leh.

Ladakh and Leh border on Pakistan, and have been the scene of extended fighting between Indian and Pakistani forces, most recently in the Kargil war that took place between May and July of 1999. It is not far from the contested Siachen glacier, the most high-altitude war front in the world, where Indian and Pakistani forces are in a seemingly perpetual military standoff in an area well-above the tree line in perpetual snow and ice.

The region is in the high Himalayas, with altitudes from 10,000 to 18,000 feet. It is one of the most sparsely populated regions in India, with a population of approximately 250,000. Almost every resident of Ladakh is of Tibetan descent and Tibetan religion and culture are the norm.

The principal town is Leh, and this is where we began our journey. We flew from Delhi to Leh, a flight of only a few hours duration. The airstrips in the Himalayas are small, and therefore the airplanes are as well. The airstrips are located in small valleys surrounded by high mountains. The small planes must veer between the high peaks and land on a small airstrip, often in poor weather, as cloud, rain, and snow are commonplace. The ride in is often turbulent. When we set up our tour, we were told that Ladakh is of such high elevation that we must simply stay in our hotel room for an entire day until our lungs adjust to breathing the thin air. We thought this was exaggerated, but it turned out to be quite true.

We stayed in small lodge in Leh. The buildings are simple, sand colored, with lots of wooden railings. Our room was also simple. By the time we made it to our room, we were so weak we could do nothing but lie in our beds and sleep throughout the day. After about eight hours, we emerged from our beds and went downstairs for our simple meal. We could breathe normally and never had any problems during our remaining time in Ladakh.

Because I was an American diplomat, I was not allowed to visit the "sensitive" border regions, where Indian military forces are entrenched and facing off against the Pakistanis. Leh, at about 10,000 feet had some vegetation, but the next morning we boarded a jeep and started driving ever higher into the Himalayas. It did not take us long to get above the tree line, and soon there was no vegetation at all, only snow-capped peaks and lots of rocks, snow, and ice.

When the sun shines on this environment, it reflects off the rocks, snow and ice and gives everything a bright appearance that can be overwhelming. Anything that breaks up this dominant whiteness stands out. When we approached bodies of water, they were bright blue surrounded by white. We drove for hours to various Buddhist sites. The monasteries and temples stand out in this environment. They seem to be tiny oases of human habitation in a vast and unpopulated mountain vastness.

The buildings are typically Tibetan, made of large rocks and plaster with sloping wooden roofs and windows. We visited a Tibetan temple built around a reclining image of the Buddha. The statue was so large that it could not be contained by any one room of the building. Front one room, we viewed the head, and from the other rooms, the other parts of the body. At another location, we viewed ancient wall paintings depicting the life of the Buddha. In the high and thin air the paintings were well preserved.

I notice that when I leave Tucson and venture up into the mountains or out into the desert, the sounds of the city are left behind and I am able to perceive the stillness that is the natural state of existence. It is then when I realize that I am perpetually surrounded by the sounds of engines, automobiles, air-conditioning, airplanes, and machinery. Sometimes, I take an early morning walk from my house along the arroyo just outside my door. I stop and listen, and immediately discern a low and continuous rumble that permeates the air. Because this noise is inescapable for us, we adjust ourselves to it. We tune it out. It is only during those rare moments that we are away from the sounds of "civilization" that we are able to perceive true stillness.

This effect was magnified a thousand fold in Ladakh. There were no human beings for many miles in any direction and no machinery of any kind anywhere. There was only the sound of the wind blowing. Whenever I travel in Buddhist areas of the Himalayas I come across Buddhist prayer flags. These contain religious messages in Tibetan, and many colored, and are strung across seemingly random areas. In these areas, I am usually on foot and come across them.

Prayer flags are supposed to be reminders of the basic temporality of existence. They are put up to decay, and their decay serves to provide us with a lesson, that we should not become overly attached to Maya and should focus our minds on what is truly important. We came across many such areas while wandering around Ladakh.

The high point of our visit occurred at an enormous Buddhist monastery. It rose out of the white rock, multistoried and long, and filled with long rooms. It so happened that a Buddhist festival was taking place when we arrived. It was sheer serendipity, as we had no idea of such an event. It was something meant to happen. It was another Asian function, so I sat down in a long prayer-hall/temple besides the monks and local villagers and spent several hours immersed in our shared experience.

The monks at the head sat in a long row facing us and chanted Tibetan chants. These have become quite popular. No one seems to be able to figure out how the monks perform these chants. They are low sustained tones that reverberate throughout the room and into your heart and consciousness. It is timelessness personified, as without timelessness, there is no way to appreciate or understand the chants. I let myself be swept away into another place and stayed there as long as the chanting continued.

The chants were broken up by religious addresses, periods of eating, musical performances, and dramas. The monks wore otherworldly Tibetan masks and performed plays about the Buddha Dharma. I did not know how long we were there, as I lost all track of time.

While in South Asia, I am often in spaces that are totally free of other Westerners, in which I am the only "foreigner" present. But this never seems to matter. From my very first sojourn into India and Nepal as a teenager until the present, the space has always opened up to include me. When in Nepal during that first trip, I inexplicably climbed a ladder to enter a room with devotees on all sides. They could have been Indian or Nepali. They were chanting Hare Krishna, and I joined in. Nary an eyelash was raised and they opened up and let me in and included me. The same experience has happened again and again. It also happened in Ladakh.

Retracing the footsteps of the Buddha
Buddhist Pilgrimage

India is the origin of Buddhism. The Buddha gave up his princely life in Nepal when he discovered the reality of suffering. He discovered that suffering permeates the human condition. He did not want to live the princely life if it was only a denial of reality (maya). He was determined to discover the truth and embraced an extreme form of asceticism, thinking that denial of all things pleasurable would be a denial of maya, itself. One of the most famous of Buddhist statues is that of the starving Buddha, meant to capture him at the height of this ascetic phase. His rib cage pokes through his skin and his face is thin and emaciated. It is a graphic portrayal.

This ascetic path led him to India, where he sat under the Bodhi tree in present-day Bodh Gaya in the Indian state of Bihar. That is where he obtained enlightenment and cast off extreme asceticism. Instead, he promulgated the doctrine of moderation in all things. Gathering a group of disciples around him, he journeyed from Bodh Gaya to Varanasi in the present-day Indian state of Uttar Pradesh. In the deer park, outside the city, he delivered his first sermon.

In 2014, I stayed in India for three and one half months. In the final phase of that journey, I started in the city of Jamshedpur in the Indian state of Uttarakhand, and made my way across Bihar, retracing the path of the Buddha.[87]

The Final Phase Begins

The final phase of the yatra is a trip through the state of Bihar. The focus is on Buddhism. Bihar borders Nepal on the North, the state of West Bengal in the East, and Uttar Pradesh in the West.

---

[87] The following is an excerpt from, *My Indian Journey (Mera Bharatiya Yatra)*, CreateSpace Independent Publishing Platform (June 18, 2015), San Bernadino, California

We three travelers piled our luggage into the motor Rickshaw for the ride to the Jamshedpur railway station. We caught an evening train from Jamshedpur to the town of Gaya in Bihar. The train travelled through the rural darkness of Jharkhand and Bihar, passing village after village. There was little electricity and most villages were dark.

I had made reservations at a hotel in Bodh Gaya, the site of Buddha's enlightenment and one of Buddhism's principal pilgrimage spots. The driver from the hotel met us at the railway station. It was late at night and Gaya was dark. The car drove through the narrow streets, out into the countryside and into the sleeping town of Bodh Gaya.

Buddhism dominates Bodh Gaya. It is the Buddhist equivalent of Vrindavan. Buddhist shrines and temples are everywhere. Buddhists from throughout the world have built shrines there. The car passed them on the way to the hotel, including several massive sculptures of Lord Buddha. The car drove through the foggy night, past the Buddhist gardens and down a dirt road to the hotel. It was located in the middle of what used to be a farm fields. Agricultural land stretched out on all sides.

The hotel lobby was simple, with no decoration except a Buddhist picture and a small statue of Buddha. White cloth covered the few pieces of simple furniture. Although the proprietor and all the workers were Indian Hindus, the hotel was built for the Buddhist pilgrim trade. Most guests are Buddhists from Japan and other Buddhist countries. Our party was the exception to the rule. The rooms were cold. It was late at night. Everyone went to bed.

Buddhist Pilgrimage II

Like Vrindavan, Bodh Gaya is a vegetarian environment. No one consumes meat. We awoke early and ate a simple vegetarian breakfast at a small coffee table in the lobby. Although rickshaws are available, everything in Bodh Gaya is within walking distance from the hotel.

We finished our breakfast and headed out the door. The hotel is only half built. An entire wing is simply concrete and a wire frame heading into the sky. There is space for a restaurant, but it is empty. The road is an old farmers' track, formerly used for tractors. Buddhist monks in saffron robes and Buddhist pilgrims, mostly from the Far East, walk calmly along the road. A sense of peace permeates the environment. There is no rush and no stress. No one is in a hurry to get anywhere. If only the entire world could be like Bodh Gaya.

We walked for some time until we came to a T-junction. To our right stood the gardens we had passed in the car in the middle of the night. We are standing directly behind three enormous statues. We take the path to the right and go through the gate into the garden. It is still early morning. The rickshaw wallahs and various vendors and hawkers sleep outdoors by their booths and rickshaws. They are just getting up and starting their day, and the pilgrims and tourists just starting to arrive. The vendors and rickshaw wallahs are boiling water for tea and eating chapattis.

Once we are inside the garden, a straight path leads to the three enormous statues. Smaller statues around the perimeter depict Buddhist saints. The three central statues are of Lord Buddha. Japanese Buddhists built the garden. We follow the straight path to its conclusion and stand below the central statue. There is a small altar there for burning incense and saying prayers. We circumambulate the three statues, looking at them from all sides. It is quite formidable and quite impressive. We are getting into the spirit of Bodh Gaya, and enjoying the peace and serenity of the Garden.

After some time, we leave the garden, take a left and enter the Bhutanese monastery on our left. Each variant of Buddhism has built a temple in Bodh Gaya in its own particular architectural style. This Bhutanese temple is no exception. It looks like it was lifted straight from Bhutan and dropped in Bihar. This is the sensation at every temple. Whether the temple is from Sri Lanka, Bhutan, Japan, China or Thailand, it reflects the culture from which it originates.

Workmen are working to restore the elaborate reliefs in the Tibetan style on the outer walls of the temple. We take off our shoes, go inside, and are amazed at the giant Tibetan style statue of the Buddha inside. Beautiful murals illustrating the life of the Buddha decorate the ceiling and walls. By the end of the day, we will absorb all the Buddhist motifs and symbols. We will see a variety of Buddhist wheels of dharma, pictures of cranes, monks, and lone Buddhist ascetics absorbed into foggy landscapes, the Buddha as a starving ascetic, the Buddha preaching enlightenment.

The temple next door is Japanese. It features a "peace garden" outside. This is a feature of Japanese Buddhist establishments. Japan reels from the aftermath of World War Two and the nuclear bombing of Hiroshima and Nagasaki. The Japanese see Buddhism as the hope for not only inner peace, but peace in the world. They do not want to be responsible for inflicting the suffering of war on anyone ever again. They want to bring conflict to an end, and replace violence with non-violence.

The Buddhist temple is the same as the temples Nilu and I visited in Kyoto, the Zen Buddhist center of Japan. It has the same rock gardens and the same Zen monks, and a hostel where pilgrims can stay for a nominal fee. When Ranu and I had originally conceived this trip, we did not know that Nilu would be joining us. We originally planned to stay there, but changed the plan to a hotel later. Nini and her children were planning to accompany us to Bodh Gaya. Ranu and I had determined that Nini's family would not be up to the total Zen Buddhist pilgrim experience, so made reservations at a hotel. At the last minute, Nini became ill and dropped out. Ranu and I agreed that at some future date we will return to Body Gaya and stay with the pilgrims in the hostel.

The temple itself is totally Japanese and incorporates the total Japanese aesthetic. A railing separates the public space from the private space. The altar and statue of Lord Buddha are far to the back and bathed in a half light. The public space is for meditation. Meditation cushions and Buddhist prayer books are in racks along the walls.

The Japanese center has its own attached school. As part of their religious obligation, Japanese Buddhists funded this school for local children. It is based on the teaching of principals of peace and compassion. The children must gain enormous benefit from this education.

After leaving the Japanese space, we passed through its gate. The gate marks the boundary between Japan and Bihar, India. The transition is seamless. We continued down the shaded tree-lined street past pilgrim hotels and restaurants to the main intersection. This is another T-junction. Off to the left is a huge Thai Buddhist temple. Down the road from this temple is the local museum. Off to the right are a series of Buddhist temples from Buddhist countries all over the world. The road curve offs to the right and leads directly to a giant park. The Bodh Gaya temple and shrine are the focal point of the pilgrimage center, and the Bodhi tree under which the Buddha meditated and obtained enlightenment is the focal point of the shrine.

Before making our way to the shrine, we stopped at the Thai temple. It is massive and a piece of Thailand transplanted into Bodh Gaya. Worshippers and curious Indians crowd the temple. They walk through the long hall decorated with Thai motifs to the railing in front of the altar. There are donation boxes just over the railing. Pilgrims can donate money to education, poverty relief, and temple maintenance. In addition to the obvious East Asian worshippers, many Indians pay their respects as well. Few, if any, of these Indian worshippers are Buddhists. The vast majority is Hindu. In typical Hindu fashion, they have no problem folding their hands, showing their respect to Lord Buddha and saying a personal prayer.

Outside the temple is an exhibit devoted to the Thai monarchy. It shows the King visiting the site and showing his respects to the Buddhist monks. Thailand is a Theravada Buddhist country with a strong stress on asceticism. Monks are revered in Thailand and everyone, including the King, pays respect to monks.

After leaving the Thai temple, we turned right at the gate, walking along the road toward the Bodh Gaya Shrine. On our left is a Chinese Buddhist temple, with everything written in Chinese. We passed through a pagoda arch, over a small Chinese bridge, through a small garden and up the steps. The temple is dark inside. The walls are covered with tiles depicting hundreds of Buddhas. Just behind the temple is a hostel for Chinese pilgrims.

Next door to the Chinese temple is a Tibetan Buddhist complex. It is large containing a series of buildings. We passed through a Tibetan gate and a garden and into the first building. It is multi-storied, with small Buddhist temple rooms on all floors. Downstairs inside a large room is a giant Buddhist prayer wheel. The Tibetans use this as a rosary and repeat the mantra:

Om Mani Padmi Hum

while turning the wheel. This wheel is several stories tall. An Indian family is inside the room. The father spins the wheel around along with his children. They are having a lot of fun. They are laughing and making a lot of noise. The Tibetan temple worker sits at the counter in front of the prayer wheel and is nonplussed and not disturbed. He lets the family play and make noise. After some time, the Indians conclude their play and leave.

All visitors must pass through this room to get to the rest of the complex. After leaving the temple through the back door, we find ourselves in a walled garden with Tibetan statues. The temple is closing for lunch so we must quickly go inside and have a look. Since I have been in many Tibetan temples before, I volunteer to stay outside and guard the shoes and watch the tourists/pilgrims, while the other two go into the temple.

Afterwards, we strolled slowly through the Tibetan garden. Tibetan boys become monks at a young age. They are barely teenagers when they start the process. Two of these young monks in their purple/ochre robes and shaved heads are playing with a dog on the lawn. For westerners it seems incongruous to see children who are monks, and to see monks engaging in horseplay, laughing and joking. The two monks lay on the lawn with the dog and watch the clouds move slowly across the sky.

Having worked our way slowly across Bodh Gaya on foot, the time has come to finally enter the Bodh Gaya shrine. As we walked towards the entrance, there was a high stone wall on our right. This is the boundary wall of the park in which the shrine is located. In front of the wall is a continuous line of carts selling trinkets of all kinds. These are the ubiquitous "*teeli*" (bicycle wheel carts), which serve as the common man's store. The carts sell all manner of Buddhist paraphernalia, as well as ordinary trinkets, such as plastic jewelry, and postcards and cheap plastic sunglasses. The street is very noisy.

We walked along the wall and turned right into the shrine gate. There are little booths there to leave shoes and luggage. We passed these by and entered the line for the obligatory security check. Buddhists initially erected a temple on this site where Lord Buddha obtained enlightenment. When the Muslims arrived in the area, they destroyed this original shrine. When Hindus regained control, they erected a Hindu-style temple at the spot of the destroyed Buddhist one. In the course of history, Muslims would destroy the temple two more times. The one currently existing on the spot was the latest rebuilt temple. In the 21st Century, Muslim extremists assisted by Pakistan have targeted famous non-Muslim sites in India for terrorist attack. This results in extensive security at all sites such as Bodh

271

Gaya. We passed through the metal detectors and the pat down, and made it inside the secure zone.

We must now find a place to park our shoes where they will not be stolen. Just in front of the pat down area is the reception house, where the temple management receives guests and donors. We find a place off to the side to unobtrusively leave our shoes. The other visitors have left their shoes in the public racks in a nearby narrow lane. This is an odd procedure necessitated by our footwear. Most pilgrims were simple rubber slippers, costing only a few cents and of little or no interest to shoe thieves. Our shoes are more expensive and therefore more desirable.

The temple loomed above us. We walked down ancient steps to go towards the temple entrance. Off to the side are small rooms where visiting Buddhist monks once stayed and meditated. Monks and pilgrims are seated in the lotus position all around the temple meditating. The park is specifically set-aside for meditation. Visitors can find a spot anywhere and stay there until the park closes. We inspected the small stone cells and got into line to enter the temple.
Although there is a tall *shikara* looming over the building and it is quite large, the interior space is small. There is only room for a small passageway and a statue of the Buddha. The line moves slowly, as pilgrims make their way to the statue and pay their respects.

Once outside, we walked around the perimeter the building perimeter, walking slowly towards the back where the Bodhi Tree is located. We stopped at the side of the temple to watch two young Tibetan monks playing. They sit with the young monks and chat. They state that they are in Bodh Gaya for the summer and will return to Dharamshala after their studies are over.

We now approached the epicenter of Bodh Gaya, the Bodhi tree. It is a large tree surrounded by a high brick wall. There are many spaces in the wall and the tree is clearly visible inside. There are so many people meditating around the tree that no one speaks loudly. Everyone takes pictures of the spot from all angles. I sat with the meditators for a time and soaked up the experience.

On the other side of the temple is a long space marked out with stone vases filled with flowers. It is here that the Buddha, after obtaining enlightenment walked back and forth in meditation and absorbed the experience. Each vase marks a step of the Buddha.

After leaving the temple area, we looked for a place to eat, wandering around a long open field looking for a restaurant recommended by the guidebook. Unable to find it, we crossed the street into a Tibetan enclave to eat with the Tibetans. It is a compound. A single building of several stories, surrounding a courtyard. We entered a gateway, walked through the building and into the courtyard.

Rows of Tibetan merchants man small stalls selling every kind of Tibetan handicraft, including antiques. Crossing the courtyard to the opposite side, we entered the restaurant. It is the kind of restaurant beloved by hippie travelers to India. Customers can stay as long as they like. The food is cheap, and there are all manner of clothing, books, jewelry, and paraphernalia of all kinds for sale. We enjoyed a long leisurely lunch there, rested, relaxed, and absorbed our experience.

After lunch, we retraced our steps and returned to the intersection of the Thai temple and continued past the temple to the museum. It is about to close, so we quickly went inside. It features a series of Buddhist carvings excavated from this area where Buddhists have been building temples for over 2,000 years. The carvings are exquisite. They are mounted in bits and pieces on the wall, and the larger pieces are in the center of big rooms. We have time only for a cursory tour of the museum before the staff herds us out. They are eager to shut down and head home for the day.

It is now evening and the winter sun is going down. We walk slowly towards the hotel. On the way, we stopped again at the Japanese temple. It is dusk and night is arriving. Pilgrims are quietly entering the temple and sitting quietly on meditation cushions in the public space. The room is dark. The only light is from candles on the altar. We take meditation cushions, sit in the lotus posture on the floor, and join in. There is no sound. The room is filled with meditators. There is hardly any light. Outside, the sun disappears. At the conclusion of the session, everyone replaces their cushion in the rack and silently goes on their way.

Buddhist Trek – Day Two

Ranu has negotiated with the hotel. They will provide a car and driver for the trip to Patna. On the way, we will drive through the Nalanda district and visit two Buddhist sites, Raj Gir and Nalanda. We got up early, ate a traditional Indian breakfast of tea and parathas, and loaded our luggage into the car while it is still dark and headed out onto the road to Raj Gir.

Rajgir was the first capital of the Magadha state that would later evolve into the Mauryan Empire. The site is revered because both Buddha and Mahavira, the founder of Jainism liked the spot and spent time there.

After obtaining enlightenment, Lord Buddha spent several months at Rajgir immersed in meditation at the site called Gridhrakuta (hill of the vultures). He delivered a famous sermon at the site and the early Buddhists held a council meeting there. In modern day India it is both a Buddhist pilgrimage site and a tourist destination for non-Buddhist Indians.

To reach the site, the car turns off of the highway and drives slowly up a hill to the parking lot. Horse carts (tongas) are driving up and down along the side of the road filled with tourists. They come to Rajgir for a pleasant day in a pleasant spot and take tonga rides with their families. The car reaches the parking lot. There are tour busses there. These are usually for the foreign pilgrims. Most foreigners are Buddhists from East Asia. There are few Western tourists.

The central Buddhist location is the Vishwa Shanti Stupa, (Universal Peace Stupa) built by Japanese Buddhists. It is on top of a hill overlooking the entire region. Visitors ride a ski lift to reach the stupa. The ski lift is a series of individual seats suspended on a cable. They are in perpetual motion. The visitor must stand at the specified location, wait for the seat to move towards him and jump on. Many Indian tourists have never seen a ski lift before and are not sure what to do. The staff helps them by holding on to them to anchor them to the right spot and tapping them when it is time to enter the chair.

As soon as I was in the chair, I pulled down the cross bar and locked it in place. The chair quickly ascended towards the summit. Going up, the only view is of the face of the hill. When visitors reach the summit, they must get out of the moving chair. After taking the ride, we reunited at the summit and took the path leading to the stupa, which is round and white and faced with gold.

There is a circumambulation path around the stupa, walked around the stupa and stopped at the front entrance. This spot provided a spectacular view of the mountain valleys on all sides. It is a hazy day, and the peaks are covered with a fine haze.

There is loud drumming coming from a location just past the stupa. It is Buddhist monks engaged in a ceremony in the attached temple. We went into the temple and watched the ceremony until it ended. It has a special sanctity, as it is taking place in such a sacred spot, where Lord Buddha himself was present. After leaving the temple, we spotted a group of Tibetan monks in full ceremonial regalia. They had long horns and were participating in a ceremony, which called for them to play long notes in the Tibetan style on the horns. They are on the overlook from which it is possible to see Gridhrakuta (hill of the vultures) where the Buddha gave his famous sermon. The Indian tourists quickly tire of the ceremony and the music and drift away. I stayed with the monks and took it all in.

Afterwards, we got back onto the ski lift and went back to the base of the hill, found our driver and drove on to Nalanda, the next destination. Nalanda was a Buddhist monastery in the ancient state of Magadha. It functioned from the 5th Century until the 12th Century. The Gupta and Pala Empires patronized the monastery and it attracted students from Tibet, China, Korea and Central Asia. Scholars believe it was destroyed by Muslim troops in the 13th Century.

After a long drive through the Bihar countryside the car arrives at the town of Nalanda. The entire town is devoted to the Nalanda site. It is a tourist attraction for Indian tourists who are there in large numbers. After finding a place to park, the group stops for some lunch at a small restaurant on the path leading to the museum. It is a very quiet rural setting with tall trees and green fields in all directions. A slight breeze rustles the leaves on the trees.

The museum provides some information as to what Nalanda was and includes some artifacts excavated from the site. I also watched a short video in Hindi about Nalanda. Now that everyone is sufficiently oriented we are ready to go to the site itself.

Although Muslim troops sacked and razed the site as part of their extensive anti-Buddhism campaign, it was so enormous that even after the passage of nine centuries, impressive structures remain. Archeologists have excavated most of the site, and the Indian government has completed considerable restoration. A large group of workers were reconstructing one of the buildings. The site is beautifully landscaped and well maintained. There are numerous guards to ensure tourists do not climb on the buildings or cause damage.

In India there remain many who are illiterate, poorly educated, or unsophisticated. They have no concept of historical or archeological sites and often try to take home souvenirs or climb on the ruins. White Americans demonstrated the same behavior when visiting ancient Indian cliff dwellings in Arizona. In the 19th Century, white tourists systematically looted these sites, even digging into Native American gravesites and removing bones and ceremonial items. It is only extensive and systematic education that changes such behaviors. In the interim, the guards spend their days trying to protect India's heritage.

It is easy to make out the layout of the original institution. There is a large mall, which must have been paved, with large buildings on each side. These are where the monks lived, ate, meditated and studied. Scattered about the mall were Buddhist temples, shrines, and stapes. It took hours to see all of the buildings. Some are multi-storied even today. The ones being restored by the Indian government demonstrate the sophistication of the architecture and the beauty of the craftsmanship.

It had been a full day. We had been driving and sightseeing all day, starting in Bodhgaya, then through Gaya District, on to Rajgir and Nalanda in Nalanda District and crossed the entire district to Patna, where we would bed down for the night. The following day, my family members start back for Jamshedpur, and I fly to Delhi to start my long journey back to Tucson.

Chapter XVII

Islam

It has become standard practice in the popular media to speak of Islam as a monolithic entity. In reality, no major religion is a monolithic entity, and Islam is no exception. Like with so many things in life, as one grows more familiar with something, its complexity increases.

I can provide an example from my own experience. When one reads a basic primer on India, it states that approximately 15% of the Indian population is Muslim. That is fine as far as it goes. However, to get a truly accurate picture, one has to examine the subdivisions within Indian Islam. Indian Muslims profess a wide variety of beliefs depending on their sectarian tradition. These broad differences make it impossible to generalize about the attitudes and behavior of Indian Muslims.

The principal division within international Islam is that between the Sunni and Shia sects. Sunni Islam, is centered in Saudi Arabia, which is the custodian of the holy places associated with the Prophet Muhammad (Mecca and Medina). It is India's predominant Muslim sect. Between 87 and 90% of the world's Muslims are Sunni.[88] Shia Islam is the country's minority Muslim sect, with approximately 10 to 13% of the world's Muslim population. Shias, like their Sunni brethren, pay reverence to Mecca and Medina, and its adherents, like the Sunnis, undertake the Haj (pilgrimage) to Mecca. However, Shia Islam, centered in Iran, maintains an additional set of holy places in Iran and Iraq, and Shia Muslims journey to those two countries for pilgrimage, as well.

This basic divide between Sunni and Shia is also found in India. While it is difficult to obtain precise figures, the common estimate is that between 10 to 13% of India's Muslims are Shia. This is much higher than in the vast majority of countries with Muslim populations. This is because Shia Muslims predominate in Iran and a few sultanates in the region of Saudi Arabia, with other Muslim countries having much smaller Shia populations. Shia Muslims emigrated from Iran and elsewhere to India in large numbers and thrived within India's liberal and tolerant society, facing none of the prejudice and acrimony they endured in Sunni majority states. They subsequently established sophisticated and vibrant cultures in Indian cities such as Lucknow and Hyderabad, famous for their music, cuisine, dance, architecture and poetry. Similar to situations faced by Jewish adherents around the world, Shia Muslims in India often gravitated towards business, as they were discouraged from going into government, and the military. Shia Muslims within India are further divided into numerous subsects.

[88] These figures were compiled by Pew Research and are available on their website

To substantiate the broad diversity within Indian Islam, we will concentrate on India's Sunni majority. It is possible to construct an ideological line of Indian Sunni sectarianism going from left to right, from most liberal to most conservative. On the far left are the Sufis, an inherently mystical sect essentially non-sectarian. As mystics, the Sufis do not differentiate between people. They see all human beings as "children of Allah," and welcome anyone and everyone. Sufis, as mystics, accent the personal experience of the divine, and deemphasize rigidity and orthodoxy. To Sunnis the essential experience of the divine is beyond definition and therefore cannot be confined within the boundaries of any sect or tradition. As part of their attempt to communicate that which cannot be communicated, Sufis have embraced the arts and are noted for their love of music and poetry. Needless to say, Sufis do not embrace the concept of "jihad" as a literal war. They are not concerned with proselytization or converting non-Muslims to Islam. Nor do Sufis discriminate between Islamic sects. Ultimately, Sufis downplay religious divisions altogether.

The next major Islamic group within Indian Muslim society is the Barelvis. While Sufism originated in the Middle East, the Barelvi sect of Islam is a wholly Indian phenomenon. It originated in the town of Bareilly in the modern Indian state of Uttar Pradesh and its founder was Ahmed Reza Khan (1856-1921). Khan preached that Islam should be centered on a personal relationship between the individual Muslim and Allah. While he called on his followers to adhere to Sharia law, his principal influences were Sufi. There is thus considerable overlap between Sufi and Barelvi Islam. The Barelvi sect is the largest in India, with approximately 75% of India's Sunnis identifying as Barelvi.

Hindu nationalists like to contend that Indian Hindus were converted to Islam by force ("by the sword"). This has not been borne out by the historical record. Most scholars now agree that Islam became entrenched for two reasons. Many dalit and lower-caste Hindus were suffering from the inherent injustice of the caste system, which precluded social mobility and doomed those at the bottom of the caste ladder to suffering and discrimination for no fault of their own, and furthermore doomed all subsequent generations to the same wretched existence. These Hindus were eager for an alternative and were attracted by the open and tolerant beliefs of Sufism and the personal example of the Sufi saints (pir) who had journeyed to India from the Middle East. They were attracted to Islam as a means of escaping caste prejudice and subjugation and the dominance of the upper castes, most particularly the Brahmins. These low-caste Hindu converts constituted a large majority of Hindu converts to Islam.

A second, much smaller group, consisted of higher caste Hindus who most likely converted for political reasons. They wanted to occupy high-ranking positions within the Muslim administration and saw conversion to Islam as a means of securing them. High-caste Muslim converts not only occupied high-level positions, but encouraged a "composite culture" that became the norm for India's Muslim elites. The males often converted to Islam, but often continued to marry

Hindu women. Any psychologist will tell you that mothers are the primary determinants of personality formation, as they interact intensively with their offspring during the crucial years between birth and five, when the foundations of individual personality are constructed. This resulted in a culture that freely adopted and combined Hindu and Islamic elements. Increasingly, educated persons around the world have embraced such multi-cultural interaction, arguing that this exposure to differing cultural influences results in a more cosmopolitan, sophisticated and tolerant individual. Research has confirmed that this is a positive thing.

Later, a faction within India's elite Muslims would rebel against this liberal outlook and embrace a harsher, more intolerant view of Islam. This culminated in the ascent of Aurangzeb to the Mughul throne. He attempted to forcibly impose his strict Islamic views on the Indian population, which was overwhelmingly Hindu, launching anti-iconoclastic persecution, hence the damaged temples found throughout Vrindavan. Aurangzeb's efforts touched off revolts all over India, as the formerly quiescent Hindu population rose to defend their faith. Aurangzeb spent the final years of his reign marching armies from one end of the empire to the other trying to suppress Hindu and Sikh rebellions. Regional leaders took advantage of the resulting power vacuum to break away from the Mughul Empire and set up their own independent "princely states." Historians view Aurangzeb's rule as the beginning of the death knell for the Mughul Empire, one of the most powerful, sophisticated and significant in Human history.

By the 19th Century, the Sufi approach and interpretation of Islam was well-entrenched within Indian Muslim society. Barelvi Islam appeared in the 19th Century as a codification of this South Asian orientation, with its particular South Asian concerns. Barelvi Islam also appeared as a reaction against both a shift within Indian Islam towards a more conservative doctrine, and to the suppression of Indians and their civilization under British colonialism.

More conservative Indian Muslims wanted to reorient Indian Islam away from South Asia, Sufism and liberalism, towards Arabia and Islamic orthodoxy. These issues became particularly important after the failure of the 1857 Sepoy revolt. Many of the Indian soldiers (sepoys) within the army of the East India Company who joined the revolt were Muslims. They were fed up with East India Company rule and longed to return to a perceived golden age of Muslim rule over India. They wanted to expel the British and re-establish the Mughul Dynasty.

When the British and East India Company armies defeated the rebels and recaptured the capital in Delhi, Queen Victoria determined that the revolt indicated a major failure of the East India Company to rule over India. She ended Company rule and absorbed India into the British Empire. This change of status opened the door to active efforts by British colonialists to impose British culture and attitudes on their colonial subjects. The East India Company had long avoided such efforts. The Company was in India solely to make money. The Englishmen who joined the Company and went to India did so because they wanted to return to England as wealthy men. They believed that interfering in Indian culture would only incite the population and would be bad for business. However, in the years prior to the 1857 revolt, this hands-off position was undermined by an evangelical revival sweeping Britain. The East India Company was a business enterprise, but maintained one of the largest armies in the world. While the officers were British, almost all of the enlisted men were Indians, primarily Sikhs, Hindus, and Muslims. Evangelical officers began to see it as their Christian duty to convert their troops to Christianity. It was this proselytization, coupled with intolerant practices that fed sepoy resentment culminating in the violent revolt against Company rule.

Indian Muslims were devastated by this defeat. Proud of their heritage as the former rulers of India, they now had to accept British dominance and a change of status to colonial subjects. Some Indian Muslims were heavily influenced by the British, took up the English language and Western education and were determined to carve out a spot in the upper ranks of colonial society. Another group clung more tenaciously to their Islamic identity.

These more conservative Muslims embraced the Deobandi sect founded by Shahwaliullah Delawi (1703-1762) in Deoband. Delawi argued that Indian Muslims were in this subordinate position because they had abandoned the true Islam propounded in Saudi Arabia and embraced heretical Sufi beliefs. Because of its inherent liberalism, Indian Muslims were syncretic, blending Islamic beliefs with traditional Hindu beliefs. Sufi Muslims had a strong belief in the power of spiritually advanced beings, who they believed had mystical powers. This belief system was readily intelligible to Indians, who had a long tradition of reverence for holy men and a belief in their mystical powers.

These Sufi Saints (pir) established their own religious centers and taught by example and were widely respected and admired by Indians of all faiths and backgrounds, including large numbers of Hindus. Upon their deaths, the tombs of the pirs became shrines, with devotees (Muslim and non-Muslim) journeying to these tombs as supplicants praying for divine intervention or illumination. These shrines (also called pirs) are common today throughout India, Pakistan, and Bangladesh.

The Deobandis believed that Indian Muslims who adopted this belief system were apostates. They called on Indian Muslims to abandon pirs, religious practices originating in Hinduism or folk belief, and embrace a stark Arabic style of Islamic culture that emphasized Islam as the true religion and discouraged social interaction with non-Muslims. As part of this process, Deobandis were encouraged to adopt distinctive Islamic dress, beards for men, and veils for women, further isolating Indian Muslims from their non-Muslim neighbors.

Today, Deobandis have turned to Saudi Arabia and other Sunni countries for financial assistance and are building *madrassas* (religious schools) and mosques all over India to propound their orthodox brand of Islam. This process has made great strides in Pakistan, where Deobandis have grown powerful, often with government encouragement and assistance, and have begun to challenge Barelvi dominance of Pakistani society.

This has not been the case in India. There is little evidence of such a major shift within Indian Islam. For a variety of reasons, most Indian Muslims seem happy with their Sufi-oriented belief system and wary of Islamic Orthodoxy that alienates them from their native culture, way of life, and non-Muslim neighbors and keeps them out of the Indian mainstream. During my intensive interaction with Indian Sunnis, they often told me that their primary interest of in social mobility. Unlike Pakistan, where the economy has been largely stagnant, India's economy is now the fastest growing in the world. Indian Muslims, who are generally poorer than non-Muslim Indians, want to take advantage of this improving economy to better their lot in life. Furthermore, Indian Muslims have grown up in a society that has discouraged the formal practice of separating the sexes, as found in many Muslim majority countries. Co-education is becoming more and more popular in India, and, unlike Pakistan, education in India is widespread, with girls encouraged to go to school, aspire to higher education, and pursue their own careers. Many Muslim parents told me that their aspirations for their daughters are high, and no different than those for their sons. Deobandi Islam rejects these modernizing influences.

On the far right are the Wahhabis who have embraced the ultra-orthodox brand of Islam that is the state religion of Saudi Arabia. While Deobandis are conscious of their South Asian identity and tend to tread lightly when discussing religious beliefs with others, the Wahhabis are openly contemptuous of Indian culture and most particularly Hindu culture, which they believe is based on idolatry and superstition. Indian Wahhabis, like many of their Arabian counterparts are attracted to extremist groups such as al Qaeda and the Islamic State. These far right Muslim are a tiny minority within the greater Indian Muslim community. While it is difficult to provide precise figures, my Muslim informants often told me that Wahhabi Muslims constitute less than five percent of Sunni Muslims in India.

Personal Interaction with Islam

For a variety of reasons, I have had extensive interaction with Indian Muslims. By coincidence, my home village is located less than 10 kilometers from Deoband, and I travelled there frequently while living in Rankhandi, and visit and spend time in Deoband whenever I travel to Rankhandi. While living in the village, I availed myself of the opportunity to visit the seminary and familiarize myself with it.

After I was assigned to the US Embassy in Delhi, I was made the "Islamic Affairs Officer" (among many other things). After 9/11 American Embassies launched Muslim outreach programs to interact with Muslim populations and counter the growing influence of Muslim jihadi groups. I was made Islamic affairs officer because I had served two tours in Pakistan, one tour in Bangladesh, and one tour in Nigeria, and had acquired an extensive background in Islam through years of intensive interaction with Muslims on a daily basis. I was also a certified Urdu speaker and Urdu is the language of India's Muslims. I was actually the only American officer in the Embassy with any substantive background in Islam or Islamic affairs.

Since no one else had sufficient background, or much interest to understand and relate to the intricacies of Indian Islam, I was left to oversee Islamic affairs on my own. I supervised a staff of Indian assistants (then called Foreign Service Nationals or FSNs), and junior officers. Our little group covered all aspects of Islam in India and how it influenced India's relations with the United States and the rest of the world.

I traveled all over North India in this official capacity interacting with a cross-section of Indian Muslims. Over the course of my travels, I visited Deoband many times. On one visit, I accompanied the Deputy Chief of Mission (DCM), the number two person in the Embassy directly below the Ambassador, and acted as his translator and advisor. The US Embassy had not paid much attention to this community in the past. In addition, I travelled extensively in areas of India that were off the beaten path, away from the urban centers usually frequented by American diplomats. As a result, my visits attracted considerable attention and were widely covered on television and in the newspapers and I found myself being interviewed by print, and television journalists often.

I also traveled to Bareilly, the headquarters of India's dominant Sunni sect and the Deobandis principal competitor. I met with the leadership of the Barelvi sect and had long discussions with them covering many topics. The city of Lucknow, the capital of Uttar Pradesh, India's largest state, is home to a large and well-established Shia community. Shias had ruled Lucknow during the Mughul era, dominated Lucknow during colonial times, and remained politically significant.[89]

I traveled there on a regular basis and became well-acquainted with the community leaders. Lucknow is home to a number of Shia shrines called the Imambara. Shia Muslims come from all over the world to visit these shrines. Iran views itself as the leader of all Shias around the world and intervenes actively in Shia affairs in India. The Iranian Embassy was courting the Indian Shia community and trying to turn it against the United States, (This was during the period following the US invasion of Iraq, which Iran and its followers in Iraq viewed as an American war against Shia Islam). The Iranians tracked my visits to Lucknow very closely and, at their behest, the administrators of the Imambaras painted a large American flag

---

[89] To gain insight into Lucknow's vibrant Shia culture, I recommend. "Umrao Jaan, (the courtesan of Lucknow), by Mirza Muhammad Hadi Ruswa, Orient Paperbacks, Delhi, India, 2005.

on the floor of the walkway leading into the shrine. This compelled all entrants to walk on the American flag. Before one of my visits, a majority of the administrators revolted, told the Iranians they would not accept their dictation, and painted over the American flag. While this angered the Iranians, my friends argued that this was an inhospitable gesture and ran counter to the courtly system of manners propounded by Indian Muslims. They told me that my presence in Lucknow was controversial and that I was in some danger. A large group of friendly Shias accompanied me during my visit to preclude any untoward incident.

I also kept my pulse on Delhi, visiting the head of the Jumma Masjid, the largest Mosque in Delhi. I met regularly with the Imam of the Masjid, who was known for his anti-American views. As head of one of the largest and most significant mosques in India, he had a lot of influence. I would like to believe that my friendly interaction with him moderated his behavior and perhaps kept him from making anti-American outbursts or encouraging anti-American demonstrations by Indian Sunnis.

The Jumma Masjid is a beautiful building in the heart of old Delhi adjacent to the palace of the Mughul Emperors. It was here that the Emperors, their wives and retainers, performed their namaz (prayers) every Jumma (Friday, the Islamic holy day). Although the Palace was practically across the street from the Mosque, the Emperor and his retinue would form a grand procession to enter the mosque for prayers.
It was difficult for Muslim opinion leaders to turn down their anti-American rhetoric, as the US was deeply engaged in the war in Iraq and the American invasion of that country and the subsequent war between Muslim insurgents and the American armed forces there, angered many Indian Muslims. We should not forget that historians estimate that the American invasion and the insurgency caused 400,000 civilian casualties in Iraq, and culminated in the scandalous Abu Gharaib incident in which American military personnel systematically tortured and humiliated Muslim prisoners in their custody.

Hazrat Nizamuddin

Delhi is a sprawling historical city. In the older parts of the city it is almost impossible to go very far without bumping into ruins, and sometimes fully-intact historical buildings, palaces, fortresses, temples, mosques, and tombs. I lived in Delhi for four years and attempted to explore every nook and cranny, but the task is so immense that I sometimes think I have only scratched the surface.

One of the most interesting neighborhoods of Delhi is Nizamuddin. It is a Muslim enclave that has grown up around the tomb of Syed Muhammad Nizamuddin Auliya (1238-1325). A Sufi Saint of the Chishti Order, Nizamuddin Auliya was one of the most significant Sufis of South Asia, and pilgrims come from all over the world to pay their respects at his tomb. Buried close to the tomb of

Nizamuddin Auliya is Amir Khusrao, Nizamuddin's closest disciple and one of India's leading cultural figures. Here is how Khusrao is described in Wikipedia:

Amir Khusrao was a prolific classical poet associated with the royal courts of more than seven rulers of the Delhi Sultanate. He wrote many playful riddles, songs and legends which have become a part of popular culture in South Asia. His riddles are one of the most popular forms of Hindavi poetry today. It is a genre that involves double entendre or wordplay. Innumerable riddles by the poet have been passed through oral tradition over the last seven centuries. Through his literary output, Khusrao represents of the first recorded Indian personages with a true multicultural or pluralistic identity. Musicians credit Khusrau with the creation of six styles of music: qual, qalbana, naqsh, gul, tarana and khyal, but there is insufficient evidence for this.[90]

The official website of the Nizamuddin Shrine has this to say about the saint:

Nizamuddin Auliya was a great Sufi saint from the Chishti Order. An order with a mystic Sufi tradition, which is based on love and humanity. Sufism is love, which starts from a master and ends upon the whole world. Sufi saints start their life with love and devotion. ... He always lived for others and loved everyone. Love is like fuel for a soul, with which life seems like a fair.

Hazrat Nizamuddin taught lots of things to this world along with the Sufi manner. He also taught to his disciples that "ego" is the main block between God and Human beings. When Ego is finished, only then can we truly love our master, and only then can we become honest on our path to God.

His key beliefs for humanity:

Women should have the same rights as men

Food should be distributed at all religious places

Do not hesitate to make contact with the poor

Always think about mankind and honesty

Help the needy and feed the hungry

Love should be your prayer for your master

Helping others is our social responsibility.[91]

---

[90] Wikipedia

[91]From the official website

While I enjoyed meeting with my Muslim brothers from all sects and backgrounds, it was the Sufis at Nizamuddin that I truly fell in love with. My assistant Dinesh Dubey made my appointments and took me all over India, introducing me to some of the most interesting personalities on Earth. Dinesh knew anyone and everyone that mattered, and made sure that I cut a wide swathe through the disparate Indian Muslim community. As part of this effort, he took me to Nizamuddin and introduced me to Musa Sahib, the General Secretary of the Shrine. His ancestors have held this position for the past eight centuries, and his son his set to take over after he leaves the scene.

Musa Sahib and all the people at Nizamuddin radiated the love preached by the saint as the bedrock of religion and spirituality. We hit it off from our first meeting. We always speak only in Urdu, although his son sometimes attempts short phrases in English. No matter how busy he is, Musa Sahib stops everything to greet me and spend some time with me. Nizamuddin is famous for Qawwali, the mystical music of the Sufis. When I lived in Pakistan, I watched television on Friday night, just before the only station shut down. The closing program consisted of Qawwali, followed by a sermon delivered by a Maulvi. Qawwali is traditional South Asian music played by groups of men. They usually sit in a line on a carpet and at Nizamuddin shrine always are accompanied by a harmonium. The lyrics consist of mystical poetry, often metaphors comparing one's loving relationship with Allah to the relationship between earthly lovers. The music puts both the musicians and the listeners into a trance. The singers clap loudly and interject with shouts as the intensity increases. The musicians of Nizamuddin live on the compound. The job is hereditary, passed on from father to son. The musicians are in high demand, playing concerts, weddings, and private parties all over Delhi. Nizamuddin's Qawwali singers are universally revered in Delhi society. They make no distinction between religious and secular events and perform for Muslims and non-Muslims alike.

When I visit with Musa Sahib, we retire to his office in an ancient building adjacent to the tomb. We chat, drink tea and eat lots of food, and then a troupe of Qawwali singers entertain us in a private performance. Afterwards, Musa Sahib wraps my head in a green turban and wraps a green and gold prayer shawl around my neck and takes me inside the tomb. I carry a basket of rose petals. The tomb is almost always filled with worshippers engaged in private prayer, and the room filled with incense smoke with a thick flowery scent. I put my head down on the tomb and Musa Sahib says prayers in immaculate Urdu, calling for the saint to shower me with his blessings. After the prayer, I, in usual Muslim fashion, place my two hands on my face before leaving the room.

Nizamuddin is famous for its Qawwali Music and I could not get enough of it. I not only heard the music during my visits to Musa Sahib, I came for the weekly Qawwali nights that took place every Thursday. The Sufis of Nizamuddin welcome everyone and do not discriminate against anyone. The shrine is particularly welcoming to those with nothing, the poorest of the poor, who are always fed and blessed. Many non-Muslims come to the Thursday Qawwali singing sessions, which start after dark and go on well into the morning. They are held in the courtyard in front of the ancient mosque at the heart of the shrine. The building is one of the originals, built over eight hundred years ago. We sit on mats in the courtyard with bright stars overhead and are immersed in Qawwali, losing all track of time.

My wife and children accompanied me several times to Nizamuddin and everyone was as entranced with the shrine as I was. Musa Sahib is a living example of Sufi values in action. Although most Muslim shrines highly restrict entrance of women and their participation, Musa warmly welcomed my female family members, making a special exception for my wife and daughter to enter the shrine and perform Namaz.

Here is a description of my 2014 visit to the shrine.[92]

We walked through the crowds to Baoli Gate to meet Musa Sahib's son. We were a few minutes early and stopped in front of the gate to wait. A family running a religious goods shop harassed us. They insisted we were blocking access to their open-air shop and told us to move on. This seemed to be a repeat of what had happened to us at the Juma Masjid earlier and reflects the influence of the doctrinaire Sunni Salafists, who are inherently anti-Western.

Musa Sahib and the Nizamuddin Shrine are part of the Sufi sect of Islam. Sufis have no problems with anyone. It is their duty to extend Allah's love to all without discrimination. Salafists cannot stomach the Sufi worldview, despise the Sufis and take great delight in discriminating against non-Muslims whenever they get a chance. When these things happen, there is no real issue. It is just a case of Islamic resentment against Americans, and a reflection of this messy world we currently live in.

Musa's son was at the gate at the correct time. He was very happy to see Me and I happy to see him. We had first met when he was a gangly and awkward teenager, and he is now a grown man. We gave each other a long hug in the fashion practiced by Muslims meeting good friends. I have shared this bear hug with Muslims all over India, Pakistan, and Bangladesh.

He arranged for someone to watch over our shoes, and provided us with skullcaps to cover our heads. We walked through the crooked covered corridors connecting the vast complex of medieval buildings, past the pool of water attached to the shrine, and through the gate into the tomb area at the center. All roads lead to the tomb, the epicenter of pilgrimage. We made a bumpy passage through a sea of human beings. Musa's office was at the opposite end of the courtyard. We squeezed through an entire crowd to get to him. The noise was deafening, with devotees practicing all manner of private devotions at once (loudly).

---

[92] This is excerpted from *My Indian Journey, (Mera Bharatiya Yatra), Phase Two*

Musa Sahib was delighted to see us and gave me a big hug. Everyone chatted, while his assistants prepared the flower petals for the worship ceremony. Ranu and I spoke with Musa Sahib in Urdu and translated for William. Once everything was prepared, we again plunged into the crowd to head to the tomb. The crowd was thick, with many people pushing and shoving, making it impossible to move. Long lines of men holding trays with offerings waited in the courtyard to get inside (women are not allowed into the shrine). Musa Sahib's son was ahead of us. He made a path for us, shouting loudly and pushing people aside.

We followed traditional protocol, first visiting the tomb of Amir Khusrau, Nizamuddin's principal disciple. He had requested to be buried together with Nizamuddin, but such burials are not permitted in Islam, so his tomb is built off to the side of his master's, as close as possible under religious strictures. Worshippers first seek Khusrau's blessing before entering the most holy shrine of Hazrat Nizamuddin.

Both shrines are very small, and worshippers stream inside until no one can move. Each pilgrim wants to get close to the tomb, make an offering, and touch it, resulting in considerable pushing and shoving. According to popular belief, Nizamuddin is present at his shrine and listens to all requests for his intervention presented by the worshippers. People of all types thus come to the shrine praying for the Saint's intervention.

We made our way to the very edge of the pir (tomb) and Musa Sahib began to recite the namaz. Everyone held out his hands palms up in the attitude of Muslim prayer, but no one could hear what Musa Sahib was reciting. Before praying, we took the rose petals out of the basket that William had carried into the shrine on his head, keeping it above the throng. We threw the petals over the raised sarcophagus (the actual body is located nine feet below the sarcophagus). It was already deeply covered in red rose petals left there by previous devotees. This is the epicenter of the epicenter, the most sacred spot in the shrine, the most beneficial for divine supplication.

Worshippers throw brightly colored cloths (often all green, covered with Arabic inscriptions and fringed in silver) over the sarcophagus. Dargah workers then remove these and put them aside for disposal.

We repeated the process at the tomb of Hazrat Nizamuddin.

After we left the tomb, Musa Sahib took us on a tour, showing us the feeding hall and the mosque, which was undergoing restoration.

We adjourned to a corner of courtyard to burn incense and make further supplications. We placed the smoking sticks in a giant incense holder filled with sand. A cloud of thick fragrant smoke rose from the holder into the Delhi air.

Back in Musa Sahib's office, we had tea, ate snacks, chatted and looked at photos. Musa Sahib took the green and red cloths used in the ceremony and made turbans on our heads over our skullcaps. We concluded our visit sitting on the floor next to Musa Sahib's son. He entered our names on a register as we made donations. He explained that the shrine maintains living records of every donation, dating back to the Mughul era and including donations from specific Mughul emperors.

At the end, we bade farewell to Musa Sahib. His son led us back to the Baoli Gate. We put on our shoes and returned to the mundane world. I forgot to remove my skullcap. Ranu noticed and reminded me. It would not do to wear it outside the confines of the shrine.

Ajmer

Sufi pirs are found all over India and Pakistan. Most are village affairs, the burial places of a local saint who was never famous, and is unknown to anyone outside the village. We had such a shrine in Rankhandi. Once a year, the entire village (90% Hindu), congregated at the pir to pay respects to our very own Sufi saint. It was like a religious festival, with families bringing large amounts of food, which we shared with each other while sitting on the steps leading up to the Pir and on the verandah surrounding it.

Nizamuddin is one of two Sufi Shrines in India known around the world. The other is the Ajmer Shrine, located in the state of Rajasthan. The shrine is an extensive complex surrounding the tomb of Moinuddin Chishti (1142-1236), perhaps the most influential and revered of all Islamic figures in India and South Asia. He emigrated from Iran to India as a young man and lived there for the rest of his life. Chishti wholeheartedly embraced Sufi Islam and is responsible for introducing music into Sufi Muslim worship, hence the origination of Qawwali and other Sufi devotional music in India.

Chishti was well-aware of the subtleties of Indian culture and determined that the spartan and harsh Islam of Saudi Arabia would not prove desirable to the Indian population. He therefore deliberately softened the Muslim message, emphasizing love, mysticism, and tolerance. He founded the Chishti order of Sufism and his followers had an enormous impact on India (and Pakistan). Historians agree that Islam would likely not have been successfully introduced into South Asia were it not for the likes of Moinuddin Chishti. This is borne out by the fact that the overwhelming majority of South Asian Muslims practice some form of Sunni Islam heavily influenced by Sufism.

After our experiences at Hazrat Nizamuddin, my wife and I were eager to go to Ajmer and see it for ourselves. We traveled there as tourists during one of our many visits to Rajasthan. The vibes were the same as at Nizamuddin, except on a much grander scale. The enormous site was packed with pilgrims from all over the world, both Muslim and non-Muslim. The pir was established soon after Chishti's death in 1236, and the site has been in continuous operation ever since. As per Sufi custom and doctrine, the shrine management feeds thousands of poor people every day, no questions asked, and there are no restrictions on who can enter the shrine and pray. This wholescale feeding of anyone and everyone together cannot be overemphasized in the South Asian cultural context. Because of the all-pervasive influence of caste, which is not restricted only to Hindus, there are deeply entrenched restrictions in India regarding who it is proper to eat with. Orthodox Indians are deeply aware of ritual pollution and will not accept food from a person of a lower caste, and would not socially interact with dalits (formerly untouchables). At Sufi shrines everyone is thrown together, eats together, and rubs shoulders with each other. This is a living rejection of caste.

At Ajmer, we had no Musa Sahib to take care of us. We were only anonymous tourists. Although obviously foreigners and non-Muslims, we were greeted warmly by everyone we met. But the shrine is much larger than Nizamuddin and we knew no one there, so we did not personally interact with the management. We were just two pilgrims. I truthfully cannot recall whether my wife was allowed into the tomb itself or had to wait outside. We did everything that any other pilgrim does at the shrine, including eating the food readily proffered to one and all. The belief is that if you sincerely perform namaz at Ajmer, Khawaja Moinuddin Chishti will bless you, freeing your soul to get closer to Allah.

We certainly felt that way.

Chapter XVII

The Never-Ending Saga

Star Trek Discovery – Season Two – Episode Two – New Eden

Star Trek Discovery is the latest iteration of the Star Trek franchise, and is radically different in many ways from those that preceded it. The principal character in this series is Michael Burnham. Orphaned as a child when her parents are murdered in a Klingon attack, Michael is adopted by the Vulcan family of Spock, and becomes his foster-sister. She is science officer on the Starship Discovery. Its new Captain is Christopher Pike, whose previous command was the Starship Enterprise.

In this episode, the Discovery is led by a mysterious red beacon to a planet on the far side of the galaxy, where they discover a colony of humans. In 2053, Earth was engulfed in a traumatic nuclear war that resulted in 600 million deaths. At the height of the conflict, humans from a wide variety of religious backgrounds seek shelter in a church. A nuclear warhead is launched at the structure and they face imminent death. However, a "red angel" appears and transports them to their current location. It is now 200 years later, and Earth has been completely transformed.

Before beaming down to the planet to investigate Pike explains to Burnham that his father was a science teacher, who also taught comparative religion. He tells Burnham that "this led to considerable confusion in our household." This exchange is filled with nuance and implication. Burnham's surprise suggests that religious observance has all but died out on Earth and has been replaced by a secular humanism. Pike then infers that he does not embrace this consensus, but it rather open to religious/spiritual ideas and respects them. Burnham finds this shocking and disturbing.

Pike confirms his orientation when he quotes Shakespeare, saying, "There are more things under Heaven and Earth, Horatio,"

Burnham immediately reacts, saying "Are you suggesting some kind of divine intervention?"

Pike reminds her of "Clarke's Third Law." "Yes," she says, "Any sufficiently advanced technology is indistinguishable from magic."

Pike notes that after considerable debate among philosophers and theologians, the law was changed to read:

"Any sufficiently advanced extraterrestrial intelligence is indistinguishable from God."

Burnham, incredulous, states, "are you stating that this is not an accident?"

Burnham, calls the building they are about to enter a "structure." Pike corrects her, stating, "it is a church Burnham," implying that she is being dismissive and intentionally irreverent.

After they enter Pike asks Burnham and the other crew member whether they have ever been inside a church.

The crewmember says, "No, my family are unbelievers."

Burnham icily replies, "I am familiar with the texts of Earth's religions."

They discover that the church has been converted from a Christian structure to the center of a new faith that is based on the synthesis of Christianity, Judaism, Islam, Hinduism, Buddhism, Shinto and Wicca.

Since Burnham and the crewman are ignorant of Church architecture, Pike explains that its stained glass windows are pictorial representations of religious truths.

Burnham is clearly appalled, reminding Pike, yet again, that "my religion is science, and I believe in rational theories."

The New Eden colonists welcome the strangers and they attend a religious service and meet the priestess. Burnham aggressively challenges her, almost demanding that they seek out a "rational" explanation for their transportation from Earth to New Eden. She replies that, "We have no need of proof. We are guided by the existence of something much greater than ourselves, our faith."

Burnham turns away in disgust.

When they depart, Christopher Pike again demonstrates his familiarity with Christianity, telling the priestess, "thank you for the fellowship."

When the Priestess says, "Peace be with you," Pike automatically replies with the standard Christian liturgical statement, "and also with you."

When they are in private, Burnham insists that Starship Discovery evacuate all the New Eden Colonists, saying, "These people are kin to us. They deserve to be reintegrated into modern society. The faith they cling to is a lie."

"Can you prove that?" Pike asks.

This entire story is an allegory. Burnham, Pike, and the Priestess represent three different ways to approach our existence. Burnham and the Priestess represent two opposing extremes who can never meet. Burnham is a Newtonian rationalist who has expunged all faith in the supernatural and replaced it with a faith in science, as a new religion based on rationality. However, her view does not allow any space for compromise with religious belief, she condemns all religiosity as superstition. The Priestess, for her part, is gentle and open, but, like Burnham, sees the world as a polarity. She is content to rest on faith and is not overly concerned about science and technology and the possible answers and insights they may provide.

In my view, Burnham is a deeply flawed main character. She has benefitted from a unique life experience. Raised as a human being from Earth until the age of ten, she then is totally immersed in the radically different Vulcan culture. She is unable to synthesize these two often contradictory approaches to life. She cannot embrace the stoic almost Zen Buddhist approach to life provided to her by the Vulcans, she also cannot fully embrace the irrationality and emotionalism of human existence. This failure to integrate leaves her constantly conflicted. In this allegory, she overcompensates and embraces an extreme rationality that is incapable of accepting any spiritual premise.

In this allegory, it is Pike that has risen above these dualities and provided a way out of this conflict. Pike is comfortable in his own skin. He is not embarrassed to pay due credence to his spiritual impulses and due reverence for spiritual traditions. However, this does not prevent him from embracing the latest scientific discoveries and applying scientific knowledge on a daily basis to benefit mankind. However, he does not embrace a metallic materialism, but rather lives out what can only be described as a highly developed set of Christian ethics. This enables him to respect the diversity of life he encounters, to be non-judgmental and to love others regardless of their faults and failings. He also exhibits Christian humility. Although he is the highest ranking person on the ship, he does not assume superiority over others and takes a genuine interest in the crew members regardless of their station or rank.

Where Does That Leave Us?

It should have become apparent to you by now that religion can be approached and defined many different ways. This two-volume work has explored my individual spirituality, with discussions and explication of its intellectual roots, and descriptions of the actual experience. It is my particular way to approach religion. As part of this process, I tried to answer the question "Why India." The answer is not possible without relating personal experiences based on innate spiritual messages stemming from an early age.

Life itself is inherently paradoxical. We all therefore go to great lengths in our attempt to impose a rational construction on life because we are unable to process the paradoxical. This is true whether we are overtly religious or not. Atheism is itself a construction meant to impose rationality on something inherently irrational. An atheist is correct when he/she states that, "Science, based on rationality, is my religion."

"Religion" is our attempt to make sense of the inconceivable because we are overwhelmed by it and are, as a result, overcome with fear. We demand closure. We demand that life "make sense," and when life fails to accede to our demands, (as it will certainly do), we jam that round peg into a square hole, attempting to make it fit, and are greeted with endless frustration. Many of us are convinced that the purpose of religion is to provide us with a readily apparent and simple explanation, that will make sense of everything for us. When this process fails to provide the required result, we give up, saying there is no meaning to life and adopt some variant of nihilism, (Nihilism can be cloaked in political and religious extremism that seemingly removes the boundaries of morality. Examples abound, such as the "Islamic State" terrorist group, or Stalinist Communism.)

Yet this embrace of nihilism often makes it even more difficult to get through the day, and those that embrace nihilism often end up self-destructing. As John Lennon said, "whatever gets you through the night, is alright."

Another thing that should have become apparent to you by now is that there is no hierarchy of religion. There are no higher and lower faiths. There is only the variegatedness of faith itself. There are so many different religions because we are human beings. Each human being is individual and has his/her own perception and experience of life. We attempt to share our individual perceptions and influence each other, but that only goes so far. Our inherent individuality makes it impossible for any two human beings to mesh their beliefs into a totally common belief system. Instead, we embrace the illusion that all Muslims, Christians, Hindus, or whatever believe the same things, taking a steam roller to the myriad differences and the inherent nuances of individual thought and perception.

Organized religion is man's grandest attempt to construct and impose a common narrative. It must go awry, however. Those purportedly sharing this narrative convince themselves their narrative has successfully answered all the questions and provided absolute certainty. Once they have convinced themselves they have discovered the one true faith, they take the next logical step and conclude that everyone else is wrong, because in our limited mindset we cannot have two radically different versions of the truth occupying the same space. This, to us, is an inherent contradiction. This is because we inhabit a mechanical universe with no possibility of paradox. This is, say the sages, nothing but an artificial construct. Human history has also taught us that this elaborate social/political construct leads to the odd paradox of religiously motivated hatred, conflict, and violence.

Religion should, by definition, be all about love. While the variation in religious belief and practice is as variable as human personality, love is what ideally should be at the core of this seemingly endless diversity. As a child growing up in New Mexico, my family used to pile into the massive station wagon for family outings in the Sandia Mountains. There, on the rocks by the side of the highway, nameless persons had painted, "God is Love." Those nameless persons were right.

Why do we insist on making everything so complicated? Why do we devise so many elaborate ways of making sense of our experience? We should instead go to the basics and try to agree on the few universal truths, like "God is Love." "God so loved the world that He gave his own begotten son." "Love they neighbor as thyself." God loves us and wants us to reciprocate that love, but we fail to do so. He keeps trying to connect with us, but we push Him away.

Why India? First it is about *prajna*, that inner voice, that speaks to each of us and provides us with insights. The other elements then follow. Prajna is our inner guide, nudging us along our path as we aspire more and more to be closer to the divine. Everyone is suffering here on planet Earth, because everyone longs for something better. It takes only a quick look around (or one daily newscast) to determine that we are surrounded by suffering. This is compounded by the fact that on this planet we inhabit, it is quite often that the innocent that bear the brunt of this suffering, and that this is inherently unjust.

We blame God for this suffering. We say that God is omnipotent, why does He allow suffering? But suffering is part of our finite experience. Our entire approach to existence is rooted in our finite life. Yes, we all suffer, and some suffer more than others. Everyone has been exposed to stories of persons whose entire life consists of suffering beyond our wildest imagination. Such stories are so powerfully overwhelming that we do not know how to respond. These accounts of unbearable suffering cause us to question everything we have devised to make sense of our existence.

Historically, one only has to be reminded of the Holocaust, the systematic degradation of slavery in the United States, or the genocidal eradication of the American Indian. But we are fooling ourselves if we think such massive, pointless suffering of the innocent ended in the 19th Century. It goes on all around us every day. I am deeply moved, for example when I read of the suffering endured by Yazidi community at the hands of the Islamic State. They are totally innocent, yet endured this incomprehensible pain, just because of their identity. This is inherently unjust. God is immanent and transcendental. He suffers with us and feels for our suffering, while being omnipotent. Whenever anyone reaches out to relieve the suffering of another human being, it is evidence of God's love. We are tempted to say that God stands by and does nothing to relieve the suffering of the innocent, yet amazing human beings sacrifice all they have every day to help their fellow man, plants and animals, and our suffering planet, and they are able to make these sacrifices because of their devotion to God. We should see such unbelievable acts of kindness as evidence of God's love.

We are rooted in time and everything we experience within our insignificant time frame is of the utmost importance to us, for we are ego first and foremost, and what happens to each of us is what we consider to be the most important. God, however, is rooted in infinity and is unrestricted. He sees our suffering, but knows it is a blink of an eye in the eternal unfolding of time. Krishna says in the *Bhagavad Gita* that "I am time the destroyer of worlds." Time is that which destroys everything in the material world, both suffering and happiness. All is transient. Nothing is permanent.

God wants to relieve us of our suffering, but knows that true relief can only take place when we make a conscious decision to reciprocate His love. This is what will allow us to transcend the material and discover our true state of existence. This existence will be free of suffering, for it will be free of time. It is based on love, and love is not love if coerced. Love based on fear is not genuine. Love is love only when it is a willing relationship of two beings. That is why religion requires faith. It requires a "leap of faith" to enter into this transcendental relationship with God. If God appeared before us in the flesh. If He allowed us to touch him and see him and remove all shred of doubt from our minds, we would naturally accept His existence and enter into a relationship with him, but that relationship would not be real. A reciprocal loving relationship can only be based on faith. As Jesus Christ told the apostle Thomas, "blessed are those who believe but do not see."

Yes, India is home to its own unique approach to the divine. Yes, India is rightfully famous for its spirituality. There are solid reasons why spiritually-minded persons have been attracted to India for millennia. However, this does not make India better than any other place we know of. In many ways India is worse off than most other countries. Only the most naïve go to India expecting to find heaven on earth. Indians live in a spiritually-infused culture, but there is no guarantee that Indians will be more spiritually advanced than anyone else. Liberation is not tied to geography. Since God is immanent and transcendent, we can encounter Him and interact with Him anywhere.

The trick is to go to India with an open mind. Go there fully prepared to experience the good and the bad. India is perhaps the most intense culture on the planet. This means that when things are good, they are intensely good, and when things are bad, they are intensely bad. All of this intensity can, in the end, by simply overwhelming; too much of a good thing is still too much. Yes, there are profound spiritual insights to be gained in India, but it requires an enormous amount of effort, patience, and forbearance to plow through the bucketfuls of bad to get to the good.

Because I am experiencing my own individual life, India has had a lot to teach me. This does not mean that you will have the same experience or the same attraction to India that I do. I perfectly understand that. For many other people, who, like me, were born and raised in the West, India has nothing whatsoever to offer. That is OK. That is fine. Each of us has to make our own path, find our own way. Just because India is known for its spirituality, that does not mean that you must go to India to experience spirituality. You can find spiritually enlightened personalities anywhere. Anyone can gain enlightenment without ever encountering India. Every culture and religious tradition has its own unique merits and is fully capable of providing enlightenment to its proponents.

This brings me to my second major point. Prajna led me to India, but after experiencing prajna I began to examine the Indian religious tradition. This led me to conclude that Indian metaphysics provides the foundation for the experience of Indian spirituality. Without a thorough grounding in metaphysics, it would be all but impossible to put Indian spirituality in its proper context. I would argue that India's metaphysics is one of the principal Indian contributions to human civilization.

What specific metaphysical ideas would I point to?

India attracted me because the Indian approach rendered the question of the hierarchy of religions irrelevant. We call Hinduism a "religion" because that enables us to place it squarely within our intellectual construct. However, Hinduism is not really a religion the way that Christianity, Judaism, and Islam are religions. Indian metaphysics provided Indian religious seekers the philosophical basis to aspire to a higher truth that transcends division and to search for overarching unity. Intellectually, this appeals to persons who, like me, are inclusive, rather than exclusive.

Hinduism is in no way the end-all of religious experience. It, like all religious traditions, is deeply flawed. The abuse of the concepts of Karma and rebirth have undermined the Hindu ethical system, resulting in the social abomination we call the caste system. There is no religious justification for such a system, and most especially the creation of a perpetually degraded group as the dalits. That is religious justification for injustice plain and simple.

By contrast, I would contend that Christianity's strongest component is its amazing and highly-developed ethical system. Just as Christians have a lot to learn from Hindus about metaphysics, Hindus have a lot to learn from Christians about ethics. For example, Christian ethics provides a divinely inspired systematic rejection of caste. Hindus such as Mahatma Gandhi and other Hindu reformers over the ages have long called for just such a thing. The Hindu reformers of the 19th and 20th Centuries were heavily influenced by their contact with Christian ethics. Mahatma Gandhi combined the Christian emphasis on social justice with the Hindu emphasis on non-violence to provide the tool for Indians to gain their freedom from British colonialism, and later for Martin Luther King to non-violently push for the eradication of Jim Crow. Hindus and Christians should not look at this mutual borrowing as a bad thing. For whenever there are two sides, contending that both are in the right, the only way out is to devise a third way by being open to change and open to learning from each other.

This is not to say that all Hindus have embraced and continue to embrace caste or that Hindus need Christians to provide them with the ethical means to finally reject caste and eradicate the caste system. Hinduism is not a static religion, although it has gone through long periods of decadence and stasis. Over the long term, the Hindu ethical system would likely have evolved on its own to the point where the caste system would have been untenable and would have been dispensed with.

We Americans went through the same process when we finally eradicated slavery from our shores. Yes, American abolitionists were encouraged and influenced by British abolitionists, but once that train left the station, the end of slavery was inevitable.

When Hindus encountered other social systems, they began to challenge their own beliefs regarding caste, and the impetus to eradicate this system increased exponentially. We must keep in mind, however, that this system has been in place for millennia and will not disappear overnight.

I would argue that there are a number of concepts that serve as the basis for Hindu metaphysics, and that these concepts are quite profound. For example, the law of karma and reincarnation are basic Hindu metaphysical concepts. Westerners often dismiss them out of hand as "primitive" or "superstitious," but both have entered common parlance in Western society and have become widely acknowledged, if not accepted.

One of the big shortcomings of Christian metaphysics is the belief that human beings are a unique species and are the epitome of God's creation. Christians have traditionally believed that Earth is a unique place, as it is the only inhabited planet in the universe. While Christian theology and metaphysics are themselves rapidly evolving, Christians traditionally believed that the soul is created by God at conception and placed only in human bodies. Plants and animals, while animate, do not have souls, and were purportedly created by God to serve man. While God loves mankind, He traditionally does not love animals or plants. When men die, their souls face divine judgment and, are sent by God either to heaven, to live eternally with Him, or to hell to face eternal damnation. From an early age, I found this metaphysical construct to be unsatisfying. This is because it appeared artificial and inconsistent with the facts.

As soon as I started studying the Christian faith, I could not accept the Christian teaching that human beings have only one life, that this Earth is the only inhabited planet in the universe, and that God puts human beings on this planet for a short time, during which they must make decisions that will determine the fate of their soul for eternity. It was impossible for me to accept that God punishes sinners by sending them to hell, to suffer torment for eternity. There is no activity undertaken by any person that would justify such a punishment. Surely, there would be a point in eternity at which any rational person would agree that even Joseph Stalin or Adolph Hitler had suffered enough for their egregious sins and had atoned for their atrocities.

Christians also face the quandary of the deaths of innocents. For example, Christians believed that God created a soul and put it into the body of a baby in the womb. That baby has only one chance to experience eternal salvation. What happens when that baby dies in the womb or in childbirth. That baby never had a chance to accept Jesus Christ as his/her savior, and therefore, as some Christians believe, experience salvation. Likewise, that baby never had a chance to lead a Godly life on earth, which some other Christians believe leads to salvation.

Christian theologians wrestled with this problem for centuries, but have, in my view, never come up with a plausible way out of this quandary. Catholic theologians in the Middle Ages, devised the concepts of purgatory in response to these dilemmas, and then introduced the concept of limbo. Both concepts failed to be convincing and are largely rejected by modern Catholics.

Another common Christian belief, which some Christians still subscribe to is that non-Christians will experience damnation, because they have not accepted Jesus Christ as their personal savior. Theologians of this particular belief system have been challenged by the question of what happens to non-Christians who have never even heard of the Christian religion and have therefore never had an opportunity to determine whether they should accept or reject Jesus Christ.

The response to this particular quandary was to espouse missionary proselytization movements. Under this doctrine Christian missionaries journeyed to the ends of the earth, to its most remote corners, to ensure that every human being on the planet had a chance to encounter the Christian faith, Jesus Christ and his teachings. This concept does not really resolve the quandary. It does not answer the question as to what has happened to the millions of human beings that have existed on this planet before and after the advent of Christianity, who were never exposed to this religion. Such persons are, by any definition, innocent, and therefore undeserving of eternal damnation. How could a loving God cast them into hell when they did nothing to deserve such a fate.

In my view, the two Hindu concepts of the law of karma and reincarnation largely resolve these quandaries. Human beings are not the only creatures with a soul. All living things possess a soul that evolves and devolves according to the law of karma. Human beings are provided freedom of choice under the law of karma and their every action has a reaction that can be positive or negative. Human beings are not the epitome of God's creation, but just one of many species that inhabit the universe. Human beings have an infinite number of chances to establish a loving relationship with God and ultimately transcend the material world and live with God for eternity.

Babies who die in childbirth or in the womb, are simply born again and given another chance.

This picture ultimately provides a much more merciful concept of God, in that He is not going to subject human beings to eternal punishment for their actions in one short lifetime, but is rather engaged in an eternal relationship with us that has its ups and downs.

One shortcoming in these Hindu doctrines is that they can be subject to abuse. For example, Hindus can argue (and many have) that persons born with diseases or born into poverty are suffering because of bad karma accumulated in a previous life. This makes it possible for an individual Hindu to argue that there is no need for empathy or charity because the poor, diseased, and those suffering from a bad break in life, are just getting their just desserts.

These concepts, of course, have been used to justify the ludicrous idea that there are "untouchables" who have no option but to be subjected to humiliation and depravity solely because of an accident of birth. Hindu proponents of untouchability have argued that the dalits occupy the bottom rung of the caste system because of bad karma accrued over a former life. They argue that if the dalits accrue good karma over the course of their lifetime, they will be reborn in a higher caste next time. This enables the caste Hindus to accrue the social and economic benefits of an exploitative social system without any sense of empathy or guilt.

This is mirrored in American history. Southern slave owners bent and twisted the Christian religion to preach that God created Negroes as inferior beings meant for slavery and that the save owners were "saving" them by removing them from heathen Africa and providing them with Christianity. This provided them to live lives of privilege and prosperity based on the misery and suffering of their fellow human beings, and not to feel one shred of guilt or empathy.

Hindu reformers, such as Sri Krishna Chaitanya have responded to these specious arguments by emphasizing God's love and God's grace. Some misguided Christian theologians have mistakenly stated that Christianity is the only religion with the concept of grace, and that Hindus believe that salvation is attained only through good works. One has to only examine the writings of Hindu thinkers from the earliest times up to the periods of reform and modernism to see ample confirmation of grace in action.

Sri Chaitanya plainly stated that God's love and grace is the heart and soul of the divine relationship between human beings and Krishna. Without love and grace, there is no divine relationship. Sri Chaitanya never taught that the mechanical following of Hindu orthodoxy and its complicated set of laws, and emphasis on ritual purity will bring the individual believer closer to Krishna. It is rather the cultivation of a loving relationship that lifts the devotee out of this material world and into the arms of God. A common Vaishnava iconographic work illustrates this. A man is drowning in the ocean and is about to go under the waves for the last time. He lifts his hands to Krishna, who appears above him and lifts the suffering man out of the water and carries him to his heavenly abode to live side by side with Him forever. Krishna does not stop and ask the drowning man whether he has committed good works and attained ritual purity. Krishna extends his hand with no questions asked. If this is not a pictorial description of grace, I do not know what is.

Likewise, Sri Chaitanya said that one can practice Yoga and austerities (tapasya), and this will bring one closer to Krishna, but without the cultivation of genuine love in the heart, liberation cannot take place.

Another example of Krishna's grace is described in the Bhagavad Gita. Krishna tells Arjuna that, "I am seated in everyone's heart, and from Me come remembrance, knowledge and forgetfulness."[93]

Likewise, it was always difficult for me to grasp the concept that only Christian religious figures were holy and that only Christian things were sacred. As a child, I visited native American pueblos and witnessed ceremonials. According to traditional Christian doctrine, the Pueblo Indians were "pagans" and "heathens," and therefore destined for hell. I always found this traditional doctrine difficult to accept.

The Pueblo people lived in the Southwest for thousands of years before any White Christian person ever arrived. During this period, they followed their own religion and found fulfillment and contentment within it. Most Pueblos continue to practice their traditional faith today. It is impossible for me to conceive that God would punish these innocent, earnest and well-meaning people purely because they have never heard of Christianity, or in the case of many modern Pueblos, practice their traditional faith and Catholicism side by side.

I quickly ascertained that all human beings share the same characteristics. Human society has used religion to divide human beings from each other. That is a political exercise, not a religious/spiritual one. We are all human beings and share the same fate. We have all been born here on this planet and must endure suffering and experience elation. But neither state is eternal, for in this material world, nothing is eternal.

India is home to Hinduism, the oldest of the world religions. Hinduism is far older than the Semitic faiths, and spawned the religions of Jainism, Buddhism, and Sikhism. The concepts elucidated by Hindu philosophers from Vedic times to the present, have challenged and mystified great thinkers from all over the world.

Hindus have become "technicians of the sacred." They have codified the ways and means to experience the divine, and ways to interpret this existence we are immersed in. Hinduism has transcended the boundary between the "sacred" and the "secular," defining religion not as a set of specific activities, rituals, and ideas, separate and apart from daily life, but rather as life itself.

This has vexed me from a young age. I could never understand the neat compartmentalization so often found in Western countries, in which religion is viewed as something separate from life, and making it possible to exile the

---

[93] A.C. Bhaktivedanta Swami, *The Bhagavad Gita as it is*, page 730

spiritual to a certain time of the day, or a certain day of the week, or a certain building, and to totally ignore it most of the time.

There should be, in essence, no religion, only the experience of life, for life itself is religion. Religion is not a set of doctrines or dogmas, but rather all-encompassing experience. Yes, experience is the essence, and Hinduism has been for me first and foremost an experience.

Thousands of tomes are written by learned scholars attempting to conceptualize religion. Hinduism very quickly determined that this is a fool's errand, because no words can ever capture the essence of life.

Instead, there is only the experience. Experience transcends the moment and is rooted in eternity, and therefore transcends this individual life we are leading on this particular planet right now. Hinduism exists in a world where it is possible for the individual person to "break through" this mundane experience of life and experience the divine, if only for an instant. This breakthrough is a foretaste of eternity, and allows the individual to temporarily transcend the material and experience the spiritual.

Life is not a short journey from one point to another. It is rather an eternal quest, a never-ending saga. With each successive life, we gain further insight and get closer to our ultimate goal.

In the end, I cannot help harking back to the story quite common in India.

A group of blind men were asked to describe an elephant. They all relied on their sense of touch, as they had no sight. Each felt a different part of the elephant. One felt the trunk said that the elephant was like a long snake. One felt the elephant's ears and said it was like a bird with large floppy wings. Another felt the elephant's leg and said an elephant was like a huge tree trunk. Each had a totally different description of what an elephant was. Each was correct. None was wrong. It was only when putting all the parts together that the blind me were able to accurately describe the elephant in its totality.

Appendix A

Solitary Journeys

During the course of conversation with my nephew Christopher, a pattern emerged. I have engaged in a lot of travel ever since I was attending high school in Germany, and much of that travel has been undertaken alone.

My friend William and I purchased a VW van intending to drive, along with Eric, from Germany to India. Because of the various wars plaguing the region, we drove across France, stayed on the beach, and crossed the Pyrenees, in the dead of winter, into Spain.

For one night, I slept alone in the grounds of an abandoned monastery. Then it come to light in my mind that I had slept alone and under the stars on numerous other occasions.

The night I graduated from high school in Frankfurt, I arranged to spend the night at the home of a friend of mine, whose name I have long forgotten. I took a free military bus to the Air Force base where he lived, but did not stay with him as planned. Instead, I slept in a clearing in the nearby woods. I must have had a sleeping bag with me. The next day, I walked to the bus stop and returned to Frankfurt.

Another time, my friend Michael and I went up into the Taunus Mountains. We found a clearing in the woods and erected a pup tent. We planned to spend an entire vacation living in the woods, but were rousted out of our tent by the forest ranger in the morning and sent packing.

On another occasion, while still in high school, I determined I would travel alone to Dubrovnik in Yugoslavia. I walked out of my front door and started hitchhiking. After many adventures, I found myself in the middle of the Italian Alps. I slept in my sleeping bad on a ledge overlooking an alpine valley. When I awoke, I discovered I found a plaque describing the area as the site of a very bloody World War I battle.

I hitchhiked to Turkey once from Germany with a college friend. We hitched through Bulgaria to Turkey and through Yugoslavia. On the way back, we stopped in Athens, Greece. One night on that trip we slept under the portico of a tiny village church in Yugoslavia next to the cemetery.

While in high school and college, I hitchhiked and took trains and busses to the following countries:

France – beach, nameless people's apartments

England – a friend's home, cheap hotel

Germany – people's homes and the woods

The Netherlands – city park, hippie hostel

Spain – monastery, friend's home

Greece – friend's home

Slovenia – hostels

Croatia – hostels, churchyard

Serbia – hostels, cheap hotel

Italy – cheap hotel, mountainside

Turkey – hostels

Bulgaria – no stopping there

Liechtenstein – cheap hotel

In addition, after starting college, we went on school trips to:

Czechoslovakia

Berlin

Denmark and Sweden

I attended college in Boennigheim in Swabia. I wore the same clothes for weeks, and accumulated them in a bag. We, William and I, hitchhiked back to Frankfurt in Hesse, where I washed my clothes in my parent's washing machine.

Once I was traveling alone on a train and ran out of money. I panhandled in the train station and a GI gave me money to get back home.

We took a semester off and lived Frankfurt. Four of us lived in a one room rental flat, sleeping in bunkbeds we had stolen from an Army warehouse. We shared the building with hookers and drug dealers. I tired of the cramped quarters and moved alone into a pup tent in the back yard.

Our entire floor shared one bathroom and one bathtub. We put money into a geezer to get our hot water.

One day I answered a knock on the door and a man stuck a loaded pistol in my face. He looked around and left, without saying a word.

I returned to the USA. I hitchhiked around the country alone and had more adventures.

I stayed one night in a commune, and returned to the West, where I reconnected with William.

William, myself, and his then girlfriend drove across the country in his big car. One night, I slept alone on the side of a mountain in the Appalachians, while they slept in the car.

I went to college in Maine. My friends and I traveled to Quebec City in Canada and shared a single hotel room.

I rode the Greyhound in the dead of night across the country, stopping for donuts in fog and thick blackness. Stopping in small southwest towns to change busses at trading posts at the edge of town with concrete Tipis in front.

I traveled to India and Nepal for the first time with a group. The group went home, and I stayed on in South Asia alone. I slowly made my way back to Delhi. It took several weeks. I traveled through Nepal, Khajaraho, Varanasi, Agra, and Vrindavan before arriving in Delhi.

I loaded all my earthly possessions into a trunk, placed it in the back of a van, and we drove across the country from Maine to Arizona. William, Eric and I stayed at another commune on the way.

My friend Dave, from Maine, visited me with his then girlfriend. We loaded into a car and drove across Mexico. We slept on a beach in Baja, facing the Pacific Ocean. The only people around were fishermen living in huts.

I traveled alone by train from Tucson to Los Angeles and stayed in the ISKCON temple there. I remember the brahmacharya ashram. I met Achutyananda and Brahmananda.

I traveled with friends to the Apache reservation to attend a puberty ceremony. We did not stay anywhere, because we spent the entire night with the dancers. The Crown Dancers came in the middle of the night. They jumped out of the darkness into the light of the fire, and whirled their stringed fetishes that made frightening and unearthly sounds.

I went to Rankhandi village in India alone to complete my doctoral research. I flew across the world by myself and was so frightened when I got off the plane, that I wanted to turn around and fly right back to Tucson.

I steeled my courage and took the train from Delhi to Rankhandi. I traveled all over North India with my Rajput family, by train, bus, oxcart, and on foot.

After graduation, I went to Vrindavan alone to participate in the Braj padayatra. I joined a group of devotees headed by Lokanath Swami. We stayed in temple courtyards, and took cold baths outdoors, using hand pumps. We walked hundreds of miles visiting sacred spots.

I accompanied a devotee to the baitak of Sri Chaitanya Mahaprabhu in Vrindavan. I helped him do a dandavat circumambulation around the sacred tank.

I traveled alone to Mayapur, staying first in Calcutta and then taking an ISKCON pilgrim bus to Mayapur. I stayed in the temple there and met with the Swami in charge of ISKCON's varied presence in that city. I toured the holy sites associated with Sri Chaitanya Mahaprabhu.

I later returned alone to the ashram in Kesava Bharati dasa Goswami in Govardhana. I stayed for Diwali and Govardhan puja. I made the Govardhan padayatra by myself in my bare feet. Afterwards, my feet were all cut up. I feasted with much of the top leadership of ISKCON at the ashram. I had to go to the health unit when I returned to Delhi to care for my feet.

My family was evacuated twice, once in Bangladesh and once in Nigeria. We were in India, when we received word of the Nigeria evacuation. My family flew off to Arizona, and I returned to Nigeria, alone.

I went to Iraq, alone and spent a year there, immersed in war and loneliness.

While posted to Washington, I volunteered for a one month TDY in Dhaka, Bangladesh. I traveled to Bangladesh alone, and lived in a hotel. It may have been six weeks before I returned to Washington.

Two years ago, I got on a plane and flew to India, alone. I stayed at the YMCA alone, until William arrived to start on our journey.

What does it all mean?

Expound....

There are no coincidences, especially when a pattern emerges.

The hardest person to get along with is yourself. That is why so many people go to such great lengths to avoid having to spend time with themselves.

The easy thing to do is to seek the most comfortable alternative. However, what is most comfortable is not always the most meaningful.

I read short obituaries every day in the newspaper of those who chose the most comfortable.

One often chooses to take the difficult path. It can be painful, but it often is the path laced with meaning.

There are far worse things in life than spending time alone.

Appendix Two

Over the course of this work, you have heard me allude to my foreign service career. I have deliberately kept such references to a minimum, as I see this topic as outside of my current frame of reference. However, I leave you with the essay below, just to give you some idea of what my job entailed. I believe it encapsulates a lot of material within a page and a half.

How Did the United States Devise Such a Thoughtless and Incoherent South Asia Policy?

American Pakistan policy has been beset by a series of blunders dating back to the founding of the Pakistani state. The biggest blunder made by the US in regards to Pakistan was to give it far more weight than it warranted. Students taking my International Relations class, must learn all about realism, which ranks all countries in the international system into three categories - significant, major regional powers, and world powers. Afghanistan is an insignificant state in realist eyes. Under the tenets of realism, it therefore does not deserve much attention from the US, which falls into the world power category.

Right wing ideologues in the Reagan administration abandoned their own realist principles when they decided the United States must get deeply involved in Afghanistan. They justified this decision by stating that the Soviet invasion necessitated a US response. However, under the tenets of realism, this is no justification, as the Soviet invasion was not relevant to the US. The invasion for all of its drama, posed no threat to American national interests. Realism defines relevance in terms of national interest. To realists, any issue that does not threaten or favor national interest, is by definition, irrelevant. If the US had applied this standard realist analysis to Afghanistan, it would have quickly determined that no US national interests were at stake there, and would have left Afghanistan under Soviet occupation. Such a policy would likely have prevented the subsequent deleterious events, such as the 9/11 attack, and the never-ending Afghan War.

The US did not just fail to follow its realist principals in Afghanistan, it abandoned these principals throughout the South Asian region throughout the cold war. The British did this also, when during the colonial period, they allowed themselves to become entangled in a "great game" with the Russian Empire. The British mistakenly convinced themselves that Russia wanted to absorb Afghanistan into its empire and that this presented an inherent threat to the British empire in India. As a result, the British fought two disastrous wars in Afghanistan. The United States inherited the mantle of world hegemon from the UK, after its decline, and made the same mistakes in the region. When the USSR got involved in Afghanistan, US policy makers were mistakenly convinced that this development posed a major threat to the region. This underlies the US decision to become

306

actively involved, first in Pakistan, and later in Afghanistan. This involvement in both countries has proved to be disastrous.

Pakistan welcomed US support and quickly became adept at playing on US cold war delusions. Pakistan convinced US policy makers that the Pakistani military would stand as a bulwark against Soviet and Chinese expansion and stop the spread of communism in the region. The Pakistani Army artfully extracted billions of dollars in US military and economic aid. In reality, Pakistan also falls into the realist category of an insignificant country, as the South Asian region is dominated by its major power regional hegemon – India, with the other countries in the subcontinent playing a subsidiary role.

Despite its claims to anti-Communist credentials, Pakistan never had any intention to commit its military to an anti-Soviet campaign sponsored by the United States. Pakistan's primary interest was, and remains, its rivalry with India. Pakistan intended from the outset to use American military and economic aid to build up its capabilities against India, and to acquire from India, the territory it claimed in Kashmir. Rational analysis would have determined that Pakistan never had much to offer the US, and certainly nothing that justified such an outrageous expenditure of taxpayer money. It should have been readily apparent to any thoughtful American observer that Pakistan was playing a double game.

The basic principles of International Relations dictate that the US relationship with Pakistan should have been no different than that with any small to middle-ranked developing country. The United States should have cultivated normal diplomatic relations with Pakistan, with little or no military aid and limited economic aid. Under this logical scenario, the Pakistani Army would have had to fend for itself, as no other country would have been willing to so generously provide military aid. In addition, any military aid provided by another state would not have matched the technological sophistication of American weaponry. There was no credible reason for the United States to arm one antagonist in a regional dispute in which it had no national interests at stake.

The former colonial power, the UK, had already come to this conclusion and was not willing or able to build up and support Pakistan's military. If the United States had refrained from providing military aid to Pakistan, it would have eventually turned to China for this assistance, but Chinese aid would not have provided Pakistan with sufficient military capability to pose a threat to India. China has also rightfully indicated that it will not allow itself to be drawn into any India/Pakistan military conflict. Without access to American military technology, Pakistan would not have had the military capability to fight repeated wars against India and would not have been so eager to sponsor terrorist groups and terrorist attacks against India. Without the active sponsorship of a major world power, the risk of military defeat for Pakistan would have been too great. It is ironic that India defeated Pakistan decisively in the Bangladesh war, despite the enormous military support provided by the United States. Imagine Pakistan's position without US military assistance.

If the United States was not sponsoring Pakistan, it would have been easier for the US to work in concert with other nations to address the major issues of the region. Should Pakistan have developed nuclear weapons under these circumstances, the United States would have enjoyed considerable leverage to take concerted action with the world community to compel Pakistan to roll back its nuclear weapons program. It would also have been more likely that nuclear weapons would make their appearance on the subcontinent at all. Pakistan developed nuclear weapons in response to what it viewed as the Indian conventional military and nuclear weapons threat. It developed nuclear weapons while enjoying continuing American military aid. The ill-advised decision by US policy makers to sponsor an anti-Soviet insurgency in Afghanistan, provided Pakistan with additional leverage. The US was well-aware of Pakistan's nuclear weapons program, but chose to look the other way because Pakistan threatened to abandon its anti-Soviet alliance and end the covert war in Afghanistan.

Because of its alliance with Pakistan the US was compromised and felt incapable of taking effective action to prevent Pakistan from acquiring nuclear weapons capability. Likewise, the world community, which could have worked with Israel, India, and other interested states to take strong action against Pakistan's nuclear program, could not do so, as long as Pakistan enjoyed US sponsorship. Likewise, if Pakistan were not in a military alliance with the US, it would not pose a sufficient threat to Indian security, and the US and the world community could have made a serious case to India, that it had no impetus to develop its own nuclear capability. The US and the international community could have moved forward with a program to work with both India and Pakistan to ensure a nuclear weapons free South Asia.

It has been American long-term support for the Pakistani military that has allowed it to acquire dominance over the Pakistani state. The Pakistani military has an existential fear of India, but it is not shared by the Pakistani population at large. The Punjabi group, which directly experienced the horrors of partition is the most anti Indian, and dominates the Pakistani Army. Other Pakistani ethnic groups do not share this inherent hatred of all things Indian. In fact, the Pathan group, found in both Pakistan and Afghanistan, is arguably the most pro-Indian group in the region. This explains why the Pakistani Army has such an inherent fear of Afghanistan falling under Indian influence. Should the Pathans in Afghanistan enjoy a period of peace and stability, they would likely start commiserating with their brethren in Pakistan, making it more attractive for the Pathans in Pakistan to become more assertive, demand more autonomy and threaten to leave the Pakistani state. This underlies Pakistan's determination to prevent the Pathans from integrating into a secular Afghanistan friendly to India. The Pakistani military wants to use its Interservices Intelligence (ISI) to keep the Pathans stirred up and at war with other Afghan ethnic groups. ISI also tries to use Islam to keep

Pathans from reviving their former friendly relationship with India and to encourage Pathan hostility against "Hindu" Indians.

If the United States had not entered into an alliance with Pakistan, it would have been free to play the role of a neutral power interested only in the region's continued economic development and democratization. The United States could then have chosen to confront the Pakistani military's dominance of Pakistan and worked in concert with other countries to encourage a democratic, civilian run Pakistan that poses no threat to its neighbors. The United States should have worked assiduously to encourage normal economic and diplomatic relations between India and Pakistan. The militarization of Pakistan has drained valuable resources from economic development into military spending. It has also threatened the long-term viability of Pakistan. The Pakistani state of Baluchistan is in the midst of a long-term uprising against the Pakistani state, which the Pakistani Army is brutally suppressing. Many Balochis are resentful of their region's dominance by what they view as the "Punjabi" Army, and are tired of seeing their state's natural resources drained off to benefit other states. They would like to have their independence, so they could focus on their own economic development and no longer have to subsidize the Pakistani Army and its endless dispute with India.

Unlike Pakistan, India has never sought an active alliance, military or otherwise, with the United States. Despite the many provocations provided by Pakistani support for terrorism directed against India, it has strong reasons not to get involved in a tit for tat unconventional warfare conflict with Pakistan. India is focused on economic development and playing its rightful role as a world power, as well as facing the growing challenge presented by Chinese expansionism. India and China will be in perpetual conflict in the coming decades over dominance of the Asian continent. The Indian military is focused on China, not Pakistan. India has concluded that Pakistan is a failed state in all but name (an army with a country) that cannot pose a viable challenge to India in the region.

India, therefore wants simply to manage Pakistan, keep it from imploding, avoid another Indo/Pakistan war, and prevent Pakistan from using a nuclear weapon. India has rightfully concluded that time is running out for Pakistan. Its inability to address its demographic, environmental, and economic problems, is likely to doom it to oblivion over the long term (Somalia on a massive scale), unless it is able to diplomatically address its many disputes with India, reduce the size of its military, and channel it resources from military spending to economic development.

This dynamic has been in place since the partition of British India in 1947. The rational choice for the United States at that point would have been to announce its desire to play the role of an objective and benign world hegemon. The United States should have made it clear at the outset that it desired no alliances with any state in the South Asian region, was not interested in supplying military aid to any South Asian state, and had no desire whatsoever to favor any side in the

India/Pakistan dispute. The United States could then have offered its good offices to help both countries address their dispute, and many economic problems, and encouraged normal India Pakistan diplomatic and economic relations.

Sad to say, American leaders took a series of conscious decisions over several decades that ran counter to every principal of foreign relations, and precluded these positive outcomes. Instead, we are left with the dismal situation of today, and we have only ourselves to blame.

Glossary

Words are in chronological order, as they appear in the work. They are marked as follows:

(S) – Sanskrit

(H) – Hindi

(U) – Urdu

(B) – Bengali

Please note that Hindi and Urdu experience considerable overlap, as many Hindi words are taken directly from Sanskrit.

Likewise, Urdu contains many loanwords from Arabic and Persian

I have not included terms in Japanese or Anglo-Indian terminology

Prajna (S) – divine intuition

Gaudiya (B) – adjective relating to the medieval Indian state of Gaud (now Bengal)

Vaishnava – (S) – Hindu sect centered on the worship of the God Vishnu

Sampradaya – (S) – A sect

Kshatriya (S) – The second highest of the Hindu castes. The warrior ruler caste

Varna (S) – Any of the four principal castes of Hinduism

Jati (S) – subcaste, the thousands of occupational specialties that subdivide the varnas

Rajput (S) – a subcaste of the Kshatriya varna

Maharaja – (S) "great ruler" – any monarchical ruler

Deobandi – (U) A Sunni Muslim sect founded in Deoband, India

Madrassa – (U) An Islamic school centered on teaching the Qu'ran

Talib – (U) Student, most particularly a madrassa student

Khandan – (H) The extended family, covering at least three generations and including cousins, aunts, and uncles

Patti – (H) Neighborhood

Tonga – (H) Horse cart

Kurta – (H) Long shirt with long sleeves that goes over the head and has buttons only at the collar

Buggi (or Bugghi) (H) Colloquial Hindi to denote a village made ox cart that incorporates the axle and tires of an automobile

Jugard – (H) Improvisation – in colloquial Hindi denotes a Buggi powered by an irrigation pump rather than oxen

Dal – (H) Lentils. A staple of the North Indian diet, it comes in many varieties

Charpoy (H) String cot. A wooden frame with twine strung between

Rezai (U) Quilt

Bidi (H) Filterless cigarette made of a rolled up piece of tobacco leaf

Dhoti (H) Traditional Hindu garment for men made of a single piece of cloth wrapped around the waist

Pajama (H) Baggy trousers tied with a draw string. Traditional outfits for men include "kurta-pajama," and "kurta-dhoti"

Dalit (H) Politically correct term for those on the bottom of the caste ladder, formerly called "Harijan" (child of God), or "untouchable"

Lotha (H) A small water pitcher, often with a long spout

Bhangi (H) A subcaste of the dalits whose caste duty is to remove human excrement from latrines

Brahmacharya (H) celibacy

Brahmachari (H) celibate

Rajasic (S) passionate

Rajas (S) passion. One of the three modes of material nature

Roti (H) Generic term for Indian flat bread. A staple of the North Indian diet, which is often described as "roti-dal"

Chapatti (H) The most basic form of flat bread, most commonly consumed. There are many different varieties, with some reserved for special occasions

Chulla (H) Hearth. Indian housewives cook sitting on the floor using a small portable hearth, in which a small fire can be made. They are often made of adobe bricks and caked with dry mud

Gobar (H) Cow dung cakes. Cow dung is gathered, dried, and made into cakes for fuel

Zenana (U) The women's quarters within the Purdah system

Mardana (U) The men's quarters within the Purdah system

Purdah (U) The system that divides the sexes, restricts women to the house, and forces them to cover themselves when out in public

Shalwar Kameez (U) An outfit (for both men and women) consisting of a Shalwar, a longer variation of the Kurta, and a variation of pajama pants

Lathi (H) A stock similar to those used in medieval Europe. A common weapon in North India

Dakku (H) Dacoit (Anglo Indian) – A robber

Mataji (S) Honorific title applied to older women with children. Mata means mother, with the honorific "ji" attached

Gharwalli (H) colloquial Hindi, literally "house person." A politically incorrect term for a housewife

Lungi (H) A variation on the dhoti, it is a much smaller piece of cloth than a dhoti and is tied differently

Bhagat (H) A religious devotee. In colloquial Hindi the term is used for secular purposes. For example a "filmi bhagat" is a person fanatical about Hindi movies

Gotra (S) The clan within the Varna system. The Gotra is a subset of the Varna and persons often combine the two terms when describing themselves. For example, I am a Rajput Pundir

Mantra (S) A holy incantation. It can consist of just a few words or an entire phrase, that is repeated to induce a religious state

Banyaan (H) Undershirt

Sadhu (S) A generic term for an ascetic. There are many kinds of ascetics and renunciates

Ghee (H) Clarified butter. It can be applied in a paste state but is usually heated and poured on food

Rakhee (H) A piece of red string tied around the wrist for religious purposes. It is also a holiday when women and girls tie rakhees around the wrists of close male friends to make them "brothers" and signify their close relationship

Kereela (H) Bitter Gourd. A popular vegetarian main course in North India

Hijra (U) A hermaphrodite. A hijra can be a genuine hermaphrodite or a castrated male. They dress in women's clothing and entertain at parties, and sometimes practice prostitution

Langur (H) A Punjabi loan word. The practice of seating large numbers of people in rows on the ground and serving them. The server walks between the rows carrying a large pot of food and doles it out to the rows on both sides

Puja (S) Religious worship. It can consist of formal pujas conducted by a priest, or informal personal pujas. They can be conducted at home, at roadside shrines, or in temples

Bhajan (S) A religious song, primarily Hindu

Darshan (S) Literally "view." It denotes getting a blessing by seeing a holy person or object, most especially a statue. It can also have a secular meaning, as to gain darshan of a great person

Jeneuu (S) The sacred thread worn by male members of the top three varnas (the twice born castes). Wearers must recite specific mantras and fulfill religious duties while wearing the jeneuu

Dhaba (H) Colloquial Hindi, denoting a small usually outdoor eating establishment, usually serving a few simple dishes such as "roti dal." They are often found on sidewalks and beside the highway

Chole (H) Chickpeas. This is a popular Punjabi dish beloved all over North India

Chopal (H) The family compound of an extended family (Khandan)

Brahman (S) This is the all-pervasive spirit found throughout the universe. Monist Hindus (Vedantists) aspire to merge with it

Avatar (S) Literally "to descend." An incarnation of God. God descending to the world to share the life of humankind and correct wrongs

Maya (S) Literally "illusion." The tendency of human beings to be lead astray and mistake the false for the real, the material for the spiritual

Lila (S) Literally "play." Used most often with Lord Krishna, it has deep philosophical meaning in that for God what we think of as momentous can be mere play. God with a sense of humor

Yuga (S) Literally "an age." The evolution and devolution is divided into four descending Yugas

Siddhi (S) Literally "powers." Persons adept at spiritual practice can acquire special powers such as the power to read minds, fly, or pass through solid objects

Farishta (U) Literally "angel." Muslims share this concept with Christians and Jews and Farishtas are found throughout Islamic culture

Ishta Devta (S) Literally "personal God." God appears to His devotees in the form most beloved by them

Vishwa (S) Universal

Rupa (S) Form

Arathi (S) A special form of Puja that takes place in the early morning

Prasad (S) Literally "grace." Food shared with God by offering it to Him first on the altar before consumption

Archa (S) Literally "secret." Something beyond man's comprehension

Vigraha (S) A representation of God, usually as a statue

Archa Vigraha (S) The incomprehensible process that allows God to inhabit a statue

Shikha (S) Literally "steeple." The steeple that rises over the inner sanctum of a Hindu temple. It also denotes the top lock of long hair worn by priests and religious devotees

Rasa (S) Literally flavor. In Hindu philosophy it denotes specific types of experience

Japa (S) The private recitation of a personal mantra, either aloud or silently. It is often performed on japa beads (similar to a Catholic rosary)

Sannyasi (S) A type of Sadhu who takes formal vows of renunciation, chastity, and poverty

Sannyas (S) The last stage of human life when men and women separate from their spouses and families and go to the forest alone to pursue spiritual life

Vedanta (S) The monist Hindu philosophy that espouses unification with the divine (Brahman)

Achintya (S) Inconceivable

Bheda (S) Difference

Abheda (S) Oneness. In Sanskrit, the syllable "A" at the beginning of a word negates its meaning

Achintya Bheda Abheda (S) - The Vaishnava doctrine of the inconceivable oneness and difference of God and the Soul

Dvaita (S) Unified. The doctrine of the monists that all existence is one

Advaita (S) Different. The doctrine of the dualists that God and the individual soul are infinitely different

Sankirtan (S) Kirtan is the individual performance of mantra/bhajan in front of an audience. Sankirtan is the group performance of the same, with no barrier between performer and audience

Karma (S) A basic Hindu doctrine, that for every action, there is a reaction. It is coupled with the doctrine of reincarnation of the soul to make a unified concept

Kartal (H) Thick brass finger cymbals of some 3" diameter that make a distinctive ringing sound

Tilak (S) Markings made on the body with colored clay. Vaishnavas, for example, make distinctive marks on their forehead, chest, and forearms with white clay

Dham (S) A holy place

Tirtha Stan (S) A pilgrimage place

Kunda (S) A "tank" in Anglo Indian, a manmade pond

Brahmamahurta (S) The early hours of the morning before sunrise. The most auspicious time to engage in spiritual practice

Dandavat (S) Danda is Sanskrit for "Stick." To make your body like a stick and fully prostrate before a holy thing or person

Kutira (S) Hermitage. Residence of a holy person

Samadhi (S) In Hindu philosophy denotes liberation from earthly existence. In Vaishnava terminology, it is the tomb of a liberated person who will never be reborn in the material world

Parikrama (S) A circumambulation of a holy place or object

Yatra (S) A trip

Tirtha Yatra (S) A pilgrimage

Panda (H) Colloquial Hindi – a deliberate mispronunciation of Pundit (learned Brahmin). It denotes a false pundit

Gurukul (S) Traditionally a religious school in which celibate students reside with and study with a guru, religious teacher

Dharamshala (S) A rest house for pilgrims at a pilgrimage center

Chappal (H) Sandals

Hawaii Chappal (H) colloquial Hindi – flip flops

Bhang (H) Marijuana

Charras (H) Hashish

Bhang Sharbat (H) colloquial Hindi for a powerful concoction made of Bhang/Charras, Yogurt and sugar or honey

Brijabasi (H) A native of the Braj region of India

Braj (H) The region of India associated with Lord Krishna and His childhood/adolescent pastimes

Holi (H) The Hindu holiday celebrating the advent of Spring. The festival of colors

Saddharan (S) Simplicity/simple. Simplicity is held up as one of the highest Hindu virtues

Shila (S) Sacred stones. In Vaishnava doctrine these can only be collected in certain places under certain circumstances and only then are worthy of worship. Often found on Vaishnava altars

Guru Parampara – (S) The disciplic succession. A lineage of gurus tracing back to a revered founder

Sawal (H) Question

Jawab (H) Answer

Sawal/Jawab (H) a musical convention in which a soloist plays or sings a phrase and it is repeated by a group/band, or another musician. We see the same convention in Jazz

Shloka (S) A couplet of poetry or prose/poetry

Pujari (S) One who performs the puja. In formal settings this is a highly-regarded Brahmin priest

Sattva (S) Goodness. The material world has three attributes. This is the highest, and is also found in the spiritual world

Tamas (S) Ignorance

Rajas (S) Passion

Jiva (S) A divine being

Van (S) Forest. For example, Vrindavan is a forest of Vrinda trees

Agarbatti (H) Incense, it can be sticks, cones, or powders

Goshalla (S) A refuge for cows. When cows grow old, they can be put out to pasture and not slaughtered

Aparadh (S) An offense. In the religious sense, an offense against God, a holy place, or one of God's representatives

Manas (S) The mind

Manasic (S) Of the mind. Something conceived in the mind

Snan (S) A bath. In the religious context to bathe in a holy body of water

Mleccha (S) Literally "dog-eater." Meaning someone who is totally outside the boundaries of religion

Hare Namer Chaddor (B) – A scarf/shawl printed with the Hare Krishna Mantra. Usually yellow with red lettering in Bengali or Sanskrit

Sadhana (S) Renunciation. The religious path is never easy. It requires sacrifice and hardship. Those who practice true Sadhana acquire Siddhi

Saali (H) Sister in Law

Dasya (S) Servitude. In Vaishnava philosophy to serve God is the highest aspiration. This is why Vaishnavas can adopt Das (servant) as their last name

Murti (S) A religious statue

Shtala (S) A column

Kunja (S) A grove

Pratibha (S) Talented

Manjari (S) A prepubescent female who waits on and associates with a divine woman, such as Radha

Venu (S) A pond

Diwa (S) A traditional lamp made of clay, with a simple wick, and burns ghee for light

Diwali (S) The Hindu festival of lights, when Hindus burn diwas to mark the return of Ram and Sita to Ayodhya

Juma (U) Friday. The Muslim holy day when the community goes to the mosque for prayers

Acharya (S) An esteemed holy personality that is the founder of a sect (sampradaya)

Moksha (S) In dvaita philosophy, the unification of the individual with the divine, a type of liberation

Shudh (S) pure. Purity is a highly-esteemed virtue

Shakahari (S) vegetarian

Shudh Shakahari (S) pure vegetarian, with no trace of animal products

Thalli (H) A plate, often made of aluminum with places for the different foods. Indian restaurants often sell an unending thalli, in that waiters fill up your plate as long as you keep eating

Trishul (S) Trident. This is associated with Lord Shiva, who is depicted in iconography carrying one

Tapasya (S) Sacrifices made for religious reasons. Persons who willingly undergo hardship to gain spiritual merit

Jholla (H) A cloth shoulder bag used by men and women

Chowkidar (H) A watchman or gatekeeper

Brahmin (S) A member of the Brahmin Varna, the highest, priestly, varna

Mahatma (S) Literally "great soul." Maha means great. Atman means soul. A title given to anyone deemed to be holy and worthy of respect and admiration, such as Mahatma Gandhi

Mahayana (S) The "great vehicle," used to denote the largest of Buddhism's two divisions

Teeli (H) A homemade cart, consisting of a wooden pallet mounted on four bicycle wheels. These serve as portable shops for enterprising small businessmen. An example of jugard

Sepahi (H) Anglo Indian Sepoy. A common soldier

Pir (U) A Sufi Saint. Also the tomb of a Sufi Saint

Namaz (U) Muslim prayer

Qawwali (U) A form of music associated with Sufism. A leader leads a group of men in devotional and highly rhythmic singing

CPSIA information can be obtained
at www.ICGtesting.com
Printed in the USA
FSHW022001030821
83802FS

9 798639 773075